Creativity and Cultural Improvisation

ASA Monographs

ISSN 0066-9679

1. *The Relevance of Models for Social Anthropology*, ed M. Banton
2. *Political Systems and the Distribution of Power*, ed M. Banton
3. *Anthropological Approaches to the Study of Religion*, ed M. Banton
4. *The Social Anthropology of Complex Societies*, ed M. Banton
5. *The Structural Study of Myth and Totemism*, ed E.R. Leach
6. *Themes in Economic Anthropology*, ed R. Firth
7. *History and Social Anthropology*, ed I.M. Lewis
8. *Socialization: The Approach from Social Anthropology*, ed P. Mayer
9. *Witchcraft Confessions and Accusations*, ed M. Douglas
10. *Social Anthropology and Language*, ed E. Ardener
11. *Rethinking Kinship and Marriage*, ed R. Needham
12. *Urban Ethnicity*, ed A. Cohen
13. *Social Anthropology and Medicine*, ed J.B. Loudon
14. *Social Anthropology and Law*, ed I. Hamnett
15. *The Anthropology of the Body*, ed J. Blacking
16. *Regional Cults*, ed R.P. Werbner
17. *Sex and Age as Principles of Social Differentiation*, ed J. La Fontaine
18. *Social and Ecological Systems*, ed P. C. Burnham and R.F. Ellen
19. *Social Anthropology of Work*, ed S. Wallman
20. *The Structure of Folk Models*, ed L. Holy and L. Stuchlik
21. *Religious Organization and Religious Experience*, ed J. Davis
22. *Semantic Anthropology*, ed D. Parkin
23. *Social Anthropology and Development Policy*, ed R. Grillo and A. Rew
24. *Reason and Morality*, ed J. Overing
25. *Anthropology at Home*, ed A. Jackson
26. *Migrants, Workers, and the Social Order*, ed J.S. Eades
27. *History and Ethnicity*, ed E. Tonkin, M. McDonald and M. Chapman
28. *Anthropology and the Riddle of the Sphinx: Paradox and Change in the Life Course*, ed P. Spencer
29. *Anthropology and Autobiography*, ed J. Okely and H. Callaway
30. *Contemporary Futures: Perspectives from Social Anthropology*, ed S. Wallman
31. *Socialism: Ideals, Ideologies and Local Practice*, ed C.M. Hann
32. *Environmentalism: The View from Anthropology*, ed K. Milton
33. *Questions of Consciousness*, ed A.P. Cohen and N. Rapport
34. *After Writing Culture: Epistemology and Praxis in Contemporary Anthropology*, ed A. James, A. Dawson and J. Hockey
35. *Ritual, Performance, Media*, ed F. Hughes-Freeland
36. *The Anthropology of Power*, ed A. Cheater
37. *An Anthropology of Indirect Communication*, ed J. Hendry and C.W. Watson
38. *Elite Cultures*, ed C. Shore and S. Nugent
39. *Participating in Development*, ed P. Sillitoe, A. Bicker and J. Pottier
40. *Human Rights in Global Perspective*, ed R.A. Wilson and J.P. Mitchell
41. *The Qualities of Time*, ed W. James and D. Mills
42. *Locating the Field: Space, Place and Context in Anthropology,* ed S. Coleman and P. Collins
43. *Anthropology and Science: Epistemologies in Practice*, ed J. Edwards, P. Harvey and P. Wade

Creativity and Cultural Improvisation

Edited by
Elizabeth Hallam and Tim Ingold

Oxford • New York

First published in 2007 by
Berg
Editorial offices:
1st Floor, Angel Court, 81 St Clements Street, Oxford, OX4 1AW, UK
175 Fifth Avenue, New York, NY 10010, USA

© Elizabeth Hallam and Tim Ingold 2007

All rights reserved.
No part of this publication may be reproduced in any form
or by any means without the written permission of Berg.

Berg is the imprint of Oxford International Publishers Ltd.

Library of Congress Cataloging in Publication Data

Creativity and cultural improvisation / edited by Elizabeth Hallam and Tim Ingold.
   p. cm.
  Includes bibliographical references and index.
  ISBN-13: 978-1-84520-526-3 (cloth)
  ISBN-10: 1-84520-526-X (cloth)
  ISBN-13: 978-1-84520-527-0 (pbk.)
  ISBN-10: 1-84520-527-8 (pbk.)
  1. Creation (Literary, artistic, etc.)—Social aspects. 2. Culture—Social aspects. I. Hallam, Elizabeth, 1967- II. Ingold, Tim, 1948-

BH301.C84C734 2007
306.4'2—dc22

                                             2006102149

British Library Cataloguing-in-Publication Data

A catalogue record for this book is available from the British Library.

ISBN 978 1 84520 526 3 (Cloth)
ISBN 978 1 84520 527 0 (Paper)

Typeset by JS Typesetting Ltd, Porthcawl, Mid Glamorgan
Printed in the United Kingdom by Biddles Ltd, King's Lynn

www.bergpublishers.com

Contents

List of Illustrations		ix
List of Contributors		xiii
Preface		xix
1	Creativity and Cultural Improvisation: An Introduction *Tim Ingold* and *Elizabeth Hallam*	1
2	Improvisation and the Art of Making Things Stick *Karin Barber*	25

Part I Modes of Creativity in Life and Art

	Introduction *Tim Ingold*	45
3	Structure, Innovation and Agency in Pattern Construction: The *Kōlam* of Southern India *Amar S. Mall*	55
4	Creating or Performing Words? Observations on Contemporary Japanese Calligraphy *Fuyubi Nakamura*	79
5	Creativity, Subjectivity and the Dynamic of Possessive Individualism *James Leach*	99

Part II Creative Appropriations and Institutional Contexts

	Introduction *Melissa Demian* and *Sari Wastell*	119

Contents

6	Locating Authorship: Creativity and Borrowing in the Writing of Ethnography and the Production of Anthropological Knowledge *Elizabeth Cory-Pearce*	127
7	Revolution as a Convention: Rebellion and Political Change in Kabylia *Judith Scheele*	151
8	'You knit me together in my mother's womb': English Baptists and Assisted Procreation *Jeanette Edwards*	167

Part III Creativity and the Passage of Time: History, Tradition and the Life-course

	Introduction *Eric Hirsch* and *Sharon Macdonald*	185
9	Performing the World: Agency, Anticipation and Creativity *Kirsten Hastrup*	193
10	'Tradition and the individual talent': T.S. Eliot for Anthropologists *Felicia Hughes-Freeland*	207
11	Back to the Future: Temporality, Narrative and the Ageing Self *Cathrine Degnen*	223

Part IV The Creativity of Anthropological Scholarship

	Introduction *Mark Harris*	239
12	From Documenting Culture to Experimenting with Cultural Phenomena: Using Fine Art Pedagogies with Visual Anthropology Students *Amanda Ravetz*	247
13	Creativity in Advertising, Fiction and Ethnography *Robey Callahan* and *Trevor Stack*	267

14 (Re)constructing the Field through Sound: Actor-networks, Ethnographic Representation and 'Radio Elicitation' in South-western Uganda
Richard Vokes 285

Epilogue

15 A World Without Anthropology
Clara Mafra 307

Index 321

List of Illustrations

3.1	*Kōlam* placed for deities at a Hindu temple. Chennai, Tamil Nadu, 2004	56
3.2	Basic *kōlam* executed without *puḷḷi* on threshold of private residence. Chennai, Tamil Nadu, 2004	57
3.3	Leaf from the 1901 Tamil publication *Arpatha Colamanjeri*, showing referents for *kampi kōlam* designs	59
3.4	*Nērpuḷḷi* (left) and *cuṇṭapuḷḷi* (right) grid structures	63
3.5	A demonstration of the distinction between *nēr* and *cunṭa puḷḷi* and the resulting *kōlam*. Chengelpet District, Tamil Nadu 2004	63
3.6	Leaf from a practitioner's notebook containing hand-drawn *kōlam* designs	64
3.7.1–3.7.9	Determining the grid structure required to extend a five *puḷḷi kōlam* to nine *puḷḷi*. Chengelpet District, Tamil Nadu 2004	67–69
3.8.1–3.8.9	Determining the position of the *kampi* for the nine *puḷḷi* design. Chengelpet District, Tamil Nadu, 2004	71–73
4.1	*The Stains/07, Mumi Mushū (No Taste, No Smell)*, by Yugami Hisao, Kyoto, Japan, 2002	79
4.2	*Traces of Lines*, Kimura Tsubasa, Kyoto, Japan, 2004	84
4.3	Hidai Nankoku at the Modern Music Festival, Middelburg, the Netherlands, 1979 © Tenrai Shoin	87
4.4	*Work 1: Den no variēshion* ('Variation on Lightning'), Hidai Nankoku, 1945, Chiba City Museum of Art, Japan, © Tenrai Shoin	88
4.5	Various kinds of *fude*, Toyohashi, Japan, 2002. Photograph by F. Nakamura	90
4.6	The *Sumi* Exhibition, Tokyo, Japan, 2001. Photograph by F. Nakamura	90
4.7	The process of making liquid *sumi*, © Tenrai Shoin	91
4.8	*Mitsu (Honey)*, by Yugami Hisao, Kyoto, Japan, 1999	93
4.9	Yugami Hisao at his exhibition, *The Stains of Words*, at the Gallery Maronie in Kyoto, Japan, August 2002. Photograph by F. Nakamura	94

List of Illustrations

4.10	Scene from Kimura Tsubasa's exhibition, *Crowd*, Kyoto, Japan, April 2005	95
6.1	Portrait of Makereti (centre rear), her mother, Pia Te Ngarotu (front right), and her great aunt, Marara Marotaua (front left). B43A. 64, © Pitt Rivers Museum, University of Oxford	130
6.2	Postcard of Whakarewarewa village, Rotorua, postmarked 1911 (author's collection)	131
6.3	Makereti writing at her desk in her house, Tuhoromatakaka, at Whakarewarewa in 1910. B43A. 19 B, © Pitt Rivers Museum, University of Oxford	132
6.4	The interior of Makereti's house, Tuhoromatakaka, at Whakarewarewa, in 1910. B43A. 20 A, © Pitt Rivers Museum, University of Oxford	133
6.5	Postcard depicting Guide Maggie (Makereti), greeting the ancestor Tane-Te-Pupuke with the *hongi* (pressing noses together), juxtaposed on a New Zealand Ensign. Rauru Meetinghouse, Whakarewarewa, early 1900s (author's collection)	135
6.6	'Hera with Curios'. Photograph of Hera selling photographic portraits, *poi* balls and miniature *kete* (woven baskets) from Makereti's carved *pataka* at Melbourne Oval, Victoria, 1910. M2420–1 © Pitt Rivers Museum, University of Oxford	136
6.7	Makereti's son, William Te Aonui Dennan (seated, front row, second from left), with a group (possibly of Oxford University students) probably taken at their home in Oddington, Oxfordshire, dressed with garments, weaponry and *poi* balls from her collection. B43A 82 © Pitt Rivers Museum, University of Oxford	137
6.8	Questions set by T.K. Penniman with Makereti's handwritten responses. Makereti Collection, Box 1, Section C, © Pitt Rivers Museum, University of Oxford	141
6.9	Letter from T.K. Penniman to Mrs Staples-Browne (Makereti), Oxford, 1929. Makereti Collection, Box 1, Section C, © Pitt Rivers Museum, University of Oxford	142
6.10	Makereti's response overwritten on the reverse side of the letter from T.K. Penniman, Oxford, 1929. Makereti Collection, Box 1, Section C, © Pitt Rivers Museum, University of Oxford	142

List of Illustrations

7.1	Monument to the victims of the war of independence in Ighzer Amokrane, spring 2004. Photograph by Judith Scheele	159
7.2	Monument to the victims of 2001, Ighzer Amokrane, spring 2004. Photograph by Judith Scheele	160
10.1	The *Saritunggal* for six dancers. Photograph by Felicia Hughes-Freeland	216
10.2	Didik Nini Thowok plays with Sundanese mask dancing. Photograph reproduced by permission of Didik Nini Thowok	217

Contributors

Karin Barber is Professor of African Cultural Anthropology at the University of Birmingham. She works on Yoruba language and culture, and on African orature and popular culture more generally. Her books include *I Could Speak Until Tomorrow: Oriki, women and the past in a Yoruba town* (1991) and *The Generation of Plays: Yoruba popular life in theatre* (2000).

Robey Callahan received his PhD in Cultural and Linguistic Anthropology from the University of Pennsylvania in December 2005. His main regional focus is the Maya of Yucatán. His theoretical interests include creativity, emotions and cognition, dreams and their interpretation, and the interactions of scientific and magico-religious modes of thought.

Elizabeth Cory-Pearce is Lecturer-Curator in the School of Anthropology and the Pitt Rivers Museum at the University of Oxford. Her research and publications focus on the material and visual culture of tourism locales in Rotorua, New Zealand, and the Canadian northwest coast, and the mediation of cross-cultural social relations.

Cathrine Degnen is Lecturer in Social Anthropology at the University of Newcastle. She gained her MA and PhD in Medical Anthropology at McGill University and was then a postdoctoral research fellow at the University of Manchester. Her research interests include experience and the ageing self; social memory, place and temporality; and public understandings of genetics.

Melissa Demian is Lecturer in Social Anthropology at the University of Kent. She completed her PhD at the University of Cambridge in 1999, and has since published on the subjects of adoption, legal pluralism, property theory and 'culture loss' in Papua New Guinea.

Jeanette Edwards is Senior Lecturer in Social Anthropology at Manchester University. She has carried out extensive ethnographic fieldwork in the north of England and has published widely on kinship and new reproductive technologies. Author of *Born and Bred: Idioms of Kinship and New Reproductive Technologies in England* (2000), she recently coordinated a European-funded project on 'the

The Contributors

public understanding of genetics' and from that research is co-editing *Kinship Matters: European Cultures of Kinship in the Age of Biotechnology* (forthcoming from Berghahn Books).

Mark Harris is Senior Lecturer in Social Anthropology at the University of St Andrews. He has carried out fieldwork with people who live on the banks of the river Amazon in Brazil. Recently he started archival research on the history of the region, and is currently writing a book entitled *Rebellion on the Amazon: race, popular culture and the Cabanagem in Northern Brazil, 1798–1840*. His publications include *Life on the Amazon* (2000), *Some other Amazonians* (edited with Stephen Nugent, 2004) and *The Child in the City* (edited with Anna Grimshaw, 2000). He was awarded a British Academy Postdoctoral Fellowship in 1996 and a Philip Leverhulme Prize in 2004.

Elizabeth Hallam is Senior Lecturer in Social Anthropology at the University of Aberdeen. She has researched and taught in the fields of anthropology and cultural history at the Universities of Kent and Sussex. Her publications include *Beyond the Body: Death and Social Identity* (with J. Hockey and G. Howarth, 1999), *Cultural Encounters: Representing Otherness* (edited with B. Street, 2000), and *Death, Memory and Material Culture* (with J. Hockey, 2001). She is currently writing *Anatomy Museum. The Body, Death and Display* for Reaktion Books. Her research and publications focus on the historical anthropology of the body, death and dying, visual and material cultures, and histories of collecting and museums. She is also involved in collaborative museum, exhibition and digitization projects.

Kirsten Hastrup is Professor of Anthropology at the University of Copenhagen. She has published some 30 books and 200 articles. Among them are monographs on Icelandic history and society, works exploring the foundations of anthropology, edited volumes on human rights and a number of textbooks. A recent monograph entitled *Action: Anthropology in the Company of Shakespeare* (2004) provides an important background for the chapter presented in this volume.

Eric Hirsch is Reader in Social Anthropology at Brunel University. He has a long-standing interest in the ethnography and history of Melanesian societies, most especially those of Papua New Guinea. He recently co-edited (with Marilyn Strathern) *Transactions and Creations: Property debates and the stimulus of Melanesia* (2004).

Felicia Hughes-Freeland is Senior Lecturer in Anthropology at the University of Wales, Swansea. Her regional research interests focus on Indonesia, and she has carried out fieldwork in Java and Bali over the course of twenty years. Her areas of interest are cultural politics, performance, media, gender and social change. She also works in the field of visual anthropology, and her films include *The Dancer and the Dance* and *Tayuban: Dancing the Spirit in Java.* She has just completed a book about Javanese dance.

Tim Ingold is Professor of Social Anthropology at the University of Aberdeen. He has carried out ethnographic fieldwork among Saami and Finnish people in Lapland, and has written extensively on comparative questions of environment, technology and social organization in the circumpolar North, as well as on evolutionary theory in anthropology, biology and history, on the role of animals in human society, on issues in human ecology, language and tool use, and on environmental perception and skilled practice. His latest book, *The Perception of the Environment*, was published by Routledge in 2000. He is currently writing and teaching on the comparative anthropology of the line, and on issues on the interface between anthropology, archaeology, art and architecture.

James Leach is Research Fellow in Anthropology, King's College, Cambridge. He has carried out field research in Madang Province, Papua New Guinea, resulting in published works on kinship and place, creativity, artistic production, ownership and cultural/intellectual property. These include *Creative Land: Place and Procreation on the Rai Coast of Papua New Guinea* (2003) and *Rationales of Ownership: Transactions and Claims to Ownership in Contemporary Papua New Guinea* (edited with Lawrence Kalinoe, 2004). He has worked in the UK with artists' placements in industry and science, on constructions of gender among Open Source software programmers, and on artists' relation to the law.

Sharon Macdonald is Professor of Social Anthropology at the University of Manchester. Her recent publications include *Behind the Scenes at the Science Museum* (2002), *A Companion to Museum Studies* (edited, 2006) and *Exhibition Experiments* (co-edited with Paul Basu, 2007). She is currently working on a project about post-war cultural policy in relation to the Nazi past, and especially Fascist architecture, in Nuremberg, Germany.

Clara Mafra is Lecturer in Anthropology at the Department of Social Sciences, State University of Rio de Janeiro, Brazil. Her research interests include Pentecostalism and popular religiosity in Brazil and Portugal, migration, skills and urban transformations, and conversion, ritual and cosmology. Her publications include *Na Posse da Palavra – religião, conversão e liberdade pessoal em dois contextos nacionais* (2002) and *Os evangélicos* (2001).

The Contributors

Amar S. Mall is a doctoral candidate at the Department of Anthropology, University College London, with research interests in material and visual culture. His chapter in this volume is based on fieldwork conducted in India during summer 2004, in fulfilment of a Master of Research degree funded by an ESRC studentship at University College London. Mall has previously worked in the area of museum access and collections management.

Fuyubi Nakamura obtained a doctorate in Social Anthropology for her thesis about contemporary Japanese calligraphy from the University of Oxford in 2006. She started her anthropology career at the University of Sussex, and specializes in the fields of museology and visual and material culture. Her other research interests include the historical reception of Japan in Britain by examining ethnographic collections, especially the Basil Hall Chamberlain collection at the Pitt Rivers Museum, Oxford.

Amanda Ravetz is currently AHRC Research Fellow at MIRIAD, Manchester Metropolitan University, where she is carrying out research into aesthetic ethnography. She studied painting at the Central School of Art and Design and later completed a doctorate in Social Anthropology with Visual Media at the University of Manchester. Her edited volume *Visualizing Anthropology* (with Anna Grimshaw) was published by Intellect Books in 2005. She has contributed to a number of panel discussions on anthropology and art, including *Fieldworks: dialogues between anthropology and art*, at Tate Modern in 2003, and the *Leventritt Symposium*, Harvard University, in 2004.

Judith Scheele is Junior Research Fellow at Magdalen College, Oxford. Her research and publications focus on issues of community, knowledge and local politics in Kabylia, a Berber-speaking area in north-eastern Algeria. Her current research investigates past and present connections between Algeria and Mali, and local perceptions and practices of trans-Saharan exchange.

Trevor Stack holds a PhD in Anthropology from the University of Pennsylvania and is a Lecturer in Hispanic Studies at the University of Aberdeen. He has carried out extensive fieldwork in west Mexico, including a period among Mexican migrants in the United States. His research has focused on two topics: the politics of historical knowledge, and citizenship beyond the State. He also has an interest in the anthropology of creativity in fictional writing.

Richard Vokes is Lecturer in Anthropology at the University of Canterbury, New Zealand. His research is concerned with ethnic identity and ethnic violence, political patronage and new religious movements in the Great Lakes region of

The Contributors

Eastern Central Africa. His new book *Shadows in the Fire: Secrecy, Exchange and the Kanungu Inferno of March 2000*, an exploration of millenarian religion in south-western Uganda, is forthcoming from James Currey. He was trained at the Universities of Kent and Oxford.

Sari Wastell is Lecturer in Anthropology at Goldsmiths College, University of London, where she teaches on social theory and the anthropology of rights. She has worked in Swaziland since 1997, studying divine kingship and the legal forms, political subjectivities and social improvisations divine kingship fosters. Her forthcoming monograph, *The Mouth that Tells No Lies: Kingship, Law and Sovereignty in Swaziland*, consolidates these interests. More recently, she has begun work on international humanitarian law and its institutions, focusing on the International Criminal Tribunals for the former Yugoslavia in The Hague and the national War Crimes Chambers of the ex-Yugoslav states.

Preface

This volume is an outcome of the 2005 Conference of the Association of Social Anthropologists of the Commonwealth, held at King's College, University of Aberdeen, in April of that year. The theme of the conference, *Creativity and Cultural Improvisation*, was chosen to capture the dynamism and vigour of our subject, and of the people around the world among whom we work, in coping with the challenges that face us all. But it also reflects the outlook of our new Department of Anthropology here at Aberdeen. The youngest in Scotland, and one of the most recently founded in the UK, the Department has already won international recognition for its research in the complementary fields of the 'Anthropology of the North' and 'Culture, Creativity and Perception'. The conference and now this book have given us the opportunity, which we much appreciate, to place our work in this latter field in a much wider context of anthropological research, not only in the UK, but also in Europe and beyond.

In planning the conference, we were determined to move the subject on rather than simply to provide a forum for participants to display their assorted wares. To this end, we decided to set a clear intellectual agenda for the conference in advance. This took the form of a tightly structured programme of sessions based on four themes, originally entitled 'Creativity, visual perception and material culture', 'The creativity of social, political and religious life', 'Creativity and temporality' and 'The creativity of anthropological scholarship'. We have retained the four-theme structure in this book, devoting a separate part to each, with minor changes in the titles for each part to reflect the interests and emphases that emerged during the conference discussion. We also asked the conference convenors for each theme to contribute an introduction to the corresponding part of the volume (an exception is Part 1, which is introduced by one of us, since the co-convenor, James Leach, is himself the author of a chapter). It was with their advice, too, that we selected the papers that would eventually be included in the volume, from the three times as many that were actually presented in the conference. As editors, we would like to pay tribute to the contributions of all who presented. By all accounts, the standard of presentations and the discussion that ensued was very high, and the task of selecting papers for publication was not easy. Inevitably, our choices were guided not only by quality but also with an eye to the thematic coherence of the volume as a whole.

Preface

Immediately following our general introduction in the opening section of the book is a chapter by Karin Barber. This is closely based on Karin's brilliant opening address at the conference. It made for a wonderful start to the proceedings, and we are privileged to be able to include it in the volume. The book closes with a final epilogue by Clara Mafra, on 'A World Without Anthropology'. Clara deserves a special mention here. Normally based at the State University of Rio de Janeiro, Brazil, she was with us in Aberdeen as a Visiting Research Fellow for the academic year 2002–3, and played an important role in the discussions leading up to the proposal for the conference. We toyed with many alternatives for the title, but it was Clara who came up with the final one. It was an inspired idea!

Along the way from the initial conference proposal to the book we have been encouraged, helped and cajoled by too many friends and colleagues to list. However, we would like to extend particular thanks to the following: Richard Fardon, then Chair of the ASA, who took the initiative in encouraging us to submit a proposal in the first place and whose continuing support and confidence in our capacity to deliver meant a great deal to us; Rohan Jackson, whose supreme organizational skills and unflappability made the whole task of running a conference so much easier; Trevor Marchand, in his capacity as coordinator for the ASA Monographs series, for enthusiastically backing the volume; and Hannah Shakespeare, of Berg Publishers, for being patient with our procrastinations and for seeing the volume through to press.

Finally, we would like to acknowledge the generous support of the British Academy, the Royal Society of Edinburgh, the Royal Anthropological Institute and – last but not least – both the City and the University of Aberdeen for their generous support, without which neither the conference nor this book would have been possible.

Elizabeth Hallam and Tim Ingold
Aberdeen, August 2006

–1–

Creativity and Cultural Improvisation: An Introduction
Tim Ingold and *Elizabeth Hallam*

There is no script for social and cultural life. People have to work it out as they go along. In a word, they have to *improvise*. To introduce the themes of this volume, we want to make four points about improvisation. First, it is *generative*, in the sense that it gives rise to the phenomenal forms of culture as experienced by those who live by them or in accord with them. Second, it is *relational*, in that it is continually attuned and responsive to the performance of others. Third, it is *temporal*, meaning that it cannot be collapsed into an instant, or even a series of instants, but embodies a certain duration. Finally, improvisation is the *way we work*, not only in the ordinary conduct of our everyday lives, but also in our studied reflections on these lives in fields of art, literature and science. In the following paragraphs we expand on each of these points in turn.

Before we begin, however, we have an observation to make. The title of this volume, *Creativity and Cultural Improvisation*, was also that of the conference from which its chapters were drawn. Throughout the conference we heard a great deal about the concept of creativity. Its possible definitions, uses and abuses, and resonances in the contemporary world were discussed at length. The concept of improvisation, by contrast, was discussed hardly at all. Though slipped in every so often as a relatively unmarked term, it did not capture the attention of conference participants in the way that the concept of creativity did, nor was it perceived to be especially problematic or to call for the same degree of unpacking. Whereas 'creativity' appeared to conceal a cornucopia of meaning between its covers, 'improvisation' seemed like an open book.

Though this imbalance surprised us at the time, in retrospect the reasons for it are fairly obvious. As John Liep explains, introducing an earlier collection of anthropological papers on the topic, creativity is on everyone's lips these days. Apparently we cannot have enough of it (Liep 2001: 5)! In a global commodity market with an insatiable appetite for new things, where every aspect of life and art is convertible into an object of fascination or desire to be appropriated and consumed, creativity has come to be seen as a major driver of economic prosperity and social well-being. A quick glance through the list of recent books with 'creativity' in the title, in any library catalogue, will reveal that the majority are in the fields of business or organizational management, where creativity is seen as the key to commercial success, and in education, which is supposed to produce the kinds of creative individuals who will go on to succeed in a knowledge-based economy.

Anthropology, Liep argues, cannot escape the processes in which it is enmeshed, of cultural commoditization and the consequent aestheticization of everyday life. Thus it is no wonder that the preoccupation with creativity affects the life and thinking of anthropologists as much as everyone else (ibid.: 4). Indeed Liep himself swims with the current, along with his fellow contributors, in associating creativity with the production of novelty *as opposed* to the 'more conventional exploration of possibilities within a certain framework of rules' (ibid.: 2; see also Schade-Poulsen 2001: 106). For the former he uses the term *innovation* – which he regards as a virtual synonym for creativity – while reserving the term *improvisation* for the latter. Though the improvisation that undoubtedly goes on everywhere and all the time in the course of quotidian life may appear to lend it a creative aspect, this, he tells us, is merely a 'conventional creativity', as distinct from the 'true creativity' that stands out here and there, marking unique moments of radical disjuncture. An anthropological approach to creativity, Liep contends, would do well to focus on the latter (ibid.: 12).

We disagree. In our view anthropology can best contribute to debates around creativity by challenging – rather than reproducing – the polarity between novelty and convention, or between the innovative dynamic of the present and the traditionalism of the past, that has long formed such a powerful undercurrent to the discourses of modernity. In this respect our approach comes closer to that of Edward Bruner, in his epilogue to a still earlier collection of essays on anthropology and creativity. As Bruner observes, people everywhere 'construct culture as they go along and as they respond to life's contingencies' (Bruner 1993: 326). In this process they are compelled to improvise, not because they are operating *on the inside* of an established body of convention, but because no system of codes, rules and norms can anticipate every possible circumstance. At best it can provide general guidelines or rules of thumb whose very power lies in their vagueness or non-specificity. The gap between these non-specific guidelines and the specific conditions of a world that is never the same from one moment to the next not only opens up a space for improvisation, but also demands it, if people are to respond to these conditions with judgement and precision. 'Improvisation', as Bruner puts it, 'is a cultural imperative' (ibid.: 322).

The difference between improvisation and innovation, then, is not that the one works within established convention while the other breaks with it, but that the former characterizes creativity by way of its processes, the latter by way of its products. To read creativity as innovation is, if you will, to read it backwards, in terms of its results, instead of forwards, in terms of the movements that gave rise to them. This backwards reading, symptomatic of modernity, finds in creativity a power not so much of adjustment and response to the conditions of a world-in-formation as of liberation from the constraints of a world that is already made. It is a reading that celebrates the freedom of the human imagination – in fields of scientific and artistic endeavour – to transcend the determinations of both nature and society. In this reading, creativity is on the side not only of innovation against convention, but also of the exceptional individual against the collectivity, of the present moment against the weight of the past, and of mind or intelligence against inert matter.

By harnessing our understanding of creativity to improvisation rather than innovation we propose a forward reading that would recover the productive processes that have been neglected in cultural studies due to their almost exclusive concentration on consumable products (Friedman 2001: 48). The improvisational creativity of which we speak is that of a world that is crescent rather than created; that is 'always in the making' (Jackson 1996: 4) rather than ready-made. Because improvisation is generative, it is not conditional upon judgements of the novelty or otherwise of the forms it yields. Because it is relational, it does not pit the individual against either nature or society. Because it is temporal, it inheres in the onward propulsion of life rather than being broken off, as a new present, from a past that is already over. And because it is the way we work, the creativity of our imaginative reflections is inseparable from our performative engagements with the materials that surround us. In all four respects our focus on improvisation challenges the backwards reading of modernity.

We consider each below: roughly speaking, they correspond respectively to the themes of the four parts of this book. Then, in the penultimate section of this introductory chapter, we place alternative forward and backwards readings of creativity in their context in the history of ideas, showing how, following their long co-existence, the rise of modernity tipped the balance towards the latter. Finally and briefly, we map out the overall thematic structure of the volume as a whole, leaving it to the authors of separate introductions for each part to discuss the chapters it includes in more detail.

Improvisation is Generative

A famous modern architect designs a building, the like of which the world has never seen before. He is celebrated for his creativity. Yet his design will get no further than the drawing board or portfolio until the builders step in to implement it. Building is not straightforward. It takes time, during which the world will not stop still: when the work is complete the building will stand in an environment that could not have been envisioned when it started. It takes materials, which have properties of their own and are not predisposed to fall into the shapes and configurations required of them, let alone to stay in them indefinitely. And it takes people, who have to make the most of their own skill and experience in order to cajole the materials into doing what the architect wants. In order to accommodate the inflexible design to the realities of a fickle and inconstant world, builders have to improvise all the way. There is a kink, as Stewart Brand writes, between the world and the architect's idea of it: 'The idea is crystalline, the fact fluid' (Brand 1994: 2). Builders inhabit that kink.

Why, then, do we not celebrate the creativity of their work, as we do that of the architect? And why, for that matter, do we not celebrate equally the creativity of those who subsequently use the building in the course of their own lives? For the reality is that no building remains – as the architect might wish – forever unchanged, but has to be continually modified and adapted to fit in with manifold and ever-shifting purposes. At the same time it is constantly buffeted by the elements, the forces of wear and tear, and the visitations of birds, rodents, arachnids and fungi, all calling for the equally improvisatory interventions of workmen of diverse trades – plumbers, joiners, window cleaners, roofing specialists and a host of others – merely in order to shore it up against the tide of destruction. Do they not also, along with inhabitants' efforts to do-it-themselves, play their part in the building's ongoing creation? As the distinguished Portuguese architect Alvaro Siza admits, he has never been able to design, let alone build a *real* house, by which he means 'a complicated machine in which every day something breaks down' (Siza 1997: 47).

A rather similar puzzle emerges if we turn from artificially built structures to organically grown ones. Wherever life is going on, solid, liquid and gaseous materials are binding in the formation of stupendously complex, organic tissues. Human beings are as much caught up in this process as creatures of any other kind. What can be more creative than the growth of a human infant – 'knit together', in the wonderfully poetic words of the biblical psalm (cited by Jeanette Edwards, this volume), in its mother's womb? Most biologists, however, are remarkably reluctant to acknowledge the creativity of organic life. They are understandably nervous that any admission of creativity would attract charges of creationism. If they speak of creativity at all, it is with regard to the origin and diversification of species, that is, to evolutionary phylogeny rather than ontogenetic development. Evolution, they point out, is a result of natural selection, and the first thing to understand about natural selection is that it explains how creativity can occur in a world of living things, in the *absence* of a creator.

But if we pause to inquire what has been created, the answer turns out to be not the organism itself but a *design* for the organism, supposedly encoded in the materials of heredity. Indeed one of the ironies of the current spat between Darwinian evolutionary biologists and the advocates of so-called 'intelligent design' is that if there is one thing that both sides take for granted, it is that such design exists, at the heart of every organism and expressed in its development. The issue at stake is merely whether the intelligence of this design is that of Science reflected in the mirror of nature, or of Theodicy reflected in the mirror of God. Only a hair's breadth separates the two positions. Either way, it is assumed that organic form issues directly and unproblematically from the pre-created design. To account for the form, all you have to do is to 'read back' to the design of which it is supposed to be the expression, albeit modulated by environmental circumstances. And just as with the building, what this leaves out are the myriad tactical improvisations by which actual living organisms co-opt whatever possibilities their environments may afford to make their ways in the tangle of the world. Neither natural selection nor an intelligent designer can build a *real* organism, any more than the modern architect can build a *real* house.

The belief that in the building of a house or the growth of an organism – or more generally, in the activities by which living beings of all kinds, human and non-human, sustain themselves in their environments – nothing is created that was not designed in advance, pre-existing in virtual form the processes that give rise to it, is deeply rooted in modern thought. It is this belief that leads us to look to innovations in design as the source of all creation. We are inclined to say that something is created only when it is *new*, meaning not that it has been newly produced, but that it is the manifest outcome of a newly concocted plan, formula, programme or recipe. Everything else is a copy. Notwithstanding the effort, attention and even problem-solving that goes into reproducing an existing model, the process of copying – by this logic – *cannot be creative*. It can only replicate what is already there. A fundamental opposition is thereby set up between creativity and imitation. We challenge this opposition, as do many of the contributions to this book.

Copying or imitation, we argue, is not the simple, mechanical process of replication that it is often taken to be, of running off duplicates from a template, but entails a complex and ongoing alignment of observation of the model with action in the world. In this alignment lies the work of improvisation. The formal resemblance between the copy and the model is an *outcome* of this process, not given in advance. It is a horizon of attainment, to be judged in retrospect. Indeed the more strictly standards are observed, the greater are the improvisational demands placed on performers to 'get it right'. Precision – as Felicia Hughes-Freeland shows in her study of Javanese dance, and Fuyubi Nakamura in her account of Japanese calligraphy – demands a heightened responsiveness which, for practitioners who are truly skilled, can be truly liberating. That is why there is creativity even and especially in the maintenance of an established tradition. Just as a building that is not kept in repair soon disintegrates, so traditions have to be worked at to be sustained. The continuity of tradition is due not to its passive inertia but to its active regeneration – in the tasks of *carrying on*.

For this reason the metaphor of transmission has to be used with great care. In a loose sense we can of course speak of generations passing on their skills and knowledge to successors. There has been a tendency, however, to interpret the metaphor much more literally, as though in the performance of tradition people do not so much emulate their predecessors by copying their actions, as act out, or 'convert into behaviour', prototypical schemas that have already been copied into their heads by a prior process of replication (Sperber 1996: 61). Some anthropologists and psychologists have even taken to calling these schemas 'memes', information-bearing nodules that are supposed to inhabit the mind as genes inhabit the body, whence they control the carrier's thought and behaviour. Creativity, for meme-theorists, lies not in what people do but in the potential for mutation and recombination of its memetic determinants (Aunger 2000). However, just as natural selection can no more build a *real* organism than can an architect build a *real* house, so no amount of meme-juggling, intentional or otherwise, can build a *real* human being. Real people, as the living organisms they are, continually create themselves and one another, forging their histories and traditions as they go along.

Improvisation is Relational

We are talking here about the process of social life. By this we mean the life of persons in those mutually constitutive relationships through which, as they grow older together, they continually participate in each other's coming-into-being. We do *not* mean the life of some hypostatized, superorganic entity – namely 'society' – as it unfolds over and above that of the solitary individual. It is this latter view that, in classical social theory, sets the freedom of the individual on a collision course with the external determinations of society, and it is reproduced every time the exercise of creativity is associated with individual talent and expression.

The creative individual, it is commonly supposed, is one who is prepared and able to make a break with socially imposed convention. This can sometimes lead to the paradoxical results that Judith Scheele observes in her study of the political rhetoric of revolution in Algeria. For where collective identity is defined by revolutionary commitment, the only way to swim against the tide is by adherence to tradition! It can be unconventional to be conventional, just as it can be traditional to change. Even the most creative of individuals, by this account, can never fully escape what Friedman (2001) has called the 'iron cage' of social constraint, since their nonconformity – if it is not to be dismissed as mere idiosyncrasy – must 'make sense' within a more widely inhabited universe of meaning and accord with its communicative conventions. Creativity, as Kirsten Hastrup points out in this volume, cannot totally cut loose from the social whole, lest it register as madness.

In this imagined tussle between individual and society, the stature of the former appears proportional to the gravitas of the latter. It takes a giant to move a mountain, and it is generally assumed that since society is a totality of an altogether larger scale than the individuals that make it up, no ordinary person can shift it. That is why creative individuals tend to be credited with extraordinary powers, of intellect or charisma. In his epilogue to *Creativity/Anthropology*, to which we have already referred, Bruner goes some way towards reducing the deadweight of society, and by the same token, recognising that 'even little people in the routine and everyday' can change the world (Bruner 1993: 321). The assumption nevertheless remains that in the 'mix of tradition and change' (Rosaldo, Lavie and Narayan 1993: 5), creativity is about change, and moreover that its source lies with the agency of the individuals who initiate it, as against the inertia of tradition induced by social conditioning. It is precisely this assumption that we seek to challenge.

Following a tradition, as we have shown, is a matter not of replicating a fixed pattern of behaviour, but of *carrying on* from predecessors. Social life is a task, and for those engaged in it the overriding concern is to keep going, rather than coming to a dead end or becoming caught in a loop of ever-repeating cycles. There is no opposition here between continuity and change: rather, change is what we observe if we look *back* over the ground covered, comparing a present state of affairs with those of select points in the past (Ingold 2000: 147). The forward movement of keeping life going, however, can involve a good measure of creative improvisation, not unlike that required of pedestrians on a busy street who have continually to negotiate a path through what Michel de Certeau (1984: xviii–xix) would call tactical manoeuvrings – that is, through those improvisational adjustments of posture, pace and bearing by which one's own movement is attuned on the one hand to that of companions with whom one wishes to keep abreast or in file, and on the other to strangers coming from different directions with whom one does not wish to collide (Lee and Ingold 2006: 79–82). Nor is this attunement limited to human others, for it must also take account of non-human presences of all sorts, both mobile and stationary. There is no reason, as Vokes points out in this volume (after Latour 1993), to limit the scope of social life to *human* actants.

Improvisation is relational, then, because it goes on along 'ways of life' that are as entangled and mutually responsive as are the paths of pedestrians on the street. And by the same token, the creativity it manifests is not distributed among all the individuals of a society as an agency that each is supposed to possess a priori – an internal capacity of mind to come up with intentions and to act upon them, causing effects in the vicinity (Gell 1999: 16–17) – but rather lies in the dynamic potential of an entire field of relationships to bring forth the persons situated in it.

We find a precedent for this view in the writings of the theologian H.N. Wieman. It is necessary, Wieman writes, to distinguish two senses of creativity: 'One is a characteristic doing of the human person. The other is what personality undergoes but cannot do'. A human being is creative in the first sense 'when he constructs something according to a new design which has already come within reach of his imagination… The second kind of creativity is *what progressively creates personality in community*' (Wieman 1961: 65–6, our emphasis).

Now in the first sense, the meanings of creativity and agency coincide in the notion of the 'doing' of the person. However, the creativity of social life, we contend, has to be understood in Wieman's second sense. As one of us has argued elsewhere, 'social life is not something the person does but rather what the person undergoes' – a process in which people 'do not make societies but, living socially, make themselves' (Ingold 1986: 247). Another way of saying that people make themselves is to say they not only *grow* but are also *grown*, in that they undergo histories of development and maturation within fields of relationships established through the presence and activities of others (Ingold 2000: 144). Critically, this growth is not just in strength and stature, but also in knowledge, in the work of the imagination and the formation of ideas. The latter is, after all, as much a full-bodied knitting together of materials and experience as the former.

Returning to the analogy with the pedestrian wayfarer, every idea is like a place you visit. You may arrive there along one or several paths, and linger for a while before moving on, perhaps to circle around and return some time later. Each time you revisit the idea it is a little different, enriched by the memories and experience of your previous stay. Leading others along the same pathways, you may also share the idea with them, though again, as each brings along the particularities of their own previous experience, it will not be quite the same for one individual as for anyone else. But there would be no ideas, just as there would be no places, were it not for the movements of people towards, around and away from them. Only when we look back, searching for antecedents for new things, do ideas appear as the spontaneous creations of an isolated mind encased in a body, rather than way stations along the trails of living beings, moving through a world.

Perhaps that is how we might have viewed the creativity of the fictitious architect, introduced in the last section, who has produced a design for a revolutionary new building. His design would exemplify what the philosopher and psychologist Margaret Boden, a pioneer in the study of artificial intelligence, calls a 'creative idea'. There are two senses, she writes, in which ideas can be deemed creative. One sense is psychological, the other historical, and she calls them *P-creative* and *H-creative* for short. Basically, an idea is P-creative when it is fundamentally novel with respect to the mind of the individual who had it. It is H-creative when it is novel with respect to *the whole of human history* (Boden 1990: 32). Thus our architect, having produced a totally unprecedented design, could claim to be H-creative. This is not a claim, however, to the effect that his design took shape within the historical current of social life, or through any such worldly engagements. To the contrary, it is a claim to total independence from any external influence whatever! Social relations and historical engagements, in Boden's world, have a bearing only on the dissemination and recognition of ideas, not on their origination. In coming up with creative ideas it seems that every mind is on its own, effectively cut off from the world of persons, objects and relations in which it necessarily subsists. As Boden states, quite categorically, 'the mind's creations must be produced by the mind's resources' (ibid.: 29).

Even architects, however, are human beings. They move in the same circles as those who walk the streets of the cities they have helped to design. And it is surely in these movements, not in splendid isolation, that their ideas take shape. For the mind, as Andy Clark has observed, is a notoriously 'leaky organ' that refuses to stay inside the skull, but shamelessly mingles with the body and the world in the conduct of its operations, turning whatever it finds there into resources for the solution of its own problems (Clark 1997: 53; see Ingold 2001: 138). Thus, far from being a strategic planner, aloof from the material world upon which its designs are inscribed, the mind is in practice a hotbed of tactical and relational improvisation. As it mingles with the world, the mind's creativity is inseparable from that of the total matrix of relations in which it is embedded and into which it extends, and whose unfolding is constitutive of the process of social life.

Improvisation is Temporal

According to what might be called the 'traditional view of tradition', its enactment is rather like the derivation of a sequence of numbers from the iteration of a basic formula. As the formula is passed down from generation to generation as part of a schema or code of conduct, so its recipients are destined to replicate the same sequence. Against this background, creative innovations stand out like prime numbers: they resist decomposition into already existing ideas or entities just as prime numbers cannot be divided by any integers other than themselves. This parallel is suggested by the art historian George Kubler (1962: 39), in an essay in which he attempts to link the distinction between the conventional outcomes of routine, traditional performance and the novel products of creative design to the perception of time and history.

> Our actual perception of time depends on regularly recurrent events, unlike the awareness of history, which depends upon unforeseeable change and variety. Without change there is no history; without regularity there is no time. Time and history are related as rule and variation: time is the regular setting for the vagaries of history. (ibid.: 71–2)

Thus the replications of tradition, endlessly repeated, belong to time; the novelties of invention, each a one-off, belong to history.

Time, in this view, is not creative; it brings nothing forth. Rather, what has once been brought forth, through a unique historical event of creation, ultimately sinks back into time through its subsequent replication. The first house to be built from the design of our revolutionary architect, for example, marks a historical moment, but the hundredth has already faded into the backdrop of time against which a succession of other inventions make their entrance (Ingold 1986: 340). Thus history is configured as a sequence of creative innovations, cast upon the ground of the repetition of their antecedents. Though new things can turn out to be long-lasting, they are dated to their first appearance, and vanish from history as soon as the present-day of this appearance has fallen back into the past and the novelty of their impact has worn off. They become old: no longer of the present, they mark past time. The same can happen to people too, as Cathrine Degnen shows in this volume. 'Old people' are deemed to belong to time and not to history: we celebrate their anniversaries but do not expect them to *do* anything except repeat themselves, even in contexts that demand otherwise. Their moment is past, and the past is over, finished.

The notion that once they cease to be 'new', persons and things can no longer be deemed creative or have any bearing on what comes to pass, is a corollary of the backwards reading that judges creativity by the innovativeness of its results rather than by the improvisations that went into the processes of producing them. Why should building the hundredth house be any less creative than building the first, even if the design remains unchanged? To be sure, some procedures may have become routine, but as the world will not stand still the challenge remains of accommodating a fixed plan to a fluid reality. Or more generally, nothing that people (or indeed, other organisms) do ever exactly repeats. No repeating system in the living world can be perfect, and it is precisely because imperfections in the system call for continual correction that all repetition involves improvisation. That is why life is rhythmic rather then metronomic, for the essence of rhythm, as the philosopher Henri Lefebvre has shown in his essay on *Rhythmanalysis*, lies in the 'movements and differences within repetition', rather than in repetition per se (Lefebvre 2004: 90).

Whereas innovation, in the backwards reading of creativity, lies outside of time, improvisation, in a forward reading, is inherently temporal. This is a time, however, that is not marked out by the oscillations of a perfectly repeating system such as a clock or metronome, or by the revolutions of the planets, but one that is lived and felt in the pulsating rhythms of life itself. Though it is a linear time, its linearity is of a particular kind. It is not the kind of line that goes from point to point, connecting up a succession of present instants arrayed diachronically as locations in space might be arrayed synchronically. It is rather a line that grows, issuing forth from its advancing tip rather like a root or creeper probes the earth. More than any other philosopher, we owe our understanding of this sense of time, as *duration*, to Henri Bergson. 'Our duration', Bergson wrote, 'is not merely one instant replacing another; if it were, there would never be anything but present – no prolonging of the past in the actual... Duration is the continuous progress of the past which gnaws into the future and which swells as it advances' (Bergson 1911: 4–5).

For Bergson, then, growing older is not the falling back of an already completed, uniquely historical being into time – as the sand falls back into an upended hourglass (ibid.: 18) – but the advance of time itself as it brings forth being in an ongoing generative movement that, since it is open-ended and never complete, is carried on rather than replicated by generations following. Thus the past, far from being set off against the present as a repository of finished business, is continually active in the present, pressing against the future. In this pressure lies the work of memory, imagined not as a register or drawer in which records of past events are filed away, but as the guiding hand of a consciousness that, as it goes along, also remembers the way. 'There is no register, no drawer... In reality, the past ... follows us at every instant; all that we have felt, thought and willed from our earliest infancy is there, leaning over the present that is about to join it, pressing against the portals of consciousness that would fain leave it outside' (ibid.: 5).

What Bergson is describing here is the duration of a consciousness that is improvisatory: guided by the past but not determined by it; heading into a future that is essentially unforeseeable. Only when we look back over the ground covered do we account for our actions as the step-by-step realization of plans or prior intentions, as though for every act there was a novel intention that precisely anticipated its outcome. What this account offers is a retrospective reconstruction of conduct that breaks the forward movement of consciousness into a succession of fragments, each initiated by a wilfully creative (or innovative) act of design followed by its determined execution (Ingold 1986: 210). In this backwards reading, the concrete line that 'goes along' and grows as it advances, is replaced by an abstract geometry of linear connections between points that are already given before the journey begins. Such, argued Bergson, is the perspective of the intellect, 'whose eyes are ever turned to the rear' (Bergson 1911: 49).

Our argument that creativity is a process that living beings undergo as they make their ways through the world carries a corollary of capital importance. It is that this process is going on, all the time, in the circulations and fluxes of the materials that surround us and indeed of which we are made – of the earth we stand on, the water that allows it to bear fruit, the air we breathe, and so on. These materials are life-giving, and their movements, mixtures and bindings are creative in themselves. The ancients knew this when they derived the term 'material' from *mater*, meaning 'mother' (Allen 1998: 177). And they knew, too, that even the generation of ideas involves sweat, blood and tears when they extended the meaning of the verb to 'conceive' from the development of an embryo in the womb to that of ideas in the mind.[1] But by the same token, creativity is *not* a faculty of the disembodied mind, as it is taken to be in most psychological treatments of the subject, whose designs are actively imposed upon a world of matter that is effectively dead. Indeed the idea that the mind's creations figure against the ground of a material world that is lifeless and inert is a product of exactly the same backwards reading that, as we have seen, sets the innovations of the present over against the dead weight of the past.

Improvisation is the Way we Work

We began with the assertion that there is no script for social and cultural life. But there are most certainly scripts *within* it. In our capacity as ethnographers, we write, and so – as Robey Callahan and Trevor Stack point out in this volume – do advertising copywriters and authors of fiction. Though these kinds of writing, with the possible exception of advertisements, do not tell people exactly what they should do, there are plenty of other examples of scripts that do. More or less explicit instructions abound. They may be variously notated: writing is just one of many possibilities that also include signs, diagrams and the notational systems used for music and dance. Indeed it might be objected that our initial assertion is unjustified: that lives *are* scripted, at least to some extent, and therefore that people do *not* have to improvise all the time. Have we not been led, by a faulty initial premise, to exaggerate the importance of improvisation?

We believe not. Our claim is not just that life is unscripted, but more fundamentally, that it is unscriptable. Or to put it another way, it cannot be fully codified as the output of any system of rules and representations. This is because life does not pick its way across the surface of a world where everything is fixed and in its proper place, but is a movement through a world that is crescent. To keep on going, it has to be open and responsive to continually changing environmental conditions. A system that was strictly bound to the execution of a pre-composed script would be unable to respond and would be thrown off course by the slightest deviation. This, indeed, is the typical predicament of the novice in any craft who has, of necessity, first to learn by the rules. Fluent response calls for a degree of precision in the coordination of perception and action that can only be achieved through practice. But it is this, rather than a knowledge of the rules, that distinguishes the skilled practitioner from the novice. And in this, too, we find the essence of improvisation.

The theorist of design, David Pye, has distinguished between two kinds of workmanship, respectively of 'risk' and 'certainty'. In the workmanship of risk the quality of the outcome depends at every moment on the exercise of care, judgement and dexterity. The practitioner has continually to make fine adjustments to keep on course, in response to a sensitive monitoring of the conditions of the task as it unfolds. Throughout the work there is an ever-present risk that it will go awry and that the result will be spoiled. The workmanship of certainty, by contrast, proceeds by way of a pre-planned series of operations, each of which is mechanically constrained to the extent that the result is predetermined and outside the operative's control. He cannot alter course in mid-flow, but must stop, alter the settings of the apparatus, and start again. The pure form of the workmanship of certainty, of course, would be full automation (Pye 1968: 4–5). To exemplify the contrast, Pye compares handwriting and printing. It is an example worth following up.

In writing with a pen, nothing guides the tip save the movement of the hand and fingers with their characteristic penhold. The line rendered on paper is the trace of an ongoing gestural improvisation. Though we may have been taught the 'correct' ways to form letters by copying models, a person's handwriting is as distinctive and recognizable an aspect of their being, as it issues forth into the world, as is their voice. 'Writing is more than a means of communication', observes handwriting specialist Rosemary Sassoon, 'it is oneself on paper' (Sassoon 2000: 103). As Elizabeth Cory-Pearce points out in this volume, the handwritten text of archival documents is a tangible and relatively durable manifestation of the presence of identifiable persons. This personal style is not planned or designed, but emerges through a history of improvisation, above all in finding ways to connect letters in the cursive script in the interests of speed and efficiency. In 'joined-up' writing we fashion the joins, each in our own way, as we go along. Most writers of English, for example, when they write the word *the*, eventually find themselves running the cross of the *t* into the following *h*, despite having been taught that the join should be formed from the loop at the bottom of the first letter (Sassoon 2000: 40–50).

There is, in short, no script for script. Even the hand of the traditional scribe, trained through a more rigorous discipline in the art of beautiful writing, has to find its own way. It would indeed be a mistake, as Karin Barber emphasizes in the next chapter, to suppose that a disciplined performance that strains after the perceived perfection of its model is any less improvisatory than one that celebrates the leeway of performers to follow any path they choose. Citing from the work of the music psychologist Nicholas Cook (1990: 113), Barber observes that a classical musician who plays from a score improvises just as much as a jazz musician who does not. The difference lies in their aims. The former is, as it were, centripetal, aiming for the bull's eye; the latter centrifugal, seeking to cast wide. This same variation, from the centripetal to the centrifugal, can be discerned in many other fields of performance, such as calligraphy, dance and athletics. One has only to compare archery with shot-putting!

But it is perhaps in the art of walking that we find closest parallel to handwriting. For although walking can be analysed into discrete steps, as handwriting into discrete letters, in the actual *practice* of walking, steps do not follow one another like beads on a string, any more than do the letters of writing. Rather, each is simultaneously a following-through of the one before and a preparation for the one following. Their order is processional rather than successional (Ingold 2006a: 67). But the same is true of any other skilled practice involving rhythmically repeated movements. One may learn the practice as a string of beads, as John Gatewood (1985) showed in his classic study of learning the ropes on board a fishing vessel, but proficiency lies in being able to run operations together – to *move through* them with the fluency of a dancer instead of executing each in a linear series of point-to-point connections. 'Rather than speaking of ideas, concepts, categories and links', Gatewood suggests, 'we should think of flows, contours, intensities and resonances' (Gatewood 1985: 216). Precisely the same point emerges from Hughes-Freeland's study, in this volume, of Javanese dance. Though the dance is explained to novices as a punctuated sequence of prescribed steps, the aesthetic aim is to emulate the ceaseless movement of flowing water.

Let us now return to printing, which Pye compared to handwriting as a workmanship of certainty rather than risk. In this case, surely, the order of letters *is* successional; they follow one another as discrete entities. Moreover both their shapes and their sequence are predetermined, the first by the engraving of the type, the second by the work of the compositor who sets it. Has the development of printing, then, reduced the scope of improvisation in the world of letters? Pye's answer is that it has not; it has simply moved it forward. For there is no doubt that engraving and typesetting are instances of the workmanship of risk, both – if anything – requiring even more care, judgement and dexterity than handwriting itself. Once again, this is a point that applies more generally. As the historian François Sigaut has shown, the story of technology is one of constantly renewed attempts to codify skilled practice and to build machines that would embody these codes in the principles of their operation. Yet these attempts chase an ever-receding target, for as fast as skills are incorporated by technology into mechanical devices, new skills develop around the machines themselves (Sigaut 1994: 446). So universally is this the case that Sigaut feels justified in referring to the 'law of the irreducibility of skills'.

Our claim, fully consistent with Sigaut's law, is that the improvisational creativity of skilled practice is foundational to the way we work. This does not mean, however, that life is unpredictable. Predictability, as we have seen, is a hallmark of the workmanship of certainty. And unpredictability, conversely, is often taken to be of the essence of creativity. Boden, for example, links unpredictability explicitly to what she calls the 'surprise-value' of creativity (Boden 1990: 227). But this is to look back on the creative process, finding results considered so innovative that they cannot be explained by their antecedent conditions. We may indeed be surprised when things do not turn out as predicted, and science – on the principle of conjecture and refutation – has even turned its record of predictive failure into a history of advance. Improvisation, however, augurs no surprise for the simple reason that it does not endeavour to predict (Ingold 2006b: 18–19). To borrow a formulation by which Pierre Bourdieu (1977: 95) characterized the generative capacity of the *habitus*, the improvisation of the way we work is 'as remote from a creation of unpredictable novelty as it is from a simple mechanical reproduction of the initial conditionings'. Its aim is not to project future states, but to follow the paths along which such projections take shape. Far from attempting to bring closure to the world, or to tie up loose ends, improvisation makes the most of the multiple possibilities they afford for *keeping life going*. For the world will not be closed, and goes its own way regardless of what we may have to say about it. The creativity of this world may be a source of perpetual astonishment, and indeed – as we show below – of *wonder*, but so long as we do not pretend to control it or to hold it to account, it occasions no surprise.

Histories of Creativity, Creativities in History

So far we have focused on the ways in which the idea of creativity enters contemporary discussions of making and doing things, of innovation and tradition, and of the generativity of social and cultural processes. Most of the chapters in this book do indeed situate 'creativity' in its present-day settings, reflecting on currents of lived time and on lifetimes. However, the idea itself has a past, and several of our contributing authors also allude to longer-term histories that reveal the ways in which it has emerged and the transformations it has undergone. Eric Hirsch and Sharon Macdonald, for example, relate changing connotations of creativity to conceptions of the individual and of identity from the seventeenth century onwards, while James Leach considers the implications of the link between creativity and property that was established in eighteenth-century European and American political philosophy. Moreover, granted that creativity – as we have already argued – is inherently temporal, its unfolding in time has to be grounded in deeper historical processes. As Wendy James and David Mills explain, introducing a volume resulting from the 2002 ASA conference on *Time and Society*, the flow of human action is always part of the 'flow of history' (James and Mills 2005: 2). This is not to deny that social and cultural change occurs, or that it may be marked by radical breaks with the past. The point, as James and Mills argue, is that the relationships between ongoing lived time and what comes to be retrospectively constituted as history are not given. They require analysis.

As we have already noted, Western views of creativity are associated with modernity, allowing Liep (2001), for instance, to link intensified interest in forms of creativity with economic changes that assign high value to innovation in the production of new commodities. In the context of 'late modernity' Liep defines creativity as a form of 'cross-fertilization' that occurs with the 'fusion of disparate cultural configurations' (ibid.: 12). Creativity and improvisation have also been interpreted as modes of response to rapid social and technological change associated with 'modernization' in different contexts (for example, Volkman 1994). More specifically, the idea of creativity as a unique faculty that human beings 'have', namely a capacity to create, appears to have come into common usage from the early to mid-twentieth century onwards (Kristeller 1983; Pope 2005). Yet these latter-day notions of creativity have not come from nowhere, but are rooted in much older ideas about creation and what it means to be creative (see Pope 2005).

In his Introduction to Part I of this volume, Ingold contrasts two notions of creativity that can be discerned in early twentieth-century philosophical works. It may be understood, on the one hand, as the production of novelty through the recombination of already extant elements, or on the other, as a process of growth, becoming and change. The former view posits the world as an assemblage of discrete parts; the latter as a continuous movement or flow. Both these formulations of creativity, however, can be traced historically to earlier understandings of novelty, seen in conceptions – not necessarily opposed or mutually exclusive – both of the assemblage of parts and of more fluid processes of coming-into-being. In what follows we place these formulations in the context of medieval views, before turning to early modern as well as more recent conceptions of creativity. Our aim is to show that while both forward and backwards readings of creativity, as growing emergence and produced novelty, have coexisted throughout the history of European ideas, their balance eventually shifted decisively towards the latter.

We can begin by returning to the notion of wonder. For medieval people, as Lorraine Daston and Katharine Park have shown in their study of the history of this notion from the twelfth to the eighteenth century, wonder was situated 'between the known and the unknown' (Daston and Park 2001: 13). In this respect it was an apprehension of novelty, of the unexpected, which also arose out of an acknowledged 'ignorance of cause' (ibid.: 23). Wonder was associated with what were perceived to be rare phenomena that were unfamiliar in relation to customary or everyday experience. Medieval catalogues of wonders embraced a rich assortment of entities, from magnets to werewolves. In travel writing and maps novelty and variety were located in what were seen as the margins of the world. Thus thirteenth-century maps depicting Europe, the Mediterranean and the Holy Land at the centre also positioned Africa and Asia at the periphery, and it was here that wonders such as the winged salamander and humans with one leg (*Sciopodes*) or no head (*Blemmyes*) were thought to gather. Daston and Park (2001: 25) quote one source as claiming that 'at the farthest reaches of the world often occur new marvels and wonders, as though Nature plays with greater freedom secretly at the edges of the world'. These wonders were characterized by their composition, with parts missing or exaggerated, or with parts rearranged to produce what were sometimes appreciated and at other times denigrated as 'monstrous' creatures.

Novelty as recombination was also found in the hybrid animal-human figures with which many medieval and early modern writings were illustrated. These comprised disparate elements such as a human body and a dog's head. Drawings of combinatory creatures, such as the fish-man, were often inserted in the margins of medieval manuscripts (Camille 1992). The 'exotic races' at the edge of the world, however, were perceived to differ crucially from the individual 'monsters' that emerged in Europe. The former were supposed to have been generated by nature; the latter by the intervention of divine will. These monsters, moreover, were interpreted negatively as omens from God of future unwelcome happenings. Though, in the Judeo-Christian view, God had created the universe, in the twelfth century nature was not absolutely tied to divine command, but was rather thought to possess 'an independent internal order located in the chains of causes that produced particular phenomena' (Daston and Park 2001: 49). Wonders in the form of rare and novel combinations of parts were created, then, through the agency of nature and of God.

The rearrangement of components present in God's creations and in the playfulness of nature was also a feature of human works. Camille points out that 'the medieval artist's ability was measured not in terms of invention, as today, but in the capacity to combine traditional motifs in new and challenging ways' (Camille 1992: 36). The compositions illuminating the borders of manuscripts, for instance, would newly gloss, undermine or mock written texts with drawings, often taken from pattern-books, of already familiar figures such as monkeys and snails. Novelty in these manuscripts therefore worked through supplementation as well as through the juxtaposition of elements. It also operated through extensions and flows wherein the flourishes of letters would merge with creatures and other motifs.

A similar appreciation of combinatory and heterogeneous assemblages was registered in early modern cabinets of curiosities that displayed wonders in the form of *naturalia*, the products of nature, and *artificialia*, the products of human contriving. At the turn of the seventeenth century the Aristotelian opposition of nature and art still held, and in this construal the things constituted by nature possessed motion or an 'innate impulse to change', whereas the products of art did not (Daston and Park 1998: 264). Furthermore, whereas God was regarded as the 'supreme artisan of all natural forms', human designers often sought to imitate or to 'ape' natural wonders (Kemp 1995: 178). In the objects of wonder displayed in cabinets, the natural and the artificial were brought together, intricately interwoven and fused. Natural products provided the impetus for human designs, for example in the work of embellishing and amplifying the contours of shells that were incorporated into gold settings to form goblets. Such objects were identifiably 'compound ensembles', but they also sometimes erased distinctions between art and nature – in their appearance rather than in the mode of their formation (ibid.: 183). In this respect high value was placed on verisimilitude, and 'creative fantasy' was subordinated to the 'technical virtuosity of mimesis' (Daston and Park 2001: 284). Novelty in the form of recombination was joined by wonders in the form of copies.

Medieval and early modern understandings of wonder and novelty, as forms of recombination and assemblage of disparate elements, were not necessarily distinct from those that emphasized emergence through flows and growth. This is attested, for example, by Bakhtin's (1984 [1965]) analysis of medieval European popular culture and folk humour. Central to popular cultural forms, especially carnival, was the imagery of grotesque realism that rejected the notion of finished forms, be they animal, vegetable or human, and presented these not in a static world, but in terms of their movement, blending and merging. Thus 'the grotesque image reflects a phenomenon in transformation, an as yet unfinished metamorphosis, of death and birth, growing and becoming' (ibid.: 24). One of the central grotesque images was that of the open human body which was blended with other bodies, with animals and objects: this was an 'ever unfinished, ever creating body' (ibid.: 26). And among the principal sources for this grotesque conception of the body was the very tradition of wonders, with its hybrid figures of mixed parts, which we have already described. Thus in the medieval popular imagery of the grotesque we find a fusion rather than a division between the combinatorial assembly of hybrid forms and the processual generation of a world of movement and becoming.

The classical aesthetics of the Renaissance, however, brought a shift of emphasis in conceptions of the body, away from principles of flux and generativity, towards a notion of the completed, clearly bounded body of the individual separated from the world. As Stallybrass and White (1986) have shown, the canon of the classical body, with stable boundaries, underwrote the formation of individual identity throughout the seventeenth century. This shift from conceptions of a relational body that was open, heterogeneous and part of generative processes, to an individuated body with stable boundaries and fixed form, may, we suggest, be correlated with changing understandings of what it means to create: from a formulation in which to create is to be part of an ongoing process, to one that 'reads back' from the finished product to the capacity that produced it. And as this capacity became more closely associated, in the eighteenth century, with individual agency and built-in human faculties, a further differentiation took place: anything defined as truly creative had to be 'original' rather than 'derivative' or 'copied' (Pope 2005). To create, thenceforth, was to orchestrate discontinuity rather than to participate in a constantly emerging process.

A Volume of Creativity

This book challenges the idea that the capacity for creative improvisation is exercised by individuals against the conventions of culture and society. Improvisation and creativity, we contend, are intrinsic to the very processes of social and cultural life. The chapters that follow highlight the creative dynamic of cultural processes: the extent to which cultural forms are produced and reproduced, rather than merely replicated and transmitted, through active and experimental engagement over time and in the generation of persons within their social and material environments. They describe the ways in which creative and improvisational action emerges in writing, drawing, pattern-making, dreaming, poetry, drama and dance, politics, photography, narrative, commercial industry, radio and the practice of anthropology. They report on studies carried out in countries and regions as diverse as Japan, Papua New Guinea, England, Southern India, Uganda, Algeria, Java and New Zealand. Departing from the conventional characterization of creativity as an ability of gifted persons, they show how creativity is not necessarily sought after or celebrated in contexts where continuities with established cultural forms and models are valued. Emphasizing the collaborative and political dimensions of creative performance, they demonstrate the ways in which the reproduction of existing forms leads in practice to variations in their situated enactments. And with an eye to how the meaning of creativity has itself changed throughout the history of ideas, they consider its applicability as a term of cross-cultural analysis, as well as the potential of a focus on creative improvisation to support or subvert existing paradigms both within and beyond the discipline of anthropology.

The issue of how form is generated from precedent is central to the chapters by Amar S. Mall and Fuyubi Nakamura, who explore the dynamics of making in the respective fields of pattern-drawing and calligraphic writing in order to trace the material engagements entailed in creative practice. Such exploration prompts questions about the relationships between repetition and deviation, and between replication and variation. That there is creativity in the following of tradition is a theme pursued in chapters throughout this volume, ranging from Felicia Hughes-Freeland's discussion of Javanese dance to Jeanette Edwards' demonstration of how Baptists explore innovative techniques of human conception through ancient texts. These chapters are concerned with nuances and complexities, questioning the black-and-white simplicity of such received oppositions as invention versus convention, and innovation versus tradition. In this they show how ethnographically informed anthropological research can make a quite distinctive contribution to the contemporary understanding of creative processes (see Glaskin 2005).

Creativity, with its improvisational dynamic, calls for analysis of the social relations and cultural formations that guide it and in terms of which it has effects. Accordingly, many chapters explore processes of creativity in relation to definitions of personhood, sources of agency, patterns of ownership and notions of authorship. As Karin Barber explains in the next chapter, creativity is shaped by models of social being. Given these entanglements, it is better approached as socially embedded and culturally diffuse than as a clearly defined act or bounded product. These qualities of creativity are described in subsequent chapters in terms of fluidity and flows. Rather than associating creativity with newness and the disjunctures this is often taken to imply, several authors stress continuity and connection as ways through which creativity emerges. Treating creativity as a social and cultural process, these authors bring into critical focus the limitations entailed in conceptualizing creativity as a form of invention exercised by the autonomous individual.

As a social process in which persons are engaged, creativity is at the same time configured, narrated and reflected upon in discourse. While emergent in ongoing social action, it is also often marked and framed. These reflexive dimensions, as Barber shows, can be integral to performances that bring their own processes of production into focus. Relations of power and authority are often important in determining what is considered to be creative and what is not. Judith Scheele's chapter draws attention to the workings of these relations alongside the characterization of tradition in local political discourses. James Leach's contribution also underlines the politics implicit in anthropological interpretations that deploy Western concepts of creativity in places where they do not necessarily belong. He warns that such deployment can amount to a kind of 'conceptual colonialism'. The cross-cultural dynamics entailed in the construal of creativity are central to the chapter by Elizabeth Cory-Pearce, in which she questions the stability of the categories 'self' and 'other', and asks where creativity is located in a world of historical interconnections and migrations. Such questions are pertinent, especially in the light of concerns with how innovation works in colonial and post-colonial contexts (see Küchler and Were 2003).

These contexts, of course, include those of anthropological research and teaching. If, as John Davis (1999) has asserted, anthropological description is itself a creative practice, then our investigations of creativity cannot be confined to the settings of fieldwork, as portrayed for example in the chapters by Richard Vokes and Clara Mafra, but must extend to the environments of the ethnographer's study, in which he or she sits down to write, not to mention the classroom or teaching workshop where professional anthropologists and students together wrestle with the problems of what anthropological knowledge is, how it is created and how it should be conveyed. Robey Callahan and Trevor Stack, in their chapter, describe how the struggling ethnographer attempts to reconcile the flux and immersion of the field experience with the isolation and critical distance required of the writer who is under pressure to produce new knowledge. Amanda Ravetz, for her part, analyses the tension between the pedagogical principles embedded in the training of students, respectively, in fine art and social anthropology, through the example of a workshop for students in visual anthropology. As both these chapters show, and as Mark Harris points out in his Introduction to Part IV, there are good grounds for opening up the notion of the field to include the labours of both writing and teaching, and the settings in which they are conducted, since they are as much implicated in the creation of anthropological knowledge as is the labour of fieldwork, conventionally understood.

Apart from an opening chapter by Karin Barber and a closing epilogue by Clara Mafra, this book is divided into four parts. The first, corresponding to the generative aspect of improvisation, explores the creativities of life and art, and considers the issues involved in the attribution of creative agency, for example in the fields of the graphic and performing arts, and of intellectual property law. The second part, corresponding to the relational aspect of improvisation, shows how the sources of creativity are practically embedded in social, political and religious institutions, and in dispositions of power and authority. Part III is concerned with improvisation in its temporal aspect, focusing on the relation between creativity and the perception and passage of time in history, tradition and the life-course. The final part takes up the improvisational quality of the way we work, looking at the creativity of anthropological scholarship itself. How, if at all, does the generation of new knowledge in the dialogic contexts of encounters between ethnographers and their subjects, or between teachers of anthropology and their students, differ from the generativity of those interpersonal encounters in which all social and cultural life subsists? For some of the answers, and for many more questions, read on!

Notes

1. We are grateful to Margherita Pieraccini for this observation.

References

Allen, N. (1998), 'The category of substance: a Maussian theme revisited', in W. James and N.J. Allen (eds), *Marcel Mauss: A Centenary Tribute*, New York: Berghahn Books.

Aunger, R. (2000), *Darwinizing Culture*, Oxford: Oxford University Press.

Bakhtin, M. (1984 [1965]), *Rabelais and His World* (trans. Hélène Iswolsky), Bloomington: Indiana University Press.

Bergson, H. (1911), *Creative Evolution* (trans. A. Mitchell), London: Macmillan.

Boden, M. (1990), *The Creative Mind: Myths and Mechanisms*, London: Weidenfeld and Nicolson.

Bourdieu, P. (1977), *Outline of a Theory of Practice* (trans. R. Nice), Cambridge: Cambridge University Press.

Brand, S. (1994), *How Buildings Learn: What Happens to Them After They're Built*, London: Penguin.

Bruner, E. (1993), 'Epilogue: Creative persona and the problem of authenticity', in S. Lavie, K. Narayan and R. Rosaldo (eds), *Creativity/Anthropology*, Ithaca, NY: Cornell University Press.

Camille, M. (1992), *Image on the Edge. The Margins of Medieval Art*, London: Reaktion Books.

Certeau, M. de (1984), *The Practice of Everyday Life* (trans. S. Rendall), Berkeley: University of California Press.

Clark, A. (1997), *Being There: Putting Brain, Body and the World Together Again*, Cambridge, Mass.: MIT Press.

Cook, N. (1990), *Music, Imagination and Culture*, Oxford: Oxford University Press.

Daston, L. and Park, K. (2001), *Wonders and the Order of Nature, 1150–1750*, New York: Zone Books.

Davis, J. (1999), 'Administering creativity', *Anthropology Today*, 15(2): 4–9.

Friedman, J. (2001), 'The iron cage of creativity: an exploration', in J. Liep (ed), *Locating Cultural Creativity*, London: Pluto Press.

Gatewood, J. (1985), 'Actions speak louder than words', in J.W. Dougherty (ed), *Directions in Cognitive Anthropology*, Urbana: University of Illinois Press.

Gell, A. (1999), *Art and Agency: An Anthropological Theory*, Oxford: Clarendon Press.

Glaskin, K. (2005), 'Innovation and ancestral revelation: The case of dreams', *Journal of the Royal Anthropological Institute*, 11: 297–314.

Ingold, T. (1986), *Evolution and Social Life*, Cambridge: Cambridge University Press.

—— (2000), *The Perception of the Environment: Essays on Livelihood, Dwelling and Skill*, London: Routledge.

—— (2001), 'From the transmission of representations to the education of attention', in H. Whitehouse (ed), *The Debated Mind: Evolutionary Psychology versus Ethnography*, Oxford: Berg.

—— (2006a), 'Walking the plank: meditations on a process of skill', in J. Dakers (ed), *Defining Technological Literacy: Towards an Epistemological Framework*, New York: Palgrave Macmillan.

—— (2006b), 'Rethinking the animate, re-animating thought', *Ethnos*, 71: 9–20.
Jackson, M. (1996), *Things As They Are: New Directions in Phenomenological Anthropology*, Bloomington: Indiana University Press.
James, W. and Mills, D. (2005), 'Introduction: From representation to action in the flow of time', in W. James and D. Mills (eds), *The Qualities of Time: Anthropological Approaches* (ASA Monographs 41), Oxford: Berg.
Kemp, M. (1995), '"Wrought by no artist's hand": The natural, the artificial, the exotic, and the scientific in some artefacts from the Renaissance', in C. Farago (ed), *Reframing the Renaissance. Visual Culture in Europe and Latin America 1450–1650*, New Haven: Yale University Press.
Kristeller, P.O. (1983), '"Creativity" and "Tradition"', *Journal of the History of Ideas*, 44(1): 105–13.
Kubler, G. (1962), *The Shape of Time: Remarks on the History of Things*, New Haven: Yale University Press.
Küchler, S. and Were, G. (2003), 'Clothing and innovation: A Pacific perspective', *Anthropology Today*, 19(2): 3–5.
Latour, B. (1993), *We Have Never Been Modern*, Hemel Hempstead: Harvester Wheatsheaf.
Lee, J. and Ingold, T. (2006), 'Fieldwork on foot: perceiving, routing, socializing', in S. Coleman and P. Collins (eds), *Locating the Field: Space, Place and Context in Anthropology* (ASA Monographs 42), Oxford: Berg.
Lefebvre, H. (2004), *Rhythmanalysis: Space, Time and Everyday Life* (trans. S. Elden and G. Moore), London: Continuum.
Liep, J. (2001), 'Introduction', in J. Liep (ed), *Locating Cultural Creativity*, London: Pluto Press.
Pope, R. (2005), *Creativity. Theory, History and Practice*, London: Routledge.
Pye, D. (1968), *The Nature and Art of Workmanship*, Cambridge: Cambridge University Press.
Rosaldo, R., Lavie, S. and Narayan, K. (1993), 'Introduction: Creativity in anthropology', in S. Lavie, K. Narayan and R. Rosaldo (eds), *Creativity/Anthropology*, Ithaca, NY: Cornell University Press.
Sassoon, R. (2000), *The Art and Science of Handwriting*, Bristol: Intellect.
Schade-Poulsen, M. (2001), 'The "playing" of music in a state of crisis: Gender and Rai music in Algeria', in J. Liep (ed), *Locating Cultural Creativity*, London: Pluto Press.
Sigaut, F. (1994), 'Technology', in T. Ingold (ed), *Companion Encyclopedia of Anthropology: Humanity, Culture and Social Life*, London: Routledge.
Siza, A. (1997), *Architecture Writings*, ed. A. Angelillo, Milan: Skira Editore.
Sperber, D. (1996), *Explaining Culture: A Naturalistic Approach*. Oxford: Blackwell.
Stallybrass, P. and White, A. (1986), *The Politics and Poetics of Transgression*, London: Methuen.

Volkman, T.A. (1994), 'Our garden in the sea: contingency and improvisation in Mandar women's work', *American Ethnologist*, 21(3): 564–85.

Wieman, H.N. (1961), *Intellectual Foundations of Faith*, London: Vision.

–2–

Improvisation and the Art of Making Things Stick
Karin Barber

The concepts of creativity and cultural improvisation invite us to focus on the growing points of social life: to ask how new ideas, genres, forms of social being come into existence. They present a challenge to anthropology to try to trace the most elusive and fluid aspects of reality. But they also challenge us to understand the fluidity of social processes in relation to the almost universal human effort to fix things – to nail cultural arrangements down, to produce forms that will endure. People's ceaseless innovative and re-creative activity is often directed precisely towards making a mark that transcends space and time. Improvisation and the art of making things stick cannot be separated: we find them everywhere fused and intertwined.

Two venerable models of the nature, place and scope of social innovation lie behind current thinking. One proposes that the normal situation is inertia, stability and repetition. What needs to be explained is how and why change happens. Bascom, for example, suggested that conformity is taken for granted in most social institutions. A preferred site in which to trace the movements of change and innovation, therefore, is art forms, where a greater degree of innovation and creativity may be expected. This, he suggested, may serve to shed light on less visible processes of social and political change in the wider society. Even so, the problem is to explain how traditional, routine repetition with variations – in folk music, for example – can sometimes jump to a qualitative transformation involving genuine originality (Bascom 1959). So in traditional societies, stability and continuity are the default situation and are associated with conformity and a lack of originality; change is exceptional and – when it is not the result of external forces – it is associated with individual innovation and creativity.

The other model starts from the opposite assumption – that everything that happens is new, unrepeatable and not wholly predictable from what went before. G.H. Mead, in *The Philosophy of the Present*, called this the 'emergent'. The present 'is not a piece cut out anywhere from the temporal dimension of uniformly passing reality. Its chief reference is to the emergent event, that is, to the occurrence of something which is more than the processes that have led up to it' (Mead 1932: 23). Scientists and historians seek to find rational order and stretch this back so that the present may be seen to follow from the past; but in fact time itself is constituted out of a succession of 'interruptions'. What takes place does so 'under necessary conditions', but these 'do not determine in its full reality that which emerges' (ibid.: 16). The past is 'as hypothetical as the future'; the present, defined by the emergent, is constantly breaking new ground. The problem here, then, is not how to explain change, but how to account for the social creation of continuity.

In trying to think about how new things emerge from the matrix of the customary on the one hand, and how people go about solidifying the flux of social life on the other – issues which clearly lie at the very centre of anthropology – we find ourselves ambushed at every turn by latent binary distinctions: between 'text' and 'performance'; between scripted and improvised enactment; between memorization and composition; between the creativity that leads to a concrete 'product' and the creativity which is an end in itself.[1] It is worth noting, before we go any further, that in many cultures the ideational repertoire suffers no such handicap. There are local models of being-in-society which effortlessly combine what our own vocabulary keeps separating. Early in the history of our discipline, Malinowski (1935) provided riveting evidence of this in *Coral Gardens and their Magic*.

Growth and Imperishability

Malinowski tells us that Trobrianders cultivated their yam gardens with passion, devotion and artistic care. They grew far more yams than they needed for consumption. They did far more work on the yam gardens than was required in strictly biological terms for successful growth and maturation of the crop – tidying the plots, building beautiful fences. The growth of the yams, and the appearance of the yam garden, reflected, or embodied, the personal and social enhancement of the gardener. As your garden flourished, so did you and your reputation. Gardening, then, was about change, emergence and the progressive manifestation of qualities that were never fixed but constantly crescent. Not only that, but once harvested, the yams did not stay put. Every man grew the bulk of his yams to give to someone else – to his married sister and her husband, or to a chief as tribute. Every man's storehouse was filled by someone else. If the yams were plentiful, both giver and receiver stood to gain in prestige from the transaction. People calculated whether to give or to withhold, and how to conceal the extent to which they did the latter. Both giving and withholding yams were strategies of personal social navigation. Yams, then, moved along the circuits of social relationships and were mobilized in games of alliance and clientship.

Here was a local model of social being which envisaged enormous scope for negotiation and improvisation. It was a model in which personal success was understood as analogous to and deeply connected with growth, increase and change; and in which persons were constituted through constantly renegotiated relations with others, witnessed in the flow of goods from one person to another. But this picture has another equally striking aspect. When people harvested their yams, they built them into towering conical structures of perfect symmetry on the perimeters of their gardens, sheltered by a bower, and put on display to all comers. Then, when it was time to present them to the designated recipient, the tower would be dismantled, carried to the recipient's village and rebuilt in front of his house. After being carefully counted, admired and acknowledged, the pile would be dismantled for a second time and carried into the recipient's storehouse, where again the yams would be arranged meticulously. Malinowski states that the *bwaymas* (the storehouses), especially those of aristocrats and chiefs, were more beautiful than their dwelling houses – better kept, more prominent, more elaborately decorated. And the desire of the storehouse owner is that the yams should remain there permanently: magic is performed to reduce human appetites so that the full storehouse, dark with its freight, will not be depleted.

Their garden magic combined encouraging change and growth ('Shoot up, shoot up, shoot up, *O taytu*'), and striving intensely to stabilize and fix. At key points in the cycle, the garden magician pronounces a spell which reiterates:

> It shall be anchored, it shall be anchored!
> ...It is anchored, my garden is anchored
> Like an immoveable stone is my garden
> Like the bedrock is my garden
> Like a deep-rooted stone is my garden
> My garden is anchored, it is anchored for good and all
>
> (Malinowski 1935: 130).

The garden is 'anchored' before planting; the tubers, once growing, are 'anchored' to secure them with deep roots; and finally, as the storehouse is prepared to receive its pile of donated yams, every component of the building is enumerated – from the corner stone to the ornamented end of the ridge pole – and 'anchored'; eventually, at the end of the harvest process, the magician can sum up, 'my village is anchored'.

What huge effort goes into making things stable, fixing things, and attempting to arrest the processes of consumption and decay! What an extraordinary ambition, to turn piles of perishable yams into monuments outlasting human appetite! The gardeners and the magicians appear to be converting the yams into imperishable wealth. Prosperity is yams that last, that remain so long in the storehouse that the floor becomes black with their dust.

Here, then, is a way of looking at things which has no trouble combining concepts of fluid emergence and fixed stability. The yams must grow and change; shoots must emerge; the tubers must be dug up and circulated through social networks. But for their embodied value to be realized, they must also be fixed and preserved.[2] The human community takes responsibility for both processes, bending their powers of action, volition and utterance both to promote movement and to arrest it. What is most important for the purposes of this chapter is that perdurance is conceived as the outcome of vigorous, unremitting activity. Things do not last through inertia: they are made to last, through intense human creative efforts. Making things stick, then, is most definitely flagged up here as a practice, a process in itself.

Do all human societies share the propensity to build things that transcend time and space? Clearly, not all in the same way. Not far from the Trobriands, the Sabarl islanders developed what Debbora Battaglia has described as a deconstructive philosophy of transience and dissipation, a distrust in language as a vehicle of memory, a diffidence about the possibility of preserving anything or ever knowing anything for sure – a philosophy she contrasts strongly with those of monument-building cultures (Battaglia 1990). It is an outlook that can be explained partly by the Sabarls' peculiar history, which involved a nineteenth-century migration to an infertile rock-fortress without adequate soil or water, resulting in dependence on other islands even for basic necessities. Nonetheless, the central ceremonial and social event, into which Sabarl people poured their resources and effort, was the mortuary feast, precisely designed to recuperate and preserve memory. In these ceremonies, the kin of the deceased extracted and fixed a usable residue of the dead person's persona; at the same time, the event offered a fresh start, realigning the survivors in new configurations of alliance and obligation. Thus the act of fixing and the act of innovative reconfiguration happened simultaneously, and were in fact the same thing. Perhaps what we need, then, is not a binary division between cultures that build monuments and those that do not, but a comparative view of what kind of fixing they do, what models and idioms they use to describe it, and how they provide for the continued generation of novelty in the very act of consolidating tradition.[3]

Performance Theory and Entextualization

If understanding social life is at least partly about understanding how people give form to their activities, then kinds of behaviour often consigned to the margins of social theory – dance, song, verbal art – become central, as Wendy James has demonstrated in her 'new portrait' of anthropology (James 2003). This is not so much (or not only) because, as Bascom thought, performance genres are a privileged place where there is more innovation and creativity, but because the effort to give form here has a reflexive, demonstrative dimension in which its own processes are, as it were, brought to the surface. Gilbert Lewis, in *Day of Shining Red*, alludes to 'the positive alerting peculiar aspect of ritual which calls to us for attention as it does to the performers' (Lewis 1980: 20). Performances attract attention by framing and staging creative, form-giving processes, and in doing so, they not only designate themselves for future re-creation, but also bring to view the operations by which they are constituted. All cultures, I believe, produce forms that are marked out for special attention – whether or not they are thought of, locally, as something we could translate as 'art forms'.

Performance theory, emerging simultaneously in anthropology, folklore and theatre studies and gathering strength in the 1980s and 1990s, greatly enhanced our capacity to recognize and talk about the fluid, processual and emergent properties of performance genres. Battling against long-standing tendencies to reify and freeze them, this theory strongly contrasted 'performance' with 'text', declaring that the two were utterly different in kind. Text implied a view of society as prescriptive, fixed and adhering to rigid structures; performance implied a focus on what was improvised, ephemeral, fluid, of the moment only – but in that moment, vital and responsive to contingencies of context. The habit of reducing performances to fixed written texts was deplored, and a methodology was developed to capture the performance event itself rather than some presumed antecedent script – to capture the unfolding moment of performance in its living, richly context-embedded immediacy. Richard Bauman (1977) speaks of the severe limitations a 'text-centered' approach imposes on the study of oral verbal art. 'Performance can never be text', in Edward Schieffelin's view, for 'performativity is located at the creative, improvisatory edge of practice in the moment it is carried out', whereas 'texts are changeless and enduring' (Schieffelin 1998: 198–9). Dwight Conquergood elegantly sums up the opposition as a war of vocabulary, where the benign forces of 'improvisation', 'flow', 'process', 'participation', 'embodiment', and 'dialogue' are ranged against the enemy lexicon – 'fixity', 'structure', 'objectification', 'reification', 'system', 'distance', and 'detachment' (Conquergood 1989). But while performance theory provided wonderful conceptual tools for thinking about emergence, it had a tendency to dismiss the whole idea of the aspiration to fixity as a scriptocentric imposition. It thus offered inadequate resources for understanding how the fluid is consolidated, and why stunningly creative oral performers so often claim that their texts have never changed by so much as a syllable.

But out of performance theory came its own inverse and complement: the concept of 'entextualization'. The idea was demonstrated in an ethnography of ritual speech by Joel Kuipers (1990) and in Greg Urban's study of Amerindian genres (1991); further developed in *Natural Histories of Discourse*, edited by

Michael Silverstein and Greg Urban (1996); and later extended into a general theory of cultural transmission and dissemination by Urban in *Metaculture* (2001). Entextualization is the 'process of rendering a given instance of discourse as text, detachable from its local context', as Silverstein and Urban put it (1996: 21). Discourse is the unremarked and unrepeated flow of utterances in which most human activities are bathed. Text is created when instances of discourse, by being rendered detachable from their immediate context of emission, are made available for reproduction in other contexts. In other words, they are stretches of discourse which can be transmitted over time and space. According to *Natural Histories of Discourse*, detachability is achieved by a variety of devices. It can of course be accomplished by writing down a stretch of utterance, but it can also be achieved wholly within an oral context. In myth, narratives are put into the remote past tense, detaching them from the immediate context of the listener; they are put into the third person, thus escaping the tendency of first- and second-person discourse to suck the listener into a dialogic engagement with the speaker; and they are often structured from a series of parallel formulations which, by establishing internal patterns of repetition, encourage the repetition of the whole text.

This concept of entextualization can be pushed further, in two directions. The first is that it could be extended downwards into the very plane of 'discourse' from which it risks being too sharply distinguished. Studies of language acquisition have shown that, contrary to Chomsky's assumptions, language learning is not a matter of intuiting a complex set of rules (whether or not these are already 'hard-wired' into cognition) and then freely operationalizing these rules by feeding into them a collection of individually acquired words, to generate a potentially infinite number of original utterances. Rather, people learn languages by long exposure to prefabricated and semi-prefabricated chunks of utterance which they may only later break down into separable, constituent parts. We learn idioms, formulae, turns of phrase, standardized expressions, and then we learn to vary them. MacKenzie (2000) suggests that ordinary speech is therefore not unlike the oral formulaic mode of composition attributed to Homer and to the epic bards of old Yugoslavia (Lord 1974 [1960]). This means that 'ordinary' everyday discourse should not be conceptualized as a neutral, evenly flowing stream out of which the rocky outcrops of entextualized text emerge. Rather, all utterance is made up of verbal chunks in varying stages of solidification, susceptible to varying degrees of free play and reformulation. There is an internal propensity to text formation from the very first words we utter.

But conversely – and this is the second point – the notion of entextualization should be expanded to encompass further processes of creativity and improvisation. Kuipers' and Urban's early concentration on sacred speech and myth allowed the conclusion that entextualized utterance is typically frozen utterance, detached from living interpersonal exchange. Myth's concern with events remote in time, ritual speech's numinous aura, inevitably set them apart from other discourse. In relation to myth and ritual speech, the need to think of entextualization *together* with fluidity and improvisation was not so apparent as it would be with many other oral genres. Genres like African praise poetry, for example, are constituted out of lapidary fragments that are 'fixed' by being rendered compact, dense, allusive and obscure. In many cases these formulations are believed to be ancient and unchanging. They are clearly recognized as text which pre-existed the moment of utterance, and will outlast it. They are quoted; they are subjected to elaborate exegetical attention; and they may be given objective correlatives in the gold-weights, umbrella finials and pot-lids which are used to recall them. But performances are assembled in always changing configurations, drawing different selections from the open-ended corpus, linking them in different ways, and inflecting them to speak to an addressee in the present context of utterance. In the case of Yoruba *oriki*, the more skilled and experienced a performer is, the more fluid her performance: it is the inexperienced girls who chant blocks of barely changing lines. The *oriki* chant is valued because it mobilizes something believed to be of permanent worth, inscribed in changeless formulations, and in so doing, charges the addressee with the accumulated powers of the *alaseku*, 'those whose deeds remain'. But to activate and release those powers the performer uses every art at her disposal, expanding her resources by raiding other subjects' collections of epithets and even other genres, and incorporating her own observations and witticisms. Thus the consolidation of chunks of text is what makes possible, and gives point to, the performer's fluid displays of competence, while it is only in full-blown performative utterance that the powers stored in these condensed, obscure formulations can be released (Barber 1991, 1999, 2003).

Memory, Composition and Improvisation

The concept of entextualization, thus expanded, opens the way to an integrated vision of the generation of cultural forms from the bottom up, in which misleadingly sharp binary oppositions can be allowed to fade away. Much recent work supports such a move.

The conceptual split between text and performance gets in the way of understanding the links between the emergence of new things and the effort to achieve permanence. It is echoed in equally categorical divisions between improvising and performing from a script, and between memorizing and composing a text. In the field of music, Nicholas Cook has shown how closely related and interdependent all these activities are. Listening is not a matter of simply receiving all the sound impressions that enter your ears: as you listen, you disassemble and reconstruct the sounds in accordance with stylistic schemes which you build up as you go along, but which you also bring with you in the form of expectations created by previous exposure to music. This same process underlies remembering, improvising and composing. Remembering is not a matter of recording the full panoply of sounds that your sensory organs register, but rather of reconstructing a 'stylistically plausible whole' from a set of attributes or aspects – whether structural or incidental – that you analysed out of those sounds in the process of listening (Cook 1990: 108). Similarly, playing a piece of music from a score involves the same processes as improvisation, and is 'undoubtedly generative'. 'Psychologically speaking, both jazz and classical pianists are improvising, in the sense that they are creatively synthesizing performance schemes in the real time of performance; the difference is merely in the nature of the constraints within which this creativity operates' (ibid.: 113). And finally, there is a 'continuity between what it means to know a pre-existing piece of music … and what it means to compose music' (ibid.). It seems to me that much the same could be said about oral verbal genres: memorizing an oral text is not the opposite of improvising a new one, but rather is in a continuum with it. The text is reconstructed from salient cues and recurrent patterns, not simply reproduced like a photocopy.

Form-giving activity – of a kind that constitutes cultural entities which are recognized as preceding and outlasting the moment of their performance – always draws upon the conventions of genre, and at the same time subtly modifies them.

> To hear a symphony as a symphony, to hear a fugue as a fugue – in short, to hear any music as form – is then to hear it as repeatable, and hence as independent of its realization in sound on any particular occasion. (Cook 1990: 36)

To recognize a symphony as a symphony, an epic as an epic, or a yam-growing incantation as such, requires a consciousness of genre. Genre conventions are not usually reducible to 'rules'; rather, they are a bundle of attributes adding up to an overall impression, which is recognized as one would recognize personality (Fowler 1982). Recognition is built up through exposure to numerous instantiations of the genre; but each instantiation also adds an increment, and thus subtly adds to the genre's range of possibilities.[4] Genre, therefore, is like the past in G.H. Mead's philosophy: it is continually reconstructed retrospectively, as every new thing that happens occasions a readjustment in the perception of those that preceded it. Genre, then, arises from memory – the composite memory of overlaid, overlapping experiences of individual performances or texts. But genre is also prospective: it is a set of expectations of form. Composers create in the expectation that certain formal attributes will be recognized and understood as such; audiences interpret in accordance with expectations which the genre's conventions have aroused. Even when the composer's aim is to rupture the conventions and generate something wholly novel, the effect depends on both composer and listeners recognizing and expecting the conventions that are being broken.

Drawing from performances of Shakespeare's plays, Kirsten Hastrup suggests that 'agency ... is closely tied to a vision of plot, to the anticipation of a story, a line of future development' (Hastrup 2004: 155). The recognition and recreation of *all* form in social life can be seen as simultaneously recapitulatory and anticipatory. To establish form is to abstract key attributes from past and current instantiations with a view to re-embodying them in future ones (cf. Urban 2001). Entextualization, or the art of making things stick, is therefore really the art of laying down the means for new creation.

This double process happens in all domains of social life. Leo Howe takes up the performance/text distinction in order to suggest that 'inscription' – the establishment of text – is itself a process, an activity involving risk, competition and struggle over what gets inscribed. He goes on to propose that inscription 'is just as applicable to acts, skills, abilities, operations and procedures, as it is to meanings' (Howe 2000: 65–6). In an argument that is congenial to the perspective I am outlining here, he captures in this formulation the inseparability of fixing and improvisation: 'As a performance proceeds it is simultaneously inscribed in the very acts which make up the performance' (ibid.: 66). By doing, you lay down a track which can be retraced, though never exactly replicated.[5]

Collaborative Improvisation

The idea that innovation and creativity are necessarily the results of departures from convention by gifted individuals has also been comprehensively revised. Improvisation is a matter of give and take; innovation can arise *between* people and not only from *within* people. In ensemble work, the participants arrive at a kind of unanimity, an ability to function not as a collection of individuals but as something approaching an organism. In some cases, this is achieved by a kind of merging of functions, in which all participants become interchangeable. In the directorless group theatre improvisation described by Theodore Shank, everyone can do everything: 'each member of a group combines the specialized traditional functions of playwright, director, designer etc' (Shank 1972: 30). In other cases, however, group unanimity arises from a high degree of specialization, in which each participant occupies a well-defined, distinct role and contributes one component to a larger mechanism. Hutchins' extraordinary analysis of the navigational system onboard a US steamship – which, he concludes, works like a supra-personal brain (Hutchins 1995) – is an extreme and striking case of this kind of ensemble. Playing Stockhausen's atonal music, the score of which looks like a mathematical puzzle, is another case where each participant slots in his or her own component according to instructions, producing an overall effect beyond what any individual could envisage (Cook 1990). But most often we seem to see both these kinds of procedure combined – a distribution of specialized tasks, but also a blending of individual autonomy in mutual attunement that may take the form of a kind of interpersonal shadowing. In chamber music the performers keep together because, rather than abiding by a uniformly agreed beat, 'they are, in a quite literal sense, playing by ear' (ibid.: 130), each listening to the others and accommodating him or herself to them in a 'mutuality of performance' that is like the rapport of a conversation.

The Woi epic of the Kpelle people of Liberia (Stone 1988) demonstrates the combination of distribution of roles and merging of competences in exemplary form. This enigmatic narrative is improvised by a peripatetic specialist storyteller, but only with the skilled and alert cooperation of multiple, distinct, well-defined segments of the participating audience. The percussionists, the main chorus, the support chorus, the 'song-catcher', the '*muu*-raising people' and the 'questioner' all play defined roles, interacting with each other, in structured dialogic exchanges, as well as with the principal narrator. The narrator sets out an obscure fragment; the questioner elicits expansion and explanation: 'What is that? Who is saying that? Has he died now?' Other participants, in turn, prompt the questioner if he misses a beat. Thus the narrative is pieced together bit by bit. The narrator frequently calls on the participants to play their part, while the participants prompt the narrator to fill out the story. The segments are artfully joined to defer closure; among the reflexive remarks that pepper the performance are repeated comments that 'the head of an epic does not come out: you just keep bouncing'. Here we see a form that highlights – and renders visible by overt staging – the collaborative nature of its production: it involves an artful *foregrounding* of co-narration, with its profusion of designated roles paired off into dialogic dyads. The Woi epic is a mythical story, regarded as ancient, certainly recognized by the participants as pre-existing and outlasting the moment of performance – but its telling is staged to dramatize the fact that with each performance it has to be, as it were, coaxed out, pieced together and collectively rediscovered. This is how the consolidation of text happens. And in their own reflexive self-commentary, the performers express the view that the epic never can come out fully: its telling will always be ongoing and incomplete.

In such episodes of cooperative mutual attunement, it is clear that something happens that exceeds the sum of the individual contributions. Participants may collectively generate a textual environment which then inspires further production. I have described in detail how this happens in the case of Yoruba popular theatre, in which a company of twenty to thirty male and female itinerant professional actors mounted long, complex, coherent but unscripted dramas, some of which would remain in the company's repertoire for as long as thirty years, gradually evolving in response to audience taste and changing theatrical fashion. Each actor conceived of him- or herself as bringing a unique individual resource of personality, experience and gifts to the collective enterprise, and to some extent the actors were in competition with each other, each striving to expand his or her own part, fuelled and vindicated by audience acclamation. However, in the course of participating in the activities (including live stage performances) of the Oyin Adejobi Theatre Company over a number of years, I gradually realized that the company collectively improvised a linguistic medium suited to the subject matter of each play. The style, consistent right through the performance, could vary markedly from one play to another, even if they were being improvised by the same actors on successive nights. *Folajiyo*, a folkloric play set in a traditional kingdom, abounded in homely proverbs and idioms referring to a familiar rural and domestic environment. 'New water has flowed in, new fish have entered it'. 'You have eyes like the eyes of a frog'. 'He's piled his ragged clothes on in layers like the palm frond'. There were no instances of modern slang or English loanwords. But *Morawo* – which was created around the same time as *Folajiyo* and coexisted with it in the repertoire for a number of years – had an entirely different style, suited to its theme of a young white-collar city woman playing one man off against another in her pursuit of wealth and security. The first words of this play, uttered by an *aladuura* preacher, were 'Ẹ gbàdúrà! Gbogbo èyin ọlọ́mọge tí *bọ́ìfùrẹ́ńdì* yín jà yín jùúlẹ̀ bí *típà* bá ja èèpẹ̀ẹ́ lẹ̀ – ẹ gbàdúrà!' 'Pray! All you young girls whose "boyfriends" have dumped you like a "tipper" dumping soil – pray!' Thus, in the first sentences, we hear two loanwords and a contemporary metaphor; and *Morawo* went on from there to unleash a cornucopia of slang, neologisms, Anglicisms and novel turns of speech (Barber 2000: 404–16).

This production of a specific linguistic medium was not imposed on the actors by the manager or boss of the company. Through hours and hours of hanging around backstage and hearing the plays over and over again, I was gradually able to pick up the subtle transit of verbal ideas through the texture of the play – a kind of ripple effect, where a key word or expression introduced by one actor would be registered and echoed in different ways right across the performance, even by bit-part actors who had no on-stage interaction with the originator of the expression. Through this sensitive mutual stylistic awareness, a sense of the appropriate medium seemed to be arrived at as they went along, led by the more experienced and dominant actors. It was made possible by the actors' sense that each of them, though endowed with distinctive gifts and competences, could potentially play any part; all listened to everyone else's words as if they could potentially be their own. Here, then, we see how a form established its own space in which to provide for innovation of a particular kind. Although the improvised dramas often appeared exuberant, freewheeling and at times bordering on the chaotic, their improvisations were actually both inspired and regulated by a medium of the actors' own joint making.

Karin Barber

The Lengths People Go To

People go to extraordinary lengths to make a mark that transcends time. Greg Urban's recent reworkings of the notion of entextualization have focused on the question of 'how culture moves in the world'. His question is how and why some kinds of cultural elements are more successful at being transmitted through time and space than others. This opens up brilliant possibilities, bringing within a single comparative explanatory framework oral and literate cultures, 'traditional' and 'modern' ones. The perspective of entextualization, or the rendering of discourse into detachable, repeatable text, is now expanded into a general theory of culture which takes the variability of elements and their uneven distribution as its starting point. Though his evocation of culture's movements has a curiously idealist cast to it – culture is an 'immaterial, ghostlike form' (Urban 2001: 2) which 'wants to continue on its journey through space and time' (ibid.: 19) – it has much in common with Sperber's (1996) materialist, 'epidemiological' approach and the distributional models of culture developed by evolutionary cognitive sciences (for example, Durham 2002). All these approaches do away with the idea of 'a' culture as a stable, integrated structure shared by all the members of the relevant group. Instead culture is treated more like a population, a congeries of individual elements which move around, mutate, cluster in certain areas and are more or less successful in reproducing themselves. Describing culture is more like giving a statistical profile of a population than drawing an architectural plan. As Sperber (1996) cogently argues, this approach dispenses with many of the theoretical problems associated with trying to describe 'the belief system of the X'. However, it also dispenses with – or at best shifts attention away from – human agency. Human populations become mere carriers of cultural elements, which move, mutate, colonize new territory and propagate themselves, and whose success or otherwise is ascribed to their inherent properties rather than to what human beings decide to do with them. In a strong version of this approach, cultural elements (called 'memes', in parallel to genes) are propelled by a drive to reproduce and perpetuate themselves, as genes are also said to be (Dawkins 1976; Blackmore 1999). The human effort and ingenuity expended to make things stick has dropped from view – and with it, history, intertextuality, genre and the collective creation that happens between people and exceeds the sum of their individual representations.

What makes cultural elements 'fit' to survive? One of the startling facts about human cultures is their sheer excess, the inordinate expenditure of energy, skill and attention on the creation of form. Many cultural forms, far from being in any obvious sense 'naturally' fitted for self-reproduction and self-propulsion through time and space, seem to be created to advertise the high human cost of their production and reproduction. Take – as one example out of the millions available – *igisigo*, a genre of oral praise poetry that was part of the aristocratic court culture of Old Rwanda. It was produced and transmitted by a specialized guild of hereditary bards, and was the oldest and most rigorously transmitted of the many court genres, reputedly dating back fourteen generations. The poems were so constructed that only specialized rhetoricians could compose and interpret them, and the oblique and evasive style of the genre is signalled in its very name, the root of which, according to Alexis Kagame, means 'to compose in a figurative style, incomprehensible on first hearing' (Kagame 1969: 152). What makes many of the allusions in *igisigo* incomprehensible on the first hearing is the artful construction of a series of departures from the initial idea, a process of 'veiling' or 'making disappear' (*kuzimiza*) through synonyms, homonyms and metonyms. A single word could require a whole sequence of steps to retrace the composer's thought-path and retrieve the 'disappeared' meaning. The art of composing and interpreting Rwandan dynastic poetry involved deliberately going out of one's way to avoid the linear narrative and vivid imagery that would make the text spontaneously memorable. Great ingenuity went into constituting these texts as obscure, and then into ensuring that despite their difficulty they would be meticulously transmitted and widely known. People went to great lengths to learn them because their obscurity conferred prestige. Associated with the Mwami's court and aristocratic culture, their creation and decipherment could be seen as a kind of conspicuous consumption of creative energy. The powerful royal dynasty, surrounded by the Tutsi aristocracy, defined themselves as distinct and aloof by creating and perpetuating a genre that cost a lot in terms of training, time and effort to master and to transmit; and the fact that the genre was indeed successfully transmitted for long periods was simultaneously a cause, a result and a sign of its immense prestige (and hence that of its owners). Here we seem to see a deliberate repudiation of what is easily memorable in order to draw attention to the creative resources at the king's command.

Such lavish form-giving effort – examples of which could be adduced from almost anywhere in the world – seems to require a focus on the people who expend it, and the historically and culturally specific projects in which they are engaged. We need to ask by what specific methods people simultaneously improvise and make things stick, and why they do it. What are their own conceptions of innovation and perdurance? To what source do they ascribe creativity – where do they say new things come from? How do they build loopholes into their most binding customs, thus creating a space for future innovation? How do they create occasions and contexts in which supra-individual improvisation can occur?

Again we may look for clues in the reflexive commentaries embedded in entextualized forms. Let me offer a final example from the vast corpus of Yoruba oral divination poems, running to many thousand verses, which are carefully and systematically learned by all Ifá priests. The core formulations in each verse are believed never to have varied over hundreds of years, and the corpus as a whole is widely regarded in western Nigeria (and beyond) as the repository of all Yoruba wisdom. This huge effort of 'inscription' was doubly inscribed when nineteenth-century Yoruba cultural nationalists began to write the corpus down, in order to create literary monuments that would testify to their advanced civilization. In one such collection, published by the Reverend E.M. Lijadu in 1898, there occurs the following verse:

> Hoes can't hoe the farm by themselves
> If it were not for us humans who back them up
> If it were not for us humans.
> Axes could not blaze their way through the wood
> If it were not for us humans who back them up
> If it were not for us humans.
> Cutlasses can't slash through the forest by themselves
> It's we human beings who support them and back them up,
> We human beings.
> We bring the yams home, the mortar can't pound the yam by itself
> But only with the help of humans who back it up.
> Only us humans.
> And what is it that backs human beings up?
> Only God, only people.[6]

This potent verse remarks upon the human capacity both to make things and to make things happen. Hoes, axes, cutlasses, mortars are potential-filled, purpose-oriented entities, but their potential and purpose can only be realized when human beings 'back them up', supplying the energy that sets them in motion. People in turn are backed up, given the power to make things happen, by God – and by other people. This wonderful image of human mutuality suggests a model in which agency itself is generated cooperatively. In divination this verse, like all the verses in the Ifá corpus, is activated by diviners to steer clients' future life-courses in the light of precedent. Just as the human being in the verse above energetically sets his own creations in motion, thus enabling them to realize their potential, so the diviner sets the scrupulously preserved, carefully transmitted Ifá texts in motion – releasing their stored power by creatively applying them to fresh situations – and thus enables his clients to act effectively in the world.

Forms like these verses embody and reflect upon creativity and cultural improvisation in stimulating, provocative ways. Particularly enchanting is the way they can fuse into one concept what our own vocabulary keeps encouraging us to split. They thus provide food for thought about the human habit of simultaneously improvising and striving to make things stick.

Notes

1. For a discussion of this last distinction and the role it plays in the aesthetic theories of the philosophers R.G. Collingwood and John Dewey, see Sawyer (2000).
2. The political economy of Trobriand yam culture was socially non-egalitarian, and from a nutritional point of view it wasted resources. However, my aim here is not to evaluate its effects, but merely to highlight the idiom in which it was conducted.
3. Maurice Bloch (1998) has suggested that the tendency to memorialize – to preserve and refer back to the past – varies in form and degree according to social structure and historical experience. He compares the lineage-based Sadah of northern Yemen, who have a long-term genealogical view of knowledge and virtue, and the Bicolanos of central Philippines, who see themselves as 'people who have nothing', and whose view of human existence centres upon mutability – even their icons are believed to grow and decline.
4. Cook draws a strong distinction between pre-nineteenth-century music, where composers remained wholly within the conventions of a genre, so that what was produced and approved was not an individual creation but a perfect instantiation of a genre, and post-eighteenth-century music, where originality and innovation were valued and conventions were broken (Cook 1990: 36–7). This is an important historical shift, also documented in other European arts. But even very conformist instantiations of a genre usually add something new to the field of resources on which subsequent compositions draw.
5. Performance theory opened the way to the development of this perspective: see Richard Schechner's (1985) use of the idea of theatrical and ritual performance as 'restored behaviour', in which 'strips of behaviour' are as it were demarcated for recreation, but never exact replication.
6. My translation, from E.M. Lijadu, *Ifá*. The Yoruba text (with the original spelling) runs as follows: 'Awọn ọkọ ko le fi ara-wọn r'oko, afi awa enia ti işe elegbè lẹhin wọn, afi awa enia: aake ko le gbiyanju tèfetefe, afi awa enia ti işe elegbè lẹhin rẹ̀, afi awa enia: awọn àdá kò le fi ara wọn şan inu igbó lọ, awa enia ni işe elegbè lẹhin wọn, awa enia: a mu işu wa ile, odó kò le tikararẹ̀ gún u n'iyán, afi awa enia ti işe elegbè lẹhin rẹ̀, afi awa enia. Njẹ kini işe elegbè lẹhin enia? Afi Ajalọrun afi enia – Ọkanran-Sá' (1908 [1898]: 40).

References

Barber, K. (1991), *I Could Speak Until Tomorrow: Oríkì, Women and the Past in a Yorùbá Town*, Edinburgh: Edinburgh University Press.

—— (1999), 'Quotation in the constitution of Yorùbá oral texts', *Research in African Literatures*, 30(3): 17–41.

—— (2000), *The Generation of Plays: Yoruba Popular Life in Theatre*, Bloomington: Indiana University Press.

—— (2003), 'Text and performance in Africa', *Bulletin of the School of Oriental and African Studies*, 66(3): 324–33. Revised and republished (2005) in *Oral Tradition* 20(2): 264–77.

Bascom, W. (1959), 'The main problems of stability and change in tradition', *Journal of the International Folk Music Council*, 11: 7–12.

Battaglia, D. (1990), *On the Bones of the Serpent: Person, Memory, and Mortality in Sabarl Island Society*, Chicago: University of Chicago Press.

Bauman, R. (1977), *Verbal Art as Performance*, Prospect Heights Il.: Waveland Press.

Blackmore, S. (1999), *The Meme Machine*, Oxford: Oxford University Press.

Bloch, M. (1998), *How We Think They Think: Anthropological Approaches to Cognition, Memory and Literacy*, Boulder, Colo.: Westview Press.

Conquergood, D. (1989), 'Poetics, play, process and power: the performance turn in anthropology', *Text and Performance Quarterly* 9(1): 82–95.

Cook, N. (1990), *Music, Imagination and Culture*, Oxford: Oxford University Press.

Dawkins, R. (1976), *The Selfish Gene*, Oxford: Oxford University Press.

Durham, W.H. (2002), 'Cultural variation in time and space: the case for a population theory of culture', in R.G. Fox and B.J. King (eds), *Anthropology Beyond Culture*, Oxford and New York: Berg.

Fowler, A. (1982), *Kinds of Literature: An Introduction to the Theory of Genres and Modes*, Oxford: Clarendon Press.

Hastrup, K. (2004), *Action: Anthropology in the Company of Shakespeare*, Copenhagen: Museum Tusculanum Press.

Howe, L. (2000), 'Risk, ritual and performance', *Journal of the Royal Anthropological Institute* 6(1): 63–79.

Hutchins, E. (1995), *Cognition in the Wild*, Cambridge, Mass.: MIT Press.

James, W. (2003), *The Ceremonial Animal: A New Portrait of Anthropology*, Oxford: Oxford University Press.

Kagame, A. (1969), *Introduction aux grands genres lyriques de l'Ancien Rwanda*, Butare, Rwanda: Editions Universitaires du Rwanda.

Kuipers, J.C. (1990), *Power in Performance: The Creation of Textual Authority in Weyewa Ritual Speech*, Philadelphia: University of Pennsylvania Press.

Lewis, G. (1980), *Day of Shining Red: an essay on understanding ritual*, Cambridge: Cambridge University Press.

Lijadu, E.M. (1908 [1898]), *Ifá: Ìmọlẹ̀ rẹ̀ tí íṣe Ìpilẹ̀ Ìsìn ní ilẹ̀ Yorùbá*, Ado-Ekiti: Omolayo Standard Press.

Lord, A.B. (1974 [1960]), *The Singer of Tales*, New York: Atheneum.
MacKenzie, I. (2000), 'Improvisation, creativity, and formulaic language', *The Journal of Aesthetics and Art Criticism*, 58(2): 173–9.
Malinowski, B. (1935), *Coral Gardens and their Magic: A Study of the Methods of Tilling the Soil and of Agricultural Rites in the Trobriand Islands*, Volume 1, London: Allen and Unwin.
Mead, G.H. (1932), *The Philosophy of the Present*, ed A.E. Murphy, LaSalle, Ill.: Open Court.
Sawyer, R.K. (2000), 'Improvisation and the creative process: Dewey, Collingwood and the aesthetics of spontaneity', *The Journal of Aesthetics and Art Criticism*, 58(2): 149–61.
Schechner, R. (1985), *Between Theatre and Anthropology*, Philadelphia: University of Pennsylvania Press.
Schieffelin, E.L. (1998), 'Problematizing performance', in F. Hughes-Freeland (ed), *Ritual, Performance, Media* (ASA Monographs 35), London and New York: Routledge.
Shank, T. (1972), 'Collective creation', *The Drama Review*, 16(2): 3–31.
Silverstein, M. and Urban, G. (eds) (1996), *Natural Histories of Discourse*, Chicago: University of Chicago Press.
Sperber, D. (1996), *Explaining Culture: A Naturalistic Approach*, Oxford: Blackwell.
Stone, R. (1988), *Dried Millet Breaking: Time, Words and Song in the Woi Epic of the Kpelle*, Bloomington: Indiana University Press.
Urban, G. (1991), *A Discourse-centered Approach to Culture*, Austin: University of Texas Press.
—— (2001), *Metaculture: How Culture Moves Through the World*, Minneapolis: University of Minnesota Press.

Part I
Modes of Creativity in Life and Art

Introduction
Tim Ingold

In 1970 the distinguished French biochemist, Jacques Monod, published a little book entitled *Chance and Necessity*. Along with his colleagues André Lwoff and François Jacob, Monod had been awarded the Nobel Prize in 1965 for groundbreaking work on the mechanisms of genetic replication and protein synthesis. The book amounted to a forthright declaration of his scientific credo, and of the potential of the molecular biology he had helped establish to unravel, once and for all, the secrets of life and its evolution. Monod's philosophy is uncompromisingly mechanistic: every living creature, so far as he is concerned, is a chemical machine whose structure and patterns of behaviour are fully determined by interactions among its molecular constituents, principally proteins. Fundamentally, all the information specifying these constituents is encoded in the materials of heredity – that is, in strands of DNA. From this it follows that the growth or development of the organism is, in Monod's words, 'not a *creation*; it is a *revelation*' (Monod 1972: 87, original emphases). It is, in other words, no more than the realization of a design that is already there, albeit in the virtual form of a blueprint installed at the point of inception of the organism-to-be, independently and in advance of its life in the world.

By the same token, creativity is excluded from the life-process itself. The source of all creation in the biosphere, Monod claims, is not life but those chance events, of genetic mutation, that alter the design specifications underwriting the construction of living things. Evolution occurs precisely because the mechanism of replication that otherwise ensures the high-fidelity copying of elements across generations does not work perfectly. It is this indeterminacy that allows for the creative emergence of new designs.

> According to modern theory, the idea of 'revelation' applies to epigenetic development, but not of course to evolutionary emergence, which, owing to the fact that it arises from the essentially unforeseeable, is the creator of *absolute* newness. (Monod 1972: 113)

Not all advocates of the so-called 'modern synthesis' of neo-Darwinian evolutionary theory were quite so outspoken. One of them was Theodosius Dobzhansky. Chance, Dobzhansky argued, may be the source of all *variation* in the biosphere, but it is not, in itself, the source of all creation. Evolution occurs not because of variations alone, but because these variations undergo a process of selection in which they are tested in manifold combinations and recombinations. The relative viability of these combinations, under specific environmental conditions, then determines the frequency with which their elements are represented in future generations. Thus the creativity of evolution, for Dobzhansky, lay in what he called the 'antichance factor' of selection, working on the raw material of variation supplied by chance. What are created, however, are not living organisms, but rather designs for life that are subsequently realized in the forms we actually observe. 'Every new form of life that appears in evolution', writes Dobzhansky, 'can, with only moderate semantic license, be regarded as an artistic embodiment of a new concept of living' (Dobzhansky 1974: 329).

I return below to the analogy between the organism and the work of art. What matters now is that for Dobzhansky as much as for Monod, life is a movement of revelation, and not of creation. It is no more than the writing out of a genetic text that has been pre-composed through a reshuffling of elements. Nor was this view limited to those whose approach to science was similarly reductionist. No one could have been more opposed to reductionism than Gregory Bateson, yet in his *Mind and Nature* Bateson compares the process of epigenesis – that is, the emergence of the form of an organism through its life in the world – to 'the development of a complex tautology ... in which nothing is added after the axioms and definitions have been laid down' (Bateson 1980: 57). He goes on to set up a radical opposition between, on the one hand, epigenesis and tautology, and on the other, art, learning and evolution. Whereas the former entail a working out, or unfolding, of what is already given, the latter comprise 'the whole realm of creativity ... in which the ongoing processes of change *feed on the random*' (ibid., original emphasis). Thus in art as in life, the creative element lies in the sheer novelty of the conception, not in its subsequent realization. Yet just as in evolution, every new design emerges through the recombination of elements, so in thought, according to Bateson, 'the genesis of new notions is almost totally ... dependent upon reshuffling and recombining ideas we already have' (ibid.: 201). Learning is like evolution in that the testing of these ideas, in different combinations, affects the probability of their recurrence.

This combinatory view of creativity, as the endless generation of first-time novelties through the rearrangement of elements (Boden 1990: 38), is deeply embedded not only in biology and psychology but in many other fields of academic discourse as well, not least in anthropology (Friedman 2001: 46–8). For example, it underlies Lévi-Strauss's celebrated notion of the creative mind as a *bricoleur* that is for ever engaged in the novel assembly of structures of thought out of the bits and pieces of old ones. And in linguistics, it reappears in Chomsky's notion of 'rule-governed creativity' as the capacity to construct an infinite variety of comprehensible expressions from a finite repertoire of lexical items (Lévi-Strauss

1966: 17; Chomsky 1964: 22–3). Yet this view has always existed side by side with another, less mainstream perhaps, which would *deny* that there is anything intrinsically creative about the recombinatory generation of novelty. In his *Science and the Modern World*, first published in 1926, the philosopher Alfred North Whitehead insisted that the creativity of the evolutionary process was to be found in something other than the mechanism of variation under natural selection (Whitehead 1938 [1926]: 134–5). For the world we inhabit is not made up of static and discrete bits and pieces that may be connected up in myriad ways into ever-changing patterns. It is rather a movement, or flow, in which every element we might identify is but a moment. Creativity, for Whitehead, lay in that very movement of becoming by which the world, as it unfolds, continually surpasses itself. Whitehead's term for this unfolding was 'concrescence' (Ingold 1986: 173; cf. Whitehead 1929: 410).

It was in the philosophy of Henri Bergson – which Monod would later dismiss as 'almost completely discredited' (Monod 1972: 34) – that Whitehead found inspiration. In his *Creative Evolution* of 1911, Bergson had been quite explicit in repudiating the creativity of the kind of invention that proceeds 'by a new arrangement of elements already known' (Bergson 1911: 48). Thus an evolutionary mechanism that worked in this way, through mutation and recombination, although it might generate an ever-changeful sequence of non-recurrent patterns, would not in itself be creative. To the contrary, the creativity of evolution, for Bergson, lay precisely in the life process itself – that is, in the very process that writers like Monod, Dobzhansky and Bateson regarded as revelatory or expressive *rather than* creative. To highlight the contrast between these two views of creativity we can return to the analogy between the living organism and the work of art. For as Bergson insisted, the artist's invention is inseparable from the progress of his work. If he is painting a picture, the picture is not already created before the painting begins. This is what makes painting different from solving a jigsaw puzzle. With the puzzle the result is already given; 'to obtain it requires only a work of recomposing and rearranging – a work that can be supposed going faster and faster, and even infinitely fast, up to the point of being instantaneous'. With painting, by contrast,

> the time taken up by the invention is one with the invention itself. It is the progress of a thought which is changing in the degree and measure that it is taking form. It is a vital process, something like the ripening of an idea. (Bergson 1911: 359–60)

Thus the movement of consciousness, in the painter's work, is creative in bringing forth the idea it embodies; it does not merely give outward expression to a conception that has sprung ready-formed to his mind. In just the same the life of the organism is generative of form rather than merely the reve pre-existing design.

y that is inherent in the flow of life or consciousness, however, is ...er than punctual. It cannot be collapsed into a sequence of one-off ...s or novelties, nor can it be reconstructed by joining them up. The artist's invention, in this view, does not end with the completion of his work, any more than it began with a preconceived idea of its final form. It is not, in other words, encompassed within the bounds of any specific project. Rather, every work encapsulates the movement that brought it forth, and is in turn encapsulated in the maturation of what follows. Likewise the life of the organism is not simply expended in the translation of an initial, genetically encoded design into a material end-product. If we ask what organisms and persons create, the answer must be that they create one another and themselves, playing their part in the never-ending and non-specific project of *keeping life going*. 'For a conscious being', as Bergson reasoned, 'to exist is to change, to change is to mature, to mature is to go on creating oneself endlessly. Should not the same be said of existence in general?' (Bergson 1911: 8). To answer Bergson's question in the affirmative is to acknowledge that while no artist is immortal, and while every creature dies in the end, the process of life nevertheless goes on in a world that has been unalterably affected by their presence.

I have dwelt on the contrast between these two views of creativity since I believe it accounts for many of the tensions that come to light in the three chapters that follow. In his discussion of the *kōlam* – beautiful patterns of interwoven lines traditionally drawn by Tamil women in southern India to cleanse and protect their homes and temples – Amar Mall notes the concern of many scholars that the widespread publication of pattern books will thwart local creativity, encouraging women to copy existing patterns rather than invent their own. These books, however, reproduce ready-made patterns and say little or nothing about the techniques involved in forming them. The perception that copying is inimical to the exercise of the creative imagination betrays an approach to creativity that sees in technique nothing more than the revelation or transcription of a design that already stands fully formed before the practitioner's mind. If one follows this approach, then technique becomes irrelevant to the explanation of form or pattern, since it adds nothing to what has been laid down from the start. Drawing a *kōlam*, to recall Bateson's analogy, would be equivalent to the development of a complex tautology. But as Mall shows, it is very far from the case, especially with more convoluted patterns, that the design precedes its execution. It rather develops or matures as the work proceeds, so that the final form of the pattern only emerges when it is virtually complete – when the meandering line (*kampi*), having made any number of possibly unanticipated twists and turns, eventually finds its way home, or at least when journey's end is in sight. Only then, as *kōlam*-makers say, has the pattern 'come' or been 'brought back' to its starting point, so as to form a

Part I, Introduction

closed loop that has neither beginning nor end. And the practitioner may be both surprised and delighted by the result: surprised, since it may be far from what was expected; delighted, because the innovation has come out of the work itself.

The capacity of the *kampi kōlam* patterns – as indeed of their makers – to 'go on creating themselves endlessly' (to borrow Bergson's words) is even more striking by contrast to *kōlam* different sort, in which the lines connect fixed points rather than weaving around them, so as to reveal a structure that, rather like in a 'join-the-dots' puzzle, is already given in advance of its execution. Whereas it might be said of the maker of a *kampi kōlam*, in the memorable phrase of the painter Paul Klee (1961: 105), that her line 'goes out for a walk', always developing as it goes, in *kōlam* of this other sort every constituent line is preconceived as a link between points even before it is marked out on the ground. These lines are inflexible, of finite length, and static rather than dynamic, welding the points they connect into a rigid assembly. The contrast between these two species of *kōlam*, and the kinds of line involved in each, is clearly recognized by practitioners. Moreover a quite different sense of innovation is entailed in each case. To create a new assembly means shattering the original connections between its elements and reconnecting or recombining them in novel configurations, in the manner of the *bricoleur*. The makers of *kampi kōlam*, however, find their way *as they go along*, so that the novelty of their patterns is apparent only when they have finally arrived rather than prior to setting out.

It would be a great mistake, then, to regard every sort of pattern as the realization of a preformed cognitive assembly, or as the embodiment of a 'conception' that has lodged itself in the maker's mind. And for the same reason, it would be wrong to suppose that the pattern necessarily appears to those who come across it as an intellectual puzzle to be solved. This, for example, is how Alfred Gell, in his study of complex pattern, understands the *kōlam*. It is a 'mind-trap' (Gell 1998: 80) that ensnares anyone – including, in this case, potentially malevolent demons – who would attempt to figure out the generative principles of its construction, or to unpack the tautology it represents. Yet what surely distinguishes the *kampi kōlam* from *kōlam* of other kinds is not a difference of degree of complexity, as Gell suggests, but one of kind, corresponding quite precisely to Bergson's distinction between painting and puzzle-making. As Bergson said of the work of art, so one could also say of the *kampi kōlam*, that it 'embodies the process of thinking rather than the detached thought, a consciousness rather than a conception, life itself rather than a way of living' (Ingold 1986: 182). The meaning of the pattern, therefore, can be grasped only by an intuition that enters into it, or that follows its trails, rather than by an intellect that, in contemplating the finished work, attempts to reconstruct the puzzle from its solution.

Much the same conclusion can be drawn from Fuyubi Nakamura's study of contemporary Japanese calligraphic art. Indeed the lines of the *kampi kōlam* and those of calligraphy have much in common. In both cases they find their own way, flexibly and organically, rather than connecting fixed points. In both, too, they are learned and remembered as rhythmic gestures. While these gestures leave their traces in the lines we see, it is thanks to their very rhythmicity that these traces are woven into recognizable patterns. Rhythms, as André Leroi-Gourhan has observed, are in this sense 'the creators of forms' (Leroi-Gourhan 1993: 309). Thus the calligraphic line is 'read' by reliving the gestural movement that gave rise to it, rather than by contemplating its final form and seeking to extrapolate to some concept of which it might be supposed to be the expression. Again, the same is true of the line of the *kampi kōlam*. Both, in this sense, can be compared in their performance to music or dance (cf. Gell 1998: 95). As Nakamura shows, one can never grasp the meaning of calligraphy simply by looking *at* it and wondering what it might express or reveal. One has to enter *into* it and to join in the process of its production – in other words, to be reunited with the calligrapher in his or her 'inked traces' (see also Yen 2005: 89–90). Yet to be able to do that, one must have some knowledge of calligraphy's history and techniques.

Moreover, while the conventions of the art world might lead us to speak of calligraphic 'works', no work is ever finished. It cannot be contained within the bounds of a project that originates with a conception and is fulfilled in its material expression. The work might rather be compared to a never-ending story whose every telling is shaped by previous relations and goes on to shape subsequent ones. In this sense, it evolves through time: it has no determinate point of origin, nor any final destination. Far from yielding a concrete and objectified end-product, every performance is just one moment in the work's concrescence – its ongoing generation. This idea is reinforced by a method of learning in which, through repetitive practice in copying or imitating previous or classic exemplars, novices incorporate the movements and sensibilities of the masters into their own bodily comportment, only to surpass them in the development of their own personal style. At no point, however, do they cease to copy. For every original is a copy in that it is modelled on previous studies, and every copy is an original in that it can become a model for those who follow. There is nothing creative, for Japanese calligraphers, about the production of novelty for its own sake. What is observed in calligraphy, according to Nakamura, is a creativity of a different kind: one that is not opposed to imitation as the original is to the copy, but that finds in imitation the very impetus that keeps a work alive, allowing it to grow and flourish.

James Leach, in the final chapter of this part, shows how imitation and creativity (which the Japanese critic Kobayashi Hideo has described as 'mother' and 'child') came to be prised apart in the history of modernity, to the point at which they now appear radically opposed on either side of a master dichotomy between subject and object, intellectual freedom and mechanical necessity (see also Ingold 2000: 350). It is this that has led to the emergence of a notion of creative art or invention as the spontaneous production of novelty, feeding on the random recombination of experiences or elements of design. And by the same token, it has reduced the process of imitative learning or copying to the mere replication of these elements, in a manner analogous to genetic replication. In this view, the *practice* of imitation amounts to no more than running off identical copies from a template or schema that has already been 'downloaded' into the novice's mind. This is not, however, the way novice calligraphers learn their art. They do so, rather, by following in the footsteps of predecessors, along the same or similar trails. Novices are thereby enabled to grow into the knowledge and skills of the masters, in the very process of forming their own. The wisdom to which they aspire, far from having been transmitted at the outset, lies at the end of the journey – albeit at a horizon they can approach but never reach.

This is why, as Jerome Bruner (1986: 123) has pointed out, there can be no distinction in practice between learning culture and (re)creating culture, since the contexts of learning are the very crucibles from which the cultural process unfolds. In this process, knowledge is not so much *replicated* as *reproduced* – that is, 'produced anew, as the crystallisation of concrete, situated activity' (Ingold 2002: 62; on this distinction, see Jablonka 2000: 39). Though a piece of music is replicated each time it is played from a disk, it is reproduced each time it is performed with an instrument. A *kampi kōlam*, as Mall shows, is likewise reproduced or created anew every time it is copied. And so, too, is a calligraphic exemplar every time it is performed with the brush. No performance can be repeated, yet as a work comprises the accumulating trail of its performances – each one copying the copy of a copy – every performance becomes part and parcel of the ever-evolving work. Contemporary calligraphers, however, are torn between this understanding of their art and the demands of an art world that lays all the emphasis on the originality and creative agency of the individual artist. In this modernist conception, every trace on paper is a unique and finished 'work' which may be linked to the agency that produced it as object to subject.

In his chapter, Leach spells out the history of ideas that led to this isolation of human subjects vis-à-vis one another and their objective productions. He shows how the connections between subjects and objects came to be epitomized in the idea of property, and how these connections were guaranteed and enforced through the elaboration of property rights. In this world of subjects and objects, or persons and things, culture itself becomes a project whereby humanity inscribes its preconceived designs upon a material substrate. At the centre of this story of the emergence of possessive individualism stands the magisterial figure of John Locke, one of the founding fathers of the European Enlightenment. For Locke, property begins at the point where human subjects mix their labour with the raw materials of nature, impregnating the things they find there with their own creative agency and causing them to bear fruit (cf. Gudeman 1986: 80–4). Thus in tilling in cultivation, they mix their labour with the land. And in the measure that they transform the land, and establish control over it, they also transform themselves in the collective human project of culture-building or civilization.

Now as it turns out, calligraphers, according to Nakamura, also speak of mixing. But the mix is not just of their labour with the materials, but of the materials themselves, principally paper, ink and ink-stone. As the 'active' ingredient, the ink is said to mix with the paper – in ways that are never entirely predictable – to yield an outcome. It seems as though the agency of 'things' (the materials supplied by nature) has at least partially taken over from the agency of the 'person' (the calligrapher and his techniques), so that the outcome is a consequence of the interaction between the two. Significantly, this theme of the displacement of agency runs through all three chapters in this part. In the case of the *kōlam*, Mall contends that agency is to some degree displaced from the practitioner to the pattern, so that the outcome may surpass or confound her original intention. And of the villagers of Reite, on the Rai Coast of Papua New Guinea, Leach argues that in the creation of knowledge, agency is displaced from the people to the land in which they live. The ground, villagers say, gives people knowledge.

But the implications of Leach's argument are more profound. For the land that Reite people inhabit, contrary to the imagination of Locke and his intellectual successors, is not filled with concrete entities that have, as it were, already crystallized from the flows and circulations of substance in which they are formed. Their world is rather concrescent, in Whitehead's sense, undergoing continual formation. In such a world, creative agency resides neither in persons nor in things, nor even in persons *and* things. Indeed it is not, as Gell (1998: 16) would have it, an internal property that *resides* at all, or that either persons or things *possess*, whence it causes 'effects' in their vicinity. Attempts to move beyond the modernist polarization of subject and object, or the mental and the material, in terms of a language of agency that remains trapped in these very same categories, are bound to lead to contradiction and confusion. Contemporary anthropology, as Gell's work exemplifies, is in the thick of it. Perhaps, instead of claiming that entities possess an agency that causes them to act, we should acknowledge that agency 'possesses' the entities that – like eddies of dust raised by the wind, to adopt Bergson's (1911: 134) metaphor – are caught up in it. This agency could be none other than the generative flux of the world itself in its continual concrescence, from which persons and things emerge and take the forms they do for the duration of their existence. Thus the *kōlam* is the outline of a movement that is as much creative of the practitioner as of the pattern, the calligraphic trace captures the momentary confluence of hair, soot and morning dew in the sweep of a brush, and – in Reite – a new song comes to a man through his susceptibility to the generative power of the ground in a particular place. More generally, what these chapters show is that *humans do not, through their creative interventions, transform the world from without, but rather – belonging within it – play their part in the world's creative transformation of itself.*

References

Bateson, G. (1980), *Mind and Nature*, London: Fontana.
Bergson, H. (1911), *Creative Evolution* (trans. A. Mitchell), London: Macmillan.
Boden, M.A. (1990), *The Creative Mind*, London: Weidenfeld and Nicolson.
Bruner, J.S. (1986), *Actual Minds, Possible Worlds*, Cambridge, Mass.: Harvard University Press.
Chomsky, N. (1964), *Current Issues in Linguistic Theory*, The Hague: Mouton.
Dobzhansky, T. (1974), 'Chance and creativity in evolution', in F.J. Ayala and T. Dobzhansky (eds), *Studies in the Philosophy of Biology*, London: Macmillan.
Friedman, J. (2001), 'The iron cage of creativity: an exploration', in J. Liep (ed), *Locating Cultural Creativity*, London: Pluto Press.
Gell, A. (1998), *Art and Agency: An Anthropological Theory*, Oxford: Clarendon Press.
Gudeman, S. (1986), *Economics as Culture: Models and Metaphors of Livelihood*, London: Routledge and Kegan Paul.
Ingold, T. (1986), *Evolution and Social Life*, Cambridge: Cambridge University Press.
—— (2000), *The Perception of the Environment: Essays on Livelihood, Dwelling and Skill*, London: Routledge.
—— (2002), 'Between evolution and history: Biology, culture, and the myth of human origins', in M. Wheeler, J. Ziman and M.A. Boden (eds), *The Evolution of Cultural Entities*, Oxford: Oxford University Press.
Jablonka, E. (2000), 'Lamarckian inheritance systems in biology: a source of metaphors and models in technological evolution', in J. Ziman (ed), *Technological Innovation as an Evolutionary Process*, Cambridge: Cambridge University Press.
Klee, P. (1961), *Notebooks, Volume 1: The Thinking Eye*, London: Lund Humphries.
Leroi-Gourhan, A. (1993), *Gesture and Speech* (trans. A. Bostock Berger), Cambridge, Mass.: MIT Press.
Lévi-Strauss, C. (1966), *The Savage Mind*, London: Weidenfeld and Nicolson.
Monod, J. (1972), *Chance and Necessity* (trans. A. Wainhouse), London: Collins.
Whitehead, A.N. (1929), *Process and Reality: An Essay in Cosmology*, Cambridge: Cambridge University Press.

—— (1938 [1926]), *Science and the Modern World*, Harmondsworth: Penguin.
Yen, Y. (2005), *Calligraphy and Power in Contemporary Chinese Society*, London: Routledge Curzon.

–3–

Structure, Innovation and Agency in Pattern Construction: The *Kōlam* of Southern India
Amar S. Mall

> Originally far removed from decoration, all these ritual magic designs are forms of a will directed to an end which is to confine and control a supernatural power and to isolate it from the ground. The effect of these symbolic shapes is at one with their efficacy. They do not form abstract patterns for they are the shape of conceptions.
>
> S. Kramrisch, *Unknown India*

This chapter is concerned with the question of intentionality in the design and generation of non-representational form. It points in particular to the problem of 'locating' creativity within the design process and to the connection between redundancy and novelty in relation to technique, where technique carries with it structural implications. The case in point is that of the south Indian *kōlam*,[1] a particular but widespread form of women's folk art in South Asia. Preserved and transmitted almost exclusively by women, traditional south Indian *kōlam* are distinctive in India for taking the form of either one or several superimposed closed lines (*kampi*) that interweave around a grid of dots (*puḷḷi*). These beautiful and complex geometric and symmetrical designs form a central component of domestic and public ritual practice among the Hindu communities of the southern Indian state of Tamil Nadu, where they are commonly rendered in rice flour or rice-flour solutions on the thresholds and floors of houses and temples to ritually cleanse these areas and protect them from malevolent forces (see Figures 3.1 and 3.2). Far from manifesting an obscure ritual art, *kōlam* are ubiquitous throughout the state and in its capital, Chennai (formally known as Madras), where I conducted my fieldwork. As Renate Dohmen rightly observes, 'in terms of the sheer numbers of practitioners and households actively engaged in the practice, it could ... be said to be one of the most popular forms of visual practice in contemporary Tamil Nadu' (Dohmen 2001: 134).

Marking both space and time, *kōlam* prepare a ground, and are intimately linked to the generation of auspicious – or conversely, the prevention of inauspicious – states (see Madan 1985; Marglin 1985; Raheja 1988). It is through the placing of

Figure 3.1 *Kōlam* placed for deities at a Hindu temple. Chennai, Tamil Nadu, 2004

kōlam designs that women aim to control and manipulate these states (Kramrisch 1985), and most people I spoke to explained the practice in these terms. The notion of auspiciousness encapsulates concepts of bodily and material well-being and concomitant ideas of wealth and advantage (Marriott 1976), reflected in the oft-cited claim that *kōlam* are prayers offered by householders to *Laxmi* – the Hindu goddess of wealth and prosperity – to entice her into their homes. At increasing levels of magnitude – whether in size, number or complexity – *kōlam* usher in the beginning of the day, household worship, new life phases, annual cycles and celestial events. *Kōlam* also mark inauspicious time, being conspicuous by their absence following the death of a family member or during the annual rites to honour ancestors. These temporal 'cycles' are given spatial expression at points of transition between states, such as the threshold, the kitchen stove and the temple sanctum. The salience of these factors in local discourse accounts for the weight given to domestic ritual in scholarly analyses of *kōlam* practice, and this remains its most well-researched aspect (see Beck 1976; Hart 1973; Leslie 1991; Wadley 1991; Hancock 1999).

I do not, however, intend to rehearse these insights in this chapter, but rather to develop a novel perspective on the well-established theme of agency and action in relation to ritual art. Drawing on theoretical insights offered by Alfred Gell (1998)

The Kōlam of Southern India

Figure 3.2 Basic *kōlam* executed without *puḷḷi* on threshold of private residence. Chennai, Tamil Nadu, 2004

on agency and pattern construction, I explore the relationship between structure, innovation and agency in the implementation of traditional *kōlam* designs, which call for exacting execution of both the grid structure and the encircling line or lines. In my field research I had set out to identify the strategies and techniques adopted by women to document, learn and execute designs in the *kampi kōlam* repertoire, in order to tease out local understandings of design, structure and form. What emerged from this research was an interesting body of 'technical' lore hitherto neglected in the scholarly literature (cf. Layard 1937; Kilambi 1985; Archana 1989; Dohmen 2001), which privileges the values of openness, flexibility and receptiveness to the revelatory potential in the design's execution. I begin with a brief regional and historical contextualization of *kōlam* art during the twentieth century, highlighting the emergence of printed referents for *kōlam* designs and their significance for early anthropological work on the subject. This is followed by a description of *kōlam* categorization, the planning and preparation of grid structures and the use of printed prototypes. These procedures are illustrated through a detailed study of the successful attempt, by one of the women who participated in my study, to execute a *kōlam* design. I conclude with an analysis of the implications of the study for our understanding of pattern construction.

Print Culture, Folklore and Education in Madras

From the beginning of the twentieth century, commercially produced, printed referents for *kōlam* designs – known locally as *kōlam* 'books' – have been in widespread use. These publications vary considerably, from single sheets of paper to hardback books containing many hundreds of designs, but most are produced cheaply in pamphlet form and in local vernaculars. Most women I spoke to claimed to have ready access to this printed material at the individual or household level, and it was frequently offered as a source of illustration during interviews. Printed referents therefore provide these women with cheap access to a large corpus of design prototypes in permanent form and are now a prominent feature of *kōlam* practice in contemporary Chennai. A distinctive feature of this commercial material is that designs are often presented with minimal explanatory text or suggested methods of execution. As collations of a variety of design types and formats, the 'books' leave any formal interpretation of design elements primarily to the viewer. This style of presentation is evident in early examples and remained dominant throughout the twentieth century. One such early example is the 1901 Tamil publication *Arputha Colamanjeri* [*sic*] (Ammani Ammal 1901). Currently held in the India Office collection of the British Library, this third edition text contains a short anthology of Tamil poetry and folk songs to which is appended a compilation of over a hundred *kōlam* designs (see Figure 3.3). Originally intended for use in girls' schools, the text provides surprisingly early evidence of the use of *kōlam* in school curricula and suggests that access to printed referents during this period – at least among the metropolitan elites – may not have been as restricted as is commonly supposed. Another early text published in Tamil and Telugu in 1929 and composed entirely of *kōlam* designs, again numbering over a hundred, is also held in the British Library collection.[2]

Early scholars of *kōlam* art made good use of these printed referents as documentary sources. They were troubled not by the scarcity of designs but by the perceived deficiency in local interpretations of their meaning and symbolism. Two of the most significant attempts to fill this lacuna were made by the anthropologist John Layard (1937) and the historian Jagadisa Ayyar (1930). Both writers collected and offered interpretations for a substantial number of *kōlam* designs, Layard in particular proving a significant influence on subsequent work (Kilambi 1985; Steinmann 1989; Archana 1989). Layard's paper, published in the journal *Folklore*, analysed approximately thirty-five individual *kōlam* designs alongside comparative material, all of which was indebted to 'two books, printed in Madras, for use by Hindus' (Layard 1937: 119). From the notes in Layard's article it is clear that these 'books' contained at least ninety-five and forty-five individual designs, respectively. The first of these books, reliably dated by Layard to 1923, is almost certainly an earlier production of the 1929 publication referred to above.

The Kōlam of Southern India

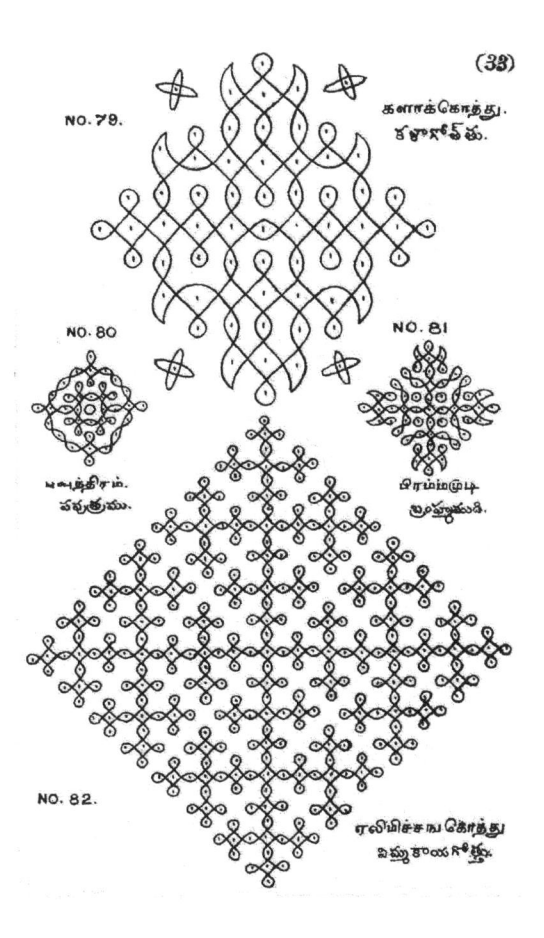

Figure 3.3 Leaf from the 1901 Tamil publication *Arpatha Colamanjeri*, showing referents for *kampi kōlam* designs

This admittedly rudimentary evidence nevertheless suggests that a commercial practice of collating and disseminating *kōlam* designs through the medium of print was beginning to be established in Madras by the early twentieth century, and that *kōlam* 'books' were being reprinted during this period for both school instruction and general consumption. Seven years prior to Layard's paper, and five years after his seminal *South Indian Customs* (1925), Jagadisa Ayyar published in Madras a two-part volume of *kōlam* designs with accompanying names and interpretation (1930). Again, it is highly likely that he exploited printed referents available in Madras at the time.[3]

The emergence of printed referents during this period is not wholly surprising. The decades of the late nineteenth and early twentieth centuries were marked by major social and political developments in colonial south India that were to affect dramatically the lives of urban women and thrust folklore to the forefront of public consciousness. Late nineteenth-century Madras had witnessed a burgeoning local culture of printed folklore, led primarily by Indian-owned commercial presses and buoyed by demand for readers from an expanding state education system introduced in the 1820s (Blackburn 2003). The primary patrons of these new educational institutions were the emerging social elites, particularly the urban middle class and, increasingly, their daughters. Private as well as state schools for girls were flourishing by the end of the nineteenth century in Madras Presidency, and the 1881 Indian census revealed that the province ranked highest in British India for female literacy. By 1902 there were over 130,000 girls' schools – a figure that more than doubled over the next decade – albeit mostly restricted to primary instruction and catering to the upper classes, higher castes and Christians (Raman 1996). Lessons in practical arts subjects had become a mainstay of the female curriculum, with the early twentieth century witnessing the introduction of examinations in singing, ornamental needlework and, later, subjects such as drawing (see Raman 1996: 82–3). It is no wonder, then, that early evidence for printed referents appears in the form of appendices to collections of folk songs produced for use in girls' schools. From the 1920s, however, the production and use of *kōlam* books appears to have increased significantly. One possible catalyst took the form of the 'populist movements' that emerged in India at that time, marking the intensification of nationalist sentiment. In Bengal, this emerging nationalist interest in folk culture was reflected in the much celebrated writing and art of Abanindranath Tagore (1871–1951), who in 1919 published a collection of Bengali *alpana* designs, entitled *Banglar Brata*, that was apparently republished in French under the title *L'Alpona au les décorations rituelles au Bengale* (see Guha Thakurta 1992: 203; Bonnerjea 1933: 163). That such a celebrated figure should publish a collection of women's ritual art testifies to how regional folk culture (increasingly interpreted as the culture of subaltern groups such as women, tribals and untouchable castes) had come to be seen as the site of an authentic, uncolonized India, upon which the emerging nation's new identity could be formed (Chatterjee 1993).

Much of what characterizes *kōlam* practice in Chennai today appears therefore to have its antecedents in this political and commercial history. *Kōlam* books are cheaply produced and readily available through most general commercial outlets; school art classes now increasingly provide young girls with their first formal introduction to *kōlam* designs; and public authorities organize *kōlam* competitions as showcases for 'living' Tamil culture. All this is clearly connected to the contemporaneous growth of popular literary print culture in south India and the development of strong Tamil regionalist sentiment (Irschick 1986; Ramaswamy 1997). Despite their limited editorial text, *kōlam* books have the capacity to standardize local discourse on the history, meaning and values associated with the practice. They certainly have significant implications for practices of learning and memory. Moreover it is unquestionably the case that women frequently draw inspiration from printed referents. Yet despite this, the attitude of scholars towards the emergence of printed referents for designs remains disparaging. Printed referents are blamed for having led to a stagnation of local creativity, a charge borne of the conjecture that to copy designs from *kōlam* books rather than to compose them anew eliminates the need for a keen eye, astute memory or geometric thought. The basis for this conjecture lies in the assumptions that these skills of eye and mind are called for only in the composition of designs as opposed to their execution, and that copying amounts to a simple, mechanical transcription that creates nothing that was not already prefigured in the initial composition. My study, however, leads me to question these assumptions. As I shall show, the processes that allow for a printed referent to be realized as a completed *kōlam* adorning a threshold are anything but simple. Not only do they call for significant technical knowledge and accomplishment on the part of practitioners, but they are also potentially generative of novel designs. It is to these processes that I now turn.

Kōlam Prototypes and the Realization of Designs

Chennai – formally known as Madras – is the fourth largest city in India and the former administrative centre of the Madras Presidency. Today a major commercial and manufacturing centre, educational hub, tourist destination and one of the principle ports of India, the modern city is marked by its cosmopolitanism, drawing temporary workers and permanent settlers of various social and cultural backgrounds from throughout India. It is currently home to a substantial and growing urban middle class, and it was largely among this Tamil middle class, and the 'lower-class' maids employed to work for them, that my research was conducted, these two groups representing the primary socio-economic categories in the urban context of the city. My study involved a sample of sixteen women and one man, aged between twenty and fifty-six, of whom seven were drawn from the educated middle class and ten from lower socio-economic groups. Respondents were contacted through informal social networks and leads offered by organizers of local *kōlam* competitions. Women of the upper socio-economic group were either in professional employment or would identify themselves as housewives, although a significant proportion engaged in additional freelance or casual work of various kinds. Women in the sample from the lower socio-economic group worked primarily as maids, although enquiries as to additional sources of income were not pursued. All women identified ethnically as Tamil and the majority of respondents were Brahmin by caste.

The study focused mainly on identifying the strategies whereby women manipulate proto-designs into different forms. Interviews began with loosely structured conversations eliciting biographical data, such as the age at which respondents first started drawing *kōlam* and from whom they had learned. They were then asked to draw a *kōlam* design, and this formed the basis for further discussion in which they were asked questions regarding their choice of execution. Typically, questions touched on the placement of dots in the underlying grid structure and the choice of starting position, but they also addressed aspects of execution peculiar to a particular respondent, such as the marking of certain *puḷḷi* (dots) before the placing of the *kampi* (line), and the practice of turning the paper relative to the body when executing certain *kōlam* designs. Once it was understood that the study was focused on technique, women proved surprisingly comfortable discussing such technical questions at length, and it soon became apparent that this formed a significant aspect of *kōlam* lore. Women were given the choice of demonstrating with pencil and paper or with rice flour, depending on the medium with which the practitioner felt most comfortable. The formality of the interview situation, however, meant that most demonstrations were provided on paper. Respondents generally appeared to be comfortable with this, often using the interview as an opportunity to present personal collections of notebooks and publications on *kōlam* designs. Where interviews had gone particularly well, further sessions were arranged with the intention of videotaping *kōlam* construction techniques. I hoped this would provide a more naturalistic record and allow for detailed analysis of the position, direction and movement of women's bodies and hands, particularly in relation to tracing paths. Following preparatory meetings, three practitioners were videotaped during two separate sessions. Of the two filmed sessions, only one continued to further editing and final analysis.

When asked questions concerning technique, respondents were unanimous on the importance of the underlying *puḷḷi* structure for the successful execution of the *kōlam* design. Although small, basic *kōlam* can be executed without *puḷḷi*, most informants agreed that *puḷḷi* were indispensable for larger or more complex *kōlam*, ensuring both accuracy and evenness in the final design. Respondents distinguished consistently between two types of grid structure (see Figure 3.4), known respectively as *nēr*, meaning 'straight', and *cuṇṭa*, a word glossed as 'between' or 'centre'. In common usage these terms indicate the general distribution of dots (*puḷḷi*) within a grid, but used in the strict sense *nēr* and *cuṇṭa* specify the relative position of particular dots within a given grid structure. *Nēr puḷḷi* appear on the same horizontal axis as *puḷḷi* in adjacent columns. As dots fall perpendicular to each other, this produces a uniform grid that forms 'straight' lines of *puḷḷi*. *Cuṇṭa puḷḷi* appear in the 'centre' or 'between' *puḷḷi* in adjacent columns. This distinction forms the basis of the categorization of *kōlam* designs into three broad types, based on technique. As a general rule, *kampi kōlam* – in which the line (*kampi*)

The Kōlam of Southern India

Figure 3.4 *Nērpuḷḷi* (left) and *cuṇṭapuḷḷi* (right) grid structures

encircles the *puḷḷi* – are executed on *nēr puḷḷi* grids; whereas *cuṇṭa puḷḷi* grids are reserved for *kōlam* in which the line *joins* the dots, rendering the *puḷḷi* structure invisible in the finished design. Completed *kōlam* of these two types appear very different in form, as is shown in Figure 3.5. The third type, known as 'line *kōlam*', is a freehand drawing that requires no underlying *puḷḷi* structure at all.

Figure 3.5 A demonstration of the distinction between *nēr* and *cuṇṭa puḷḷi* and the resulting *kōlam*. Chengelpet District, Tamil Nadu 2004

Amar S. Mall

Most respondents agreed that, with the exception of a few small designs, it was not possible to place *kampi kōlam* on *cuṇṭa puḷḷi* grids, as it would not be possible to encircle each dot. *Cuṇṭa puḷḷi* are, however, incorporated within *kampi kōlam* designs as 'fillers' for enclosed spaces generated as a function of the execution of the *kampi* on the *nēr puḷḷi* structure. These 'miscellaneous' *cuṇṭa puḷḷi* are integrated either before or after placing the *kampi* and are often used as 'markers' in the execution of more intricate designs. This is exemplified in Figure 3.6, where the practitioner has marked outlying *cuṇṭa puḷḷi* positions with a cross. Any given *kōlam* will therefore require a specific combination of *nēr* and *cuṇṭa puḷḷi* composing a grid of particular size and shape. When placing these grids, practitioners first delineate the central vertical column, commencing

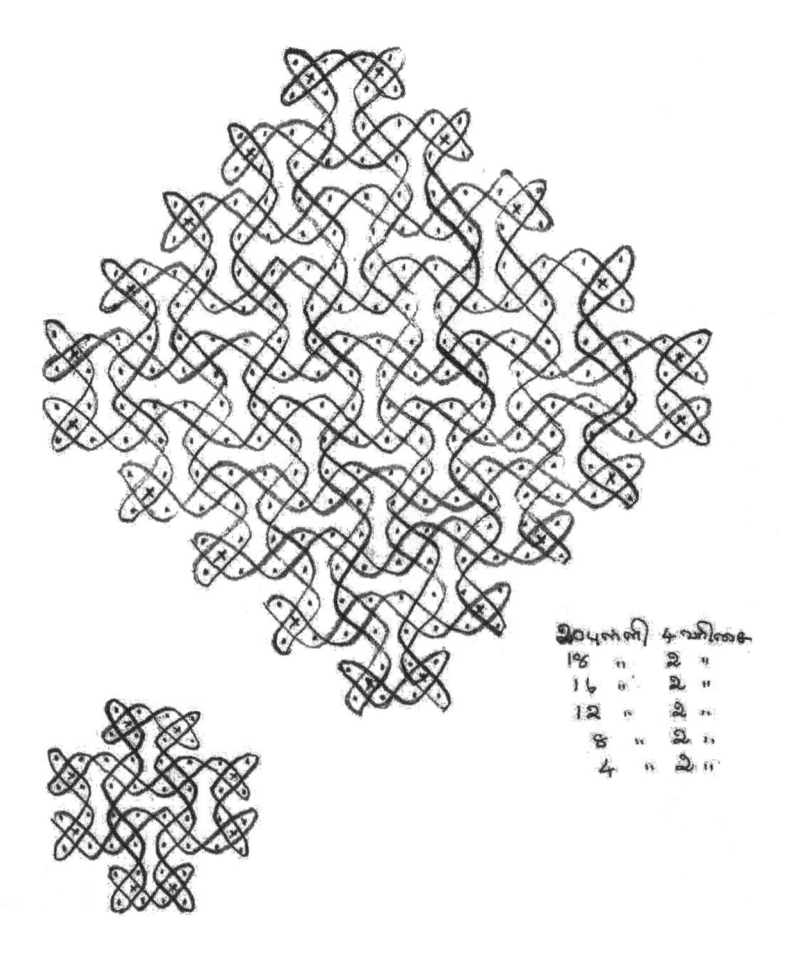

Figure 3.6 Leaf from a practitioner's notebook containing hand-drawn *kōlam* designs

-64-

from the bottom *puḷḷi* and moving up and away from their bodies – the number of *puḷḷi* in this central vertical column being given as the 'size' of the *kōlam*. This procedure is then repeated for columns on either side of this vertical axis, reducing by the number of *puḷḷi* required for that design. As well as the underlying grid, practitioners demonstrated a strong preference for initiating the *kampi* from this same position, testing compositional elements against the grid before committing themselves to completing the design.

Only *nēr puḷḷi* are therefore dominant in the execution of the *kampi*, and grid structures are nearly always symmetrical. As a result, *kōlam* designs are notated as numerical sequences corresponding to the number of *puḷḷi* in consecutive columns from the central vertical axis. Apart from these numerical sequences, however, there is little attempt to formalize the learning procedure to include any systematic description of the movement of the *kampi* through the grid structure. Women insisted that such understanding was only possible through exposure to the *kōlam* 'design' and by way of active practice. In nearly all cases the process of planning and executing designs was therefore first refined on paper, and to this end women maintained collections of *kōlam* designs in the form of personal notebooks and annotated print material. As it is considered highly inappropriate to have recourse to these paper referents when placing designs in powder, women must develop strategies for parsing designs and effectively memorizing execution sequences. Often the numerical 'algorithm' required to change the scale of a design (that is, to increase or decrease its 'size') would be calculated and recorded for future reference; alternatively, women would create a basic prototype by 'reducing' a design to the minimum number of *puḷḷi* (see Figure 3.6, above). *Kōlam* presented to me on paper were therefore described (using English loanwords) as the *kōlam*'s 'design', 'model' or 'pattern'. The use of these terms is largely contextual, as definitive prototypes were rarely identified, any transformation of the figure being interpreted as the potential 'model' for an executed 'design'. Nevertheless, it attested to a certain interrogation of designs for key structural properties that enabled the recognition of several forms as essentially 'the same' – that is, generated from the same 'model'.

In formal terms, a *kōlam* therefore comprises a 'prototypical' structure that can be subjected to certain 'prescriptive' transformations that may be pre-planned or may materialize through the act of placing the *kōlam*, which (as noted above) would rarely take place with the paper referent to hand. Numerous individual designs may therefore be identified as equivalent, in that each constitutes a distinct example of the transformative potential of a given *kōlam* form. Compositional elements, however, will set parameters on the degree to which a design can be manipulated. An appreciation of the transformative potential and limits of *kōlam* designs is integral to women's ability to both pre-empt and effectively manage problems that may occur during their execution. Despite women's rehearsal of designs on paper, the frequency of mistakes in the placing of designs is surprisingly high, occurring when grids are positioned incorrectly or the *kampi* becomes misdirected and subsequently 'gets stuck'. This is partly because designs are rarely placed with the paper referent to hand; but women also recognize that mistakes can be made easily even with relatively straightforward designs. In most cases they are rectified with simple ad hoc adjustments, but they sometimes occasion a complete innovation to the originally intended form. Effectively preventing or at least controlling such contingent factors remains a primary consideration when executing designs in powder. This is not always successfully achieved, however, and in such circumstances women must 'bring the pattern back' so that the *kōlam* may 'come'.

The term *varum* (meaning 'to come') was frequently adopted by women when discussing *kōlam* designs. Spectators watching a woman placing a *kōlam* would often observe, halfway through the execution process, that the pattern 'has come'. Rather than taking the final form as wholly given, this idiom conveyed a sense that the planning procedure and initial placing of the *kampi* had been successfully orchestrated and the intended design would manifest itself. Although presented sequentially, each of these factors – the planning and preparation of the *puḷḷi* structure, experimentation with the transformative potential and limits of the 'model', and the final delineation of the *kampi* – would coalesce in the act of placing any given design. This is presented in Figures 3.7 and 3.8, a collection of video stills in which a woman attempts to ascertain the grid structure required to extend a five-*puḷḷi* single-line *kōlam* 'model' to nine-*puḷḷi* (that is, to increase the grid 'size' by four). It was this woman who, upon inspecting the original 'model' (with which she claimed to be unfamiliar), proposed the nine-*puḷḷi* figure. Figures 3.7 and 3.8 detail the procedure whereby this particular practitioner extrapolated and subsequently delineated the nine-*puḷḷi kōlam* 'design'.

As Figures 3.7.1–3.7.6 reveal, the practitioner begins by laying the *puḷḷi* in the conventional manner, starting each row from the bottom and completing the right half of the grid to the 'standard' *nēr puḷḷi* plan, that is, with the number of *puḷḷi* in consecutive columns reducing by two. As this is a nine-*puḷḷi* design, the pattern laid down is therefore '9, 7, 5, 3, 1'. This procedure is then repeated to complete the first two columns of the left half of the grid, but in this case each contains seven *puḷḷi* (Figure 3.7.4). At this point the practitioner checks the emerging configuration against the arrangement of *puḷḷi* in the original five-*puḷḷi kōlam* design, just visible in the foreground, visualizing with her hands the position of the *kampi* by tracing the *kampi*'s movement through the *puḷḷi* structure (Figure 3.7.4). She then makes a series of adjustments to this *puḷḷi* structure (Figure 3.7.5–3.7.6) before proceeding to the bottom of the central axis (Figure 3.7.7), finally to test the movement of the *kampi* against the *puḷḷi* from this 'starting' position (Figures 3.7.7–3.7.9). Upon commencing the *kampi*, the number of *puḷḷi* is therefore provisionally set at

The Kōlam of Southern India

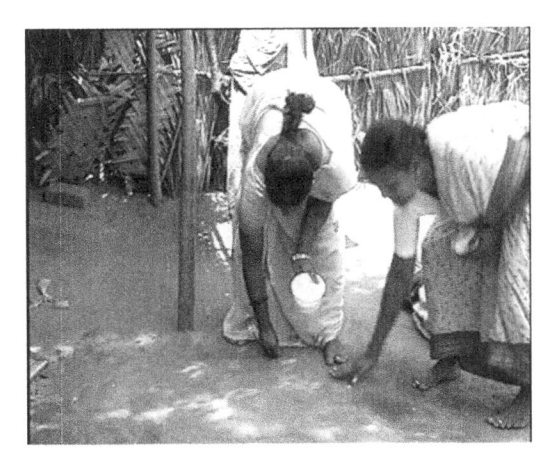

Figures 3.7.1–3.7.3 Determining the grid structure required to extend a five *puḷḷi kōlam* to nine *puḷḷi*. Chengelpet District, Tamil Nadu 2004

Figures 3.7.4–3.7.6 Determining the grid structure required to extend a five *puḷḷi kōlam* to nine *puḷḷi*. Chengelpet District, Tamil Nadu 2004

Figures 3.7.7–3.7.9 Determining the grid structure required to extend a five *puḷḷi kōlam* to nine *puḷḷi*. Chengelpet District, Tamil Nadu 2004

'9, 7, 7, 1'. Figure 3.8 illustrates the placing of the *kampi* on this provisional *puḷḷi* structure, and the manipulation of both *puḷḷi* and *kampi* during the execution of the *kōlam* design. Figure 3.8.1 illustrates the initial stages of placing the *kampi* and how *puḷḷi* operate to guide the *kampi* and ensure even distribution. Of particular interest is Figure 3.8.2, where instead of moving the *kampi* back upon itself (as seen in Figure 3.8.1), the practitioner places an additional *puḷḷi* (Figure 3.8.2) around which the *kampi* subsequently circles (Figure 3.8.3). This same procedure is repeated further in the sequence, as shown in Figure 3.8.4. After a few moments determining whether the *kampi* will 'close' correctly the practitioner returns to the 'starting' position (Figure 3.8.5) to complete the design. The placement of the *kampi* is thus effectively executed in two halves. Having successfully 'closed' the *kampi* (Figure 3.8.7), the practitioner finally finishes the *kōlam* with the addition of 'flourishes' that preserve the design's symmetry (Figure 3.8.8). The final pattern of *puḷḷi* laid for this design was '9, 7, 7, 5'.

What is significant in this sequence is the manipulation of the *puḷḷi* in order to accommodate the movement of the *kampi*. During a subsequent interview the practitioner claimed that she was initially uncertain as to whether or not the final row of *puḷḷi* on either side of the grid would be required, that is, whether or not they were integral to the pattern 'coming' (*varum*), suggesting that conceptually the *puḷḷi* structure remains 'open' during the execution of the *kampi*. The addition of these *puḷḷi* was not in fact necessary, but the practitioner chose to retain them and keep the outer *kampi* curves as attractive 'flourishes' in the final design. She pointed out that had these outer curves been removed and the *kampi* closed (in effect a reversal of the procedure illustrated in Figure 3.8.8), the 'integrity' of the design would have remained true to the basic *kōlam* 'model'. The active manipulation of different structural elements of *kampi kōlam* designs therefore forms an important aspect of women's practice. Indeed the adjustments that this practitioner can be seen to make indicate a far greater degree of flexibility in the execution of *kōlam* than that suggested by both the current literature and women's own perceptions of their practice. Following this exercise the same practitioner was able to expand the same *kōlam* to twenty-one dots, adapting the *puḷḷi* in order to make the final *kōlam* more circular.

This material presents a number of problems for locating creativity and intention in both the design and the execution of *kampi kōlam*. The *kampi kōlam*'s capacity spontaneously to transform in directions different from those originally intended locates 'creativity' somewhere *between* the intentions of the practitioner and this 'self-generating' capacity of the *kōlam* form. Although most women tried hard not to be put in a position where they would have to test their wits *against* the *kōlam* (in having to 'bring the pattern back'), they nevertheless agreed that this was the primary mechanism behind the generation of novel designs, and skilled women cultivated a receptiveness to this revelatory potential in the design's execution. It

The Kōlam of Southern India

Figures 3.8.1–3.8.3 Determining the position of the *kampi* for the nine *pul̤l̤i* design. Chengelpet District, Tamil Nadu, 2004

Figures 3.8.4–3.8.6 Determining the position of the *kampi* for the nine *pulli* design. Chengelpet District, Tamil Nadu, 2004

The Kōlam of Southern India

Figures 3.8.7–3.8.9 Determining the position of the *kampi* for the nine *puḷḷi* design. Chengelpet District, Tamil Nadu, 2004

is important to note, however, that none of these processes are ascertainable from the finished *kōlam* design. The structural constraints concomitant on placing a *kampi* on a *nēr puḷḷi* grid mean that designs will inevitably 'revert to form', and women remarked on how difficult it was to infer the *actual* technique used to produce a given *kōlam* from an examination of the finished design alone. In this respect, whenever a woman adopts a new *kōlam* for herself, she also recreates that *kōlam* anew. In short, creativity is evinced more in the practice than in the product, and as such, it is neither indexed by any accumulation of novel outcomes nor restricted by their limitation to predetermined referents.

Locating Creativity

In this chapter I have set out to demonstrate how an appreciation of technique in the context of pattern construction can provide insight into understanding agency in a local context – that of the *kampi kōlam* of southern India. I have tried to achieve this through an investigation of the interplay between structure and innovation in pattern construction, by demonstrating how agency can become displaced from the original intention of the practitioner to the self-generative capacity of the *kōlam* form itself. As I have already noted, the verb most often used in association with the execution of *kōlam* was *varum*, glossed as 'come' or 'to come'. Even highly experienced practitioners would exclaim, 'Oh! It's come!' whenever it became clear that a half-executed pattern would complete. Evidently women do not take it as a foregone conclusion that a *kōlam* will necessarily manifest itself. This may not be questioned for very simple *kōlam*, but for larger or more complex designs, where *puḷḷi* become indispensable and there is always a chance of misplacing a single *puḷḷi* or taking the *kampi* one *puḷḷi* too far or too short, women become skilled at sensing the point at which, during the execution of the *kampi*, the final shape of the pattern becomes apparent – the point at which it 'comes'. This effect is accentuated in contexts where women are executing a *kōlam* design for the first time, as in the example presented above. Although I do not wish to overstate the case, I believe that an appreciation of this facet of *kōlam* art is important in understanding the pleasure women take in *kōlam* designs. As one respondent explained:

> Sometimes we think something but something else will happen. We will set our mind on one, and decide to place that *kōlam*. Despite that, if we miss even a little, we would get a different *kōlam* for a different set of dots. Some people have even sung songs about this, saying that what they have kept is one thing but what they got was something else.

Rather than viewing this unpredictability in negative terms, women take it as the driving force behind the innovation of new and, with luck, more beautiful designs.

As the passage cited above suggests, credit for such innovation lies as much with the generative capacity of the *kōlam*, borne from the structural implications of the movement of the *kampi* on a particular *puḷḷi* grid, as with the creativity – or in the above case, the inaccuracy – of the practitioner.

Alfred Gell attributes the apotropaic capacity of the *kōlam* to the cognitive equivalent of 'unfinished business' (Gell 1998: 80): the virtual impossibility, on beholding a complex pattern, of ever being able to grasp the process of its construction. Though it appears as a fully formed figure, complete in itself, we know that the pattern was once composed and executed by a real-life practitioner, yet we remain unable to unravel the skilled movements that gave rise to it. The perceptual task is never finished; the puzzle of the pattern never solved. In the case of *kōlam*, this 'cognitive stickiness', according to Gell, ensnares potentially malevolent demons, preventing them from crossing the thresholds on which they are drawn (ibid.: 85–6). This is a sound analysis of the *kōlam* and would certainly be corroborated by local women. My observations suggest, however, that it is not only on the side of perceivers or 'recipients' of the designs that business is never finished. This is equally true on the side of the practitioners who produce them.

I have argued that the tendency of scholars to focus on the completed *kōlam* form has effectively masked the creativity of the technical practices that give rise to it. These practices are both flexible and open-ended. They do not merely transcribe onto a material surface a design already settled in the mind of the practitioner. To the contrary, a practitioner's gestures – both in the manipulation of *puḷḷi* and in the execution of the *kampi* – enact a process of design that evolves throughout the work. The maturation of the design concept, in thought, is one with its material enactment. Hence the agency that brings the *kōlam* into being is not necessarily lined up in advance, initiating a causal sequence that results in a final form matching the prior intention, but is immanent in the *kōlam*'s own potential for indefinite growth or self-generation. Yet even after a pattern has 'come' it keeps on going, suspended in perpetual motion. Like the life of the person it reflects, it remains unfinished business, creating itself endlessly. As much a path to be followed as an element of a preconceived structure, the line is learned, remembered and reproduced temporally rather than figuratively, as a rhythmic series of movements or gestures. Thus practitioners innovate by way of the improvisational exploration of novel paths around the grid, with the potential of generating previously unimagined patterns.

In this respect the *kampi* is clearly distinguished from the lines drawn on a *cuṇṭa puḷḷi* grid. In the *kōlam* drawn on a *cuṇṭa puḷḷi* grid the relation between lines and dots is quite different, as these lines join the dots rather than weaving a way around them, each having a starting point and end point that are predetermined in the placing of the grid. Thus, in this case, the *kōlam* appears as a static figure, the manifestation of a structure that cognitively precedes its execution on the ground. Innovation here entails altering the structure rather than exploring the generative potential of alternative pathways. In marking the outlines of a mosaic of shapes, the lines of such a *kōlam* are not only drawn upon a surface but define that surface as a geometrical plane. The line of the *kampi kōlam* has precisely the opposite effect, dissolving the very surface upon which it is drawn so that it appears instead as a labyrinthine mesh of threads along which all of life and existence is constrained to run. It is perhaps by entangling demons in the mesh, rather than by challenging them with insoluble cognitive conundrums, that the *kampi kōlam* exercises its protective functions.

Acknowledgements

This chapter is based on ethnographic fieldwork conducted in Chennai, India, during June and July 2004. The research was funded by a postgraduate studentship awarded by the UK Economic and Social Research Council, held at University College London. I am grateful to the Council for its support.

Notes

1. Transliteration of Tamil terms follows the standard transliteration and pronunciation scheme used by the University of Madras *Tamil Lexicon*. Where possible, I have attempted to retain the phonology of spoken Tamil.
2. *Mahalatcumi Kolapputtakam*, Amarampetu: Pumakal Accukkutam.
3. My knowledge of Jagadisa Ayyar's (1930) work is drawn from Walldén (1997).

References

Ammani Ammal, C. (1901), *Arputha Colamanjeri*, Madras.
Archana (1989), *The Language of Symbols*, Madras: Crafts Council of India.
Beck, B. (1976), 'The symbolic merger of body, space and cosmos in Hindu Tamil Nadu', *Contributions to Indian Sociology* (NS), 10(2): 213–45.
Blackburn, S.H. (2003), *Print, Folklore and Nationalism in Colonial South India*, Delhi: Permanent Black.
Bonnerjea, B. (1933), 'Note on geometrical ritual designs in India', *Man*, 33: 163–4.

Chatterjee, P. (1993), *The Nation and its Fragments*, Princeton, NJ: Princeton University Press.

Dohmen, R. (2001), 'Happy homes and the Indian nation: women's designs in post-colonial Tamil Nadu', *Journal of Design History*, 14(2): 129–39.

Gell, A. (1998), *Art and Agency: An Anthropological Theory*, Oxford: Clarendon Press.

Guha Thakurta, T. (1992), *Making of a New Indian Art: Artists, Aesthetics and Nationalism in Bengal, c.1850–1920*, Cambridge: Cambridge University Press.

Hancock, M.E. (1999), *Womanhood in the Making: Domestic Ritual and Public Culture in Urban South India*, Boulder, Colo.: Westview Press.

Hart, G.L. (1973), 'Women and the sacred in ancient Tamilnad', *Journal of Asian Studies*, 32(2): 233–50.

Irschick, E.F. (1986), *Tamil Revivalism in the 1930s*, Madras: Cre-A.

Jagadisa Ayyar, P.V. (1925), *South Indian Customs*, New Delhi: Asian Educational Services.

—— (1930), *Folk Art – South Indian Kolam, Part I and II*, Madras.

Kilambi, J.S. (1985), 'Toward an understanding of the *muggu*: threshold drawings from Hyderabad', *Res*, 10: 71–102.

Kramrisch, S. (1968), *Unknown India: Ritual Art in Tribe and Village*, Philadelphia: Philadelphia Museum of Art.

—— (1985), 'The ritual arts of India', in *Aditi: The Living Arts of India*, Washington DC: Smithsonian Institution Press.

Layard, J. (1937), 'Labyrinth rituals in S. India: threshold and tattoo designs', *Folklore,* 48: 116–82.

Leslie, J. (1991), *Roles and Rituals for Hindu Women*, London: Pinter.

Madan, T.N. (1985), 'Concerning the categories Śubha and Śuddha in Hindu Culture. An exploratory essay', *Journal of Developing Societies*, 1(1): 11–29.

Marglin, F.A. (1985), *Wives of the God King: The Rituals of the Devadasis of Puri*, Delhi: Oxford University Press.

Marriott, M. (1976), 'Interpreting Indian society: a monistic alternative to Dumont's dualism', *The Journal of Asian Studies*, 36: 189–95.

Raheja, G.G. (1988), *The Poison in the Gift: Ritual, Prestation, and the Dominant Caste in a North Indian Village*, Chicago: University of Chicago Press.

Raman, S.A. (1996), *Getting Girls to School: Social Reform in the Tamil Districts, 1870–1930*, Calcutta: Stree.

Ramaswamy, S. (1997), *Passions of the Tongue: Language Devotion in Tamil India, 1891–1970*, Berkeley: University of California Press.

Steinmann, R.M. (1989), 'Kōlam: form, technique and application of a changing ritual folk art of Tamil Nadu', in A.L. Dallapiccola (ed), *Shastric Traditions in Indian Arts*, Stuttgart: Steiner Verlag.

Wadley, S.S. (1991), *The Powers of Tamil Women*, New Delhi: Manohar Publications.

Walldén, R. (1997), 'Notes on *Cittira Kavi* in Tamil', in S. Lienhard and I. Piovano (eds), *Lex et Litterae: Studies in Honour of Professor Oscar Botto*, Torino: Edizioni dell'Orso.

–4–

Creating or Performing Words? Observations on Contemporary Japanese Calligraphy
Fuyubi Nakamura

Figure 4.1 *The Stains/07, Mumi Mushū (No Taste, No Smell)*, by Yugami Hisao, Kyoto, Japan, 2002

Through my *sho* expression, words leave their stains on paper…
What appears is something, as my expressive entity.

Yugami Hisao[1]

Creativity and Originality

What are the prerequisites for artistic creativity? Gell (1992: 56) has pointed out that the quasi-religious status of art in modern Western societies, along with the exaggerated emphasis in these societies on originality as a guarantor of authenticity, has led to a distorted view of techniques as mechanical and impersonal, by contrast to the creativity that is supposed to be embodied in art. In practice, however, the concept of art is difficult to dissociate from notions of technical skill. In this chapter I explore the meaning of artistic creativity through an examination of the practices of contemporary Japanese calligraphy. 'Creative' artistic calligraphy, in Japanese, is distinguished by the term *sho*, while *shodō* or *shohō* refers to the 'way' or method of calligraphy. Of course, calligraphy is more than just an art form; it is also a way of writing. In the modern period, however, as calligraphy has lost its primacy as a medium of written communication, it has undergone a series of dramatic transformations. Contemporary calligraphers no longer aim necessarily to convey the lexical meanings of words. Their objective is rather to give them visual and material expression. Here I shall examine how they do so, focusing on the issues of whether, in calligraphy, creativity entails originality, and on the role that different agents, both personal and material, play in the creative process.

Ever since the Renaissance, and throughout the pre-modern period, works of art were produced in Europe for specific purposes often associated with religion. Only in the modern era did artworks become truly detached from functional considerations, leading to the rise of 'art for art's sake'. Art, then, came to acquire a value in its own right (see Adorno 1991). Against this background, issues of 'creativity' and 'originality' came to the fore. Indeed these concepts are frequently and explicitly linked in the paradigm of Western modernity. According to the Western 'activist notion of artistic creativity' (Gell 1998: 30), an artwork is defined as an original object that can be created only once and is distinguished on this criterion from both mass-produced and 'traditional' objects. In short, it is characterized by individuality, singularity and novelty. In Japanese calligraphy, by contrast, 'creativity' is not always encouraged. Or, to be more precise, what is valued is a *different kind* of creativity – one that does not oppose the original to the imitation but rather has imitation at its very source. In 1961 Kobayashi Hideo, one of the most influential cultural critics of post-Second World War Japan, described 'creativity' in the following words:

> Imitation is the mother of creativity. It is the only and true mother. Mother and child were forced apart just because of the preferences of the modern period. Without even attempting to imitate, how can we ever encounter and recognise what cannot be imitated? (Kobayashi, quoted in Yamada 2002: 214)

Discussing what he calls the 'Zen arts', such as the tea ceremony and martial arts, Cox argues that 'each copy will manifest the aesthetic qualities of what is copied. The copy can evoke this original form by the "literalness", or what Taussig calls the "copiedness", of its imitation' (Cox 2003: 112; cf. Bowden 1999, Taussig 1993). In Japan, learning methods based on mimicry, imitation and copying have been vital for creativity in literature, visual and the performing arts. *Modoki* (mimicry), *utsushi* (copying) and *manebi* (learning or following examples) are the terms associated with copying practices. Similarly, various ways of quoting were considered as artistic techniques. The art of quoting, or *honkadori*, in poetry is one such example (Tsukamoto 2001; Yamada 2002). How are these methods of 'imitating' or 'quoting' translated into calligraphic practice?

Rinsho: Interpreting and Reproducing the Classics

> The beginnings of Japanese art, as of almost all things Japanese excepting cleanliness, are to be sought in China. Even after Japanese art had started on its independent career, it refreshed its inspiration from time to time by a careful study and imitation of Chinese models; and Chinese masterpieces still occupy in the estimation of Japanese connoisseurs a place only hesitatingly allowed to the best native works.
>
> Basil Hall Chamberlain, *Things Japanese*

The British Japanologist Basil Hall Chamberlain's remarks, written over a hundred years ago, capture the common attitude of contemporary Japanese calligraphers. Masterpieces of Chinese calligraphy have long been revered as models, for calligraphic training is based upon reproducing works of the ancient masters. China is still seen as a place of sacred sites, which Japanese calligraphers often visit as if they were on pilgrimage. Although Japanese calligraphy has developed its own styles, producing kinds of work not seen in China, the fundamental structures and techniques are the same because Japanese calligraphy derived from Chinese calligraphy. How, then, can we talk of Japanese calligraphy as originally and authentically Japanese? In what ways does creativity play a part in calligraphic works in differentiating among them?

Japanese calligraphy has always had to rely on the legacy of precedents, that is, on existing calligraphic writings and, in a broader sense, on written Chinese and Japanese languages. So the starting point is inevitably to 'copy' someone else's creation. Copying, however, is 'a clumsy English term' (Harrist 1999: 19) for the 'reproductive' techniques used in East Asian calligraphy. Reproduction is, of course, common in many other fields of artistic practice. The problem of copy versus original has been discussed extensively (consider, for instance, the exhaustive debate over Greek originals versus Roman copies). As Walter

Benjamin argued, 'in principle a work of art has always been reproducible. Man-made artefacts could always be imitated by men' (Benjamin 1999 [1968]: 212). But this still begs the question 'whether creativity can be copied at all' (Hannas 2003: 88–9). In other words, we have to investigate what is reproducible and what is not. Benjamin argues that it is the 'aura' of the original work that is not reproducible. Does this also apply to Japanese calligraphy?

By consciously imitating a model or *tehon* – be it an ink rubbing of the classics or *its* reproduction (a printed or hand-copied version provided by a calligraphic teacher) – Japanese calligraphers claim that they acquire the 'essence' of calligraphy. This method of learning calligraphy by freehand-copying is called *rinsho*. Some calligraphers consider *rinsho* merely a stepping stone to creative work, while others regard it as a goal in itself. Notwithstanding these contrasting views, *rinsho* remains the foundation for any type of calligraphic work. The model presents the calligrapher with an ultimate standard for which to strive. Especially in the past, the practice of *rinsho* meant far more than simply writing exercises. Produced by expert calligraphers, reproductions disseminated canonical masterpieces of calligraphy, and demonstrated the calligraphers' technical skill as well as their insight into the history of calligraphy. *Rinsho* works evince what Gell calls 'the enchantment of technology... The power that technical processes have of casting a spell over us' (Gell 1992: 44; cf. Strathern 2001: 261). Thus they are not necessarily considered derivative and are often displayed at calligraphic exhibitions as artworks in their own right. This is in striking contrast to the values of the Western art world. I doubt if a faithful reproduction of the *Mona Lisa* by a contemporary artist would be displayed alongside the original *Mona Lisa* at the Louvre and be admired for its technical virtuosity, without being labelled as a fake or viewed with postmodern cynicism.

How, then, does the calligrapher reproduce the model? The traditional, 'standard' view holds that there are three stages of *rinsho* in learning calligraphy. The first is called *keirin*. One learns the mechanics of brush techniques by imitating the forms of characters as faithfully as possible, by carefully studying them as one writes. The focus should be on the configuration of the characters and how the strokes are constructed. The second practice is *irin*, where one reproduces the model work by interpreting the intention or spirit of the brush. In other words, one is expected to understand the work beyond what is visible on paper. The last stage is called *hairin*, in which one writes or reproduces without looking at the model, by relying on one's memory. This allows for more individual freedom in executing the work.

While technical mastery is what many calligraphers seek to achieve, there is an implicit assumption that the efforts made to attain the requisite skills should not be visible in the work produced, as the masterwork should display spontaneity. After the lengthy training of *rinsho*, the calligrapher is paradoxically encouraged to discard his acquired somatic conformation. Only when he succeeds in this does a personal style emerge. This is what the third stage of *rinsho*, *hairin*, aims to achieve. The ultimate goal of calligraphy is not just to reproduce. Nor however is it simply a matter of expressing the self through an artistic medium, as in much modernist Western art, such as Jackson Pollock's 'drip' paintings which, as '(non-representational) self-portraits of a man in frenzied ballistic activity' (Gell 1998: 33), have no subject at all except the agency of the artist himself. For in calligraphy, even when a personal style has been developed, the practice of copying continues. Style is more than simply a matter of what visually appears on paper.

There is a long-standing belief in Japan and in China that one's handwriting or calligraphy reflects or reveals one's personality (this is known as *sho wa hito nari*, literally 'writing is like the person'). It is a kind of 'self portrait' (Carpenter 2002). This perception of calligraphy, or 'Confucian graphology' (Kraus 1991: 48–51), became common during the Six Dynasties period in China. During this period, the visual effects of calligraphy, rather than its literary content, attracted attention, presaging both the concept of 'art for art's sake' in nineteenth-century Europe and the autonomy of visual experience in modernist art during the twentieth century (Harrist 1999). At the selection committee meeting for a competitive calligraphic exhibition held in Kyoto in 2001, a professional calligrapher responded to my question about whether he could tell that one work was better than another in a flash, at first glance:

> Sure, I can. Imagine two men are standing there. You can tell which one looks better at once, can't you? While we cannot tell what kind of person he is just by looking at him, we can at least tell if he is good looking or not. But, in the case of calligraphy, it's a different matter. You can tell not only whether he looks good but also whether he is a good person, because calligraphy reflects his personality as well. (Personal communication, March 2002, Kyoto; cf. Yen 2005: 57)

One's handwriting is sometimes regarded as a more 'authentic' and therefore better representation of the self than one's physical appearance. This view is very common among calligraphers. However, there is a paradox. Reproducing the calligraphy of another person is a way of learning. If calligraphy embodies the person, then learning entails the incorporation of another self into one's own. It is not true, however, that everyone who successfully reproduces the model work reveals a similar personality. While this may be axiomatic, aim and outcome do not correspond in minute detail, for whether or not the calligrapher consciously strives to shake off the bodily straitjacket implanted through previous training, the limits of the physical body and those of the person do not correspond. As Yen rightly points out, echoing recent anthropological writing on 'fractal' or 'distributed' personhood (Strathern 1988; Wagner 1991; Gell 1998), the calligraphic person is not bounded by the physical body; rather, 'handwriting or calligraphy should be seen as a part of the distributed body-person' (Yen 2005: 79). This implies that while creativity is not necessarily encouraged, it is the individual qualities embodied in calligraphy that are valued, rather than the mechanical fidelity of the copy itself. How, then, do contemporary calligraphers deal with the existence of ancient masterpieces?

Inspiring the Act of Imitation

The work by Kimura Tsubasa, reproduced in Figure 4.2, is entitled *Traces of Lines*. To make things simpler for visitors to her exhibition, when they asked what she had 'written', she answered: 'They are all the same Chinese character, meaning "one" (written as 一)'. However, her lines are not actually a series of this character. Nor is the work an abstract painting consisting simply of lines. So what is it? What was Tsubasa trying to achieve in this work?

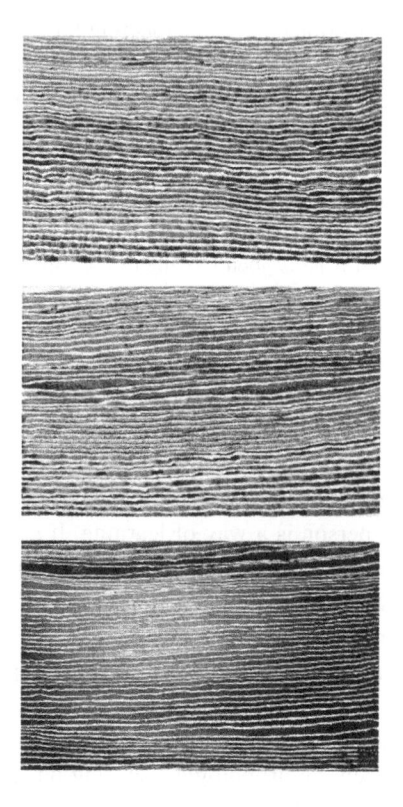

Figure 4.2 *Traces of Lines*, Kimura Tsubasa, Kyoto, Japan, 2004

Tsubasa was attempting creatively to reproduce a sequence of a specific type of line *inspired* by that of the Chinese calligrapher, Huang Tingjian (1045–1105). Huang Tingjian is considered to have been one of the four Great Masters of the Song dynasty (along with Su Shi, Mi Fu and Cai Xiang). Up to the period of the Song dynasty, the conventional brushstroke method was *sansetsu-hō*, where the calligrapher wrote in three rhythmic brush movements. This was also known as the 'new method'. Prior to the Tang dynasty, the 'old method' of two brush movements, *nisetsu-hō*, had been used. However, the so-called renaissance of calligraphy in the Song dynasty, which favoured self-expression and spontaneity, led to the development of highly personal brush styles. These were made possible by the method developed by Huang Tingjian, known as the *tasetsu-hō*, the method of multiple brush movements, and it was this *method* that Tsubasa tried to incorporate into her work.

> I repeated a sequence of *kihitsu* (starting a stroke), *sōhitsu* (pulling the stroke), and *shūhitsu* (ending the stroke). I was trying to incorporate some sort of *action* in the process, rather than merely producing lines. (Kimura Tsubasa, February 2006)

In other words, these lines are expressive gestures shaped as traces on paper, just as 'the musical phrase is an expressive gesture shaped in sound' (Ingold 2003: 7). As Ingold suggests, the physical trace is 'an almost incidental by-product, since it is the movement of forming it that counts' (ibid.: 9). To possess and utilize the brush technique means that the calligrapher knows how the movements of the body, hand and brush result in different kinds of ink traces. Consequently, to understand this piece of work one needs to visualize the gesture rather than viewing the graphic outcome. The subtlety of the work can only be appreciated with a knowledge of calligraphic techniques as well as calligraphic history.

The Illusion of the Original

A 'model' is copied in the practice of *rinsho*, or becomes the source of inspiration, as in Tsubasa's *Traces of Lines*. But this begs a question: what constitutes the model? As no copy can be made without an 'original', should we regard the model as the 'original'? If the assumption is true, then the classics of Chinese calligraphy are the 'originals' upon which copies are made. But there is an intriguing counter-instance (Harrist 1999: 18–19). *The Preface to the Orchid Pavilion* (AD 353), by the Sage of Calligraphy Wang Xizhi (303–361), is probably the best-known work of calligraphy, but is in fact a *reproduction*. The work exists only in the form of numerous copies. More precisely, Wang's style is preserved in a wide variety of later copies by other calligraphers. Some scholars believe that not a single autographed work by Wang survives today. Still, Wang's works remain the ultimate models. Certain copies of *The Orchid Pavilion*, however, notably the ink rubbing of copied versions by calligraphers such as Chu Suiliang and Ou Yangxun, made during the Tang period, have attained the status of being 'authentic'. These are the copies that are revered as the works of Wang. The technical fluency of Wang's writing is admired through these 'authentic copies'. As I have already observed, a successful copy or *rinsho* work is a result of the technical fluency of the reproducer, but does it automatically confirm the technical virtuosity of the creator as well? This case raises important questions. What makes a certain piece of work authentic or gives it authority? We should perhaps be asking, instead, *at what point* and even *why* a reproduction becomes 'authentic' or 'original'.

According to Yamada, the ubiquitous presence of 'copies' is necessary to authenticate the original and to confirm its status (Yamada 2002: 45–54). In this sense, reproduction actually enhances and increases the aura of the original, rather than reducing it. Yamada (2002: 9–12) argues that 'materials which are freely copied and have publicity' remain popular and familiar and thus are frequently reproduced. Thinking of Japanese calligraphy in these terms, its subject (that is, the Japanese writing system) is not copyrighted and is available to anyone. Reproducibility has kept calligraphy alive for thousands of years as the history of calligraphy is inseparable from that of writing. Yet it has to be noted that new models have also been created. A *rinsho* work by Empress Kōmyō, *Gakkiron* (AD 744), is a reproduction of Wang Xizhi's work, but it is now considered one of the oldest existing *Japanese* calligraphic works. Many Japanese calligraphers thus use this as a valuable model in its own right. Copied versions of the Chinese classics by Japanese calligraphers have now attained the status of 'models'. In other words, they copy copies of copies, and reproduce an already transformed version of the 'original' which itself went through various stages of interpretation by different hands and eyes at various times and places. For Japanese calligraphy, perhaps the process of 'reproduction' is more important than, or at least as important as, the finished 'reproduced' work. Authenticity is not then directly linked to originality, but to reproductive performance. What authenticates a piece of work is not fixed and can change as our interpretation changes and as a reproduction *ages*.

By reproducing the model, the calligrapher acquires not only the techniques of brush movements, but also this special insight into the history of calligraphy. *Rinsho* is a process of visually assimilating the classics by moulding 'the body in the shape of the masters' (Yen 2005: 120; cf. Cox 2003: 117). In other words, through the conscious use of his eyes and his hands or both mind and body, the calligrapher internalizes the principles embodied in the classics, eventually making them his own. Hands tamed by the practice of *rinsho* remember the movements entailed in handling the brush, so that the latter become almost effortless rather than calling for conscious endeavour.

Contemporary Japanese Calligraphy

Performing Words?

The calligrapher is not therefore necessarily aiming to create a new type of calligraphic work, particularly when it comes to *rinsho* practice. Yet differences in the interpretation of the model works and in performance by each calligrapher result in something new. In this sense, calligraphy is similar to musical performance (cf. Layton 1991: 201; Gell 1992: 54; Ingold 2003: 7). The calligrapher Hidai Nankoku (1912–99) describes calligraphy as 'an activity where one *performs* forms of words envisaged in mind' (quoted in Hidai and Uno 1983: 26).

Figure 4.3 shows Nankoku *performing* calligraphy, interestingly enough, at a music festival. Nankoku was one of the calligraphers who initiated the avant-garde movement in calligraphy after the Second World War. He was the first to have attempted to create calligraphy that did not write 'words' as we know them. *Work 1: Variation on Lightning* (Figure 4.4) looks abstract, but is based on an ancient

Figure 4.3 Hidai Nankoku at the Modern Music Festival, Middelburg, the Netherlands, 1979
© Tenrai Shoin

Chinese character for 'lightning'. By deconstructing this character, he created new forms of 'visualized words'. Nankoku's nephew, Nobuaki Yamamasu, a professional tenor singer trained and based in Germany, has a telling anecdote: Nankoku often told the young Yamamasu, 'I'm playing music by calligraphy'. Nankoku used to compare *rinsho* with musical performance, particularly of classical music. In fact, Nankoku was a keen practitioner of music and almost became a professional violinist before he seriously took up the brush instead of the bow. The analogy between doing *rinsho* and performing classical music is particularly valid, because both have a 'predominant (though not exclusive) orientation to the past' (Keen 2001: 35). Performers of the classics may be regarded, in a sense, as 'curators' of the works they perform. Both classical musicians and calligraphic practitioners interpret the old masters' works before they perform them. They both rehearse by repetitively practising the classic pieces. Furthermore, they follow a definite temporal order in the process: the order of the strokes in calligraphy, and of notation in music. But do the performers have to keep to the 'original' in an authentic manner? Is the performer 'a mere vehicle for faithfully conveying the composer's [or the author's] intentions, or a creative interpreter?' (ibid.: 43).

Despite the lengthy practice and study of the classics by both musicians and calligraphers in order to equip themselves with the necessary skills, the actual

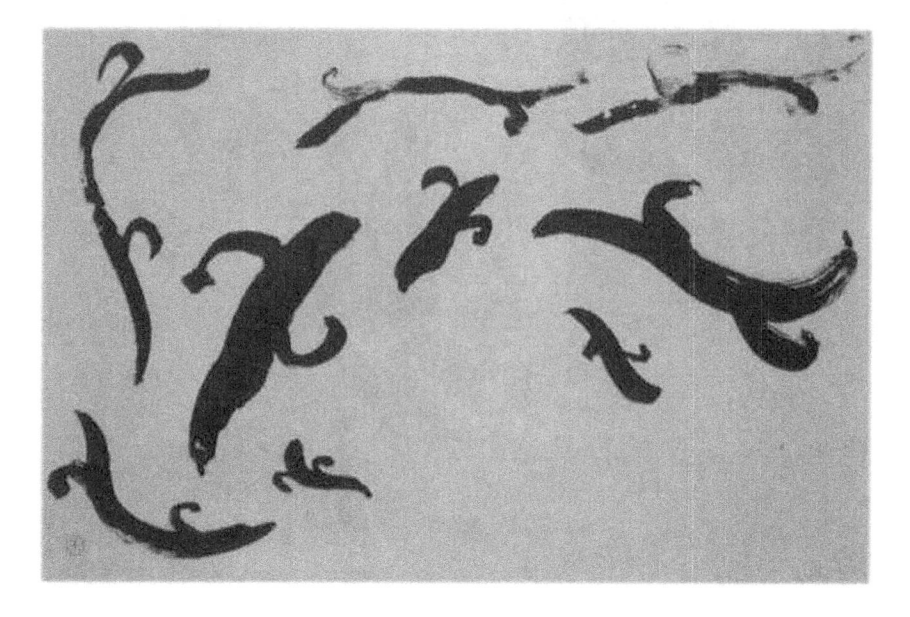

Figure 4.4 *Work 1: Den no variēshion* ('Variation on Lightning'), Hidai Nankoku, 1945, Chiba City Museum of Art, Japan, © Tenrai Shoin

performance when their interpretation is 'played out' happens only once. Music can be recorded and a calligrapher's 'visible sound' (that is, lines) remains on the paper, but the actual performance can never be repeated. The calligrapher never retouches his strokes. Irreversibility makes the moment of creation a vital part of the work, making 'the inky characters become lifelike' (Yen 2005: 89). Though invisible in the final work, the dynamics of movement of the brush, which require a definite choreography, can still be appreciated through knowledge of the process of calligraphy. 'The lack of choreography of brushwork', Tsukamoto (1984: 186) argues, is 'the factor that makes Western "calligraphic" paintings different from Japanese calligraphy'. There is a difference, however, in that 'the choreography of the brush dance is not fixed in advance' (Yen 2005: 100). That is to say, while music or dance is *composed* to be repeated, reproduced and performed, calligraphy is not. The reproduction process becomes part of the final product. In Japanese calligraphy, the actual process of creation can be 'traced' back from the final work, and this 'tracing' plays a significant role in appreciating the work, as exemplified by the act of 'writing in the air' (Tsukamoto 1984; Harrist 1999: 12; Ingold 2003: 8; Yen 2005: 109). The ephemeral aspect of performance as observed in Japanese calligraphy is in fact a characteristic of *geinō* – a term often used in describing the traditional arts of Japan. The term refers to 'the art of public entertainment' (Kumakura 1995: 59). It is not being creative to produce something new and original; rather what matters is the enjoyment of the moment. Because of this, calligraphers do not usually keep the works produced on such occasions.

The 'Natural' Creativity of Materials

Brush (*fude*, see Figure 4.5), paper (*kami*), ink (*sumi*) and ink stone (*suzuri*) are the four items that are vital for creating calligraphic works. These items are known as *bunbō shihō*, the four 'treasures of the studio'. Traditionally made from natural ingredients, these items are susceptible to changes in temperature, humidity and other environmental factors that affect their condition and performance. These are things calligraphers learn to tame, but cannot control completely. Calligraphers carefully select their 'treasures' to suit their expression. To produce the best effect, however, each material or tool is always utilized in relation to all the others. Water is an additional and key element that organically links the four items. It is therefore not only the calligrapher's technical skills, as we saw earlier in the case of *rinsho*, but also his or her knowledge and handling of materials that are combined in the production of a calligraphic work of high quality. I shall now look at how calligraphic works are created through the combination of these different agents.

Figure 4.5 Various kinds of *fude*, Toyohashi, Japan, 2002. Photograph by F. Nakamura

Figure 4.6 The *Sumi* Exhibition, Tokyo, Japan, 2001. Photograph by F. Nakamura

Contemporary Japanese Calligraphy

Sumi ink
Sumi (ink) is the actor and *kami* (paper) is the stage, while *suzuri* (ink stone) is *kuroko*, the prompter behind the scenes. The calligrapher is the director who skilfully mixes these, and produces a piece of work. The effect and colour of *sumi* ink changes depending on types of *suzuri* onto which it is rubbed... Likewise, changing the type of paper creates different nuances of *sumi* ink.
(Text panel at the *Sumi* Exhibition, at Tokyo Ginza Gallery, October 2001)

Here I would like to focus on *sumi*, the 'actor', and see how it interacts with other agents in creating the calligraphic work. *Sumi* is a crucial determinant in transforming the calligrapher's artistic intention visually on paper. Calligraphers today mainly use two kinds of *sumi*: ink stick (*kokeiboku*) and ready-made bottled liquid ink (*bokujū* or *bokueki*). The ink stick is a physical agglomerate of soot and bone glue or animal gelatine known as *nikawa*, mixed with water and perfume (Miyasaka 1965, 1994; Sakaki 1981). Traditionally, soot was obtained either from burning vegetable oils (for example, canola, sesame or camellia oils) or burning the bark of pine trees. Nowadays the soot for commercially produced *sumi* is usually made from burning mineral materials, either petroleum or coal-based materials such as naphthalene. Some calligraphers make their own *sumi*, mixing soot and other less conventional ingredients in order to achieve the result they seek. Liquid *sumi* is obtained by rubbing the *sumi* stick on the surface of an ink stone (*suzuri*) onto which a small amount of water is added (see Figure 4.7). The colour of *sumi*, while basically black, ranges widely in tone from warm to cool, and is commonly classified as 'brownish' (*chaboku*) or 'bluish' (*seiboku*) (Flint Sato 2003).

Sumi ink makers often say that *sumi* is 'alive' because the *nikawa* used in it remains alive. The protein in *nikawa* is easily affected by exposure to too much humidity or dryness. Thus the condition of *sumi* keeps changing. *Sumi* makers liken *sumi* to human beings, as they both go through different life stages. In its long process of transformation there is an ideal moment of *kare* (maturity) for each *sumi*. Great care needs to taken to provide an environment that prevents *sumi* 'getting sick' (that is, moulding, decaying and cracking up). According to a *sumi* maker in Nara, *sumi* matures very much as wine does. A freshly bottled wine has

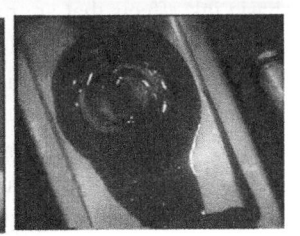

Figure 4.7 The process of making liquid *sumi*, © Tenrai Shoin

its own characteristics, but vintage wine is highly valued for its complicated but delicate taste. Time itself will not automatically enhance the quality of wine. Only with proper care and maintenance will wine mature finely over time. 'Vintage' *sumi* is highly valued for its quality, as it produces a subtle and delicate nuance of black which cannot be obtained from young *sumi*. The taste of good wine can be appreciated only when it is served properly. Likewise, it is up to calligraphers to use good *sumi* in the most appropriate way to maximize the potential that the *sumi* possesses. The subtleties of the *sumi* are due not only to the quality of its ingredients, but also to the conditions of the brush and the paper, and to the technique of execution (Boudonnat and Kushizaki 2003: 174).

As I noted earlier, water is a key factor. Traditionally, drops of morning dew accumulated on leaves are considered to be the ideal type of water for grinding *sumi*. Soft water works better to disperse the soot in *sumi* and produces smoother ink than hard water. This does not mean, however, that hard water is undesirable, as different types of water produce various effects even when the same kind of *sumi* is used. The temperature of water is another element that affects the dispersal of the soot in *sumi*. Cold water decreases the *nikawa*'s capacity to disperse soot. *Nikawa* gels at around 18 °C. Gelled *sumi* does not produce bright and strong colour. On the other hand, it can be used to produce *tanboku* (light *sumi*), which resembles the effect of old *sumi* – a popular ink effect for contemporary *sho* works.

In place of water, some calligraphers use alternative liquids. For instance, adding alcohol to the *sumi* allows for smoother writing. The resistance to the brush lessens, as alcohol reduces the *nikawa*'s capacity to disperse. It also reduces its adhesiveness, while condensing the carbon. As a result, the bleeding of ink in the paper (*nijimi*) does not produce so much blurring. Mixing *sumi* with egg white has the opposite effect. A cold *suzuri* stone will affect the condition of *sumi* as well. In order to avoid this, the *suzuri* should be warmed and the water temperature should be around 40–50 °C.

For certain genres of calligraphy, such as *bokushō* (abstract calligraphic ink impression) and one-character calligraphy, ink effects are an important element of the work. *Nijimi* (see Figure 4.8) and *kasure* (dry scratchy effect) are the two basic ink effects that are manipulated. However, like a potter who never knows exactly how his work will turn out until it is baked and taken out of the kiln, in finishing his work the calligrapher lets nature take its course. Thus the properties of materials play an important role in shaping the outcome. For instance, particles in the *sumi* ink move around and leave their traces on paper after the calligrapher has played his part in creating a work with his brush. The automatic movement of *sumi* thus becomes part of the work. Yugami entitled a series of works *The Stains of Words* (see Figure 4.9). In explaining his works he said, 'words leave their stains on paper' through his *sho* expression. There is a sense in which, in

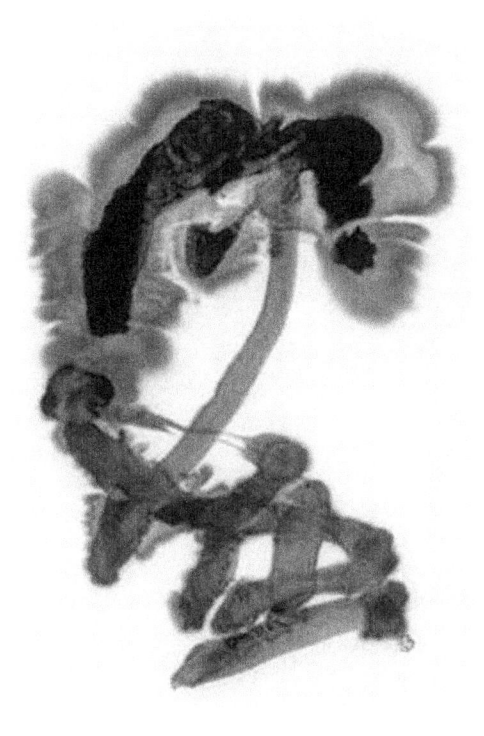

Figure 4.8 *Mitsu (Honey)*, by Yugami Hisao, Kyoto, Japan, 1999

his 'inked' words, the agency intrinsic to the materials takes over from his own. As in the doctrine of 'truth to materials' often enunciated by Western artists, architects and craftsmen, it behoves the calligrapher 'to make from his materials what "they" want, rather than what he wants' (Gell 1998: 30).

To create the ink effects he seeks, Yugami Hisao often prepares his own *sumi* mixture. When he first started *sumi*-making, he used to refer to Miyasaka Kazuo's *Sumi iro no nazo* ('The Mystery of *Sumi* Colour'), which explains *sumi* from a scientific point of view. Interestingly, Yugami remembered the title of this book wrongly as *Sumi no Majutsushi* ('The Magician of *Sumi*'). The fact that he subconsciously linked the 'mystery' of *sumi* to the ability or power of a 'magician' should not be seen as a mere coincidence. After showing me the *sumi*-making, he jokingly said, 'Well, I've just made good *sumi*, so I only have to wait for my "genius" counterpart [his way of saying inspiration] to come down to me', as if his *sho* works were created by some supernatural force.

While retaining a certain control, calligraphers often leave it to the characteristics of the *bunbō shihō* items to determine the outcome of their work. Thus the *fude* brush, too, is often regarded as having its own particular life force. A few hairs are placed at the tip of the *fude*, and they are called *inochige*, 'life

Figure 4.9 Yugami Hisao at his exhibition, *The Stains of Words*, at the Gallery Maronie in Kyoto, Japan, August 2002. Photograph by F. Nakamura

hair'. The avant-garde calligraphers, notably Morita Shiryū (1912–98) – who was influenced by Nishida Kitarō and Hisamastu Shinichi's philosophy on Zen (see Bryson 1988) – saw calligraphy not only as an embodiment of a person, but also as a manifestation of life. Morita's understanding of *sho* derives from the existential relationship he perceives between the calligrapher and the *fude* he uses: 'A brush man becomes alive when he extinguishes himself and becomes the brush' (quoted in Hughes 1978: 160–1). There is some truth in Morita's view, since calligraphers often perceive their brush to be a part of themselves, and their work is sometimes felt to be created by 'unseen' forces, particularly in large-scale works using a huge brush, as Morita did. Such works manifest a kind of 'accidentality', in so far as the intention of the calligrapher and that of his brush may not coincide.

Conclusion

Different properties of each calligraphic item are highlighted at successive stages in their lifespan. For example, the *sumi* stick can be an aesthetic item to be collected and displayed, but the liquid *sumi* ink made from the stick persists only as traces on paper. Even on paper, the properties of these traces keep changing. Both 'person-agents' and 'thing-agents', as discussed by Gell (1998), bring about intended and unintended outcomes in calligraphic works. The interaction between personal agency (the calligrapher and his techniques) and the agency of things (nature and materials) results in new types of *sho* works. In short, a calligraphic work is the outcome of an interplay between the 'natural' creativity of materials and the creative efforts of persons to resist, control, embrace or prompt it.

Creative force in calligraphy cannot therefore be judged solely in terms of the extent of innovation. It is also determined by the fusion of innovation and tradition (Biebuyck 1969). A calligraphic work cannot be a purely abstract picture detached from its precedents, since so long as calligraphers choose to operate on words, the content (that is, 'words') '*dictates* the movement of the brush' (Bryson 1988: 103). This is what makes for 'tradition' in calligraphy. Works need to stay within 'accepted canons' or an 'agreed-upon style' (Steiner 1999: 101–2), otherwise they are no longer considered calligraphic, ultimately leading to the conclusion that they are inauthentic. Thus, to a certain extent, contemporary calligraphers have to follow 'tradition' in this sense. They are constantly 'confronting the past and its traditions, asserting [their] individuality' (Aoyama 1984: 29; cf. Niessen 1999: 173–7).

The *bunbō shihō* items have always been at the heart of calligraphic production, but it was with the avant-garde calligraphic movement in the post-war period that innovative usages of these items began to be seen. For contemporary *sho* artists such as Yugami Hisao or Kimura Tsubasa (see Figure 4.10), person-agency

Figure 4.10 Scene from Kimura Tsubasa's exhibition, *Crowd*, Kyoto, Japan, April 2005

demands to be more visible than thing-agency in their work, for they are operating in a contemporary art world in which creative originality has become an issue. It is the creativity of an individual artist that is valued, not that of materials or nature. It is his or her creativity that brings together, orchestrates and conducts all the materials and instruments of 'calligraphic music'. At the same time, however, without the natural creativity and performative capacities of these things, there can be no music at all.

Acknowledgements

I would like to thank Hidai Kazuko of Tenrai Shoin, the daughter of Hidai Nankoku, Kimura Tsubasa and Yugami Hisao for kindly allowing me to reproduce the images used in this essay.

Note

1. From the flyer of his exhibition, *The Stains of Words*. Unless otherwise stated, the translation of Japanese texts, including the titles of Japanese books, is mine. Japanese names in this chapter follow the indigenous order, whereby the family name is given first, followed by the given name.

References

Adorno, T.W. (1991), *The Culture Industry: Selected Essays on Mass Culture* (ed and introduction J.M. Bernstein), London and New York: Routledge.

Aoyama, S. (1984), '*Sho* – artistic, creative calligraphy', in C. Uyehara (ed), *Words in Motion: Modern Japanese Calligraphy*, Tokyo: The Yomiuri Shimbun; Washington: The Library of Congress.

Benjamin, W. (1999 [1968]), 'The work of art in the age of mechanical reproduction', in H. Arendt (ed), *Illuminations*, London: Pimlico.

Biebuyck, D. (1969), 'Introduction', in D.P. Biebuyck (ed), *Tradition and Creativity in Tribal Art*, Berkeley: University of California Press.

Boudonnat, L. and Kushizaki, H. (2003), *Traces of the Brush: The Art of Japanese Calligraphy*, California: Chronicle Books.

Bowden, R. (1999), 'What is wrong with an art forgery? An anthropological perspective', *Journal of Aesthetics and Art Criticism*, 57(3): 333–43.

Bryson, N. (1988), 'The gaze in the expanded field', in H. Foster (ed), *Vision and Visuality*, Seattle, Wash.: Bay Press.
Chamberlain, B.H. (1890), *Things Japanese: Being Notes on Various Subjects Connected with Japan* (first edition), London: Kegan Paul, Trench, and Trübner; Tokyo: The Hakubunsha, Ginza.
Carpenter, J.T. (2002), 'Calligraphy as self-portrait: poems and letters by retired emperor Gotoba', *Orientations*, 33(2): 41–9.
Cox, R. (2003), *The Zen Arts: An Anthropological Study of the Culture of Aesthetic Form in Japan*, Richmond: Routledge Curzon in association with the Royal Asiatic Society of Great Britain and Ireland.
Flint Sato, C. (2003), 'Sumi', *Letter Arts Review*, 18(1).
Gell, A. (1992), 'The technology of enchantment and the enchantment of technology', in J. Coote and A. Shelton (eds), *Anthropology, Art and Aesthetics*, Oxford: Clarendon Press.
—— (1998), *Art and Agency: An Anthropological Theory*, Oxford: Clarendon Press.
Hannas, W.C. (2003), *The Writing on the Wall: How Asian Orthography Curbs Creativity*, Philadelphia: University of Pennsylvania Press.
Harrist, R.E. (1999), *The Embodied Image: Chinese Calligraphy from the John B. Elliott Collection*, Princeton, NJ: Art Museum, Princeton University in association with Harry N. Abrams.
Hidai, N. and Uno, S. (eds) (1983), *Gendaisho* (Contemporary Calligraphy), Vol. 1, Tokyo: Yūzankaku.
Hughes, S. (1978), *Washi: The World of Japanese Paper*, Tokyo, New York and San Francisco: Kodansha International.
Ingold, T. (2003), 'Notes toward an anthropology of the line', *Dwelling*, No 2. Coates, Glos.: Twelve Bells Press.
Keen, I. (2001), 'Agency, history and tradition in the construction of classical music: the debate over "authentic performance"', in C. Pinney and N. Thomas (eds), *Beyond Aesthetics: Art and the Technologies of Enchantment*, Oxford: Berg.
Kraus, R.C. (1991), *Brushes With Power: Modern Politics And The Chinese Art Of Calligraphy*, Berkeley and Oxford: University of California Press.
Kumakura, I. (1995), 'Geinō and Patrons', in T. Umesco, B. Powell and I. Kumakura (eds), 'Japanese Civilization in the Modern World XI: Amusement', *Senri Ethnological Studies*, 40: 59–70, Osaka: National Museum of Ethnology.
Layton, R. (1991), *The Anthropology of Art* (second edition), Cambridge: Cambridge University Press.
Miyasaka, K. (1965), *Sumi no hanashi* ('The story of *sumi*'), Tokyo: Mokujisha.
—— (1994), *Sumi iro no nazo* ('The mystery of *sumi* colour'), Tokyo: Ribun Shuppan.

Niessen, S. (1999), 'Threads of tradition, threads of invention: unravelling Toba Batak women's expressions of social change', in R. Phillips and C. Steiner (eds), *Unpacking Culture: Art and Commodity in Colonial and Postcolonial Worlds*, Berkeley: University of California Press.

Sakaki, B. (1981), *Bunbō shihō: sumi no hanashi*, Tokyo: Kadokawa Shoten.

Steiner, C. (1999), 'Authenticity, repetition, and the aesthetics of seriality: the work of tourist art in the age of mechanical reproduction', in R. Phillips and C. Steiner (eds), *Unpacking Culture: Art and Commodity in Colonial and Postcolonial Worlds*, Berkeley: University of California Press.

Strathern, M. (1988), *The Gender of the Gift*, Berkeley: University of California Press.

—— (2001), 'The patent and the malanggan', in C. Pinney and N. Thomas (eds), *Beyond Aesthetics: Art and the Technologies of Enchantment*, Oxford: Berg.

Taussig, M. (1993), *Mimesis and Alterity: A Particular History of the Senses*, London: Routledge.

Tsukamoto, A. (1984), *Art as Performance: An Essay on Comparative Aesthetics*, unpublished DPhil thesis, University of Oxford.

—— (2001), 'Modes of quoting: parody and *honkadori*', in G. Marchi and R. Milani (eds), *Frontiers of Transculturality in Contemporary Aesthetics* (Proceedings of the Intercontinental Conference, University of Bologna, Italy, October 2000), Turin: Trauben.

Wagner, R. (1991), 'The fractal person', in M. Strathern and M. Godelier (eds), *Big Men and Great Men: Personifications of Power in Melanesia*, Cambridge: Cambridge University Press.

Yamada, S. (2002), *Nihon Bunka no Mohō to Sōzō: Orijinariti to wa Nanika* ('Imitation and Creation in Japanese Culture: What is Originality?'), Tokyo: Kadokawa Shoten.

Yen, Y. (2005), *Calligraphy and Power in Contemporary Chinese Society*, London: Routledge.

–5–

Creativity, Subjectivity and the Dynamic of Possessive Individualism
James Leach

Introduction

On 16 September 1975, in Reite village on the Rai Coast of Papua New Guinea, Siriman Kumbukau dreamt a new spirit voice into being. On the same night, as his narrative reconstruction emphasized, the leader of a local politico-ritual movement for independence and self-determination died.[1] Siriman's dream gave him not only knowledge of a new spirit voice – a tune which the male cult could animate into a powerful spirit being through the ritual paraphernalia of the cult – but also a series of staccato images and metaphors that developed the power of the spirit and spoke of its achievements. This spirit was named Indepen.[2]

In this chapter I take up the issue of creativity by interrogating the assumptions behind its current manifestation as a tool in political rhetoric. I point to a series of underlying assumptions that legitimize, at a more fundamental level than just rhetoric, a global politics of homogenization and commodification of social products. In this climate it seems naive to celebrate people's creativity without understanding the effects of such transformations of people's action and effort in reinforcing particular models of the person, of culture and of the social. I point out that the common rendering of creativity is closely allied to property rights, and since these are taken for granted as the basis of our freedom (behind which lies a view of the state as guarantor of this freedom, foreshadowed in the writings of Hobbes and Locke), it is unsurprising that creativity is seen both as self-realization and as compatible with a liberal humanist political economy of individuals and states that regulates their interactions. Yet these understandings are the legacy of an emerging statecraft in Europe and America over the last few centuries. Certain kinds of person emerged along with this crafting, persons for whom the state was an appropriate adjunct. My aim is to call into question the analytic and political effects of discussing the cultural creativity of others. Contrary to intent, these effects may include a conceptual colonialism that exactly suits the spread of a notion of culture as something to be owned and claimed, and of the state as the proper guarantor of this ownership (Aragon and Leach n.d.).

The promise of property seems to exercise a strong hold over imaginations everywhere. It almost inevitably prompts visions of boundaries, exclusivity and control. We constantly hear these days about threats to people's intellectual property (IP), about individual cases in which people's creativity is either not being properly recognized or is threatened as intellectual property locks down cultural resources (Vaidhyanathan 2001; Lessig 2004). The debates and conflicts around intellectual property extend to patents upon human cell lines, and on medical drugs that are hugely inflated in price because of the monopolies that patents allow (Love 2003, 2006). Many have looked to ideas and precedents in intellectual property in order to protect indigenous knowledge or subject populations (Brown 2003, 2005). IP holds out the promise, on the one hand, of privatizing, and thus of profiting from, innovations in areas as basic to our survival as human genetics. Thus it brings activists and protesters out in droves. Yet ironically, much of the protest against the privatization of genetic materials also uses the language of property, and even of IP, in order to oppose what is seen as the undesirable control of such fundamental materials by a few self-interested individuals. To counteract commodification, various notions of common ownership, or of a public domain in knowledge, have been proposed (see Vaidhyanathan 2006).

In similar vein, complaints about the appropriation of cultural materials and the traditional knowledge of indigenous peoples are often phrased in terms of rightful ownership and property. IP is seen to offer protection against exploitation as well as being a source of inequality. Think of debates surrounding genetic modification. Much of the activist rhetoric against GM is phrased in terms of our common heritage, of the rights we all have to enjoy nature and its products, without some of them being ruined or hived off for the profit of multinational corporations. I want to examine how we have got to this point – at which the collectivity is pitted against the individual. What conception of the individual lies behind this kind of opposition, and how does creativity fit into the picture? What effect does a high valuation of knowledge, rendered specifically through IP law, have upon politics, and indeed upon social organization? To reveal this effect we must unravel a complex of assumptions about personhood, about nature and about society. This means situating the idea of knowledge as a kind of object that can be owned within a historical and cultural context in which it is inextricably linked to a particular view of creativity. Going back to John Locke, and particularly to Chapter 5 of his *Second Treatise on Government* (Locke 1960), I shall re-examine property claims in the liberal tradition of European and American political philosophy. My argument builds upon this foundation and looks at the construction, and some consequences, of a particular kind of liberal humanism that incorporates strongly determined notions of what creativity is, and of how it can and ought to be recognized.

Passions, Human Nature and Self-interested Individuals

The background to intellectual property lies in the notion of property itself, understood as a way of connecting people with what they produce. The notion has its origins in European and American political philosophy and statecraft, from the Renaissance onwards. In his book *The Passions and the Interests*, Albert Hirschman (1997) traces some of the most significant moments in the emergence of the state formations appropriate to a particular kind of property-owning individual. The process that Hirschmann documents is epitomized by Amartya Sen, in his preface to the book, by way of the following story: Imagine being pursued by a group of people hostile to you, bigots in fact, intent upon your murder because they have taken against you on the basis of the colour of your skin or of your religious belief. Fortunately, your pocket is full of high-value coins. You throw them into the air, and your pursuers turn from their collective aim of murdering you to scrabble around and collect as much of the cash as each one can.

It is a pithy and memorable rendering of an apparent truth – that self-interest overcomes other kinds of motivation. But Hirschman is concerned to highlight the particular conditions of emergence of this apparent truth, and how its form is determined by those conditions. In medieval understanding, he argues, human beings were thought to be driven by 'passions'. Religion, and the absolute authority vested in it, held these passions in check. At this stage passions were almost always seen as sinful or destructive, to be controlled or restrained by the morals and doctrines of the church and the monarch. In the sixteenth and seventeenth centuries, however, a shift occurred. As states grew in population and complexity, and as new discoveries undermined absolute confidence in religion as the basis for all knowledge and authority, there was a loss of faith in the capacity of religious precepts to keep people's passions at bay. It was noted at this time that some passions are more destructive than others. In the scenario that Sen narrates, the recognition by each and every member of the mob of their own *self-interest* saves you from a nasty fate. It is the rational and self-interested acknowledgement that collecting the cash will serve them better than indulging in murder. Here the 'passion' for individual gain – a 'rational' passion – overrides a less healthy, irrational passion for inflicting harm on another on grounds of prejudice.

Hirschman traces a trajectory of thought in which passions could be pitted against one another to suppress the worst and most destructive of them. The seventeenth century saw the elaboration and recasting of those passions supposed to be governed by reason as *interests*, so as to yield the dichotomy between brute passion and rational self-interest that subsequently became enshrined in the conventions of European thought. It is rational to pursue one's own advantage, and even if brutish elements such as avarice and greed were part of the picture, they could be harnessed by proper planning. The crucial move, according to Hirschman, was the idea that governments which took into account people's rational self-interest were more likely to succeed than those which relied merely upon suppressing 'passions' of every kind. This development is apparent in the writings of the political philosophers to whom he refers and in corresponding changes in laws and institutions. Giambattista Vico, writing in the early eighteenth century, put the idea in this way:

> Out of ferocity, avarice, and ambition, the three vices which lead all mankind astray, [the state] makes national defence, commerce, and politics, and thereby causes the strength, the wealth, and the wisdom of the republics; out of these three great vices, which would surely destroy man on earth, society thus causes the civil happiness to emerge. This principle proves the existence of divine providence: through its intelligent laws the passions of men who are entirely occupied by the pursuit of their private utility are transformed into a civil order which permits men to live in human society. (Vico 1953: 132–3)

As Hirschman comments, the expansion of commerce and industry around this time was heralded as a source of rules of conduct that might substitute for the religious precepts of medieval times, imposing much needed discipline and constraint on both rulers and ruled (Hirschman 1997: 129).

The complex of changes in notions of the passions, and of what was needed to regulate or nullify their destructive influence, was in turn based on the emerging ideal of scientific observation, applied to human beings as part of the natural world. The philosopher Spinoza professed in his *Ethics* of 1677 to 'consider human actions and appetites just as if I were considering lines, planes or bodies' (Spinoza 2000). Spinoza makes the notion of 'man as he really is' – that is, a consideration of *human nature* – the basis of his recommendations for governance. For him, how 'man really is' can be ascertained through the kind of scientific study that is more usually associated with the physical world. Hirschman also points to Rousseau, who, in the opening pages of *The Social Contract*, writes that his work has come from an examination 'taking men as they are, and the laws as they might be' (cited in Hirschman 1997: 14). Although Spinoza, Rousseau and Vico no doubt had different ways of conceptualizing human nature, the principle that one could base a prescriptive philosophy of the state upon a study of that nature was thus firmly established. Through this study the idea of interests, which substituted for that of passions, came to be narrowed in its meaning. Adam Smith took up this meaning of interest and famously outlined his vision of how, through the pursuit of individual wealth, society would be made a better and constantly developing place. Through such influential arguments, rational self-interest came to mean the interest to pursue wealth. Rational self-interest became economic interest.

The Dynamic of Possessive Individualism

Labour, Projects and Natural Reason

This development of a notion of human nature as a basis for moral philosophizing about how best to regulate human behaviour through the state also set the agenda for another great thinker, John Locke. Of course, as MacPherson (1962) points out, Locke did not himself *invent* the ideas of property on which he expounds. In fact, much like an ethnographer, Locke saw himself as recording the current state of ownership and rationalizing it in his treatise. In other words, there already was a cultural reality to the particularly clear expression of the doctrine of possessive individualism provided by Locke.

For Locke, land held an archetypal status in the development of property. Through analysis of land use and improvement, one could hypothesize a movement from the common inheritance of all mankind to individual ownership. There was a particularly obvious moral justification for a transition from holding the earth's resources in common to the private control of land. The justification ran along the following lines, which are important for my argument later on. Locke posits that the earth was given to all mankind by God for its common use and enjoyment. (In fact, it was given to his sons, who gave it to their sons, and so on.) 'Natural reason', Locke tells his readers, determines that every man has the right to preservation, and for that, he needs sustenance. But how can any man guarantee access to that which sustains him when the earth and all its products are the *common* heritage of all mankind? Spontaneous creations of nature are obviously owned by everyone. But in order to make them of use, they must be appropriated. Thus for Locke, reason shows that a man must appropriate a fruit that has fallen to the ground, and make it his own, if it is to be of any use to him. It cannot belong to another, since by nourishing this particular man – by sustaining him – it helps to achieve the end he has a right to achieve, namely his survival.

And so Locke arrives at a further principle: 'every man has property in his own person'. Through appropriating things that are commonly owned, these things become a part of him. Crucially, by mixing his labour with nature, with things that are already there in the natural world, he makes things his own. In the very act of appropriation, Locke argues, property comes about. It is the labour of picking up the apple, not the eating of it, that makes it the property of one person: 'if the first gathering made them not his, nothing else could. The labour put a distinction between them and the common' (Locke 1960: 288). The addition of labour makes a common resource into property *irrespective of others' consent*. Locke does say that reason also demands that people only appropriate enough for their needs, and thus do not waste common resources. He also discusses the advent of money and how some people could own more than others. But the important aspect for my exposition here is succinctly developed below:

> Though the things of nature are given in common, yet Man (by being master of himself and *Proprietor of his own person* and the actions of *Labour* of it) had still in himself the great *Foundation of Property*; and that which made up the great part of what he applied to the Support or Comfort of his being, when Invention and Arts had improved the conveniences of Life, was perfectly his own, and did not belong in common to others. (ibid.: 298–9)

Land was the archetypal property for Locke because through labour it could be cultivated, tilled and made productive. The importance of the plough, and thus of agriculture as a stable and enduring relation to the land, was vital. To own land it must be appropriated. And this required the mixing of labour with land. Notice that the idea of a *project*[3] comes in here. Land is turned from a common resource to private property through the project to cultivate it. Human beings own the fruits of their labours and endeavours as the outcomes of their projects. Here we already see the beginnings of the current emphasis on mental labour and intent as crucial to property. The emphasis is placed upon a kind of mixing, of intentional directed action with products of nature that are literally 'given' to all – a common heritage.

Possessive individualism had far-reaching implications for Western political philosophy, as Pocock (1985) has observed. Pocock concurs with MacPherson in suggesting that the assumptions involved predate Locke. In fact he traces elements of it to the Bible, where God's chosen people were given the Promised Land to be handed down from father to son through the generations. As he points out, 'other people' were those who wandered away from this land, roaming an earth that was nobody's to own. By the seventeenth century, as we have seen, theorists were constructing the notion of 'natural rights' on the basis of an examination of human nature. To do so, they envisaged the 'state of nature' as a primeval condition of human existence. And that condition was characterized by the image of an individual as a kind of wanderer. Pocock goes on to argue that for the political theorists of the seventeenth and eighteenth centuries, it was not until primeval individuals started to appropriate things that they needed any kind of law, and it was because they had no law that they existed in a state of nature (that is, without civilization). The individual thus *preceded* property in Enlightenment political philosophy. In the state of nature an assortment of individuals roamed the earth's surface. But appropriation, in Locke's account, led to property, which led to rights, which led to governments to enforce them. It resulted in systems of institutionalized values. In effect, the human individual as a sociable creature was defined by his property, and the individual who had still to appropriate things from the common was not yet fully human. The savage was a primeval rather than a possessive individual: 'the essential step into humanity was taken with the acceptance of law and government, and it was premised that this step could not be taken without the preceding or accompanying step of appropriation' (Pocock 1992). Primeval individuals had not appropriated the land through modification and improvement and thus did not develop laws, arts and sciences as the codified expressions of organized social relations. These social relations, when they did eventually emerge, were based on the fact that appropriation converted individuals into property owners. In other words, to use Pocock's phrase, 'property [...] was their name for relationship' (ibid.: 42). Human society is based on the ownership of property, as relationships between individuals *came into being* because of the appropriation of resources and the need to institutionalize that appropriation. 'The enlightened mind was bent upon the separation of spirit from matter, of appropriator from the substance appropriated' (ibid.: 43). So through their projects, human beings modified and improved their environment, and thus owned it as property.

For a contemporary version of the peculiar dilemma of how to regulate the passions and interests of individuals intent on maximizing their personal wealth in the absence of strong state regulation, we may turn to Garret Hardin's famous article on 'the tragedy of the commons' (Hardin 1968). Hardin took it as self-evident that people are all possessive individuals, acting in their own rational self-interest. Based on this assumption he argued that any resources held in common are likely to be either over-exploited, and therefore depleted and degraded, or underused and degenerated through lack of investment. According to Hardin, on the one hand a 'rational' user of a common resource will make demands on that resource until the expected benefits from that appropriation are overtaken by the costs of exploiting it. Because each user is an individual, and ignores costs imposed upon others by their use, individual decisions culminate in tragic overuse and, potentially, the destruction of open-access commons. On the other hand, common ownership is seen as a hindrance to economic development because it is in no one's rational self-interest to invest labour or resources in improving common land when others who stand to benefit need nevertheless not reciprocate. The bogeyman image of the freeloader is central to concerns about the commons and their rational exploitation. It is a classic economist's argument.[4] And we can see how, from being a theory of human nature, the notion of possessive individualism became a foundational assumption in making policies for governing 'economic life' that persists to this day.[5]

As Elinor Ostrom (1990) points out, the model presumes that all individuals are selfish, norm-free and motivated by short-term gain. Yet we know that there are many systems of land tenure, for example, that do not follow from these kinds of assumptions about persons (Crocombe 1971). Property tenure in the mode of possessive individualism is specific to our cultural and social history, and to the imaginative projections we make. And so, therefore, is the idea that a common resource will inevitably be misused by individuals. A commons in land of the sort

Hardin imagined is a product of a particular kind of retrospective or historical imagination. This is pertinent to Pocock's point. For Hardin's image of the commons and its users is suspiciously similar to the notion, advanced by earlier theorists, of the state of nature and of the primeval individuals who inhabited it. In this picture, individuals pursuing rational, self-interested projects will care only for what they own. Enclosure and cultivation make possible the material fulfilment of individual projects.

These distinctions, of mental from material, and of one individual's interests from another's, conjoin with the notion that invention and innovation are the driving forces behind civilization and progress. In the overall trajectory that came to be described as modernity, progress comes exactly through the inception and realization of new projects, with attendant modifications to the environment. From this point of view, if modern civilization is the most successful and powerful form of human organization that has ever existed, it is precisely because it is founded on an 'accurate' reading of human nature. This view amounts to a form of evolutionism and clearly marks a self-perception, among its adherents, that elevates them above traditional and tribal peoples. Modernity, they say, allows competition to thrive, and thus generates progress as individuals compete to outdo one another.

Culture and the Creation of Civilization

In its contemporary usage, as Roy Wagner (1981) has pointed out, the word 'culture' has a marked and an unmarked sense. 'High culture' is the civilizing influence of great art, of fine architecture, of the objects we find in museums. For Wagner, this kind of 'Culture' is closely linked to the prevalent understanding of civilization as a process, and project, of cultivation. Just as land and agriculture are improved through developments in the projects of settlement, intensification, specialization, and so forth, so human society is improved and developed through the cultivation of its public life, its institutions and its symbols. Wagner directs our attention once again to the political and moral philosophers of the Enlightenment. Through property, as Locke tells us, people came to have leisure to create institutions, and these in turn allowed the specialization of labour and the development of the arts. High culture and civilization develop together.

When anthropologists go to other parts of the world, however, and are confronted with unfamiliar behaviour and with objects and institutions they do not readily comprehend, their first inclination is to create a system of meaning analogous to that through which they would explain the emergence of their own forms of life. Agricultural practices are tied to belief systems, kinship is tied to economy, exchange is tied to kinship and myths. By placing any unfamiliar element or practice in its proper context, making it part of a wider whole, anthropologists overcome their feeling of dislocation and create the cultures of those observed. They find the *human projects*, and their backgrounds, which make order out of the apparent chaos in front of their eyes. This, in Wagner's (1981) terms, is 'culture' in the unmarked sense. It is a whole system of human creations. Culture then comes to have an existence of its own as the ultimate human project, the project of making the world that people live in. Culture as it is currently understood might be seen as the ultimate public domain, the final resource for any mental creativity that humans can engage in, as well as their creation.

The conceptual world Wagner describes, and which I have elaborated in a particular way for my own purpose here, is the world that has come down to us in part as a legacy of Locke and others. The understanding of humans within it as natural beings with a project called culture or civilization, is one in which certain human societies have progressively managed to dominate and control their environment. The notion of cultural development is crucial here. It is through manipulating plans and ideas – by using the intellect – that we are thought to have achieved this domination.

The intellect, then, is highly regarded, a hugely valuable element in human potential. Imagine if one could own the intellect. That would be tantamount to a particular kind of self-possession (which is what we have), or possession of another person (which we do not have). But while we may be in possession of ourselves, and thereby of our intellect, this is not to say that we own them as 'private property'. They belong to us without being property. We cannot dispose of them as we wish, and IP law is explicitly not the ownership of ideas, let alone creativity as a process or ability. It is an ownership of material expressions of ideas. So self-possession, which Locke talked about, is not possession of *property* until the self mixes labour with something in the world. We have property in our own person, Locke says, but this is not quite the same thing as property in the material world. The idea or the mental work, realized in the material world, is related closely to our definition of the human subject.

Creativity and the Person

John Liep has recently argued that creativity is a preoccupation of modernity (Liep 2001: 3–5). The kind of economy that supports the university in which I currently work, and the activities that make the UK one of the major economies of the world, is based on services, but also on knowledge. In a knowledge-based economy, neither labour nor even material resources are of paramount importance. What is held to be crucial is rather people's ability to think creatively, to innovate, to invent and to develop. Accordingly, educational policy places a phasis on developing creative potential. What does it mean, however, that every individual is potentially creative? Why is it so important? One answer lies in what is called 'personal self-fulfilment'. One uses one's own internal creativity to remake one's sense of worth in the world. The mechanism seems to be through producing and developing things, which in turn 'develop' the self. Thus, artistic endeavour is supposed to make a more rounded and fulfilled person, and so on. Perhaps the contemporary interest in creativity does indeed signal a preoccupation with the creation and recreation of the self, of the person. If that is so, then it is happening in a very specific way, which produces very specific kinds of person.

The relation that defines the self as a person is a subjective intervention within the world, which makes a difference to that world. This recreates the self in the same movement by which it objectifies something beyond that self. One knows one's capacity and one's 'self' through what one sees of oneself in the world. Each time a novel object is realized, as an element externalized from the person, the distinction between the self and the world is recreated. It is the very materiality of the expression that recreates the person as a locus of intelligence and agency (J. Leach 2004b: 162).

In the context of a different debate, Carol Delaney (1986) has pointed out that these conceptions of creativity are aspects of our monotheistic heritage, thereby highlighting the gender implications of the modernist version of creativity. She points out that Adam was the genitor of the line of human beings who, partaking in God's divine creativity, were able to recreate themselves. They knew themselves as God's people because of this ability to project themselves into the world through their progeny. Culture, agriculture, all those elements in our history and society that impose form upon the world, are described as versions of the primordial creativity that Adam embodied, of man planting his seed in the receptive earth, and knowing himself through his own reflection in the response. Delaney argues that the idea of 'paternity' is central to our culture and society, a core symbol around which both gender relations and relations of production are organized. This idea also has a strong influence on that of ownership, since it was God's earth (he created it) that was given to Adam, who then passed it down the male line to his descendants. Creativity, Delaney tells us, is in the image of paternity. And paternity in this construction is an act of adding life or spirit to inert but receptive matter. The current centrality of the intellect to our notions of creativity thus has a gendered dimension. Delaney's argument is that the idea of forming and transforming matter through mental work symbolically associates one gender with creative power and the other with its reception (see de Beauvoir 1953).

Presently, the UK government vigorously promotes innovation. It designs educational policies to develop flexible and creative individuals. The notions that the world is changing fast (through technology), and that people must change and adapt to keep up, are very familiar (E. Leach 1968; J. Leach 2005). Indeed, creativity and change appear caught in a relation of positive feedback: the more creative we become, the more change is embodied in technology, and so the more creative and flexible we must become to keep up with technological development. The rhetoric of creativity valorizes and celebrates entrepreneurs who, through their individual genius, can change the world. They are rewarded for this. The particular way in which creativity is imagined in these constructions of flexibility and adaptability is as an ability to meet new demands, and to combine experiences and elements of knowledge in ever new ways.

The current anthropological obsession with hybrids and creative mixings in culture could be understood as another instance of this valorization. Yet hybrids are nothing new. Property for Locke is a hybrid, a combination of the labour of a person and a natural resource. The contemporary interest in hybrids, however, is all about hybrids in ideas, in the meetings of cultures and the forms that emerge from them. Culture, then, is both a human creation and the source of human creativity. It is supposed that the whole history of ideas and knowledge is available to each and everyone as a resource from which to make new combinations, and thereby to invent and innovate. But in this general conception, what motivates the work of combination, of innovation and creativity? In choosing to cite Hardin, to dwell on the emergence of possessive individualism, and to discuss creativity through the lens of intellectual property, I have sought to show how ownership and reward are thought to motivate the work of creation. My discussion of subjectivity was intended to make this point plain. We define ourselves and our humanity, or civilization on a broad scale, through our ability to manipulate and control the material world. On an individual basis, self-expression and fulfilment emerge through creative activities such as painting or writing.

Now in IP law, it is the particular form of ownership that is the focus. Granting property in inventions is said to provide the motivation for people to create and innovate. However, IP law also works in another important respect. For once property is granted to the inventor or creator, the invention or creation can circulate. Instead of keeping knowledge secret to prevent others using it, IP law allows others to use knowledge, while at the same time ensuring that its origin is acknowledged each time they do. These two factors together – reward and circulation – are the most prevalent justifications for IP. Through the accumulation of knowledge and its development over time, science advances. If individual scientists kept all their discoveries to themselves, no advance would be possible.

The issue of reward suggests that we examine how people's labour, the outcome of their work, is attached to them (Biagioli and Galison 2003). This can perhaps best be done through establishing the particularity of the form of the person involved. In this form the person is conceived as an internally specified being, endowed with natural rights, and capable, as an individual, of labouring and creating elements in the external world to facilitate their survival, their own development and the development of a system of institutions that collectively make a 'civilization'. Other aspects are also given as internal components specified at birth: a position in a kinship system, a gendered body, and so forth. The person is partly defined by the attributes, or internal properties, that they possess. This kind of human subject controls objects in the world. The subject is defined as that which possesses attributes and controls objects.

There is a distinct connection here with ideas of creativity. And there is an interesting problem too. The subject is defined by control of the object world. It is because of projects (that is, subjective interventions) that the world is manipulated and improved. But one cannot be one's creations, for creations which one controls are by definition objects, and therefore no part of the subject. How then are they connected to the person who created them? Locke had an answer, as we have seen. The imaginative constructions of the history I have sketched out are not, however, matched elsewhere. Thus Pocock (1992: 47) describes how in Aotearoa/ New Zealand, before European colonization, there were a number of 'food gathering groups moving across an unappropriated land surface to which they relate themselves ... through song, dream, ritual and other forms of mythopoeic appropriation which may be hardly possessive at all.' In such places, knowledge is often a kind of claim over land which is not based on possessive individualism. How can this be? For an answer, we need to destabilize the divisions between the mental and the material, and between persons and things, which are the twin foundations of possessive individualism. The rest of this chapter works to this end.

Ownership and Creativity without Possessive Individuals

Joel Bonnemaison (1991) tells us that on the island of Tanna in Vanuatu, people are strongly rooted in places. In myth they were the children of stones and stumps of trees, and these stones and stumps are the basis of all magic. Gardening requires garden magic, and garden magic is specific to particular places. It is localized through the stones that are the ancestors of people in that place, and the basic power for gardening. Thus different kinds of yam appear in different places as the outcome of different kinds of magical input. This is equivalent to different kinds of person appearing in different places. Bonnemaison describes a 'biomagical heritage' in each place, and the more imbued with local magical power a crop or a person is, the more highly it will be valued on Tanna. The resource here is a mixture of knowledge, history and emplacement, all of which are enfolded in the land. Thus land both is and is not the resource. Land is not a resource without the knowledge of how to make it productive. So Tannese people enter into alliances with magicians. The knowledge needed to make land productive is part of a complex arrangement in social groups, and between them, whereby land and people become parts of one another.

Building on such indigenous understandings, Robert Lane has written that 'it is inappropriate to speak of land "ownership" [in the New Hebrides, now Vanuatu]. Land is rather one component in a total system in which people are another component' (Lane 1971: 249). Reciprocity, basic to social relations, applies between people and land. Individuals do not make rational economic calculations of how best to exploit the land in their own interests. Rather there is a complex understanding of the interconnections between people, places, knowledge and authority. Such tenure systems might be described as ones of 'multiple ownership' (J. Leach 2000a), as multiple interests are apparent in any one piece of land or piece of knowledge, or indeed in any one person. But by multiple ownership I mean something quite different from common property or common ownership. We are not looking at an undifferentiated resource in which all people have equal rights of access. Instead, people have different kinds of rights and claims, depending on their proximity, input, age and authority. Neither persons, land, nor knowledge are independent of one another.

On the Rai Coast of Papua New Guinea, the names of ancestors, and of mythic characters, are powerful. Spells are cast in the utterance of these names. People wisely said they would not reveal them to me as their ethnographer, as I might then be accused of stealing powerful knowledge and profiting from it. But they would not even tell me stories – that is, narratives of the exploits of mythic ancestors – which they did not specifically own (J. Leach 2000b). There is no power or value in these narratives according to Rai Coast people. They were afraid, however, that if the true owner of the story heard that I knew them, then the person who told me would be fined in pigs and wealth for this transgression. What possible use or value could there be in the narrative of a story that everyone knows anyway? To answer this question took some analytic work. In sum, it is because of the way people are connected to one another, through living in the same places in this area (J. Leach 2003), that knowledge of that place, its history, the ancestors who lived there and how to make it productive by invoking the right spiritual and agricultural procedures, is a way of belonging to it. Knowing the stories of the land is in many ways owning it, or rather, making a claim to be a part of the kin group which lives there (Pocock 1992). Knowledge of a place is one thing. But if, as Bonnemaison describes on Tanna, knowledge and a place are parts of the same valuable complex whole – that is, if they are dependent upon one another – then new ideas, or what the modernist outlook would regard as innovations or manifestations of creativity, also come to look very different.

Indepen and Creativity

When people in Reite dream new spirit voices, entities that are the basis of their sacred music, ritual transformations and horticulture, they do not claim authorship over the creation, or that they composed or invented the item. Instead, they displace agency from themselves and say it was the ground itself – and through the ground, the spirits – that gave them the knowledge. This displacement, far from being a disavowal of ownership, is in fact a *strong claim* to their recognition as central to a particular place, to its generativity and productivity (Strathern 2005a). But it is a claim made on very different premises to those of possessive individualism. The claim is not of individual mental labour, but of positioning on the land, and in a kin group, which is what made it *appropriate* for this new and valuable song to come to that person. There is no individual mind at work, no creative genius, hence the claim is not an individual one. Songs are owned and guarded, but by whole kin groups. Being spoken to by the land and by the ancestors of a particular place gives a composer authority and prestige in that place. The creation was not a project of an individual, but can be turned towards the projects of a kin group who wish to amaze and affect others around them by the beauty of their spirit voices (Strathern 2005b: 147–9).

If you are made up of – and manifest physically – other people's work, input, substance and knowledge, then you do not in fact own yourself or anything you produce as an individual. There is no project that is not already the project of other people as well, because they are part of you as a person. In fact, complex exchange systems that substitute persons for wealth show that there is nothing else to a person than their make-up in the work and thought of others. People, if you will, are the projects of other people. Knowledge in these places is similarly constituted. It does not come from any single creator, just as the person does not come from a single progenitor. Knowledge is part of what people are. The references here to land tenure are intended to throw into relief the assumptions of possessive individualism, particularly as Locke took land to be an archetypal case. The comparison shows that one can own knowledge, and land, and other people, without that ownership being property, or implying possessive individuals. The dreamer of a new song in Reite distinguishes himself and gains authority through connection, not through exclusive control over an object. His claim is to being an essential part of the place's identity, viability and power.

When Siriman unveiled the spirit Indepen by cooking pigs and providing meat for the male cult of his affines and kin, he used all the power and authority available to him in order to draw spectators from as wide an area of the Rai Coast as possible. He did so because, to his great excitement, the spirit appearing through him on that vital and memorable night marked him out as the local representative of a new

political order for the country as a whole, the order of an independe
spirit's value to him was not one of self-expression, much less of ec
It had nothing to do with him as a possessor, or as a creative indivi
he was possessed by the spirit rather than the other way round. His position as the
head of his particular place-based kin group was elevated to national significance
due to his connections to Yali, the emergence of the nation that night, his ancestors
and their power for generative agency, and those others who, coming to eat the
pork he provided, would in future have a relationship, through him and his kin, to
the nation as a whole. These connections were the basis of his claim, not what he
set his claim against.

The unarticulated admonition contained in this chapter is that anthropologists should be very careful when they celebrate the creativity of 'other cultures', lest that celebration should perpetrate a kind of conceptual colonialism, portraying others as making and owning the same kinds of value, and as being the same kinds of person, as anthropologists themselves. Such a move feeds directly into efforts to make cultural productions across the globe part of an encompassing version of culture and ownership, one which sees value in objects, in static items transacted as commodities or protected as heritage. We need to be more imaginative. If Papua New Guinean statecraft were to take account of those modes of personhood articulated by Pocock and others, if it were to 'take man as he is, and the law as it might be' in the specific sense of different kinds of person, and different modes of ownership for the state to administer and guarantee, a different form of state itself might emerge. Indepen is particularly apposite to this argument, as indeed is the notion of an 'independent' understanding of what is creative. Just as in colonialism, the power of colonizers was employed to force native people's acceptance of an alien set of social institutions and norms, primarily through an alien conception of property rights, so neocolonialism asks emerging nations such as Papua New Guinea to behave as if their culture was the same kind of creative force that we imagine our own civilization to be. In such a transaction they are bound to lose out.

Acknowledgements

Many people, including students in Cambridge taking the final-year course in political economy, and colleagues spread around the globe, have helped in developing the arguments I outline here. Most significantly, however, this chapter emerged from lectures I wrote in conjunction with Cori Hayden, and I am most grateful to her for her intellectual input. She is, of course, not responsible for the argument as it appears here.

Notes

1. This leader's name was Yali Singina. See Lawrence (1964), J. Leach (2003), Errington and Gewertz (2004).
2. A Tok Pisin word that abbreviates the English language root, it was part of a phrase on everyone's minds that night: 'Independence for the new state of Papua New Guinea from Australia'.
3. This term is mine, not Locke's.
4. Hardin's original article spurred a huge literature on the ways in which commons *have* been managed successfully (see Ostrom et al. 1999).
5. For example, in November 2003 I spoke at a 'Research Strategy Seminar' organized by the UK Arts and Humanities Research Board, entitled *Intellectual Property Rights in the Arts and Humanities*. One of my co-panelists, Hector McQueen (Professor of Intellectual Property Law at Edinburgh University), cited Hardin's article as unassailable evidence that creativity and cooperation do not occur without the promise of private reward (J. Leach 2004a).

References

Aragon, L. and Leach, J. (n.d.), 'The vitality of tradition. Artistic practice and the impetus to intellectual property protection in contemporary Indonesia', Unpublished ms.

Beauvoir, S. de (1953), *The Second Sex*, London: Jonathan Cape.

Biagioli, M. and Galison, P. (eds) (2003), *Scientific Authorship: Credit and Intellectual Property in Science*, London: Routledge.

Bonnemaison, J. (1991), 'Magic gardens in Tanna', *Pacific Studies*, 14(4): 71–90.

Brown, M. (2003), *Who Owns Native Culture?* Cambridge, Mass.: Harvard University Press.

—— (2005), 'Heritage trouble: recent work on the protection of intangible cultural property', *International Journal of Cultural Property*, 12(1): 40–61.

Crocombe, R. (ed) (1971), *Land Tenure in the Pacific*, Melbourne: Oxford University Press.

Delaney, C. (1986), 'The meaning of paternity and the virgin birth debate', *Man*, 21(3): 494–513.

Errington, F. and Gewertz, D. (2004), *Yali's Question. Sugar, Culture and History*, Chicago: Chicago University Press.

Hardin, G. (1968), 'The tragedy of the commons', *Science*, 162: 1243–8.

Hirschman, A. (1997), *The Passions and the Interests. Political Arguments for Capitalism Before its Triumph*, Princeton, NJ: Princeton University Press.

Lane, R. (1971), 'New Hebrides: Land tenure without land policy', in R (ed), *Land Tenure in the Pacific*, Melbourne: Oxford University Pr

Lawrence, P. (1964), *Road Belong Cargo. A Study of the Cargo Move Southern Madang District New Guinea*, Manchester: Manchester University Press.

Leach, E. (1968), *A Runaway World? The 1967 Reith Lectures*, London: British Broadcasting Corporation.

Leach, J. (2000a), 'Multiple expectations of ownership', *Melanesian Law Journal* (Special Issue on Transaction and Transmission of Indigenous Knowledge and Expressions of Culture), 27: 63–76 (online at http://www.paclii.org/journals/mlj/2000/2.html).

—— (2000b) 'Situated connections. Rights and intellectual resources in a Rai Coast society', *Social Anthropology*, 8(2): 163–79.

—— (2003), *Creative Land. Place and Procreation on the Rai Coast of Papua New Guinea*, Oxford: Berghahn.

—— (2004a), 'A dispersed creativity, or, persons and their boundaries: some broader issues involved in the ownership of intellectual property', *Cambridge Anthropology*, 24(1): 21–27.

—— (2004b) 'Modes of creativity', in E. Hirsch and M. Strathern (eds), *Transactions and Creations. Property Debates and the Stimulus of Melanesia*, Oxford: Berghahn Books.

—— (2005), 'Being in between. Art-science collaborations and a technological culture', *Social Analysis*, 49(1): 141–60.

Liep, J. (2001), 'Introduction', in J. Liep (ed), *Locating Cultural Creativity*, London: Pluto Press.

Lessig, L. (2004), *Free Culture: How Big Media Uses Technology and the Law to Lock Down Culture and Control Creativity*, New York: Penguin.

Locke, J. (1960), *The Second Treatise of Civil Government, and a Letter Concerning Toleration*, Oxford: Blackwell.

Love, J. (2003), 'Prescription for pain', *Le Monde Diplomatique* (English Edition), March, Paris (http://mondediplo.com/2003/03/12generics).

—— (2006), 'Prizes rather than prices', *Le Monde Diplomatique* (English Edition), May, Paris (http://mondediplo.com).

MacPherson, C.B. (1962), *The Political Theory of Possessive Individualism*, Oxford: Clarendon Press.

Ostrom, E. (1990), *Governing the Commons: The Evolution of Institutions for Collective Action*, Cambridge: Cambridge University Press.

——, Burger, J., Field, C.B., Norgaard, R.B. and Policansky, D. (1999), 'Revisiting the commons: local lessons, global challenges', *Science*, 284(5412): 278–82.

Pocock, J.G.A. (1985), *Virtue, Commerce, and History. Essays on Political Thought and History, Chiefly in the Eighteenth Century*, Cambridge: Cambridge University Press.

—— (1992), 'Tangata Whenua and Enlightenment anthropology', *New Zealand Journal of History*, 26(1): 28–53.

Spinoza, B. de (2000), *Ethics / Spinoza*, Oxford: Oxford University Press.

Strathern, M. (2005a), 'Imagined collectivities and multiple authorship', in R. Ghosh (ed), *CODE. Collaborative Ownership and the Digital Economy*, Cambridge, Mass.: MIT Press.

—— (2005b), *Kinship, Law and the Unexpected. Relatives are Always a Surprise*, Cambridge: Cambridge University Press.

Vaidhyanathan, S. (2001), *Copyrights and Copywrongs: The Rise of Intellectual Property and How it Threatens Creativity*, New York: New York University Press.

—— (2006), 'Afterword: Critical information studies. A bibliographic manifesto', *Cultural Studies*, 20(2–3): 292–315.

Vico, G. (1953), *Opere*, ed F. Nicolini, Milan: Ricciardi.

Wagner, R. (1981), *The Invention of Culture*, Chicago: University of Chicago Press.

Part II
Creative Appropriations and Institutional Contexts

Introduction
Melissa Demian and *Sari Wastell*

We originally conceived the conference panel from which these chapters are taken as a forum in which to explore critically the nature of creativity in social, political and religious life by considering the extent to which – or those contexts within which – 'creativity' is imagined as a social rather than an individual capacity. While anthropologists have periodically invoked creativity in their considerations of social and cultural novelty, more often than not creativity is conceived as a psychological response to radical change (Kirshenblatt-Gimblett 1978; Stephen 1997), or the novel actions of individual persons who become a focal point for others in their society (Lavie, Rosaldo and Narayan 1993). In either case, no matter how socially dispersed the effects of creativity may appear to be, creativity as a cause or source of action is still construed as an interior capacity of the autonomous individual, the 'genius' whose creations and innovations mask the social relations upon which those innovations depended (Woodmansee 1984; Biagioli 1998). In order to avoid reproducing this version of creativity, we proposed as our starting point that the innovations which appear to cause temporal or historical discontinuities are not always (if indeed ever) genius-instigated and unprecedented practices or forms of knowledge. Rather, they are appropriations in the sense that practices, information or belief systems are 'transplanted' and then recontextualized by those who appropriate them. This process of decontextualization and recontextualization generates the effect or appearance of social discontinuity.

The problem of course is that innovation might not be an appropriation of a practice at all. To play with contexts could just as easily cause long-standing practices to be recontextualized in an unanticipated milieu. Here, the appropriation would be of the context rather than the practice itself, an 'as if' scenario where dissimilar social contexts are treated as homologues to one another. This too would attest to a form of creativity that could rarely be understood in terms of individual capacities, and one that might not easily be recognizable as creativity in vernacular Western terms. The reason for this is precisely because such a form of creativity, in which enduring terms of reference are pressed into service in contexts for which they seem unwarranted, unexpected or misplaced, effects a claim to continuity. Creativity, according to its common-sense definition, is supposed to be about the new.

That the lodestar of evaluations of creativity should be a kind of social alchemy – absolute transformation – at one time privileged any number of unenunciated predicates within anthropology itself. Not only did it underscore the dispensation of possessive individualism, it also shored up temporal presumptions about the dynamism of modernity as against the stasis of the 'tradition' in which our informants were allegedly mired. Whereas the 'West' not only had a history but actively made history as well, the 'Rest' were destined to be washed over by histories of others' making and to respond in a repetitive and programmatic fashion.[1] Indeed, the measure of creativity could be scaled, a variation evaluated as less creative than a transformation, which in turn is less unprecedented than a revolution.[2] Creativity in this formulation is about action without precedent or about a self-conscious agency, but never about people doing the same thing over and over again in different or unexpected contexts. If the starting point for recognition of creativity is the combination of forms (Leach 2004: 152), it is also worth noting that some combinations are recognized as creative to the exclusion of others.

Social discontinuity, for instance, is clearly in the eye of the beholder. Discontinuity alone cannot index creativity, because it categorically precludes one rendering of what creativity might actually be. Bearing this caveat in mind, we chose to highlight the concept of appropriation in the conference panel, be it the appropriation of knowledge-and-practices or of an entire context, in order to ask how people mobilize the unfamiliar or unforeseen, either voluntarily or involuntarily, to engender or efface a sense of social distinctiveness. In doing so, we hoped to open up a space for debate about what might actually constitute creativity in disparate ethnographic settings, an aim which we think has been realized in the three chapters that follow. At the same time, we also wanted to ask who attributes 'creativity' to acts and persons, both amongst the actors concerned within the ethnographic setting, and between actor/informants and the anthropologist/observer. If creativity is not a stable term of reference, how do people claim to recognize it when they see it, and by what measure is the act or person deemed to be creative (a point to which we will return below)? Finally, we encouraged contributors to the panel to consider what is at stake when 'creativity' is invoked in either indigenous exegesis or anthropological description. What exactly is being valorized, as in the case of discontinuity, and what are the social, political and historical catalysts that prompt the invocation of idioms of creativity?

With this varied remit as our starting point for the conference panel, what we ultimately received were papers that provided critiques, implicit or explicit, of *social change*. This phrase, once popular in anthropology, has now fallen somewhat from favour, if only because of a growing recognition that if it describes anything, it describes a tautology: change is a categorical constituent of sociality.

Part II, Introduction

The fashionable line to take now is that this is especially true today, when the internally coherent and self-regulating 'hot' and 'cold' societies, as envisaged by Lévi-Strauss (1966), have been replaced by societies in an interconnected world, between which ideas flow as freely as people or commodities do. But if this is the case, where does it leave the concept of creativity in social life – is creativity just another practice of consumption? Can the concept of creativity offer any special purchase of this kind to ethnographic analysis, or is it still simply a Trojan horse for those asymmetries of modernity which allow Westerners to see themselves in both what they appropriate and what is appropriated from them (cf. Strathern 1999)?

We argue that creativity has been dogged by a tendency to link it to what might on the face of it be imagined as its polar opposite: authenticity.[3] If creativity is the capacity or process through which we are supposed to discover new social forms, authenticity is the knowledge practice through which we discover what is irrefutably endogenous to ourselves or to other people (Bendix 1997). Drawing on this tradition, some versions of cultural theory (for example, Gailey 1992) would have it that culture itself acts counter to the homogenizing effects of the market, and that as such its inherent creativity is also an inherent process of authentication against the threat of mass production and infinitely interchangeable value. But there are other ways of demonstrating ethnographically how creativity and authenticity are not so far removed from each other as they might seem. As each of the three chapters in this part reveals, creativity can be mobilized to discover 'authentic' forms of social experience. In Jeanette Edwards' chapter (Chapter 8), Baptist ministers in the north of England posit the family of God as subsuming or replacing the 'biological' family, such that discussions of the appropriateness of new reproductive technologies centre on the problem of whether the 'third parties' involved in these relationships irredeemably disrupt this family, or can unproblematically be excluded from it. In the chapter by Judith Scheele (Chapter 7), Kabyle political action in Algeria is stymied by the apparent paradox of the 'perpetual revolution', wherein the only way to claim political legitimacy is to appropriate the revolutionary rhetorics of Occupied France, the fight for Algerian independence, or the Palestinian intifada. In Elizabeth Cory-Pearce's account of early twentieth-century Maori scholarship (Chapter 6), attempts to classify the work of Makereti/Margaret Thom as stemming from either an 'indigenous' or a 'cosmopolitan' perspective are bound to run into trouble, particularly as Makereti herself appears to have declined to distinguish between anthropological and ancestral sources of knowledge about Maoridom, and instead treats one as an expression or embodiment of the other. Each of these contributions interrogates the relationship of creativity to authenticity in intriguing ways, and demonstrates that the relationship itself is predicated on a prior, but possibly spurious, association of authenticity with continuity, and creativity with discontinuity.

Cory-Pearce also points to one of the other implicit themes that, while not comprising part of our original remit, emerged in the course of the conference session: how we know when we are being creative, and whether this knowledge is a sign of creativity's moral legitimacy or illegitimacy. As intimated earlier, self-consciousness around innovation is a hallmark of Western sensibilities about creativity, and yokes creativity to autonomous efficacy. It also resonates with one of the metaphors of creativity (Joas 1996: 70–126) that has long captured the attentions and enthusiasms of Western scholars on the subject: creativity as expression. Where creativity is imagined in terms of expression, it is reliant on a subject-object distinction that has not always proved a helpful analytic across the diversity of ethnographic contexts with which anthropologists grapple (see Leach, this volume, Chapter 5). However, two other predominant metaphors for creativity explored by Joas, 'production' and 'revolution', present their own problems. Production orients creativity in the direction of the material world, positing the objective circumstances of nature as the limiting factors which both instigate and constrain creative action.[4] Revolution, on the other hand, 'assumes that there is a potential of human creativity relative to the social world, namely that we can fundamentally reorganize the social institutions that govern human co-existence' (ibid.: 71). Not only is the very stability of what constitutes the natural world as opposed to the social world a dubious starting point for anthropology, but conceiving of creativity in terms of an orientation to one over and above the other brings the question of reflexivity into acute focus. The 1990 Manchester debate concerning whether human worlds are culturally constructed couched this question in slightly different terms. Here the debate emphasized a distinction between construction as a self-conscious act which presumes both goals and the means for realizing them, and improvisation, which tends to emerge in the absence of a blueprint for action and is contingent upon what is to hand (Ingold 1996; Richards 1996). Whether both modalities are equally creative – and for whom – became a subject of serious discussion and debate within our conference session.

For example, in Edwards' contribution, 'coming to be known' is a process of creative legitimation in English Baptist narratives of conception, wherein the foetus is deemed alive or sentient when it comes to be known by God. On the other hand, suggests Scheele, reflexivity and forethought harbinger delegitimation in the perpetually revolutionary politics of Kabylia, wherein the revelation of a powerful person's motives is a sign of the waning of that person's power. If, in the words of one of Scheele's interlocutors, 'All words [have] already been taken', then the agency of political action cannot possibly have its source in living people or in contemporary political entities, but instead emanates from a past that is always just out of reach.

Part II, Introduction

The ambivalence towards creativity in these cases, and in Cory-Pearce's question of whether Makereti was an ancestral appropriator or a plagiarist (or both, or neither), is itself a suppressed aspect of the creativity concept. As Löfgren (2001) and Leach (2004; this volume, Chapter 5) have both observed, creativity is now touted as an unqualified good, desirable to fuel a 'knowledge economy' with a 'flexible workforce' and, perhaps more to the point, teachable to the children who will one day supply that workforce. But to conceive of creativity as unequivocally valuable is itself a novel position. Perhaps lurking in all three chapters in this part is the older 'tradition' of creativity, wherein creativity is regarded as the disruptive characteristic of the mythological monsters, heroes and tricksters who make us human, but also separate us irretrievably from divine law (Mason 1988). In this tradition, creativity is as terrible as it is desirable, and is further conceived in explicit opposition to society: those who create must be counterbalanced by others who assess the moral value of their creations (ibid.). With the advent of monotheistic religions, all creativity was assigned to the Creator, such that the morality of creativity was unequivocal *as long as it was attributed to divine inspiration*. The Enlightenment concept of artistic genius, in other words, was only possible because God had been removed as an agent of creativity (Kristeller 1983: 107). But as Edwards' chapter in particular shows, this feat was only partially accomplished. Contemporary English Baptists have no trouble reinscribing divine intentions in the conception of children by means of IVF, since the child so conceived is not in the end 'related' to its parents by means of biology or even technology, but by means of the knowing recognition of God. The potential disruption of creativity is thereby obviated: there are always already novel ideas that precede the novel ideas of mere humans.

We have sought to highlight some of the key questions that emerged during the conference panel, and that are raised by the chapters that follow. First, why has discontinuity become privileged as evidence for creativity, when in fact people may endeavour as far as possible to import old contexts into the background of new political forms in order to legitimize those forms (Scheele)? Second, is creativity only recognizable as such if it is self-conscious, that is, if action is undertaken with the reflexive intent to anticipate the regard of others (Cory-Pearce)? Finally, we might ask how pre-Enlightenment notions of a divine agency underlying creativity have been reinscribed into the discourse on apparently novel technological interventions (Edwards). The following chapters invite us to denaturalize the concept of creativity with the same rigour with which, say, modernity has become denaturalized, and they also ask whether creativity may be found in the appropriation of contexts rather than in the appropriation of specific social forms.

There are of course risks to finding creativity in every moment of social life, not only because of the disruption that seems invariably to be regarded as a concomitant of innovation (Strathern 1992). One risk is that we end up looking for discontinuous agency or intent in every interpolation and hybrid that appears, rather in the manner of the vogue for transgression and resistance that has characterized much anthropological writing in recent years (Brown 1996). The opposite or perhaps complementary risk is that 'change or variation can only be approached negatively, as a kind of entropy, static, or "noise"' (Wagner 1981: 29) in the social order which is itself the creation of a society imagining itself in relation to other societies. Wagner's caution is still apposite. If anthropology itself is a process of looking for social patterns that enable us to communicate our conviction that particular kinds of relationships exist, the 'noise' of social, political and religious creativity is the by-product of our attempts to convert our experience of these relationships into ethnographic description.

Notes

1. Sahlins' (1987) structural historicism can be read in just this light. History, it is proposed, arrived on Hawaiian shores and the Hawaiians met it within the enduring templates of their 'culture'. As Appadurai (1988) noted (not referring specifically to Sahlins' work), in such a model the natives do not simply *have* culture, they are trapped inside it.
2. The urge to classify innovative political forms has a long history in anthropology. Here one is reminded of Gluckman's (1963) distinction between rebellions and revolutions, or Wallace's (1956) five-stage 'life cycle' for revitalization movements. In both instances the anthropologist is faced with the improbable task of locating the level or unit of society from which new political forms emanate.
3. The extent to which authenticity, like creativity, is an intrinsic characteristic of sociality is anticipated in the word's etymology, which links authenticity to direct experience, to 'being there', and therefore to the unique and unrepeatable nature of that experience. The experiential subtext of authenticity can also be found in Heidegger's (1993) writings on authenticity as being true to one's *Dasein*.
4. One could think either of Marxist historical materialism or of Heideggerian phenomenology in this respect.

References

Appadurai, A. (1988), 'Putting hierarchy in its place', *Cultural Anthropology*, 3: 36–49.

Bendix, R. (1997), *In Search of Authenticity: The Formation of Folklore Studies*, Madison: University of Wisconsin Press.

Biagioli, M. (1998), 'The instability of authorship: Credit and responsibility in contemporary biomedicine', *The FASEB Journal*, 12: 3–16.

Brown, M.F. (1996), 'On resisting resistance', *American Anthropologist*, 98: 729–35.

Gailey, C.W. (1992), 'Introduction: The politics of culture in civilization', in C.W. Gailey (ed), *The Politics of Culture and Creativity*, Gainesville: University Press of Florida.

Gluckman, M. (1963), *Order and Rebellion in Tribal Africa*, London: Cohen & West.

Heidegger, M. (1993), *Basic Concepts*, Bloomington: Indiana University Press.

Ingold, T. (1996), 'Human worlds are culturally constructed: Against the motion (1)', in T. Ingold (ed), *Key Debates in Anthropology*, New York: Routledge.

Joas, H. (1996), *The Creativity of Action*, Chicago: University of Chicago Press.

Kirshenblatt-Gimblett, B. (1978), 'Culture shock and narrative creativity', in R.M. Dorson (ed), *Folklore in the Modern World*, The Hague: Mouton.

Kristeller, P.O. (1983), '"Creativity" and "tradition"', *Journal of the History of Ideas*, 44: 105–13.

Lavie, S., Narayan, K. and Rosaldo, R. (eds) (1993), *Creativity/Anthropology*, Ithaca, NY: Cornell University Press.

Leach, J. (2004), 'Modes of creativity', in E. Hirsch and M. Strathern (eds), *Transactions and Creations: Property Debates and the Stimulus of Melanesia*, New York: Berghahn Books.

Lévi-Strauss, C. (1966), *The Savage Mind*, London: Weidenfeld and Nicolson.

Löfgren, O. (2001), 'Celebrating creativity: The slanting of a concept', in J. Liep (ed), *Locating Cultural Creativity*, London: Pluto Press.

Mason, J.H. (1988), 'The character of creativity: Two traditions', *History of European Ideas*, 9: 697–715.

Richards, P. (1996), 'Human worlds are culturally constructed: Against the motion (2)', in T. Ingold (ed), *Key Debates in Anthropology*, New York: Routledge.

Sahlins, M. (1987), *Islands of History*, Chicago: University of Chicago Press.

Stephen, M. (1997), 'Cargo cults, cultural creativity, and autonomous imagination', *Ethos*, 25: 333–58.

Strathern, M. (1992), *Reproducing the Future: Essays on Anthropology, Kinship, and the New Reproductive Technologies*, New York: Routledge.

—— (1999), *Property, Substance, and Effect: Anthropological Essays on Persons and Things*, London: Athlone Press.

Wagner, R. (1981), *The Invention of Culture*, Chicago: University of Chicago Press.

Wallace, A.F.C. (1956), 'Revitalization movements', *American Anthropologist*, 58: 264–81.

Woodmansee, M. (1984), 'The genius and the copyright: Economic and legal conditions of the emergence of the "author"', *Eighteenth-Century Studies*, 17: 425–48.

−6−

Locating Authorship: Creativity and Borrowing in the Writing of Ethnography and the Production of Anthropological Knowledge
Elizabeth Cory-Pearce

That minor writers should fail ... is hardly to be wondered at when we find the greatest of English anthropological authors publishing such a tissue of nonsense.

Makereti, Makereti Collection[1]

[S]he could know her old people as many could not, and seeing who she was, they were willing that she should write.

Penniman, 'Makereti'

E kore e taka te parapara a ona tupuna; tukua iho ki a ia
The talents of his or her ancestors cannot fail to descend to him or her.

Maori proverb

'"Anthropology begins at home" has become a watchword of modern social science', remarked Bronislaw Malinowski (1938: vii) in his introduction to the ethnographic monograph *Facing Mount Kenya*. Written by Jomo Kenyatta, *Facing Mount Kenya* was based on fieldwork conducted among 'his own tribe' (Malinowski 1938: viii), the Giyuku people of central Kenya, in 1930 and 1931. Malinowski went on to defend the validity of a domestic anthropology, a project endorsed by the functionalist method he advocated that approved of and indeed actively sought 'the native outlook' (ibid.: xi). Displacing a previously artefact-based study of human variation and evolution, fieldwork in the Malinowskian tradition would supersede collecting as a more effective means of rendering the invisible (other, unknown peoples) visible and hence knowable (Pomian 1990). Collections – the souvenirs and objects of knowledge of eighteenth- and nineteenth-century travel and exploration – would become understood, and consequently devalued, as 'secondary' sources: material at a remove from the first-hand social experience of fieldwork and its constitution as authoritative knowledge in the form of the ethnographic monograph (Stocking 1985: 9; Thomas 1991: 142).

The immediacy of the modern ethnographer's presence in the field was a rhetorical device for authenticating his or her observations, and it thus constituted the monograph as authoritative. Furthermore, writing a monograph was also, implicitly, a claim to proprietorship of a people (Coombe 1998). In this chapter I turn to the development of fieldwork methods and ethnographic writing as particularly significant in claims to cultural authorship and proprietorship. An anthropology that begins at home, so to speak, appears to posit an alternative claim to epistemological authority than that of the modernist monograph: that of a 'belonging to' rather than the 'owning of' a people. These different articulations suggest a useful point of departure from which to evaluate conventional understandings of creativity in knowledge production as an inventive capacity or the genius of Western individuals, or, conversely, as a collectively held and shared capacity of non-Western cultures.

Illuminating the material dimensions of social life, museum collections open up the complex interconnected histories of anthropology, institutions of collecting and colonialism. Studies of such processes to date have tended to chart the role and intentions of predominantly European collectors (e.g. Gosden and Knowles 2001; O'Hanlon and Welsch 2000). Instead, considering material forms as potentially embodying an 'imprint' or 'countersign' of other presences (Douglas 1999), I extend these authors' approaches to objects and images to examine the manuscript as a cross-culturally created form of material culture. Handwritten text is, perhaps, more telling than uniform typescript. Styles are identifiable as the hands of particular persons (even if they remain unnamed), and this form tangibly manifests their presence. Archives facilitate encounters with distant 'others' (temporally, geographically, culturally), tactile encounters mediated through the material traces of human activity preserved therein. Archives prompt questions about how writing was executed in the past: with calm coherence, or a hurried, anxious or aggravated urgency, deeply indenting the surface of the page? There may be incursions: crossings-out written in the hand of the author, or in other hands, perhaps to edit or amend, or to remove or conceal. There may be absences: pages missing, lost or deliberately torn out, or in the case of correspondences, sent away. The point I want to stress is this: manuscript has a tactility and materiality that often goes overlooked in analyses, yet it remains metonymical, an aspect of a person's materially extended agency or personhood (Gell 1998; Strathern 1988), a part in relation to a whole that remains frustratingly beyond our grasp.

As O'Hanlon (1999) and Thomas (1999) suggest, in the manner of a detective inquiry, we might evaluate the worth of archives as evidence, asking what they reveal or conceal, or clarify or confuse. The central character in my 'investigation' is a remarkably creative woman – Makereti, or Margaret Staples-Brown née Thom, a student of anthropology at Oxford University in the 1920s, known in her earlier career in tourism as Guide Maggie Papakura. She bequeathed her study notes, manuscripts and personal ephemera to the Pitt Rivers Museum, where she took the Bachelor of Science degree in anthropology in 1928 (Penniman 1938: 24). Entering the discipline during a period of significant epistemological shift, from a collections- to a fieldwork-based method, her scholarship, I suggest, manifests some of the contradictions implied in this turn, contradictions that become more apparent over the course of the twentieth century.

This chapter examines these concerns through an analysis of Makereti's ethnography, investigating her manuscript notes as a material complex, to evoke a sense of ethnographic authorship as a layered and mutually (if not equitably) appropriative process. Something of this creative interaction in the authoring of ethnography might be found in study notes, and in the work of drafting and redrafting of manuscripts, as also in the acknowledgements, prefaces and footnotes of published works. Such appropriative complexity – at times seemingly ambiguous or contradictory – highlights the point that our interpretation of these past activities cannot be framed within the terms of an opposition between two camps, of colonizer and colonized, or in other words, presented as the protest of an indigenous academic who 'strikes back' against imperialist and colonialist (mis)representations of his or her people (cf. Hooper-Greenhill 2000; Awekotuku 1986, 1991). We need to go beyond a generalized critique of the negative ramifications of colonialism's hegemony, and to consider not only how collections may have emerged out of a formative nexus of social relations in the past, but also how they continue to act upon, and to be reshaped by, relations in the present.

Just as an anthropology that begins 'at home' arises at a particular point in the history of the discipline – a discipline that, for all its colonialist shortcomings, also opened up certain kinds of creative spaces in which, to a degree, the otherwise marginalized could act – so is interest in this sort of archive reignited at a particular historical moment. Why are other scholars, including myself, now returning to this archive? And how, then, do we creatively rewrite Makereti's scholarship through such acts of archival retrieval? Reflexive engagement with such questions might better enable us to understand the ways in which museum collections remain enmeshed in mutually formative social relations, as people engage and re-engage with them. Before we explore Makereti's scholarship and the processes of creativity in which it was formed, it is necessary to sketch out a biography, albeit necessarily brief, of her remarkable life.

A Remarkable Woman

In 1873, Makereti (a Maori transliteration of the name Maggie) was born Margaret Pattison Thom, in the Bay of Plenty area of the north island of New Zealand. She inherited from her mother, Pia Te Ngarotu, a Tuhourangi woman of exceptionally high *mana* (ancestral standing), a lineage connecting her to four of the founding chiefly ancestors that arrived in Aotearoa (New Zealand) on the Arawa canoe: Tama-te-kapua, Ngatoroirangi, Hei and Ika. Her father, William Arthur Thom, an English settler and storekeeper, worked in the Resident Magistrate's Court, which brought him to the Lake Rotorua region and the Tuhourangi village of Wairoa in the Bay of Plenty.

Shortly after her birth, Marara Marotaua and Maihi Te Kakau Paraoa (Makereti's maternal aunt and uncle) adopted her, and raised her for the first ten years of her life at the rural settlement of Parekarangi, near Rotorua. From these early years it is understood she acquired an intimate knowledge of her immediate landscape and her Maori heritage, learning the language, customs and history of

Figure 6.1 Portrait of Makereti (centre rear), her mother, Pia Te Ngarotu (front right), and her great aunt, Marara Marotaua (front left). B43A. 64, © Pitt Rivers Museum, University of Oxford

her people (Penniman 1938). As an *aho ariki* (born of the highest descent lines), Makereti was taught the *whakapapa* or genealogy of her ancestry, a knowledge which she recorded in vast genealogical charts that would later be deposited in the Pitt Rivers Museum in Oxford. From the age of ten, her father took an active role in her education, sending her to local schools, to a private English governess and finally to a boarding school for Maori girls, Hukarere, in Napier. The latter serendipitously saved Makereti from the terrifying experience of the eruption of Mount Tarawera in 1886, which engulfed the nearby Tuhourangi village of Te Wairoa, claiming hundreds of lives.

In 1891, at her father's home at Wairoa, Makereti married a settler, Francis Joseph Dennan, who worked as a land surveyor. They had a child, William Francis Te Aonui Dennan, and lived for a short period as a family in the Wairarapa region on the south east-coast. Later they separated, and Makereti and her son returned to her maternal village of Whakarewarewa where, in 1900, she petitioned for divorce, maintaining custody of her son. Despite the Tarawera disaster, tourism in the Rotorua region recovered quickly and continued to expand, with the focus of attention shifting to the Whakarewarewa village and valley. Visitors came to observe the Maori village where people cooked, laundered and bathed in various hot springs, and to 'take the waters' themselves. These activities became widely known through numerous publicity materials, especially the medium of the postcard (see Figure 6.2).

Figure 6.2 Postcard of Whakarewarewa village, Rotorua, postmarked 1911 (author's collection)

Makereti's fluency in both Maori and English language and social etiquette would serve her well, as she took up a career in tourguiding at Whakarewarewa, situating her as a mediator – different enough to intrigue exotica-seeking tourists, yet not so strange as to be unable to comprehend their questions and furnish a suitably beguiling response. Adopting the pseudonym Guide Maggie 'Papakura', Makereti rose to international prominence in 1901, when she, alongside her senior relative and tutor, Te Paea Hinerangi, known as Guide Sophia, guided the Duke and Duchess of Cornwall and York through the thermal village and valley of Whakarewarewa. Following this much-publicized event, Guide Maggie ventured into her first publishing activity in 1905, authoring a guidebook, *Maggie's Guide to the Hot Lakes District*, a tourist guide to the Rotorua region, of which she ordered multiple copies to sell or present to tourists and guests, along with other souvenirs. Makereti earned a comfortable living, supporting herself, raising her son and contributing to the needs of her relatives in the village and beyond. Makereti's house was also on display to visitors, and was filled with an eclectic range of belongings, old and new, from Maori cloaks to Victorian portraiture and furnishings, embodying the material culture of her times (see Figures 6.3 and 6.4).

Figure 6.3 Makereti writing at her desk in her house, Tuhoromatakaka, at Whakarewarewa in 1910. B43A. 19 B, © Pitt Rivers Museum, University of Oxford

Locating Authorship: Creativity and Borrowing

Figure 6.4 The interior of Makereti's house, Tuhoromatakaka, at Whakarewarewa, in 1910. B43A. 20 A, © Pitt Rivers Museum, University of Oxford

Not only did Makereti receive and entertain visitors in her home, she also travelled extensively with an Arawa Concert Party, led by herself and the Ngati Wahiao Chief, Mita Taupopoki, bringing her house with her as part of a full-scale model Maori village. In 1910 and 1911 the Party travelled to Australia, and then on to Britain, where they erected the village at the White City and Crystal Palace exhibitions, entertaining visitors with speeches, songs and dances, a popular format in the Great Exhibition genre of the time (Greenhalgh 1989). On the whole, the Maori village appears to have been a great success, often receiving a disproportionately large share of positive press attention. While this response may have been due to a general evolutionary thinking that ranked 'the Maori race' above other 'racial types' participating in the exhibitions, it may also have been shaped by the Arawa group's showmanship skills, honed in Rotorua's tourism industry.

Yet their successes remained limited by the overarching social and political circumstances in which the Arawa Concert Party found itself in Britain. Evolutionary attitudes percolate newspaper articles, which frequently recount in patriarchal tone the progress of 'the Maori race' from a state of 'cannibalistic savagery' to 'the most civilized of all native races' under the British protectorate.[2]

A desire to assimilate or 'tame' the exotic strangers in their midst was pervasive. For example, the postcards produced by a Kensington photographer to advertise the troupe's performances were illustrated with a series of photographic portraits in which troupe members were coloured-in with Caucasian brown wavy hair, pale skin and pink cheeks and lips. Participating in exhibitions was also fraught with economic difficulty, as the troupe experienced the financial impact of the dwindling popularity of the Great Exhibition genre compared with its 1851 inception. At the same time, Makereti, frustrated with an audience desiring entertainment, expressed her desire to write a book so that she would be taken more seriously. The troupe performed at numerous venues across the country before eventually separating. Makereti then renewed her acquaintance with Captain Richard Staples-Brown of Oxfordshire, whom she had met in New Zealand in 1907, and they became engaged. After briefly returning with some of the troupe to Whakarewarewa in 1912, Makereti relocated to England: the person popularly known as Guide Maggie Papakura of Rotorua – tour guide, society hostess and concert party leader – was about to become Mrs Margaret Staples-Brown of Oxfordshire – collector, anthropology scholar, ethnographer and author.

A Modern Social Science

Until her departure for England, Makereti had played a highly significant role in the increasingly intercultural social world of Rotorua, or 'Maoriland' as it was romantically called in tourist guidebooks. By the end of the nineteenth century, the area was considered synonymous with Maori heritage, and Makereti, as Guide Maggie, was probably its most iconic figure. To be sure, Makereti played a significant role in fashioning such an image, yet her image, and Maori heritage more generally, was also being increasingly (and selectively) appropriated as a key distinguishing feature of an emergent sense of settler nationhood (see Figure 6.5) (Cory-Pearce, forthcoming). While this may not have been something Makereti objected to at the time, with hindsight it becomes evident that appropriating native heritage as a means of securing a folkloric antiquity for a young settler nation, at the same time as encouraging the assimilation of native peoples into the colonial system, is clearly a form of displacement. It is this kind of assimilative displacement that, I suggest, Makereti's subsequent career in academia may have been concerned to renegotiate. Before addressing this issue, significant connections between tourism, exhibitions and the nascent discipline of anthropology need to be sketched out.

The emergence of the Great Exhibition genre in Britain in 1851 coincided with the rise of anthropology as an academic subject within the British university system, as part of a drive to produce a scientific understanding of the natural

Figure 6.5 Postcard depicting Guide Maggie (Makereti), greeting the ancestor Tane-Te-Pupuke with the *hongi* (pressing noses together), juxtaposed on a New Zealand Ensign. Rauru Meetinghouse, Whakarewarewa, early 1900s (author's collection)

world and the place of humankind within it. It was his experience of the Great Exhibition of 1851 that inspired General Pitt Rivers to establish a systematically ordered ethnographic collection, and by so doing, to formally establish material anthropology (Buchli 2002: 5–6; Chapman 1985: 16). Opening ethnographic collections to the general public democratized the display of previously elite cabinets of curiosities, enabling those of limited means to 'travel' the world via a visual consumption of the people and things on display. Through such displays, peoples could be represented as colonial subjects – their identities racially inscribed – as part of a project to constitute new nation states, manage political subjects and legitimate Caucasian superiority (Coombes 1994; Schnapp 1996). As with tourism industries in the colonies, exhibition displays in metropolitan centres were bound to nation- and empire-building. However, local peoples rapidly became active in these processes. They entered into exchange relations with newcomers, fashioning things in part inspired by these newcomers' preoccupations, yet also often with local desires or interests in mind. For example, models and miniatures intended for display have been fashioned for explorers, collectors, tourists and makers alike (Phillips 1998; Cory-Pearce 2005), including the miniature *kete* (woven handbags) sold by the Arawa troupe in their model village in 1910 (see Figure 6.6).

Figure 6.6 'Hera with Curios'. Photograph of Hera selling photographic portraits, *poi* balls and miniature *kete* (woven baskets) from Makereti's carved *pataka* at Melbourne Oval, Victoria, 1910. M2420–1 © Pitt Rivers Museum, University of Oxford

With regard to these processes we might ask where creativity was located. Who participated in the creation of social and material forms? Who influenced their content and meaning? While exhibitions and museums were implicated in projects of social reform and the projection of unequal relations of power, peoples participating in tourism and exhibitions may have become rapidly familiar with modes and discourses of display, and may also have developed a keen sense of their instrumentality. Some might then find a position in which to exercise a degree of influence in these and other such ideological arenas. The key character of my investigation, Makereti, is one such participant, whose career traverses the interrelated spheres of New Zealand's tourism industry, exhibitions and anthropology. When relocating to Britain, Makereti brought a substantial collection with her, re-erecting her carved house, Tuhoromatakaka, as a 'museum' in which to display her 'collection' at Bampton, her husband's Oxfordshire estate, where she entertained invited guests with informal talks (see Figure 6.7).[3] Thus Makereti entered into Oxford's social world of collectors, learned societies and scholars.

From the late nineteenth century anthropology in Oxford had been taught at the Pitt Rivers Museum, with collections regarded as central to research

Locating Authorship: Creativity and Borrowing

Figure 6.7 Makereti's son, William Te Aonui Dennan (seated, front row, second from left), with a group (possibly of Oxford University students) probably taken at their home in Oddington, Oxfordshire, dressed with garments, weaponry and *poi* balls from her collection. B43A 82 © Pitt Rivers Museum, University of Oxford

and teaching. Consistent with a period of public-participatory anthropology, Makereti's activities were well received in this academic context. Following the dissolution of her marriage in 1924, Makereti entered the University as a student of anthropology in 1926 and began compiling 'a series of books on every feature of the life of the Maori as he was' (Penniman 1938: 24). In anthropology this was a time of epistemological tension between object- and field-based methods, a tension that signalled a nascent disjuncture between popular and professional anthropology. Poised between the two – with both her material collection and her lived ethnographic experience – as a scholar Makereti was able to respond to both methodologies, deploying her field and collections knowledge in the lectures she gave to popular and scholarly audiences.

Makereti was thus a critical participant in evolutionary racial discourse articulated through modes of ethnographic display, and perhaps, to some degree, attempted to reformulate the ways in which Maori peoples were perceived in the professional and popular imagination (cf. Coombes 1994). In 1928, further to her lecturing and collections activities, she was advised to submit a part of her written material as a thesis for the BSc degree in anthropology (Penniman 1938: 24). As has been noted, this was a time in which the ethnographic monograph was emerging as the major source of authoritative knowledge in an increasingly social British anthropology – one that was concerned, through the conduct of ethnographic fieldwork, to understand and translate 'the native outlook' (Malinowski 1938: xi). On the cusp of this ethnographic turn, the timing of Makereti's entry into an anthropological career was opportune.

Nevertheless, given the immediate tension identified at Oxford – a moment in the emergence of anthropology as a modern 'social' science from the chrysalis of a previously more public-participatory and materially researched evolutionary anthropology – Makereti's anthropology might be expected to entail a constant and careful balancing of the need to demonstrate, on the one hand, a required level of 'civilizedness' (or 'assimilatableness'), in order to be acceptable to a public that perceived the world to be racially divided and evolutionarily hierarchized, with 'the Caucasian race' at its apex, and on the other, a required level of 'nativeness', in order to validate the authority of her ethnographic scholarship. Skilled, thanks to her career in tourism, in negotiating discourses of the modern, the exotic and the authentic, the inevitable tensions and contradictions surrounding this balancing act would, I suggest, manifest themselves in the materiality of her study and lecture notes, and in the creativity of her ethnographic writing.

Creating Ethnography

Writing ethnography, like biography, is a deliberate process of selecting out from the wealth of possibilities a particular imagining of peoples, places and lived experiences. Memories become reworked into accounts, with some aspects intensified, others omitted, and gaps in our recall filled or otherwise refigured. Various factors might shape this selection process. In Makereti's case, having emigrated to a distant country, writing an ethnography of her home and people may have formed a means of sustaining a relationship or connection with people and places left behind. At the same time, writing an ethnography that is also a thesis to be presented for examination is a mediated process: its content is in part shaped by the guidance of a supervisor whose thinking is in turn both formed by and formative of prevailing theoretical conventions in the discipline. My concern here is with the relationships between these two projects – writing an account of a people, place and a childhood heritage from which one has since become geographically and temporally distant, and the (somewhat precocious) ambition of a modern social science to record, before it is too late, a native understanding of society. Attention to these relationships opens our understanding of the archive as a complex modern object that is also a nexus of social relations, thereby avoiding the polarizing lens through which colonial archives, collections and histories have often been interpreted.

In her writing, as in her social life, Makereti adopted numerous different standpoints or identities, indicating the complex, shifting and at times contradictory position of the ethnographer – as someone attempting simultaneously to be both 'inside' (achieving empathetic understanding) and 'outside' (sustaining a distanced observational capacity). She explicitly championed an anthropology grounded in first-hand experience and linguistic fluency, one that endorsed her own authority on the subject. Makereti drew upon a broad range of primary sources (authored by early travellers, missionaries and, later, by travel writers, journalists, colonial administrators and ethnologists), comparing her lived experience with their first-hand observations and contributing further to their findings. For example, in a blue notebook in a section of her draft thesis manuscript entitled 'Food', Makereti cited the writings of missionary and botanist William Colenso, adding to his Latin terminology and remarks Maori translations and relevant ethnographic detail.

However, of secondary sources she was typically overtly critical. On the subject of *tangimate* (ceremonies pertaining to death) in particular, she argues, 'in no instance has the whole truth been told'. She found the writing of Cambridge anthropologist Sir James Fraser on the subject problematic, as he relied upon 'secondhand' sources rather than 'an authentic source such as a tribal leader who knew the English language as well as he knew his own traditions' (MC Box 4, Section T). At other moments, Makereti adopted the more distanced stance of the anthropologist 'participant-observer', stepping outside of praxis to draw critical comparisons between what people say they do and what they might actually be doing.

Makereti's assertions were, I suggest, timely, and likely to fall on sympathetic scholarly ears. An air of concern to demonstrate knowledge of primary sources and the linguistic skill to translate local knowledge into ethnography is apparent, for instance, in Raymond Firth's first monograph, *Primitive Economics of the New Zealand Maori* (1929). Standing on shifting epistemological ground, the library as a locus of knowledge creation was brought into question, the armchair as a seat of authorial authentication made a little less secure. Nevertheless, Firth did draw extensively upon secondary sources, and despite her assertions to the contrary, so did Makereti. For example, the following paragraph by Elsdon Best, cited by Firth (1929: 332), also appears in Makereti's notes drafted under the topic of 'Property':

> There is but little to say with regard to personal property among the Maori folk, for the individual possessed little that came under that head. He had his few garments, his few weapons, his hut, some tools, with certain fishing and snaring gear, and little else save his share of cultivated crops. Cooking utensils were unknown, house furniture did not exist. If he hewed out a canoe, why, then, any member of the family group considered that he had a right to use it. (Best 1924: 394)

In Makereti's notes the paragraph reappears almost word for word, without reference or citation, with only some minor – but I suggest deliberate – modifications.

Disparaging terms such as 'folk' and 'huts' are amended, replaced with the more equivocal 'people' and 'houses'. The description of personal possessions is made more complex through the addition of further items (ornaments, fishing and snaring gear) and the omission of commentary pointing to an absence of others (cooking utensils and house furniture):

> There is really very little to say about the personal property among the Maori people, for the individual possessed little that comes under that head. He had his few garments, ornaments, weapons, his house, with certain gear for fishing and snaring, and little else except his share of cultivated crops. If he had hewed a canoe then any member of the family group considered that he had a right to use it. (MC Box 4, Section T)

In addition to prevailing disciplinary theory and ethnographic source material, Makereti's scholarship was shaped, to a degree, by the teachers involved in her instruction and supervision. Influencing her thinking were questions posed by her supervisor, Assistant Curator T.K. Penniman, especially with regard to systems of social organization (see Figure 6.8). Makereti's diligent answers reveal a depth of kinship knowledge and, at times, a sense of exasperation as she notes the difficulty of finding enough relatives to illustrate a representative model of village kinship relations (MC Box 1, Section B). Penniman's focus on this topic resonates with a shift in emphasis away from a systematic study of material culture in evolutionary anthropology towards a sociologically framed structural functionalism – anthropology in its modern social scientific reincarnation, with kinship and lineage systems as the intellectual model and heuristic tool par excellence for understanding societies. Yet Makereti's responses at times literally overflow the ordered structure of Penniman's typescript, departing from his immediate line of questioning to convey a broader feeling of relatedness between descent lines known as *whanaungatanga* (see Figures 6.9 and 6.10).

A mutual influence upon Penniman's academic practice is evident in his concern to remove aspects of Makereti's text before publication. Makereti had been suffering from debilitating muscular rheumatism during her time as a student, which perhaps explains Penniman's involvement in compiling the typescript of her thesis manuscript. Bedridden, Makereti checked and annotated the typescript, adding further details and amendments to what would turn out to be her final draft. In 1930, just weeks before her thesis was due for examination, Makereti died suddenly and unexpectedly from a lung haemorrage and was buried at St Andrew's Church in her parish of Oddington, Oxfordshire. Penniman's efforts to publish Makereti's work in accordance with her wishes following her tragic and untimely death are ardent. Poignantly, on a piece of notepaper tucked into a small envelope, he wrote, 'four hours before she died, Makereti sent for me and asked me to delete the karakia [sacred, potentially dangerous and often restricted invocations] from this page, &c.' He impressed the importance of these amendments upon the typist,

Locating Authorship: Creativity and Borrowing

> Brothers and sisters. 3
>
> Please look at the list which I marked 2d cousins. Would you use any different words for
>
> > father's father's elder brother's older son's daughter and father's father's elder brother's younger son's daughter?
>
> *If I were speaking of my father's to elder brother's older son's daughter would be my tuakana as all his children & all the children of his brothers & sisters.*
>
> You say that a husband's brother is <u>Taokete</u> or <u>Autane</u>. If he were an elder brother of your husband, would <u>you</u> say Tuakana tane, or Taina tane if he were your husband's younger brother? *Yes*
> Would you say tungane? *not unless we were related as cousins*
> You speak of your husband's sister as <u>Taokete</u> or ~~Autane~~. If she were an elder sister of your husband, would you use tuakana or taina of her? *No. I would only say taken taokete (my sister in law) only a man can use the term Auvahine for his sister-in-law just as I can use the term for my brother-in-law as well as taokete.*
> In speaking of your husband's first and second cousins who are related to you only by marriage, do you use the words tuakana or taina or tungane? In your list you appear to sometimes, but not always. If this is too difficult, leave it until I come.
>
> *They really are my pakiwaha, or I should speak of the first cousins, as nga tuakana or nga taina o taku tane. (pakiwaha - connected by marriage)*
>
> Do you use (supposing that you are a man) the terms tuakana or taina or tuahine for your wife's brothers, sisters, first cousins, second cousins? You appear to sometimes, but not always. If this is too difficult, leave it until I come.

I should like to explain 2nd Cousins. Take as an instance

Te Pahau = Makeha

Katerina and Makereta were 1st Cousins.
Te Rangi

Nari Hurihia Paora Rakera Peate Ngaroto
Parerautuku Kiri Shipera Riki Makereti
Te Urereini Ana Apikaira Te Aomui

Katerina would refer to the children of Makereta as aku tamariki my children just as Makereta would use the same term for Katerina's children. Te Rangi would call Rakera & Peate Ngaroto his tuahine, or taina & Rakera & Te Ngaroto would call Te Rangi their tungane, or use the term tuakana & all his children Nari, Hurihia, Paora they would call their tamariki (children) — Nari, Hurihia & Paora would be tuakana to Shipera & Riki and to Makereti, but Paora would be tungane to them all I mean to Nari, Hurihia ~~Shipera~~ Shipera Riki & Makereti.

Figure 6.8 Questions set by T.K. Penniman with Makereti's handwritten responses. Makereti Collection, Box 1, Section C, © Pitt Rivers Museum, University of Oxford

Elizabeth Cory-Pearce

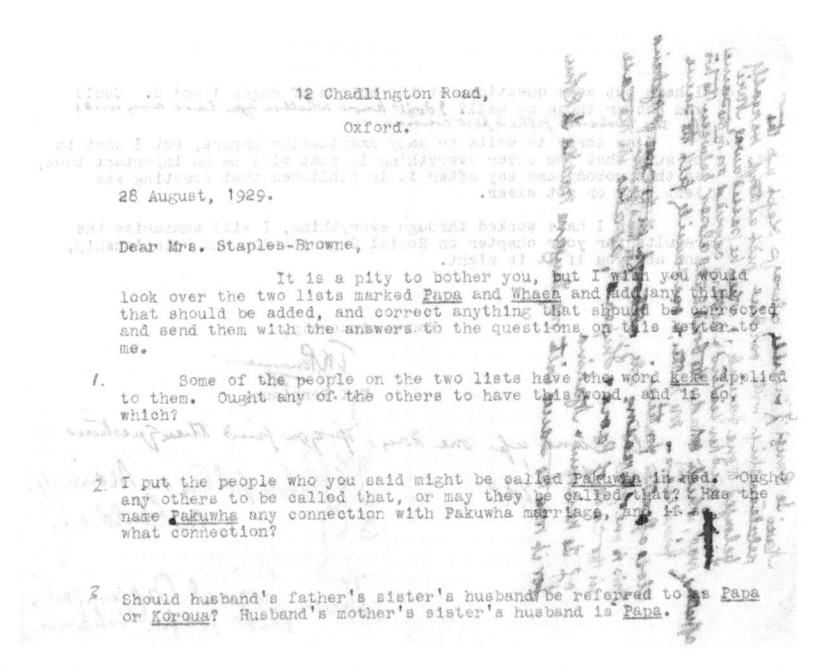

> 12 Chadlington Road,
> Oxford.
>
> 28 August, 1929.
>
> Dear Mrs. Staples-Browne,
>
> It is a pity to bother you, but I wish you would look over the two lists marked Papa and Whaea and add any think that should be added, and correct anything that should be corrected and send them with the answers to the questions on this letter to me.
>
> 1. Some of the people on the two lists have the word Keke applied to them. Ought any of the others to have this word, and if so, which?
>
> 2. I put the people who you said might be called Pakuwha in red. Ought any others to be called that, or may they be called that? Has the name Pakuwha any connection with Pakuwha marriage, and if so, what connection?
>
> 3. Should husband's father's sister's husband be referred to as Papa or Koroua? Husband's mother's sister's husband is Papa.

Figure 6.9 Letter from T.K. Penniman to Mrs Staples-Browne (Makereti), Oxford, 1929. Makereti Collection, Box 1, Section C, © Pitt Rivers Museum, University of Oxford

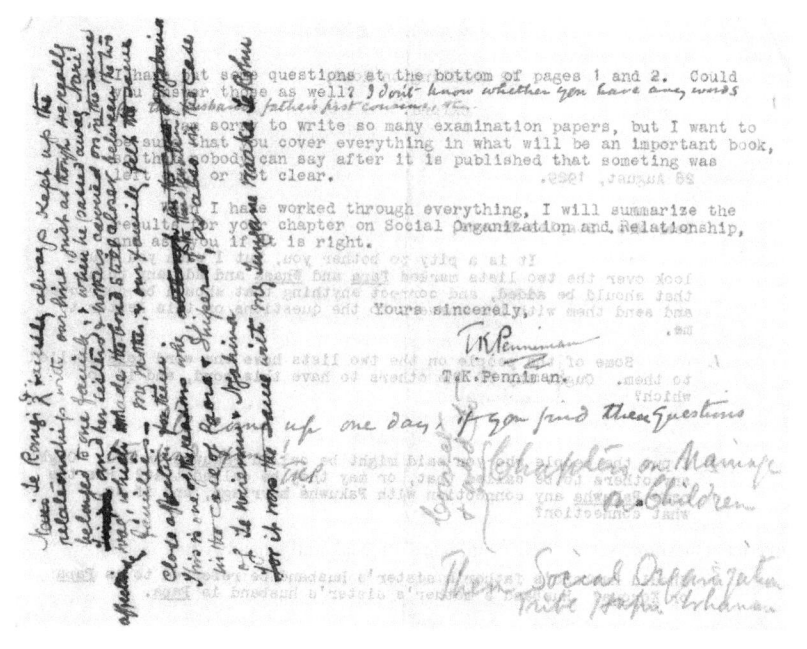

> I have put some questions at the bottom of pages 1 and 2. Could you answer those as well? I don't know whether you have any words for husband's father's first cousins, &c.
>
> I am sorry to write so many examination papers, but I want to be sure that you cover everything in what will be an important book, so that nobody can say after it is published that something was left out or not clear.
>
> When I have worked through everything, I will summarize the results for your chapter on Social Organization and Relationship, and ask you if it is right.
>
> Yours sincerely,
>
> T.K.Penniman.
> T.K. Penniman.

Figure 6.10 Makereti's response overwritten on the reverse side of the letter from T.K. Penniman, Oxford, 1929. Makereti Collection, Box 1, Section C, © Pitt Rivers Museum, University of Oxford

inscribing the typescript with red-inked and heavily underlined instructions that command attention: 'as I promised Makereta the night before she died... Not to be Published' (MC Box 1, Section A).

With these amendments in place, Penniman then consulted her relatives at Whakarewarewa, sending the typescript to them via her son, Te Aonui (William Dennan), along with a letter describing Makereti's ambition to 'publish the story of her people for future generations, to remind them of their heritage, and to make them proud of it' (MC Box 1, Section B). Three years later, he wrote again with some urgency, impressing a final deadline upon her relatives to respond, and reiterating Makereti's wish 'that those of the Arawa people who knew about the old Maori life should read the manuscript and correct it before it was published', adding that 'those of us who loved her and admired the Maori people are anxious that her work should be published without any mistakes' (MC Box 5, Section X). Finally, in 1938, Makereti's ethnography was published as *The Old Time Maori*, dedicated to the memory of Makereti's adoptive parents and first teachers, Marara Marotaua and Maihi Te Kakau Paraoa, and to all her old people.

Locating Authorship

Attention was drawn to Makereti's writing half a century later, by academic and Arawa descendant, Ngahuia Te Awekotuku, who republished *The Old Time Maori* with a New Zealand publisher in 1986. Significantly, this made Makereti's ethnography more widely available to descendants and others. A reappraisal prefaces this valuable new edition, in which Te Awekotuku highlights the significance of the work as an account of Arawa Maori customs from the point of view of a woman, covering important aspects of personal and social life, including menstruation, marriage, child-rearing, food and family relationships, that had been either ignored or treated superficially by male ethnographers (Awekotuku 1986). The republication of Makereti's ethnography, and related publications by Te Awekotuku, stimulated wider interest in Makereti's life and career amongst both academic and public audiences. Significantly, these works appeared in a decade that saw a profusion of interest in areas of museum representation and cultural ownership, in which Maori elders and scholars came to play key roles in both the orchestration of exhibitions, such as 'Te Maori' which toured the United States and New Zealand in 1984–87, and in scholarly debate.

Subsequently, Hooper-Greenhill has categorized Makereti's scholarship as a form of 'autoethnography' – ethnography 'in which colonized subjects undertake to represent themselves in ways which engage with the colonizer's own terms' (Hooper-Greenhill 2000: 86, after Pratt 1992: 7) – and also as a 'counter-ethnography', a form of 'writing back' in response to 'colonial writers

[who] observed and judged from positions of ignorance and misunderstanding' (Hooper-Greenhill: 95, after Ashcroft et al. 1995: 8). Adopting an oppositional tone, and drawing primarily on secondary sources (Awekotuku 1986, 1991), Hooper-Greenhill re-presents Makereti's scholarship as an indigenous perspective (Hooper-Greenhill 2000: 98), a 'seamless whole' positioned to 'strike against ... colonial perspectives' (ibid.: 99). However, Makereti's scholarship overlaps far too considerably, it seems to me, with a Malinowskian, positive evaluation of an anthropology that 'begins at home' for her practice to be characterized as 'counter'. On the contrary, her claim to write 'autoethnographically' is precisely what, I suggest, explains the interest and support she received from Penniman and others at Oxford. What validated her authority to write ethnography was her capacity to present 'Maori life as it appears to a Maori, rather than to an outsider' (Penniman 1938: 24).

To highlight Makereti's subaltern marginalization from Western academia as a native colonial subject and woman fails to engage with, and consequently underplays, the notable encouragement she received at the time. Furthermore, not only have recent accounts of her scholarship been overly focused on the subaltern identity of the author and the indigenousness of her knowledge, they also offer surprisingly little analysis of how Makereti's ethnography was created and what was written. What might an anthropological approach to studies of museums, archives and cultural creativity offer instead? Much may be gained by reading the archive against the grain, scrutinizing it for peculiar or intriguing presences, absences or idiosyncrasies, that may be clues to an alternative hypothesis. Given Makereti's rewriting (quite literally) of aspects of Best's authorship in her notes on the topic of property,[4] this suggests not a 'seamless' indigenous perspective positioned against 'colonial' ones, but something more complexly ravelled.

Of course, the use of another author's publication without citation or reference is highly problematic within Western academia – a system that defines and legislates knowledge as the property of persons based on the work of their individual creative genius. Reproduction without acknowledgement would constitute a transgression of proprietorship – an act of borrowing or copying that is understood negatively as plagiarism or theft of intellectual property. It is exciting to discover something so unexpected, so potentially controversial in the archive. However, my intention is not to orchestrate an exposé but rather to unpack the concepts used to evaluate knowledge-making in this period. If, in the writing of an ethnographic monograph, originality or uniqueness guaranteed intellectual proprietorship, which in turn confirmed one's authority on the subject matter, what constitutes originality or uniqueness and what might such a claim facilitate? In an anthropology that begins at home, where the topic is not 'original' but has been written on before, uniqueness might be constituted slightly differently, in the value, as a proofreader inscribed on the manuscript, of

'Maori writing as Maori', in the ethnographer's ideal of having 'lived the life' (MC Box 4, Section P).

As a modern social science, anthropology sought social knowledge from its originary source, the native person. Like an archaeological artefact retrieved from deep in the earth, this source is invested with transformative power. Things retrieved from it become invested with an aura of authenticity, one that is validated by distance. The more distant a source – whether the depth of an artefact underground, the antiquity of an object in a collection or the cultural exoticness of a native elder – the greater its worth as evidence (of other times, other cultures). Locating Best's authorship within Makereti's notes would thus be to stumble upon an idiosyncrasy. But what if we treat it as a clue to an alternative inquiry? Why might Makereti transplant aspects of Best's authorship into her notes in this way? Gaps or anomalies in the knowledge of one's culture (which are to be expected) might, in the sense of the modern presumption that epistemological totality was possible, bring the authority of the author as 'originary source' into question. Filling gaps in one's knowledge from other sources to forge a 'complete' picture might be a way of meeting this unrealistic ideal.

But does this interpretation accord too much influence to Western scholarly assumptions? What if, as Ucko[5] asks, borrowing is not necessarily anathema to knowledge production? What of culturally or historically contingent epistemologies in which copying is an acceptable, even crucial mode of practice? Reproducing knowledge would not be something dubious, but something highly regarded – the expertise of skilled practitioners. Maori conceptions of the person as a mouthpiece or vessel through which *tupuna* (ancestors) can be present, speak and act (as for example during ceremonial oratory and performance) are highly relevant here. This notion of a vessel or mouthpiece extends to things such as the carved *poupou* (wooden slabs) on meeting-house exteriors and interiors that not only depict ancestors but also physically mediate their presence in this world, as it does to paintings and photographs of ancestors hung on meeting-house walls. My argument is that it is possible to extend this notion to encompass texts.

Extending these ideas to texts complicates the location of authorship:[6] perhaps Makereti experienced Best's authorship similarly, understanding him not as 'author-creator' but as 'author-vessel', conveying the presence of the Maori elders from whom he derived his ethnological knowledge. Acknowledging a more phenomenological and less discursive encounter with texts as conduits displaces Best's authorship in what Gell (1998) might term an 'abduction of agency', in this instance from author to subject. Thus, Makereti's borrowing becomes not an act of plagiarism but a performance of relationship, an abduction that recognizes and retrieves the layers of utterances and correspondences from informant to anthropologist that sediment, often unacknowledged, into the monograph of the author.

Conclusions

This chapter has argued for an understanding of written text as a material mode for transmitting a flow of ancestral intellect. Today many Maori people talk of colonial texts as *taonga* (cherished heirloom-like valuables), as they do of photographs and paintings, and of a broad range of forms that preserve the presence and skills of forebears, from woven cloaks to colonial archives. Some describe this presence as *mana*, a metaphysical ancestral force and influence, surrounded by a protective and potentially dangerous *tapu* or sanctity, and such things, particularly the older they are, are revered accordingly. Indeed Makereti's concern to remove certain *karakia* (sacred potentially harmful chants), and to consult with her people on the advisability of publishing others, suggests that she may also have understood that the *mana* and *tapu* of ancestral *karakia* might be transferred into the materiality of texts. More significant than the idea of immediate authorship is the conception of material forms as flows or portals that connect the living to ancestors, their skills and knowledge. Whether that flow has been mediated through forms that were authored by other parties is deemed irrelevant in order to sustain rather than truncate an interpersonal flow, thus establishing an ideal of an unbroken ancestral continuity.

The notion of vesselhood appears in current discussions concerning the proper care of museum collections as repositories of the ancestral past, as does the concept of *kaitiakitanga*, or guardianship, in which people are guardians, responsible in their lifetime for maintaining and passing on valuables (objects or knowledge) from generation to generation. These notions valorize continuity at the expense of individual ingenuity. Current globally dominant discourses of intellectual property, by contrast, valorize discontinuity, so that something constituted through a complex layering of the creative work of peoples across space and time can be claimed as a product of one's own, supposedly individual and unique creativity (see Strathern 1996; Leach, this volume, Chapter 5). One approach denies rupture when discontinuity – or at least the intervention of an intermediary – may be evident. The other exaggerates rupture when degrees of overlap, continuity and borrowing are evident. Thus each misrepresents creative processes in order to approximate a social ideal: one claims knowledge as a right by articulating a continuous flow, the other by truncating a flow of interpersonal relations.

Continuous connection is typically articulated as ancestral or genealogical relationship, something akin to a hereditary right through which knowledge, like an heirloom, is received. Such a claim was articulated in Makereti's first publication, *Maggie's Guide to the Hot Lakes*. The book contains her genealogy, connecting her to an originary source and authenticating her account, not as a generic 'native outlook' (Malinowski 1938: xi), but through a specific descent line. As such, Makereti's writing does not so much 'strike against … colonial perspectives' (cf. Hooper-Greenhill 2000: 99; Awekotuku 1986) as articulate a claim to ethnological records of Maori knowledge and scholarship from within, possibly as a means to restore a continuous relationship with ancestral creativity.

From the earliest stages of European contact, Maori, and Pacific peoples more generally, have both emulated European modes of representation and, in the process, creatively refashioned them. Anthropologists interested in material and visual culture in the Pacific and elsewhere have documented the wide range of creative, interactively fashioned forms emergent from cross-cultural encounters. In this chapter I have been concerned to draw attention to another, less visually arresting, but no less significant contiguity: the intercultural creativity of ethnographic writing in an anthropology that begins at home. I have located this creative interaction in the first half of the twentieth century, when disciplinary interests in anthropology as a 'modern social science' (Malinowski 1938: vii), that adopted an 'ethnographic fieldwork method' to elucidate 'the native outlook' (ibid.: xi), overlapped with increasing local concern to record and preserve a pre-contact past for future generations, in response to the experience of rapid change brought about through colonialism, industrialization and a shift to a monetary economy. Rather than reading Makereti's scholarship within a generalized post-colonial critique that signposts indigenous resistance to colonizing representations, I have aimed to engage more fully with the complexity and contentiousness of intercultural encounters, and the often remarkable and innovative works to emerge from them.

Acknowledgements

My thinking on this subject is not entirely original. I am indebted to the late Huhana Mihinui (Guide Bubbles), and to June Northcroft Grant and Jim Te Aonui Dennan for sharing family collections and recollections with me. I thank Jeremy Coote for bringing important references and critical points to my attention. The opinions expressed here, however, are my own. Research was funded by an ESRC doctoral studentship and the RAI/Sutasoma Award (2005).

Notes

1. c. 1926, Makereti Collection (hereafter MC), Pitt Rivers Museum, University of Oxford, Box 4, Section T.
2. MC Box 9, News-Cuttings Album (Red Leather Volume).

3. Letter from Margaret Staples-Brown (Makereti) to Captain T.E. Donne, 1 May 1924. 'T.E. Donne Loose File', Alexander Turnbull Library, Wellington.
4. The extent of Makereti's use of Elsdon Best's work would require a careful comparative reading of both texts, which is beyond the scope of this chapter.
5. In his RAI Huxley Memorial Lecture, 'Forms as Never Were in Nature: Forging Authenticity', 7 December 2005, University College London.
6. My use of the term authorship is intended to evoke its multiple meanings, referring to a creator or originator of forms not necessarily literary.

References

Ashcroft, B., Griffiths, G. and Tiffin, H. (eds) (1995), *The Post-colonial Studies Reader*, London: Routledge.
Awekotuku, N. Te (1986), 'Introduction – Makereti: Guide Maggie Papakura', in Makereti, *The Old Time Maori*, Auckland: New Women's Press.
—— (1991), *Mana Wahine Maori: Selected Writings on Maori Women's Art, Culture and Politics*, Auckland: New Women's Press.
Best, E. (1924), *The Maori* (Vol. 1), Wellington: Polynesian Society.
Buchli, V. (2002), 'Introduction', in V. Buchli (ed), *The Material Culture Reader*, Oxford: Berg.
Chapman, W.R. (1985), 'Arranging ethnology: A.H.L.F. Pitt-Rivers and the typological tradition', in G.W. Stocking Jr (ed), *Objects and Others: Essays on Museums and Material Culture*, Madison: University of Wisconsin Press.
Coombe, R. (1998), *The Cultural Life of Intellectual Properties: Authorship, Appropriation and the Law*, Durham, NC: Duke University Press.
Coombes, A.E. (1994), *Reinventing Africa: Museums, Material Culture and Popular Imagination in Late Victorian and Edwardian England*, New Haven, Conn. and London: Yale University Press.
Cory-Pearce, E. (2005), 'In Touch With Things: Tourism, Arts and the Mediation of Maori/European Relationships', unpublished PhD thesis, University of London.
—— (forthcoming), 'Modernity's guises: Gifts of dress and regalia in Maori receptions to British royalty', in N. Ssorin-Chaikov (ed), *The Politics of the Gift: Empires, Diplomacies, Modernities*, Oxford: Berghahn Books.
Douglas, B. (1999), 'Art as ethnohistorical text: Indigenous presence in eighteenth and nineteenth century voyage literature', in D. Losche and N. Thomas (eds), *Double Vision: Art histories and colonial histories in the Pacific*, Cambridge: Cambridge University Press.
Firth, R. (1929), *Primitive Economics of the New Zealand Maori*, London: Routledge.

Gell, A. (1998), *Art and Agency: An Anthropological Theory*, Oxford: Clarendon Press.

Gosden, C. and Knowles, C. (2001), *Collecting Colonialism: Material Culture and Colonial Change*, Oxford: Berg.

Greenhalgh, P. (1989), 'Education, entertainment and politics: Lessons from the great international exhibitions', in P. Vergo (ed), *The New Museology*, London: Reaktion Books.

Hooper-Greenhill, E. (2000), 'Words and things: Constructing narratives, constructing the self', in *Museums and the Interpretation of Visual Culture*, London: Routledge.

Malinowski, B. (1938), 'Introduction', in J. Kenyatta, *Facing Mount Kenya: the tribal life of the Giyuku*, London: Secker & Warburg.

O'Hanlon, M. (1999), '"Mostly harmless"?: Missionaries, administrators and material culture on the coast of British New Guinea', *Journal of the Royal Anthropological Institute*, 5: 377–98.

—— and Welsch, R. (eds) (2000), *Hunting the Gatherers: Ethnographic Collectors, Agents and Agency in Melanesia, 1870–1930s*, Oxford: Berghahn Books.

Penniman, T.K. (1938), 'Makereti', in Makereti, *The Old Time Maori*, London: Gollancz.

Phillips, R. (1998), *Trading Identities: The Souvenir in Native North American Art from the Northeast, 1700–1900*, London and Seattle: University of Washington Press.

Pomian, K. (1990), 'The collection: Between the visible and the invisible', in *Collectors and Curiosities*, Oxford: Polity Press.

Pratt, M.L. (1992), *Imperial Eyes: Travel Writing and Transculturation*, London: Routledge.

Schnapp, A. (1996), *The Discovery of the Past: the Origins of Archaeology*, London: British Museum Press.

Stocking, G. (ed) (1985), *Objects and Others: Essays on Museums and Material Culture*, Madison: University of Wisconsin Press.

Strathern, M. (1988), *The Gender of the Gift*, Berkeley: University of California Press.

—— (1996), 'Cutting the network', *Journal of the Royal Anthropological Institute*, 2: 517–35.

Thomas, N. (1991), *Entangled Objects: Exchange, Material Culture and Colonialism in the Pacific*, Cambridge, Mass.: Harvard University Press.

—— (1999), 'The case of the misplaced ponchos: Speculations concerning the history of cloth in Polynesia', *Journal of Material Culture*, 4: 5–20.

–7–

Revolution as a Convention: Rebellion and Political Change in Kabylia
Judith Scheele

We were all naive. We came down from our mountains, our heads full of dreams... We were dreaming about inscribing freedom in all our acts, democracy in all hearts, justice and fraternity among all men... But while the jubilant people were celebrating their newly recovered freedom, other men, hidden in the shadows, made plans about the future... And one beautiful morning we woke up with a bitter taste in our mouth... The disaster was accomplished.

Mimmouni, Le fleuve détourné

If we want things to stay as they are, things will have to change.

Lampedusa, The Leopard

Anthropologists have long feared being accused of neglecting or even ignoring social, cultural and political change in the societies they study. Portrayals of 'timeless' societies have come to be seen – and rightly so – as morally flawed and as part of a larger political agenda, generally associated with colonialism and related evils. One recent way of avoiding such criticism has been through an emphasis on creativity, more often than not described in terms of individual agency.[1] Awareness of change, creativity and agency is crucial to analysis, and nothing could justify its absence. However, it seems to have led to the common assumption that these notions are in themselves somehow more 'accurate' than those associated with changelessness, and that they are politically and morally neutral rather than part of a larger and eminently political world view. Such an assumption is problematic, especially at a time when 'change' – often defined as brought about by the 'liberation' of individual agency and creative capacities – is being heralded as a universal goal of international politics (Hobart 1993; cf. Ho 2004).

There are two points to be made here. First, the notion of change – at least in public discourse – has come to be recognized as positive in itself and has been forcefully promoted by a long series of 'revolutionaries', often backed by international funding bodies, speaking in the name of communist or capitalist development. Political discourses of change have multiplied throughout the world, and this has happened not necessarily as a reaction to actual changes on the ground (or the lack of them, for that matter), but often as part of larger international movements. Consequently, local ideas of change might not only refer to actual changing circumstances, but also be tokens of allegiance – or resistance – to a certain model of society (cf. Herzfeld 1997: 111).

Second, since at least the 1980s, the most influential model of 'change' has been that put forward by Western liberal capitalism, which sees social and political change as essentially brought about by individual creativity and agency, often acting against the 'inertia' of society or 'tradition'. Although such a model has a long history, this history is specific to the political, economic and social development of north-western Europe and North America, whose notions of the individual and society – as summed up in the ideal both of the self-made man and of the lone political visionary, of Benjamin Franklin and Che Guevara – it necessarily reflects and furthers.[2] Without wanting to deny the ideological potency of such a model, or even its practical relevance, we need nevertheless to be aware of its limits and of its implicit moral and political implications; we also need to be aware that, due to the ideological prevalence of such a model in many places, including large parts of Europe, the notions of individual agency and creativity have themselves become conventions that mask effective continuity and a lack of local possibilities.

In the following paragraphs, I aim to show how this has happened in a recent outbreak of anti-government rebellion in Kabylia, a Berber-speaking area in north-eastern Algeria.[3] Although at first sight the rebellion seems to confirm the model of social change as brought about by individual agency and creativity outlined above – here glorified as 'revolution' brought about by individual 'heroes' – a closer look at how these categories are used locally shows that they have in themselves become conventions, widely used to legitimize the continuity and permanence of the current political system, and often also to appropriate, frustrate and repress individual energies.

The Rebellion

In April 2001, a high school student was killed inside a *gendarmerie* (paramilitary police) post in a small village in Kabylia. This event led to riots that quickly spread through the region and lasted several months (Alilat and Hadid 2002; Roberts 2002; Salhi 2002). The rioters' main grievances were the government's arbitrariness, gratuitous violence and corruption, its chronic neglect of the region and, most importantly, the *hogra*, or disrespect, of ordinary citizens displayed by state representatives. As with riots in Algeria before, the main targets of attack were police quarters, but also government buildings, party offices and travel agents.

Several weeks after the riots had first started, attempts were made by local populations to contain them and to provide the rioters with means of political expression through the constitution of local committees, labelled by some as tribal committees (*aârouch*) and by others – more commonly – as citizens' committees (*comités des citoyens*).[4] These committees, apparently inspired by the existing local village committees (*tajmaɛtin*), appointed delegates, assembled in conclaves and conducted affairs according to their own 'code of honour'. They produced a list of claims which included the demand for unemployment benefits, local development schemes, a more 'transparent' form of government, the recognition of Berber as a national language, educational reform, the end of corruption, bringing before an international court of justice those members of the security forces who had opened fire on the demonstrators, and the individual recognition of the victims of the riots as national martyrs (*shuhadâ'*), a term borrowed from the Algerian war of independence against France (CADC 2001a). The riots themselves were saturated with symbols borrowed from the national struggle for independence, the French Resistance movement during the Second World War and the Palestinian intifada, as seen on television.

The riots and the political organization to which they gave rise were interpreted in various ways by national and international observers: as a resurgence of 'tradition' (an interpretation generally adopted by the national and international press); as yet another episode in the long struggle for the official recognition of the 'Berber identity' of Kabylia as an integral part of Algerian culture;[5] as part of a still ongoing fight for national liberation (CADC 2001b); as a quasi-separatist movement (a reading espoused by some members of the government, and by a fringe of radical Kabyles themselves); as a rebellion of an economically neglected region and of disenchanted, largely unemployed youth against a central government that has long monopolized all economic resources (Salhi 2002); or as an outburst of democratic energies in a country that had too long been ruled with an iron fist (Alilat and Hadid 2002). All these interpretations, apart from the first perhaps, agree on at least one point: the riots marked a profound social change; they constituted a small revolution, in which a government that had long become alienated from 'the people' had to adjust to popular expectations.

'The people', however, came to share a very different appreciation of the riots and of the political structures that developed in their wake. After the initial popular enthusiasm had passed, claims became common that the riots themselves had been sparked by government manipulation, in order to divide and rule Kabylia and Algeria as a whole. Those who were more careful in their accusations maintained at least that the *aârouch*, or tribal committees, had initially represented the people, but that they had then been co-opted (*récupérés*) by the *pouvoir* and were now used by the government to delegitimize and ultimately destroy the two regional parties,[6] which constituted the only serious threat to the government's power locally. The movement itself quickly claimed that it was divided into 'loyal delegates' and 'Taiwan [i.e. fake] delegates', said to be on the government's payroll.[7] Yet again, all these interpretations seemed to agree on one point: the rebellion of 2001 did not mark a radical political change, but rather the permanence of existing political strategies and categories; the riots of 2001 were just another ritual of Algerian national politics. In any case, individual agency or even social change, these interpretations seemed to suggest, were impossible in the political arena. Furthermore, the variety of models and symbols that seemed to have inspired the riots were regarded as spoofs to fool a credulous public with words and images that elsewhere rhymed with heroism, freedom, democracy, peace, wealth and justice. The rioters and their families, the *aârouch* and the *gendarmes*, had all become actors, so the argument ran, in a public drama directed by the *pouvoir*, for the benefit of the local population and an international audience.

Whom to believe? As always in the Algerian context, the wisest answer – at least for the outside observer – would probably be to say both and neither, and to try to understand how and why these varying interpretations are negotiated and played off against each other, rather than to establish their absolute truth-value. However, in this case I think the question deserves further scrutiny, as it poses more general questions about how notions of political change and individual agency, couched in terms of 'revolution' and 'heroism', are applied locally, and how they relate to larger bodies of thought and political theory within which local societies are obliged to position themselves.

Kabylia and Revolution

Algeria is a revolutionary country. The most talked-about moment in its history is the 'national revolution', the official term used for the war of independence from France (1954–62); and true 'Algerian-ness' has long been perceived to be a function of nationalist commitment, or of membership in a group known for its nationalist commitment, ideally proven by death through 'martyrdom' of one of its members in the war of independence.[8] Ever since independence, Algeria has been governed by people who derive their political legitimacy from their participation in the 'national revolution'. Its memory has been enshrined in Algerian political discourse and practices through commemoration days and parades; through the development of the administrative categories of the *mujâhidîn* (fighters in the war of independence), of the *shuhadâ'* (war dead) and of their descendants; and through the resulting transformations of language that pervade all domains of life in Algeria, public or private. It has reshaped the Algerian landscape through the construction of monumental graveyards of the war dead in all but the remotest of Algerian villages. Even in the decades after independence, the notion of 'revolution' remained central to Algerian political discourse (Stora 1994). Keeping in line with the political fashions of the time, Algeria has stumbled from the 'national revolution', via the agricultural and industrial 'revolutions' of the 1970s, to the 'democratic revolution' of the late 1980s (without, one could argue, ever experiencing much political change on the ground; cf. Roberts 2003).[9]

References to 'revolution' as a constituent feature of collective identity are even more widespread in Kabylia than elsewhere in Algeria. Kabylia is a word invented and popularized by the French after the French conquest of Algiers in 1830 (Lorcin 1995). It certainly refers to a specific geographic area in the mountains of north-eastern Algeria, but it also refers to a bundle of socio-political notions; or rather, it refers to an ideal political model, to an ethnographic utopia developed in the wake and under the influence of the French Revolution (Ageron 1968; Lucas and Vatin 1975; Lorcin 1995). In the nineteenth century alone, more than forty volumes of French ethnography were produced on the Kabyles. These were written mainly by French military officers, with a good education and a strong political vision (Frémaux 1993), who saw in Kabylia an example of everything nineteenth-century France was not, but might become if a second revolution was allowed to take place. Kabylia was described as the abode of democratic, egalitarian, honest, hard-working and secular hilltop farmers, a 'kind of savage Switzerland', according to General Daumas (1864); as the 'ideal of an independent and inexpensive government, whose secret our philosophers are still searching for through a thousand utopian projects', in the words of General Hanoteau (Hanoteau and Letourneux 1873: 1). Marx himself, as contemporary Kabyles never fail to mention, is said to have been impressed with the 'truly communist society' he encountered while he sojourned in the Kabyle mountains to treat his weak lungs. A large percentage of these nineteenth-century texts have now been re-edited, often by the grandchildren of those they aimed to describe, and are widely read among contemporary Kabyles, both in France and in Algeria.

In the decades leading up to the war of independence, many early nationalists and leading nationalist politicians were from Kabylia (Stora 1985) – not least because French education and emigration to France was initially more widespread in Kabylia than elsewhere in Algeria (Colonna 1975; Direche-Slimani 1997). During the war itself, Kabylia was subject to exceedingly brutal repression by the French army, and suffered disproportionately high losses (Bouaziz and Mahé 2004). As the war was turned into a national founding myth, the idea of the 'revolutionary Kabyles' as developed by the French, and as propagated in French primary schools in the region, merged with the image of the Kabyles as 'naturally born *mujâhidîn*', and as such became firmly rooted locally. Even today, visitors to Kabylia are received with whispered suggestion that the Kabyles had actually fought and won the war of independence all by themselves, against all odds and especially against the inertia of their fellow Algerians, but that after the war, they had been excluded from government and deprived of their just rewards by 'traitors', or 'fake revolutionaries' (cf. Bessaoud 1991). In the regionalist discourse that developed after the war of independence, first among Kabyle emigrants to France, and then also in Algeria itself, democratic aspirations, individual freedom, secularism, independence, moral propriety and heroism gradually became coterminous with 'Kabyle-ness'. In the same way, the neighbouring 'Arab' populations were described as embodying 'tyranny', 'apathy' and, increasingly, also the threat of 'Islamic fanaticism', anathema to French public opinion.[10]

During the 1990s, the image of the revolutionary and democratic Kabyle seemed to be further confirmed as Kabylia was hailed by the national and international media as the last 'democratic bastion' (Lacoste-Dujardin 1992) against political Islam that had, elsewhere in the country, won a landslide victory in the first democratic elections in Algeria.[11] Locally, this notion gained further strength due to the general feeling that a disproportionately large number of Kabyles had been singled out as victims of the violence that followed the cancellation of the elections by the military in 1991. In Kabylia, rumours were heard that the *pouvoir* had just 'invented' the *barbus* ('bearded ones', i.e. Islamists) to silence the Kabyles and their democratic aspirations once and for all. Within a political climate that was less and less conducive to compromise, the 'revolutionary' and 'democratic' discourse identified with 'Kabyle-ness' left little room for flexibility, 'political creativity' or change. It allowed for anti-Arab racism and rhetorics of Kabyle exclusivity and conservatism, and defined anybody who might question the inherently democratic nature of 'the Kabyle' as a 'traitor'. Take, for example, the following messages sent to one of the most widely consulted Kabyle websites:

Why do we want to impose our democracy at all cost, they [the 'Arabs'] don't understand it, what they want is more Islam and mosques and a bit of work *hamdullah*... (www.kabylie.com 2002)

If we succeed in liberating our region and the country, we should seriously think about the expulsion of all the Arabo-Baathists (Islamists, government, Berber-traitors) to their original country, that is to say Arabia... (ibid.)

I tell you that goats will fly in a frozen paradise the day a system based on Arabo-Islamic foundations makes any concessions to the supporters of modernity and social equality. To wed the beauty democracy, you have to disinfect her future household infested with the Arabo-Islamic pest... (ibid.)

Revolution and the Rebellion of 2001

When the rioters of 2001 took care to emphasize the 'revolutionary' nature of their movement, they were thus drawing on a long tradition that had virtually equated 'Kabyle identity' with 'revolution', as well as on well-known nationalist rhetoric and symbols. How ambiguous and potentially dangerous this might be became clear in the disagreement over political terminology that soon erupted. Should the committees that developed in the wake of the riots be labelled *aârouch* ('tribes', as suggested by the national and international press), thereby implicitly referring to the 'long democratic tradition' of the region? Or was such a reference to 'tribalism' degrading, archaic or even colonialist? The committee members themselves, resolutely 'modern', chose to call themselves *comités de citoyens* (citizens' committees, always used in French), reminiscent, intentionally or not, of nineteenth-century France, and to reject any supposed connection with the 'traditional village council' – the 'local mafia', as some described it to me.[12] The most popular revolutionary rhetoric, however, was derived not from French or 'traditional' models, but from Algerian nationalism itself: the first statements made by the committees were signed in the name of the *République Algérienne Démocratique et Populaire*; the nationalist jargon was consciously copied; national memorials and national remembrance days were used as the sites and occasions for public demonstrations, and the myth of just martyrdom in the fight for freedom and democracy was heavily drawn upon (cf. CADC 2001a, 2001b). 'What else could they have done', as a friend of mine commented retrospectively, 'all words had already been taken...'

Such family resemblances, although they might at first sight seem to be merely rhetorical, bore their own dangers. What was common to all the models cited was their rejection of 'politics' in favour of direct, grass-roots action, and the constant fear of 'traitors' – which eventually caused the movement to collapse. Resemblances with 'French' models meant that the movement could be accused of having been masterminded by the French secret services, while the emphasis on 'revolution' allowed the rebellion to be made part of national history, which in itself claimed to be but a long history of revolution. The rebellion thereby lost much of its disruptive potential. This shared symbolism also meant that, before long, the committees could be accused of having been 'co-opted' (*récupéré*) by the state itself, unless – as some maintained – they had been the state's invention right from the start. The myth of the 'stolen revolution' and the 'fake revolutionary' resurfaced, and proved as effective as ever. It left everybody with a bad taste in their mouths, agreeing that, as always, nothing had changed.

Algeria, then, presents a rather puzzling – but certainly not unique – case, where all possible political legitimacy is derived from claims to being a 'revolutionary', to the point where, as most people agree, nothing ever changes; and where the most 'revolutionary' of people, the Kabyles, attempt to back up their 'revolutionary' claims with reference to 'tradition' and to nineteenth-century colonial writings, and to their anti-colonial nationalist past that helped to bring about the very system they now claim to be fighting against – using the system's own terminology and symbols.

The New Generation of Martyrs

A similar paradox appears when analysing the role of individual agency, locally most conspicuous in collective claims to 'Berber individualism' hinted at above, and in a shared rhetoric of heroism and martyrdom. One of the central demands of the committees after the riots was the official recognition of all victims of the riots as 'martyrs' or *shuhadâ'* (sing. *shahîd*), a title which usually refers to those who died fighting the French during the war of independence. To be an officially recognized *shahîd* confers certain legal rights both on the victim and on his or her family, such as priority medical care and a pension. However, the insistence that the victims of the riots be recognized as *shuhadâ'* cannot merely be explained in terms of material rewards. As indicated above, the contemporary Algerian government still derives most of its (by now hotly contested) political legitimacy from the war of independence. Rather than the surviving *mujâhidîn*, open to accusations of corruption and abuse of power, the uncontested hero of this national discourse of legitimation is the *shahîd*: forever young, he is free of any post-independence corruption; dead, he is beyond criticism and temptation; absolved by his suffering, he alone is capable of transforming the moral ambiguities of the war into a story of untainted heroism; forever silent, his voice can be claimed by many. In Algeria, as elsewhere, only dead heroes are true heroes.

Although the *shahîd* appears as the archetypical individual hero, individual memories of his actions, his personality or name are rare. I was surprised to find that, in the village where I did my fieldwork, hardly anybody could identify individual *shuhadâ'* from the village and tell me their stories, nor would they recognize individual *shuhadâ'* in the photographs I showed them. If preserved or recounted, the photographs and stories were invariably stereotyped. The same attitude seemed to be expressed in the most common national monument in the country, the graveyards of the *shuhadâ'* mentioned above: although these monuments are composed of individual and labelled tombs (in contravention of 'traditional' funerary practices), their layout and shape are all the same, and the names on the tombs have long been erased. Thus, in practice, the public emphasis on the legacy of the individual *shuhadâ'* tends to veil rather than reveal individual agency and motives, as individual heroism, much as the 'revolution' it is supposed to have brought about, has in itself become a convention that leaves little room for individual expression of any kind.

Revolution as a Convention

A similar ambiguity could be observed in the riots of 2001. Individual victims of the riots, quickly labelled *shuhadâ'*, were venerated and remembered, and the symbolic language of martyrdom was omnipresent not only in the political demands voiced by the committees, but also in the action and language used by the rioters. In the photographs the latter took of the riots, images of young men with bare chests throwing themselves into the rifle-fire of gendarmes were common, as were images that echoed television reports on the Palestinian intifada. Photographs of this type emphasized the willingness of young men to sacrifice themselves in the fight for 'freedom', and their celebration as martyrs by the community, especially by women. Similarly, victims were buried in sites reminiscent of national war monuments (see Figures 7.1 and 7.2). Again, 'individual martyrdom' was, at least in public discourse, subsumed under purely conventional models of political action and perception. Implicitly, this emphasis on death and martyrdom suggested an eternally repeated process. In the words of one of the rioters:

> We are here; we will always be here. We won't let them sleep in peace. Even when we have fallen to the ground, a real or an imaginary bullet in our flat chest, we will get up to throw yet another stone into the face of the bad guys in Algiers and elsewhere. The future young martyrs will know what to do. Our photos will be on a poster that other

Figure 7.1 Monument to the victims of the war of independence in Ighzer Amokrane, spring 2004. Photograph by Judith Scheele

Figure 7.2 Monument to the victims of 2001, Ighzer Amokrane, spring 2004. Photograph by Judith Scheele

young people will hold up when it is their turn to go and die. This is our history, and it will not betray us. The history that our generation will write with its blood on all the roads and in front of all *gendarmerie* stations... (www.kabylie.com 2001)

Despite this emphasis on individual dead heroes in the 2001 riots, individual living heroes were rare. Where they existed, their legitimacy was hotly disputed. They were rapidly accused of merely aiming to further personal motives, of being paid by the government or of being corrupted in other ways. In any case, as a friend of mine explained: 'the people you see are never the ones that really matter, they are only pawns in a game moved by people more powerful than them. Really powerful people aren't stupid enough to risk being known by everybody.' As much as true heroes are dead, truly powerful people and their individual motives are unknown – and if they come to be known, they must be just about to lose power or have already lost it. When, during my fieldwork, a young lad was pointed out to me with the comment 'that's him, the *aârouch*!', this was clearly derogatory, and meant to show both that the *aârouch* movement was morally discredited and that it had lost its power.

Such a theory of power has pervaded local discourses. It induces locally committed people to shun the centre stage, and to describe their political commitment as never quite real, and as somehow imposed upon them. Thus, in the village where I did my fieldwork, one former and one present 'activist' described the reasons for their commitment as follows:

> When the Black Spring started, we were literally paralyzed. Kamel had been killed; it was as if a war had started; and we didn't know what to do. And then, the committee in [the region's administrative centre] asked us to send delegates. The delegates were volunteers suggested by the village. I didn't really want to do anything, but people insisted so much, that I just didn't have a choice.

> When it all started, I really felt I ought to do something. I don't like politics, I am not a political person. People knew me as somebody reliable, though, so they pushed me forward. And I was practically unemployed, which meant that I had some spare time. We held meetings in the village, then in other villages in the *commune* (district); usually, two of us would go to represent our village. We were also in charge of the good conduct of the demonstrations, we had badges and professional cards to identify ourselves.

Local accounts of 'the events' de-emphasize the role of individuals as active agents. Most of those involved stressed that the riots had somehow just happened, and that the aim of their personal involvement had been merely to contain the riots.[13] The 'rioters' themselves were generally portrayed as either provoked or manipulated by the *pouvoir*. In both cases a collective and passive role was assigned to those involved, and individual agency was denied: when speaking about one's self, for fear of being accused of corruption; when speaking about others, due to the widespread belief in the omnipotence and wickedness of the *pouvoir*.

As with notions of revolution and change, a closer look at ideas about individual agency and related local categories in the context of the events of 2001 in Kabylia thus leaves us with a paradox. Despite an overwhelming public discourse of individual heroism and martyrdom, and despite a largely personal involvement of local actors, the only individuals that are truly praised as heroes are those who have died or been maimed. In other words, they are those who have no agency at all, or at best whose agency is reduced (at least from the local point of view). Furthermore, these individual 'heroes' are subsumed under a discourse that, although praising their individuality, deprives them of their individual characteristics. Rather than bringing about political change, they are made to be part of an ongoing national history of permanent revolution. I still remember my deep embarrassment when, during the celebration of a war anniversary, as I was introduced to several youths maimed for life during the 2001 riots as our 'glorious martyrs', one of my host's friends told me with a big smile: 'You are exceptionally lucky. You are witnessing the birth of a new society.'

Conclusion

Notions of change, creativity and individual agency are crucial to anthropological understanding. This does not mean, however, that they are politically neutral, or that they do not hide implicit assumptions and moral judgements. Nor does it mean that they are necessarily closer to local realities or that they need to be treated with less caution and self-awareness than notions of permanence, continuity and the emphasis on collective historical subjects or even impersonal historic forces. In the preceding paragraphs I have tried to show how notions of change and agency, once reified and imbued with moral value, can become self-fulfilling prophecies or locally manipulated categories in much the same way as, say, 'tradition' has long been known to do (Favret 1972). In this way, a fortiori in the current political climate, 'change' might become a convention, 'individual agency' a socially imposed category, and 'creativity' a constraint. This does not mean that these notions can be ignored in analysis – rather the contrary; but it does mean, much as in the case of 'tradition', that they need to be studied not only as universals or 'objective' descriptions of events, but also as part of local discourses understood in their relationship both to local practices and to international rhetoric.

Notes

1. See, for example, the collection of essays in Liep (2001), where, although 'creativity' is sometimes defined as a social process, all examples cited speak of creativity as exercised by the individual against or in modification of the norms of society.
2. For a more detailed analysis of the 'family resemblance' of socialism, conservatism and liberalism, see Wallerstein (1995).
3. Kabylia is an area that has long been central to French anthropology, from the first works of French ethnography that were written there in the nineteenth century (such as Carette 1848; Hanoteau and Letourneux 1873; Masqueray 1983 [1886]) to Bourdieu's well-known works on the area (Bourdieu 1965, 1972, 1980). For an overview of the available literature on the area, see Mahé (2001).
4. Much of the more recent political terminology commonly used in debates and conversation in Kabylia is borrowed or derived from French, such as the term *comités des citoyens* used here. The term *aârouch* is a Gallicized version of

a Kabyle word (with an Arabic root) meaning tribe, which has, in its French version and spelling, come to mean 'tribal committees (set up in 2001)', and is, in local usage, clearly distinguished from the Kabyle word *εrc* (tribe). Political terminology and spelling follows local usage throughout the chapter.

5. A political movement demanding the official recognition of the various Algerian Berber languages and the 'Berber component' of Algerian history and national identity had started to emerge among Kabyle emigrants in France from the 1960s onwards (Direche-Slimani 1997). It became popular throughout Kabylia in the late 1970s and especially from 1980 onwards, often providing an outlet for the growing frustration with the central government (see Chaker 1999; Guenoun 1999).

6. The *Front des Forces Socialistes* (FFS) and the *Rassemblement pour la Culture et la Démocratie* (RCD). Although both declare themselves to be national parties, they recruit most of their members and votes in Kabylia, and, until the events of 2001, enjoyed a certain political legitimacy unknown to any other party – apart from the FLN, the ruling party, itself – in the area.

7. The label 'Taiwan', for everything that purported to be genuine but was not, is derived from cheap and often faulty products produced in Taiwan and disguised as European or Japanese products.

8. Conversely, the *harkis*, or 'collaborators' with the French during the war of independence, had forfeited any right to an Algerian passport, and they and their children were barred from visiting the country until the late 1980s.

9. Even the government's most serious opposition, the Islamists, couched their political programme in terms of a 'second revolution' that would finally fulfil the true aims of the 'first revolution' (the war of independence) (cf. Al-Ahnaf, Botiveau, and Frégosi 1991).

10. Such a reading flourished partly because it coincided with notions both of 'revolution' and of Algerian and world politics held by the French left at that time (cf. Eisenhans 1995; Malley 1996; Le Sueur 2001).

11. Although nationwide the *Front Islamique du Salut* (FIS, Algeria's most successful Islamist party) won 55 per cent of the regional seats in 1990, and 47.27 per cent of total votes in the first round of general elections in 1991 (Martinez 1998), their success was minimal in Kabylia, where, in many cases, they had not even presented a candidate.

12. This was not the case everywhere in Kabylia, where the relationship between the *aârouch* and the village elders was often more complex.

13. Such statements are certainly also due to prudence and fear of the omnipresent secret services. However, I think there is more involved than this, as the same people have shown a total lack of prudence in my presence on other, similarly political and potentially dangerous occasions.

References

Ageron, C.-R. (1968), *Les algériens musulmans et la France (1871–1919)*, Paris: Presses universitaires de France.
Aggoun, L. and Rivoire, J.-B. (2004), *La Françalgérie. Crimes et mensonges d'Etats*, Paris: La Découverte.
Al-Ahnaf, M., Botiveau, B. and Frégosi, F. (1991), *L'Algérie par ses islamistes*, Paris: Karthala.
Alilat, F. and Hadid, S. (2002), *Vous ne pouvez pas nous tuer, nous sommes déjà morts. L'Algérie embrasée*, Paris: Editions n°1.
Bessaoud, M.-A. (1991), *Heureux les martyrs qui n'ont rien vu. La vérité sur la mort du Colonel Amirouche et de Abbane Ramdane*, Paris: Editions Berbères.
Bouaziz, M. and Mahé, A. (2004), 'La Grande Kabylie durant la guerre d'Indépendance algérienne', in M. Harbi and B. Stora (eds), *La guerre d'Algérie: 1954–2004. La fin de l'amnésie*, Paris: Robert Laffont.
Bourdieu, P. (1965), 'The sentiment of honour in Kabyle society', in J.G. Peristiany (ed), *Honour and Shame*, London: Weidenfeld and Nicolson.
—— (1972), *Esquisse d'une théorie de la pratique*, Geneva: Droz.
—— (1980), *Le sens pratique*, Paris: Editions de Minuit.
CADC (Coordination des Aarch, Douars et Communes) (2001a), *Plate-forme de revendications. Réunion inter-wilaya du 11/06/2001*, El-Kseur: http://membres.lycos.fr/archs/
—— (2001b), *1956–2001: Le combat continue*, Ifri Ouzellagen: CADC-website.
Carette, A.-E.-H. (1848), *Etudes sur la Kabilie proprement dite*, Paris: Imprimerie nationale.
Chaker, S. (1999), *Berbères aujourd'hui, Berbères dans le Maghreb contemporain*, Paris: L'Harmattan.
Colonna, F. (1975), *Instituteurs algériens*, Paris: Presses des Sciences Po.
Daumas, E. (1864), *Mœurs et coutumes de l'Algérie: Tell, Kabylie, Sahara*, Paris: Hachette.
Direche-Slimani, K. (1997), *Histoire de l'émigration kabyle en France au XXe siècle*, Paris: L'Harmattan.
Eisenhans, H. (1995), 'Du malentendu à l'échec? Guerre d'Algérie et tiers-mondialisme français entre ajustement capitaliste et engagement libéro-socialdémocrate', *Maghreb Review*, 20: 38–62.
Favret, J. (1972), 'Traditionalism through ultra-modernity', in E. Gellner and C. Micaud (eds), *Arabs and Berbers: From Tribe to Nation in North Africa*, London: Duckworth.
Frémeaux, J. (1993), *Les bureaux arabes dans l'Algérie de la conquête*, Paris: Denoël.

Guenoun, A. (1999), *Chronologie du mouvement berbère. Un combat et des hommes*, Alger: Casbah Editions.
Hanoteau, A. and Letourneux, A. (1873), *La Kabylie et les coutumes kabyles*, Paris: Challamel.
Herzfeld, M. (1997), *Cultural Intimacy: Social Poetics in the Nation-state*, London: Routledge.
Ho, E. (2004), 'Empire through diasporic eyes: a view from the other boat', *Comparative Studies in Society and History*, 46(2): 210–46.
Hobart, M. (1993), 'Introduction: the growth of ignorance ?', in M. Hobart (ed), *An Anthropological Critique of Development*, London: Routledge.
Lacoste-Dujardin, C. (1992), 'Démocratie kabyle. Les Kabyles: une chance pour la démocratie algérienne?', *Hérodote*, 65–6: 63–74.
Lampedusa, G.T. di (1991), *The Leopard*, London: Everyman's Library.
Le Sueur, J. (2001), 'Decolonising "French Universalism": reconsidering the impact of the Algerian War on French intellectuals', in J. Clancy-Smith (ed), *North Africa, Islam and the Mediterranean World*, London: Frank Cass.
Liep, J. (ed) (2001), *Locating Cultural Creativity*, London: Pluto Press.
Lorcin, P. (1995), *Imperial Identities: Stereotyping, Prejudice and Race in Colonial Algeria*, London: Tauris.
Lucas, P. and Vatin, J.-C. (1975), *L'Algérie des anthropologues*, Paris: Maspero.
Mahé, A. (2001), *Histoire de la Grande Kabylie XIXe–XXe siècles*, Paris: Bouchène.
Malley, R. (1996), *The Call from Algeria: Third Worldism, Revolution and the Turn to Islam*, Berkeley: University of California Press.
Martinez, L. (1998), *La guerre civile en Algérie*, Paris: Karthala.
Masqueray, E. (1983 [1886]), *Formation des cités chez les populations sédentaires de l'Algérie : Kabyles du Djurdjura, Chaouïa de l'Aourâs, Beni Mezâb*, Aix-en-Provence: Edisud.
Mimmouni, R. (1982), *Le fleuve détourné*, Paris: Robert Laffont.
Roberts, H. (2002), *Moral Economy or Moral Polity? The Political Anthropology of Algerian Riots*, London: LSE Working Papers.
—— (2003), *The Battlefield Algeria 1988–2002*, London: Verso.
Salhi, M.B. (2002), 'Le local en contestation: citoyenneté en construction. Le cas de la Kabylie', *Insaniyât* 16: 55–97.
Stora, B. (1985), *Dictionnaire biographique des militants nationalistes algériens. ENA – PPA – MTLD, 1926–1954*, Paris: L'Harmattan.
—— (1994), *Histoire de l'Algérie depuis l'indépendance*, Paris: La Découverte.
Wallerstein, I. (1995), *After Liberalism*, New York: The New Press.

–8–

'You knit me together in my mother's womb': English Baptists and Assisted Procreation

Jeanette Edwards

> For you created my inmost being; you knit me together in my mother's womb. I praise you because I am fearfully and wonderfully made; your works are wonderful, I know that full well. My frame was not hidden from you when I was made in the secret place. When I was woven together in the depths of the earth, your eyes saw my unformed body.
>
> <div align="right">Psalm 139, <i>New International Bible</i></div>

Religion and New Reproductive Technologies

In an intriguing study of clinical fertility services in Israel, Susan Kahn (2000) unpacks the relationship between the politics of nation-state formation, religion and new reproductive technologies (NRT). In Israel, technologies of assisted conception are widely and freely available until the birth of two live children. Kahn focuses, among other things, on the dilemmas and deliberations of Israeli rabbis who had to decide what was and was not possible under Jewish religious law. They reached some interesting and pragmatic solutions. Thus, for example, they decreed that Jewish women *may* use donated sperm, but, because of the Halakha prohibition on masturbation and the adulterous connotations of using semen from a Jewish man to inseminate a Jewish woman who is not his wife, it should ideally come from non-Jewish men. Of interest here is the way in which religious spokespersons make sense of new possibilities emerging from NRT and how they can not only accommodate those possibilities, but also enlist them into pre-existing religious understandings. My ethnographic example is from the north of England, and I am interested in how Baptist ministers draw on what they know about kinship and the origins of persons to explore novel interventions in human conception.

Chapel Country

Three towns, together with their satellite villages, make up a region in the northwest of England referred to locally as 'The Valley'.[1] The population grew with the development of the textile industry and shrank with its decline. Local historians describe the region as 'the cradle of the industrial revolution'. They also refer to it fondly and ironically as 'chapel country', with a nod to the continuing significance of nonconformist religion in the region which grew during the nineteenth century when chapels were built alongside mills and public houses.[2]

There are ten Baptist churches in The Valley, only six of which have a full-time dedicated minister. I was told that with a population of about 70,000, the Valley has the highest number of Baptist churches per capita in Britain. In 2000, while carrying out fieldwork in Alltown, I was given the opportunity of meeting and talking with the six Valley Baptist ministers about NRT.[3] This chapter draws on my recorded conversations with them and on my participation in informal Bible classes and a local Baptist men's group. I did not set out systematically to research religion (Baptist or otherwise) and NRT, and consequently this is a preliminary discussion that draws on limited ethnographic data. Nevertheless, of interest here is the way in which the Baptists with whom I spoke explore novel and innovative techniques of human conception through ancient texts and autobiographical detail. They draw on both the Bible ('the word') and their own intimate experiences of kinship to imagine the social and ethical consequences or implications of particular scientific or medical practices.

Six Baptist Ministers

The Valley ministers are all men and married with children: four are in their mid-forties, one in his late-fifties and one in his mid-thirties. They each told me about their previous jobs and careers before they trained to be ministers.[4] I have written elsewhere of how people with no vested interest in NRT draw on their own personal experiences, particularly of kinship and intimate relationships, to explore biotechnological intervention in human reproduction (e.g. Edwards 1999, 2000; Edwards and Strathern 2000). Baptist ministers are no exception. In thinking about the possibilities and limitations of NRT, they told me of what they know personally about the making and breaking of intimate family relationships. Mr Young dwells on his unhappy experience as a child, brought up by a stepmother who disliked him intensely and a father who did not notice. Mr Jones talks of his divorce and reflects on the different kinds of connection he feels with his children who live with their mother and his stepchildren who live with him. Mr Unwin muses on the relationship between his granddaughter (whom he and his wife are 'bringing up') and her father, who absented himself before she was born. Selected and considered autobiographical details illustrate and formulate ministers' views on NRT.

'Preaching with a peep'

'The Baptist church' is imagined by the ministers as a network of autonomous churches loosely linked in a Union. This model is envisaged in contradistinction to other religions that are said to have an overarching and hierarchical authority in terms of both doctrine and administration (see Cross 2000). The Valley ministers all emphasize the fact that the minister of a local church is chosen by its congregation. They talk of the matches that are made between church and minister, and of the autonomy of the church in its choice of minister. Mr Unwin describes it this way:

> ...churches opt into a system whereby names are sent to them with profiles – perhaps five or six – when they're looking for a minister. The deacons look through and they suss out who they think might be suitable. They recommend to the church that they invite that person and then that person goes and we have the famous phrase 'preaching with a view' – with a view to being appointed. We also have a phrase 'preaching with a peep' which means they invite somebody to preach as a kind of a pre-preach, if you know what I mean, because it's their choice, so they want to be sure.

In emphasizing the autonomy of a church in choosing its minister, the ministers also underline an affinity to the church in which they have ended up – and an incompatibility with those they declined. Mr Telford, for example, describes how he was initially put in touch with a church in Leicester, which gave him a unanimous call to be their minister. But, he tells me, 'I felt that that wasn't really right for me or for them because it was a church in a very, very strong multiracial area – very, very alien to what I had been used to. I felt that they would be better with a reverend who had a bit more experience of working in a multicultural city'. Mr Barnes declined the offer of a ministry in a poor area of Newcastle because he felt they needed somebody with more social work experience.

Ministers talk of a 'calling' both into the church more broadly and into their own church more specifically. This calling becomes apparent to them through their discussion with peers and mentors, their reading of the Bible and prayer. Serendipity also plays a part in 'calling' and in the will of God, although I doubt the Baptist ministers would describe it as such. Mr Rose, for example, tells of the way in which he was 'matched' with his church:

> My father-in-law is a lay preacher and he preached here and in so doing he learned that they were looking for a minister. They were in a – it's called an interregnum in Baptist

circles, when you have no minister. So he learned that and he also knew that we were considering finding ways of coming back to England. So he made that connection and he asked the people here if they would entertain a profile from someone in the States. So I sent them a profile and I didn't know whether it would work out. But it did work out.

Local churches are, in Mr Rose's words, 'self-governing' and work on a 'consensus model', with members coming to an agreement on where they 'stand' on a particular issue. Issues in need of clarification emerge from the preoccupations of church members. Individual churches, I was told, are able to define their 'position' on certain subjects and the local congregation 'seeks the mind of Christ together'.

I ask the ministers if there is a 'Baptist line' on NRT. Mr Unwin tells me that, as far as he knows, there has been nothing published in the *Baptist Times* or by the interdenominational *Evangelical Alliance* about 'cloning or IVF'. But, he explains, it is very difficult to keep abreast of everything and ministers with finite time and resources, and working on their own, struggle to 'keep up'. They have to make decisions about the 'issues' on which to focus. What gets to be an issue, of course, is of anthropological interest. Mr Unwin tells me that the previous day he preached on Harry Potter: 'Should we be recommending our children to read books about magic or shouldn't we?' It is not an issue for him, he explains, but it is for some parents: 'So it's good to have teaching on it and to look at the Bible and say "well what does the Bible say about these issues?"'

Autonomy emerges, then, as a valued and valuable feature of the Baptist church: ministers identify the autonomy of local churches in choosing their minister, in what the minister preaches and in the position they take on a particular social issue. Ministers connect the doctrinal independence of local churches to their financial independence. To return to my conversation with Mr Unwin:[5]

Unwin: All Baptist churches are totally independent – they own their own property. You see in the Methodist church it isn't like that – well certainly not in the Anglican or in the Roman Catholic Church. But we own our own property. We make our own decisions. Now if we were to make certain decisions, the Baptist Union could say 'Look, hold on a minute'... and they could say that they don't feel it's right that we should stay in the Union. If we wanted to stay in, we would change it [our decision]. But there *is* that independence.

Edwards: So does that also go for matters of ethics or morality?

Unwin: Yes.

Edwards: So I could be finding a lot of diversity within a Baptist kind of teaching?

Unwin: Yes, but the thing is you're talking to ministers and I think that we're more likely to agree having trained at probably no more than

	four different colleges. Whereas if you were talking to members – but, then again, you'd only be getting loads of individual opinions anyway, wouldn't you?
Edwards:	Would I? But that's the interesting thing. Would I be getting loads of individual opinions, or would I be getting also things that were informed by membership of the Baptist church?
Unwin:	I suppose you could take the view that gradually a minister is bound to put across his own view and take a large part of the congregation with him, if they like him and they trust him and he is convincing. But I think it does work both ways.

From this perspective, ministers are more likely to think alike than their congregation, and they may, with charisma and trust on their side, influence their congregation. But ultimately each church is independent and comprises individuals with their own individual opinions, and the individuality and independence of churches and persons are positively valued. The close and mutually informative relationship between minister and congregation is something that Baptist ministers recognize as special to Baptism. I was told over and over again that there is no *one* Baptist line, and that the Baptist Union is careful not to say, '*This* is a Baptist response'. So what holds Baptism together? What is it that members perceive themselves to share? I want to look a little closer at the idioms of kinship through which 'the church' and belonging to it are conceptualized.

The Family of God

For The Valley Baptist ministers, God has ultimately given human beings the tools and means to intervene in human suffering. He has provided the ability to overcome infertility and allowed human beings to put right what has gone wrong with nature. Nature, as we shall see, is heavily circumscribed within heterosexual marriage, which is in itself naturalized. There is a general agreement that heterosexual and married couples should be able to use NRT, and techniques such *in vitro* fertilization (IVF) and intracytoplasmic sperm injection (ICSI) are acceptable ways of achieving a pregnancy. There is less agreement about the use of donated gametes, but, as we shall see, it is not dismissed out of hand. Baptists have a powerful and prominent precedent for playing down the significance of biological connection in creating families, and it is one that they readily mobilize.

Baptists describe themselves as belonging to one family, alternatively called the family of the Church, the family of God, the family of the Word or the family of Christ. God is the father, the church the mother, and members of 'the', or 'a', church are brothers and sisters in Christ. Relatedness forged through 'the word', like that forged through biogenetic connection (as described by David Schneider (1968, 1984) for North Americans), is not optional. One can neither choose to be unrelated nor ignore its obligations. Belonging to the family of 'the word' also entails codes of conduct which include mutual support and an avoidance of gossip or criticism. Consider Mr Telford's description:

> *Telford*: When I talk about the family of the church I mean everybody who comes to Trinity, from those who are just a few months old, to those who are in their late nineties, men and women, married and single, everybody for me makes up the family of the church and when we talk about the family of the church, we constantly emphasize the importance of great relationships between all of us related in the family of the church ... the new testament says that the apostle Paul used to talk about us being brothers and sisters in Christ, which is actually quite a helpful term. Most friendships are made with people of similar interests ... but we're not talking [here] about Christian friendships, we're talking about something a lot deeper. We're talking about a relationship that's as close as a brother and a sister ... I mean, we say things like 'you can choose your friends', but actually, when you become a Christian and you become involved in the church, you can't choose your friends in a sense because you are a family. So you're brothers and sisters, like it or not.
> *Edwards*: That's interesting. But of course families are marked as much by conflict and falling-out as they are by love and care.
> *Telford*: That's right, so we are much *more* like a family. I mean we have problems in the church, people don't always hit it off, but we're always working together for all the pluses of good relationships and emphasizing to people the importance of liking one another and supporting one another and encouraging one another, being careful not to gossip, criticize and all the other things that spoil family life, and where there is breakdown, we can bring healing and reconciliation. So yes, much *more* like a family than a series of friendships.

Similar kinds of effort are required to make and sustain both the kinship described by Schneider and the kinship described by these Baptist ministers. Both are deemed non-negotiable, both are marked by 'diffuse, enduring, solidarity', both, unlike friendship, are neither chosen nor entered into voluntarily, both substantialize and essentialize relatedness, one in blood the other in the word. Mr Jones puts it this way:

We might draw on a metaphor – if you want to say that blood is thicker than water in an understanding of family ties, then that would [give] some understanding of Christian faith. We might be very different people with different lifestyles but that is the ideal of the Church – people from diverse backgrounds – and their common factor would be their faith in Christ and their experience of God. In that sense, we might say we are in the same blood family, aren't we? The family of Christ, that is the metaphor we are drawing on.

The collectivity of the church and the way in which relatedness between members is conceptualized borrows from a particular kind of kinship thinking and at the same time expands it. Mr Telford draws our attention to the way in which kinship forged through the word is as given or non-negotiable as that forged through blood – 'you can choose your friends, but not your family' – and Mr Jones expands the common idiom of blood being thicker than water to convey the thickness (and stickiness) of the connections between those who put their 'faith in Christ'. The family of God, or of the word, does not replace or subvert the family of blood, but instead extends it. I want to suggest that when it comes to NRT, Baptists already have a favourable take on the non-biological family. There is a pre-existing and central place for the creation of 'the family' through will, shared sentiment and affective ties.

Mr Unwin draws on the Bible to make his point. For him, the family of the word is 'more important' than the biological family. He finds evidence for this in the Bible in the way in which Jesus, while dying, allocates John to Mary as her son, and on other occasions proclaims his true mothers and brothers as those who 'hear the word and obey it'. Mr Unwin draws an analogy between the family of the word and the family that cares for and nurtures the infant. For him, the preference of Christ for 'the family of the word' weakens 'the biological thing'. To continue:

Edwards: Yes. But what do you think about this emphasis at present on tracing biological parents? Increasingly with DNA testing we can trace biological fathers say _

Unwin: _ I hate the word father in that sense, I really do! Hate is too strong a word, I really don't like it.

Edwards: For you, the father is the one that brings you up, who nurtures you, who wipes your nose _?

Unwin: _ of course we call God father, that is one of the names which Jesus gave to us and it is very important to us and so I would rather we had a different phrase which meant, how can I express it, the male biological.

Edwards: The genitor?

Unwin: Yes, okay, the genitor. To me it is an absolute contradiction in terms – if you're talking about somebody like the father of my granddaughter who, upon one phone call, never wanted to know, and has never been seen since – to mix the terms biological and father is a total contradiction of terms to me.

Edwards: That's interesting. But do you think culturally we do this? There does seem to be an emphasis on biological links.

Unwin: It prompts kidology doesn't it? The kidology is that the word father, meaning genitor, actually has some meaning, in terms of caring for and being part of your family. To me that just isn't true. Then it leads to this kidology which is 'if I trace my "real" father, my biological benefactor, that I will discover something about myself', and I think that what so many people discover is just huge sadness, especially where fathers are concerned. I have no statistics on that.

Mr Unwin has both the Bible and his own experience of bringing up his granddaughter with the lack of interest or care shown by her (biological) father as evidence that a distinction should be made between a (real) father and a 'male biological'. Parents are the people who bring you up and 'the biological thing is weaker' than the affective ties forged through care and attention.

The Baptist ministers are predisposed to unpack the component parts of kinship in a way that creatively undermines the privileging of biogenetic connection. This, together with an understanding that human capacity and capability are given by God and that little happens without his knowledge, means that they can accommodate many of the possibilities presented by new conceptive technologies. From one perspective, it figures that the sperm donor, like the absent father, has less claim to being a father than the man who brings up the child. But as we shall see below, when ministers look at such a procedure from the perspective of the 'sacred bond' of marriage, then the sperm donor presents an unwanted and unwarranted intrusion. Furthermore, the 'sacred bond of marriage' privileges the heterosexual couple, and indeed Scriptures and personal experience can now be drawn upon to place limits on the creative possibilities.

Intricately Woven

Over and over again I was told that 'life' starts when God *knows*. God is aware of, and works upon, the embryo or the foetus in the womb. Evidence, I was told, is found in Psalm 139. Several of the ministers turned to it in one of the number of bibles in their living room or office and read it to me; Mr Rose quoted it from memory:

> For it was you who formed my inward palms, you knit me together in my mother's womb, I praise you for I am fearfully and wonderfully made. Wonderful are your words that I know very well. My frame was not hidden from you when I was being made in secret, intricately woven in the depths of the earth.

Ideas about 'the beginning of life' emerged frequently in my conversations with the ministers about NRT. It has clearly been a topic well rehearsed in debate about abortion, and ministers acknowledge contestation within the church over how or when the beginning of a human life is defined. For some, I was told, it may be at fertilization, for others it is when the embryo attaches to the wall of the uterus, and for yet others when the foetus starts moving. All agree that the Bible suggests it is earlier rather than later and that there is evidence in the Bible that life even begins at conception. Ministers also acknowledge, however, that there are different and competing expertises. According to one minister, a theological understanding of 'the beginning of life' may differ from a physiological understanding. And in the words of another:

> Raising the question for me, it would be about when does that embryo become sentient – when does it know it exists? That is a question we can't answer because you can't take newborns in the womb and say at what point, three months [or] six months. In terms of more theological implications about when [life begins] for God, I would have to say that for God it occurs at conception. My reason for saying that for God it is at conception is because a lot of the psalms talk about being known in the womb and about God ordaining life and so. These kinds of concepts of being *known* by God, even before birth, [mean that] for me, God *knows* the individual.

Of interest here is the way in which the esoteric runs into a social pragmatism. Arguments about the omnipresence of God are interspersed with and supported by rationalizing arguments about demand and supply. Mr Unwin comments:

> I find that one of the great mysteries, one of the great ridiculous things really, about our society [is] that abortion has been allowed to go rampant, in my own view, in society, and yet there is such a desperate need for babies to be adopted. I think to myself 'why are we so crazy? Why are we killing off all these unborn infants and yet there are homes desperate for them?'

In the rhetoric of another minister: 'How can situations such as surrogacy arrangements be *concocted* when abortion is condoned'.

There is a constant tussle between tenet and pragmatism. The needs and lived experiences of church members and the responsibility of ministers for their pastoral care require some doctrinal imagination. Imperatives to alleviate suffering and the responsibility of human beings to use the capabilities provided by God cut across certain interpretations of 'the word'. NRT reveals the fault lines. Take Mr Young's comments on embryo research:

> In terms of the embryo thing, I personally wouldn't have a problem with the embryo research. I mean, I wouldn't want to go to Alder Hey[6] and have rooms and rooms and rooms of embryos just in case we wanted to do a little bit more research. Equally, I wouldn't want them produced to order. So it's about the necessity rather than the desire and I think, for me, the whole feel of scientific and medical research is this thing about necessity. The cruelty to animals – I couldn't knowingly do something to an animal that would cause it great pain and suffering but, equally, if there was a choice between doing it to me or one of my children, or doing it to an animal, I am sorry but the animal is going to lose every time. In the same way, if we can learn stuff about improving humanity on a cluster of cells, which is living by definition but has no conscious knowledge of its existence, then the group of cells is going to lose every time. But I hope that is because it is the only way we can do it.

New reproductive technologies are put into a technological bag that for one minister includes 'plastic surgery, surrogacy, Viagra, and broken families'. They are located 'in a world where one third of the population are hungry', and at a time in the UK 'when benefits to families are cut'. Ministers explore what they do not know about NRT through what they know about present-day inequalities, as well as through what they see as technological enhancement and enchantment at a time when technology appears unable to solve or resolve fundamental problems of poverty.

Nevertheless, Baptist thinking creatively accommodates technological innovation in conception and it does so in a number of ways. First, the productive and positive activities of human beings are willed by God: in the context of NRT I was asked, 'Is this not God's will?', or told that 'It must be God's will'. God, the argument goes, has given human beings intelligence and capabilities which include their ability to develop technologies of assisted conception. They may, of course, from a Baptist perspective, be applied in good or bad ways, but there is nothing intrinsically wrong in them. Second, the most significant social collectivity for Baptist ministers is the 'family of God' or 'the word', and this family is created through adoption. The prior notion that human beings are adopted into the family of God provides a precedent for demoting biological relatedness. Third, God is known to work on persons prior to birth – to begin to 'knit them together' in the womb. I suggest that, if this is the case, then it is of little consequence how the embryo got there: that is, if it is implanted or created in a Petri dish.

Biological Adultery

'The sacred bond of marriage' was a constant companion in my conversations with Baptist ministers. All the ministers see a place for NRT in the context of the married heterosexual couple unable to conceive a child. But, like the rabbis in Israel (Kahn 2000), some are concerned with the adulterous link implied in the substitution sperm. Mr Telford returns several times to the question of why using donated semen is a problem. The procedure may be unproblematic spiritually, he says, but it is a problem biologically. He explains that with what he calls 'simple IVF' (using the gametes of the married couple and would-be parents) there is a 'biological completeness'. Involving a third party, however, is 'biological adultery'.

Telford: I'm not comfortable with any third party involvement.
Edwards: Whether that was an egg donor, or sperm donor, or a surrogate?
Telford: Yes.
Edwards: Why is that?
Telford: I think if a wife goes out and sleeps with somebody else and gets pregnant, we call it adultery. I wrestle with the problem of whether this is actually biological adultery where you're introducing a third party. I also have enormous difficulties with relationships – father, mother, child – and then the third party – husband, wife, child, third party. I find that that makes it enormously muddled and complicated for the child, presumably, as he or she grows up. The amount of information they get about the donor – I'm not sure about that – whether to make that broadly available, or whether to wait till they are eighteen, or what. So I do wrestle with this concept. Firstly on the grounds that it seems to me to be biological adultery, but secondly because of the muddle and complexity and pain that you are introducing to three or four-fold relationships.

Telford struggles first with the intrusion on the bond between the married couple, and then with the additional and surplus link between the child and the sperm donor. I have written elsewhere of the analogies people draw between adultery and the substitution of gametes (Edwards 2000, 2004). There is a literalness in the way in which donated semen, for example, has the potential to forge an adulterous link. Similarly with surrogacy: 'Is there any difference', Mr Telford asks, 'between a husband going off and getting another woman pregnant and surrogacy? They're not sleeping in a bed together, and they have gone through the test-tube process, but it's still there'. While the problem might be couched in terms of biology or relationships, an overriding concern seems to be with the interjection of a 'third', unconnected, outsider into the relationship between husband and wife, which has the potential to desacralize the bond.

This argument is embedded within an explicit commitment to pastoral care. Mr Telford goes on:

> Having said that, I do have enormous sympathy for couples who haven't got children, for whatever reason, and who want them. I don't want to come across as being harsh or unfeeling because I can imagine the terrible pain that there is and we've been so fortunate – we've had two lovely girls without any problems at all. So, I mean, my position, and the Christian position I'm sure, is enormous sympathy for couples who are childless for whatever reason. I mean, they get married with the hope of having one, two, three or six children and find out that they can't. It must be enormously painful for them. My heart goes out to them, it really does.

The ministers feel keenly their obligation to keep abreast of current affairs and to be knowledgeable about the contemporary world. This is related to their role in, and concern with, the pastoral and spiritual care of their community. They need to have one eye to the future when members of their church may require access to fertility services and seek guidance from them. Their willingness to speak with me about these issues, and the care and thoughtfulness with which they engaged with my questions, was driven by a strong sense that they ought to be informed on behalf of those they serve.

Situated Morality

I was struck by the way in which Mr James described his training. He is completing a degree in contextual theology, with a part-time ministry in The Valley as his placement – a sort of 'on-the-job training'. In his words:

> A lot of what we do practically, relates to constant theological reflection and I think the difference between applied theology, as I would understand it, and contextual theology is that rather than applying your theology to context, you actually let the context speak and shape the theology... It is a different way of doing theology from the old style. You used to learn lots of doctrines and how it is supposed to be politically. This – the education model – is much more about, you know, learning [*sic*] people to think for themselves.

The notion that the context shapes theology is significant.[7] The Valley ministers concede that it is difficult to have hard and fast rules about what should and should not be allowed in terms of biomedical intervention in conception and pregnancy. Mr Young describes himself as a 'conservative evangelical', and explains what this means with reference to his views on abortion:

> I would be definitely flying against the wind [because] I would not say that there should *never* be abortion, because I think that there are circumstances where that is right... I think if you were to take a straw poll and people were to take their gut reactions, I think that I would probably be seen as going with the normal flow.... One of the first things

that I did when I came up here was to do a bible study on ethics and I had a few people saying, 'euthanasia no', 'abortion no', 'divorce no', but where that touched their lives, it put a different perspective on it. You can be very sort of hard and fast and then your daughter, who is not able to conceive, comes and says I'm going for IVF.

Mr Young is both 'flying against the wind' and 'going with the flow': out of tune with dominant Christian ideology and in tune with people in their daily lives faced with contingency and dealing with contradiction.

Of interest is the way in which The Valley ministers acknowledge the situational nature of morality. They reflect on NRT from a range of perspectives and from the point of view of a number of actors. I have written elsewhere of how other residents in this part of England reject or disagree with specific biotechnological interventions in human conception, but at the same time acknowledge that were they in a different 'position' they would think differently. They also, with great alacrity, shift perspectives and imagine the same innovation from the point of view of a different person: the gamete donor, the surrogate mother, the involuntarily childless couple, the ensuing child, the doctor, and so on.

I imagined that Baptist ministers would have less leeway in their imaginings: that their exploration of NRT would be within moral frameworks already circumscribed. To a certain extent this is the case, but only up to a point. The Baptism on which I have focused here appears to support some doctrinal flexibility without compromising certain bottom lines (which in themselves and in their turn are fuzzy). Ministers either echo the sentiments of their congregation as voices of their own, or persuade otherwise and pray for change. The Valley Baptist ministers, like other Valley people, readily rationalize and justify technological innovation in human reproduction. Their own religious technologies allow for an incorporation of reproductive techniques that encourage the heterosexual married couple to go forth and multiply.

Acknowledgements

I am grateful to the Valley Baptist ministers for their hospitality and generosity, both spiritual and intellectual.

Notes

1. 'The Valley' covers an area that roughly corresponds to the region of local government. I have been working as an anthropologist in Alltown, one of the three Valley towns, on and off since 1987.

2. See Bebbington (1994) for a discussion of the different relationship between Baptism and Evangelicalism in Britain and the United States; and Cross (2000) for further details of the particular complexion of the twentieth-century British Baptist movements.
3. I use NRT here as a shorthand for biotechnological intervention in human conception which includes artificial insemination (AI) and *in vitro* fertilization (IVF), with or without the donation of gametes.
4. Most of the ministers underlined the fact that they had been happy in their previous jobs. I think this might be partly in response to sociological analyses, which emphasize the role of deprivation and anomie in religious conversion (e.g. Robbins 2004). My sense is that in emphasizing the fact that they were happy before deciding to join the ministry they are refuting such simplistic causal arguments.
5. Here and below I present a lengthy quotation from our conversation with the aim of indicating how ideas lead on from others. I use the following conventions in the transcripts: _ at the end and at the beginning of an utterance indicates an overlap in speakers; ... indicates material omitted; italicized phrases or words indicate original emphasis; square brackets indicate my addition.
6. Alder Hey is a children's hospital in Liverpool which was recently in the news because of 'the discovery' of tissue samples and organs from dead infants and foetuses, which had been taken and stored without the consent of parents.
7. The idea is part of a contemporary zeitgeist and found across a range disciplinary practices: for example, we teach anthropology students that theory emerges from ethnography, and social workers with whom I have worked insist that their practice is shaped by the particular context and by the specific needs of the people in whose lives they intervene.

References

Bebbington, D. (1994), 'Evangelicalism in its settings: the British and American movements since 1940', in M. Noll, D. Bebbington and G. Rawlyk (eds), *Evangelicalism: Comparative Studies of Popular Protestantism in North America, the British Isles and beyond, 1700–1990*, Oxford: Oxford University Press.

Cross, A.R. (2000), *Baptism and the Baptists: Theology and Practice in Twentieth-Century Britain*, Carlisle, Cumbria: Paternoster Press.

Edwards, J. (1999), 'Explicit connections: ethnographic enquiry in north-west England', in J. Edwards, S. Franklin, E. Hirsch, F. Price and M. Strathern, *Technologies of Procreation: Kinship in the Age of Assisted Conception*, second edition, London: Routledge.

—— (2000), *Born and Bred: Idioms of Kinship and New Reproductive Technologies in England*, Oxford: Oxford University Press.

—— (2004), 'Incorporating incest: gamete, body and relation in assisted conception', *Journal of the Royal Anthropological Institute*, 10(4): 755–74.

—— (2005), 'Make-up': identity, upbringing and character', *Ethnos*, 70(3): 413–31.

—— and Strathern, M. (2000), 'Including our own', in J. Carsten (ed), *Cultures of Relatedness: New Approaches to the Study of Kinship*, Cambridge: Cambridge University Press.

Kahn, S.M. (2000), *Reproducing Jews: A cultural Account of Assisted Conception in Israel*, Durham, NC and London: Duke University Press.

Robbins, J. (2004), 'The globalization of Pentecostal and Charismatic Christianity', *Annual Review of Anthropology*, 33: 117–43.

Schneider, D. (1968), *American Kinship: A Cultural Account*, Englewood Cliffs, NJ: Prentice Hall.

—— (1984), *A Critique of the Study of Kinship*, Ann Arbor: University of Michigan Press.

Strathern, M. (2002), 'Externalities in disguise', *Economy and Society*, 31(2): 250–67.

Part III
Creativity and the Passage of Time: History, Tradition and the Life-course

Introduction
Eric Hirsch and *Sharon Macdonald*

Creativity and Temporality; Creativity or Temporality?

'Creativity and temporality' was the original title of the conference panel at which the chapters in this part were presented. One question that we raised in our panel abstract concerned the kinds of change over time that might be counted as evidence of 'creativity'. When was a change deemed 'creative' and when was it something else? Could change that was 'merely' the outcome of the passage of time or of the past somehow pressing itself into the present be considered creative or not? And should 'creativity' be seen as entailing a value judgement about particular kinds of agency that rest in culturally and historically specific interpretations of time?

After hearing the original conference papers and the comments of our discussants, Penny Harvey and Marilyn Strathern, it became clear that posing our title as a question – 'creativity *or* temporality?' – emphasized these central questions and highlighted key themes running through the papers, in particular those of agency and of how 'creativity' is defined by both 'natives' and anthropologists.[1] It also brought to the fore another question that we raised in our conference abstract: why is there so much emphasis on creativity – especially in the academy and in Western or Euro-American societies – at present?

We explore these questions below, beginning with a brief consideration of the history of the term 'creativity' itself and the constellation of notions and social forms with which it is associated, leading to reflection on its contemporary usage and spread. Then, by way of reflection on the three chapters that follow, we look at some further implications of the relationship between creativity and temporality that are opened up by our 'creativity *or* temporality' perspective.

A Temporal Perspective: From Creative to Creativity

The adjective 'creative', according to the Oxford English Dictionary, only entered conventional English usage in the seventeenth century. It did so alongside the development of particular conceptions of personhood which emphasized not only the idea of individual difference or 'individuation', but also a moral obligation to express that difference, and thus to 'work on' the self to realize individual distinctiveness (Taylor 1989: 159, 375). Such conceptions put new levels of emphasis on individual responsibility and the capacity for making opportunity, rather than seeing life trajectories as divinely plotted. Personal accumulation of wealth and success became conspicuous social values, and failure to take responsibility for the self, or 'take opportunities', could be met with disapproval. Ian Hacking (1995, following Douglas 1992) points to Locke's theory of personal identity (first published in 1689) – where he considers two concepts of identity – as a key formulation of these values. Central to the theory was the choice of the word 'person' for what Locke called a 'forensic concept', constituted via chains of memory and responsibility (Hacking 1995: 146). ('Man', by contrast, was chosen as a concept that could refer to bodily continuity in Locke's terminology.) This new conception of identity was part of the enterprise society – marked by new practices of commerce, law, property and trade – that was taking shape at the time (ibid.: 146). This was a society in which people were called upon to be 'creative' in the sense of taking individual responsibility and realizing their immanent potential.

The expressivity of this notion of 'creative' was subsequently expanded into the realms of art and literature during the Romantic period of the late eighteenth century. Here it was coupled with the idea of the imagination, which was understood as a mental faculty capable of acts of creation testifying to individual distinctiveness and personal identity. The Romantics sought further to distinguish between 'the merely reproductive imagination, which simply brings back to mind what we have already experienced ... and the creative imagination which can produce something new and unprecedented' (Taylor 1989: 378–9). This characterization of 'creative' as requiring novelty informs much subsequent discourse, though it remains contested and the subject of much philosophical and other discussion. Bergson's 'creative evolution', for example, is an attempt to expand the notion into the realm of early twentieth-century science (Ingold 1986: 173–221; this volume Introduction to Part I). By the end of that century, 'creative' had taken on other meanings too, as in the domain of financial matters – 'creative accounting'.

Despite the variability in the meanings of the term, there are two other points about the historical emergence of its use that we might note here, for they are important in subsequent characterizations of 'creative' and 'creativity', and have a bearing upon considerations of creativity or temporality. The first is the objectification of 'imagination' – the idea that there is a specific mental faculty or locus in which novelty might be produced. This lays the ground for 'creativity' later coming to be regarded as a distinctive quality, with a presumed mental location, rather than simply a temporal realization; and becoming a suitable topic for psychological – and even neurological – investigation. The second is the objectification of time, which has implications for the creative working out of individual distinctiveness.

Life-narration emerges as a key mode of self-expression, one capable of relating memory and the actions of the individual to the temporal unfolding of events (Taylor 1989: 289).

The concept of 'creativity' itself only really became conventional well into the period of the Industrial Revolution, though applied solely to individual artistic matters. Towards the end of the twentieth and into the twenty-first century, however, there has been an explosion of interest in creativity: in defining it as much as exhibiting it. In part, this seems to be bound up with what some called 'the end of history' – the 'triumph' of a neoliberal vision of the world that displaced the old certainties about East and West, capitalism and communism, society and individual – and the dominance of a world view in which the 'individual' reigns supreme. In such a world view, transnational corporations are typically conceptualized as larger versions of the private individual – super-private and super-individualistic; and changes of scale between the individual person and private company seem irrelevant. There is 'only a magnification or diminution along the same scale of virtues' (Strathern 1992: 141–2).

A key aspect of this 'creativity explosion' – or 'cult of creativity' (Eriksen 2005) – is that creativity comes to be expected and even demanded, widely and coercively. Where 'individuals' reign supreme, it seems, they need to demonstrate what is perceived to be the highest achievable good: creativity (Osborne 2003: 508; Liep 2001). What creativity is, though, is far from certain.

Creativity as a Particular Form of Agency

Considerable philosophical attention has been accorded to attempting to define what is meant by 'creativity' (see, for example, Beaney 2005: ch. 6). Such discussion typically focuses on questions of novelty (how 'new' and 'original' does a product have to be to provide evidence of 'creativity'?), value (is anything new 'creative' or does it have to be in some sense worthwhile?) and agency (e.g. is intentionality a prerequisite?). Such debate informs Kirsten Hastrup's discussion of creativity and agency below, though unlike most philosophical debate, Hastrup emphasizes the *social* nature of creativity and, in turn, the performative nature of the social. This has the effect of reframing conventional questions. In relation to time and novelty, Hastrup's account puts particular emphasis on anticipation rather than intentionality. The latter, she argues, inevitably casts creativity as a matter of individual agency; whereas anticipation is an inherent feature of all social action – we act in anticipation of future events. Creativity, however, parts company from that which is anticipated: it is 'eccentric'. Nevertheless, this does not mean that it is rare or characteristic of only some kinds of societies, for Hastrup (following Bateson) regards the social as inherently flexible and therefore as containing 'uncommitted potential for change' (Bateson 1972: 497). Because 'all social worlds have such uncommitted potential', all societies, according to Hastrup, manifest creativity.

While Hastrup's careful analysis is very useful for clarifying ways in which anthropologists might understand and use 'creativity' and allied notions, as well as showing how all societies can be understood to be creative, there remains a question over whether certain cultural conceptions of personhood, agency and temporality lead to particular kinds of concerns over creativity, as we have suggested above. As Penny Harvey and Marilyn Strathern (2005) point out in their reflection on the conference contributions, there is variability across cultures in which kinds of events are understood as evidence of human agency and creativity and which are regarded as outcomes merely of the passage of time. Particularly characteristic of Euro-Americans is

> intense concern ... in how they will get into the future ... An existential crisis is made out of what is going to occur anyway. There is a strong need felt to propel oneself forward: there is a distinctive value accorded to speed and tempo in this regard. An outcome of this is the recent value accorded to flexibility that Eriksen (2005) critically assesses. The reason for this valuation is because the future is regarded as something that has not happened yet, as a 'new' time. The existential dimension presents itself in enticing questions: what am I going to be, what kind of world will it be? ... The concept of creativity thus augments the scope of human agency, a potential that Euro-Americans see as lying in the passage of time. What is so distinctive about these Euro-American values is that they divide people that use time in this productive sense, from those who do not. A consequence of this division is that certain matters follow:
>
> Not all potential is realised
> Not all moments into the future are innovative
> Not everyone is creative
> Not all societies and cultures are creative (Harvey and Strathern 2005: 109)

Hence, the current Euro-American obsession with trying to identify, define and capture productive uses of time and the creative – and its associated downgrading of that which is not judged to be so.

Some of the implications of such notions for those living in Western societies are well illustrated by Cathrine Degnen's study of older people. The aged, with less future and uncommitted potential ahead of them, do not conform to the desired ideal of the creative self; and, as Degnen describes, they easily find themselves defined as inhabiting a different – non-productive and non-creative – temporality from that of younger people. Her sensitive analysis highlights the ways in which older people frequently employ narrative styles that differ from the linear self-narratives that emerged alongside dominant modern Lockean notions of personhood. While part of her own anthropological aim was to recover the status of 'creative' for such alternative styles, she shows how they can nevertheless feed back into stereotypes of old age. In so doing she raises important questions about anthropological attempts to identify and celebrate agency and the creative. Such attempts may, she suggests, fail to recognize important aspects of people's experience, including their own senses of loss.

Creativity and Tradition

Despite the overwhelming emphasis on novelty and the future in Western understandings of creativity, all three of the chapters that follow show that to be accorded the status of 'creative', actions must be perceived to be part of some kind of 'larger whole' (Hughes-Freeland) rather than as 'cut loose from the world (in which case [they] would register as madness)' (Hastrup) – as the actions of some of the older people in Degnen's study are indeed sometimes judged to be. This is a point well recognized by many Western artists and philosophers, who have tried variously to define the degree and nature of the relationship to what has gone before that a thing or action should have in order to be deemed creative.

One particularly interesting commentator, partly because of his unusually strong assertion of the importance of tradition over that of individual personality, was T.S. Eliot, as discussed by Felicia Hughes-Freeland. Like Degnen's account of the alternative temporalities of older people, Hughes-Freeland's attention to T.S. Eliot's ideas is important, among other reasons, for highlighting some of the variations within the Western context. For T.S. Eliot, creativity was as much if not more about being part of a tradition as about breaking free from it – a conception that entailed seeing the artist as embodying tradition, and time not as linear but, to a degree, as cyclical, with present actions altering the past as much as vice versa.

If T.S. Eliot's assertions about creativity to some extent surprise by denying the strong emphasis on individual creativity and novelty that Western artists more usually hold, Hughes-Freeland's discussion of Javanese dancers serves to disrupt further some of the ways in which creativity is typically understood in the West. As she points out, Westerners typically see Javanese dance as involving the effacement of individual creativity and the valuation instead of self-discipline and the accurate following of tradition. Her argument, however, is that this opposition is unhelpful, for it is in the achievement of total immersion, in 'getting it right', that the dancer may become creatively free and 'transcend ... any mechanical movement determinism'. With respect to choreography too, she shows that 'innovation is not always apparent, and technical expertise can dissimulate newness behind the appearance of similarity'. So whereas creativity in dominant Western conceptions is generally identified via visible 'products', such as artefacts and performances, in the world of Javanese dance, identifications of 'innovation' do not necessarily reside in the outwardly new.

Contesting the Future

As well as entailing particular though variable relationships to tradition, what constitutes creativity is often simultaneously a contest about how the future should materialize. According to Western evaluations, the future should appear as new – but not entirely new – and as a newness that others find convincing and compelling. This is glossed as creativity, while others, such as Javanese court dancers noted above, require much greater visible adherence to tradition. Among other contributions to the original conference panel, Cristina Grasseni (2005) showed how future temporalities in the competing 'foodscapes' of Italy are highlighted in public debates surrounding so-called 'slow food' and the 'fast genes' of genetically modified crops. And Joy Hendry (2005) described how 'indigenous peoples' seek to demonstrate through their material forms that they are capable of newness and change, and that they are not 'static' as they are conventionally shown to be in museum exhibits. To act and appear as capable agents, these peoples feel compelled to demonstrate their creativity. Nevertheless, as James Weiner showed in his conference contribution on indigenous tribal names in North Queensland, Australia, there can also be strong legal and political pressures against innovation – even where this is itself 'traditional' – in the contexts in which some indigenous peoples live.

An outcome of a world dominated by the Western view of the future as unknown, as potentially new, is that people seek to enter that future as capably as they can. 'Wasting time', not using all one's time productively, becomes tantamount to a relinquishment of responsibility and opportunity. Being flexible is an idiom most appropriate to such a temporal orientation: one is not constrained by context or convention, and the new technologies of the internet, DVD, video, and so on, seem to enable such a vision. However, as Thomas Hylland Eriksen (2005) argued, taking his cue from Bateson, flexibility is only really possible when all the gaps in time are *not* filled.

And this, it seems, is one of the implications of the associated explosion in audit culture – associated, that is, with the similar emphasis on creativity – and the regimes of trust it is meant to foster. According to audit culture, trust can only be attained if all relevant knowledge is rendered visible, as Alberto Corsín Jiménez (2005) pointed out in his conference contribution. But the attempt to render such knowledge evident (e.g., as isolated value-episodes in the internet language of XBRL) is analogous to trying to fill all the temporal gaps: ironically, such attempts are antithetical to the very social life and social relations they are meant to sustain.

Part III, Introduction

The Irony of Anthropological Practice

As anthropologists, we are sensitive to these limitations of Western notions creativity and temporality. At the same time, though, these notions inadvertently enter our ethnographic accounts in quite fundamental ways. The Malinowskian myth of the creative, heroic ethnographer who forges a new beginning with his or her version is one in which we all precariously participate and which we seek, albeit critically, to reproduce. But as Hastrup reminds us, it is a myth nonetheless. And yet myths, like other ways in which our perceptions of the 'presence of time' (Wagner 1986: 81–95) are manifested, are an inescapable feature of social relations. There are no ultimate beginnings, just as there is no definitive creativity. Lives are lived, just as much as they are described and interpreted, with respect to unique configurations of past, present and future, that is, in relation to what Wagner calls 'organic time'. These are constraints we can only accommodate as much as we seek continually and 'creatively' to surpass them. The chapters that follow demonstrate this tension vividly.

Notes

1. A full set of papers, with the exception of that by James Weiner which could not be completed in time, has been published in *Cambridge Anthropology* vol. 25 no. 2, 2005. This includes an afterword by Penny Harvey and Marilyn Strathern based on their discussant comments, and a short introduction on which the present contribution is based. We are grateful to *Cambridge Anthropology* for allowing us to reproduce this, and the following chapters, here.

References

Bateson, G. (1972), *Steps to an Ecology of Mind*, New York: Balantine Books.
Beaney, M. (2005), *Imagination and Creativity*, Milton Keynes: The Open University Press.
Corsín Jiménez, A. (2005), 'After Trust', *Cambridge Anthropology*, 25(2): 64–78.
Douglas, M. (1992), 'The person in an enterprise culture', in S.H. Heap and A. Ross (eds), *Understanding the Enterprise Culture: Themes in the Work of Mary Douglas*, Edinburgh: Edinburgh University Press.

Eriksen, T.H. (2005), 'New work, flexibility and the cult of creativity', *Cambridge Anthropology*, 25(2): 95–107.

Grasseni, C. (2005), 'Slow food, fast genes: timescapes of authenticity and innovation in the anthropology of food', *Cambridge Anthropology*, 25(2): 79–94.

Hacking, I. (1995), *Rewriting the Soul: Multiple Personality and the Sciences of Memory*, Princeton, NJ: Princeton University Press.

Harvey, P. and Strathern, M. (2005), 'Afterword', *Cambridge Anthropology*, 25(2): 108–10.

Hendry, J. (2005), 'Creativity as evidence of having persisted through time', *Cambridge Anthropology*, 25(2): 36–49.

Ingold, T. (1986), *Evolution and Social Life,* Cambridge: Cambridge University Press.

Liep, J. (2001), 'Introduction', in J. Liep (ed), *Locating Cultural Creativity*, London: Pluto Press.

Osborne, T. (2003), 'Against "creativity": a philistine rant', *Economy and Society*, 32(4): 507–25.

Strathern, M. (1992), *After Nature: English Kinship in the late Twentieth Century*, Cambridge: Cambridge University Press.

Taylor, C. (1989), *Sources of the Self. The Making of the Modern Identity*, Cambridge: Cambridge University Press.

Wagner, R. (1986), *Symbols that Stand for Themselves,* Chicago: University of Chicago Press.

–9–

Performing the World: Agency, Anticipation and Creativity
Kirsten Hastrup

In this chapter I shall explore a set of theoretical issues related to the way in which social worlds are performed; by this I mean that social worlds have no existence outside of practice and performance – however much they seem to be systematic in some sense or other. By their unique and unrepeatable acts, people actually contribute to a perceived pattern; social life is routinely choreographed by the ceremonial animal (James 2003). Stressing the performative rather than the semantic or the cognitive aspects of social worlds is – among other things – to acknowledge the prominence of time and temporality in their make-up. I shall argue that our apperception of the social depends on a sense of closure that is belied by life itself – always spilling over into new histories, new ways of thinking and new complexities. New histories are made in diverse ways, but in this chapter I shall concentrate on the processes of anticipation and creativity. The former is seen as an inherent feature of all social action, while the latter is eccentric in relation to the pattern as perceived.

The baseline of my argument is that humans are *social* to the core. This is the legacy of European social anthropology, and with it goes a wholeness of vision that allows for comprehensive analyses of social forms, individual actions, collective beliefs, material restraints and creative expressions. The point is that 'there cannot be a "non-social" anthropology, a human science which sets aside the kind of "sociality" we find celebrated in the humanities, in poetry, religion or music', to quote Wendy James (2003: 301). This implies that even creativity is a profoundly *social* fact – as eccentric as it may be. Addressing matters of action and creative social processes responds to the long-felt need to reintroduce time and temporality into a scientific practice that 'is so detemporalized that it tends to exclude even the idea of what it excludes' (Bourdieu 1990: 81).

My argument will start in a discussion of the eventness of being, with a view to identifying social agency and its temporality. I shall proceed to a discussion of the illusion of wholeness that pervades social life, with a view to establishing the role played by anticipation; after that I shall discuss creativity as an accordion of meaning. I shall conclude with some intimations of imagination as the link between action and history in a more general sense.

Agency: The Eventness of Being

Evans-Pritchard (1961) once noted that history is what reveals society for what it is; effectively this implied that time was an all-important parameter in the identification of social worlds. More recently, it has become acknowledged that the social is not only revealed over time, but also constructed *with* time (Bourdieu 1990; Fabian 1991). In anthropological accounts, the succession of moments and the duration and density of events have most often been subsumed under the presentation of a configuration; this is a feature of narrative, as we know (Ricoeur 1991). The challenge now is to highlight the *occurrence* of life and the variety of ways in which people construct their reality with time – in anticipation of an outcome or in the interest of invention. Social life and individual action are closely intertwined with anticipation and creativity.

Let us start with the observation that living is essentially unrepeatable; borrowing a term from Mikhail M. Bakhtin (1993), one could claim that the essence of being is its 'eventness'. The rationalist legacy had made us think that to truly understand a particular action we have to split it into its content or sense on the one hand, and its historical actuality on the other. However, no action exists beyond one's 'once-occurrent' experiencing of it (Bakhtin 1993: 2). The act is real only as an indivisible whole. It is in its entirety that the action contributes to the process of biography and history, where it has no meaning independent of the moods it releases and the motives it embodies.

Being consists in being engaged in a reality of unique, unrepeatable events, and unique, once-occurrent experiences *that are real only as wholes*. The events exist only in the moment of their realization and our experience. Similarly, *thinking* is not something that more or less successfully attaches itself to and reflects upon action. It is part of an action or even an action in its own right; according to Geertz (2000: 21), thinking is the most consequential of social acts. To acknowledge the eventness of being is to acknowledge the *undivided* experience of meaning and action as a social fact.

The eventness of being gives new substance to the idea that being is becoming. Often these two terms have been seen as opposed, 'becoming' referring to an unsteady state, leading, hopefully, to a steady state of 'being'. But as Friedrich Nietzsche (1991) realized, these two states are but one. One becomes what one is through a process by which the individual incorporates and accommodates experiences. One's identity is not dependent on being always 'the same', but on being consistently true to oneself and being able to incorporate new experiences

(Ricoeur 1992). All of a person's actions, including those performed against better judgement, contribute to his or her character. The general point is that the self has no essence, only character, *emerging* from one's actions – not the other way round (Hastrup 2004a). 'What I am has to be understood as what I have become' (Taylor 1985: 47).

The emergent nature of character and the eventness of being shed a peculiar light on the relationship between self and time, which in a sense are but abstract notions for agent and action. Agency points to the power to act responsibly within a particular social world – certainly not exclusive to Western subjects – with a view to both past and future. Curiously, what is often left out of theories of agency is the notion of time; however, the emergent nature of character implies that the agent is constantly in a process of reconciliation with the past. There may be actions one regrets, and events one would rather forget – yet on the whole, the past is what has led to the present, and only 'now' is one able to change this course, and project oneself into the future. In the process of appropriating the future, through one's actions, the nature of the past is constantly reinterpreted – this, we know also from the plays on stage, in so many ways mirroring social life in general (Hastrup 2004a). As the plot progresses, previous occurrences gain renewed significance. And the suspense of form – being the diacritical feature of dramatic illusion – makes this process end only with the curtain (Hastrup 2004b). This also pertains to our lives; only when there is no future left would we be able fully to comprehend our story – and with it our character. Then, of course, it is too late to restyle it. Incidentally, this is why the writing of autobiographies may imply a symbolic death (Hastrup 1992b).

To the extent that we cannot say of all the constitutive events of our lives that 'thus I willed it', we have to accept that we cannot *will* the future either. The eventness of being and the emergent nature of character make such control impossible. The future is orchestrated by many partly unknown players whom one cannot direct at will. This is a lesson well taken from Shakespeare's drama, whose characters are constantly caught up in their own acts. In *Macbeth*, the protagonist is caught up in the history he himself has orchestrated but cannot control. His command, 'Let every man be master of his time' (III. 1. 40), gradually loses conviction. If the question for Hamlet is to be or not to be, for Macbeth it is to kill or not to kill. Macbeth finds himself in a state of liminality, or *interim*, as he says (I. 3. 154). In *Julius Caesar*, Shakespeare's idea of this interim is powerfully depicted by Brutus:

> Between the acting of a dreadful thing
> And the first motion, all the interim is
> Like a phantasma or a hideous dream. (*Julius Caesar* II. 1. 63–5)

Who does not know this feeling from experience? Few have planned a murder, but many have considered whether to apply for a particular job, for example and found themselves in a temporal crisis akin to Macbeth's: 'a moment that seems exempt from the usual movement of time, when the future is crammed into the present' (Kermode 2000: 205). The interim is saturated with ontological uncertainty. Acting temporarily solves it. This goes for social acting in general, I would suggest, where 'the present' is always the momentous unknown (Strathern 1992: 178).

Causal explanations in history are often reduced to an identification of precedents – and more often than not the most recent and the most exceptional among all the events that preceded the phenomenon to be explained (Bloch 1956). From an anthropological perspective, the anticipated future plays an even more significant role in the understanding of history than preceding events, even if past experience does infiltrate anticipation (Hastrup 2004c). History is created by people, who act 'in character' within a plot-space that they may only partly comprehend, but to which they inevitably contribute their actions.

This poses the question of the extent to which humans are really the source of their actions – a question already raised by classical tragedy. As Vernant has said about the world of Aristotle's dramas, the individual who commits a crime is also its victim:

> The action does not emanate from the agent as from its source; rather it envelops him and carries him away, swallowing him up in a power that must perforce be beyond him since it extends, both spatially and temporally, far beyond his own person. The agent is caught in the action. He is not its author; he remains included within it... (Vernant 1992: 44)

Clearly, Macbeth was to some extent caught in his actions and thus swallowed up by his destiny; yet he also remained a responsible moral being. This feature not only relates to literary characters, whom the author can mould freely; we have seen how even the players of these characters become swallowed up in particular moral horizons and actions, once they take the internal perspective of the character. The attempt to prove that any moral (or other) justification for action will always conflate with the rational, epistemological explanation is bound to fail. Intentionality has to be separated from agency (Singer 1993: 44ff.). Intentional subjectivity often resorts to the metaphor of 'will', which displaces agency from the social to the individual domain. The agent may refer to intentionality in describing the action, but it is a description that includes the consequence of the act, and hence cannot be taken as its cause. Attribution of intention provides a justification, while attribution of agency is an assignment of responsibility (Davidson 1980: 48). Agency, therefore, is not reducible to intentionality, however much this provides the agent with a metaphor for the act.

The inherent problem in many discussions of agency and will is apparently the notion of will itself. One 'wills' so much for so many reasons, and within such different social contexts and moral horizons, that the concept of will itself is severely weakened as a rational explanation for action. By itself, 'will' explains only a fraction of the course of events, be they on the level of biography or world history. Willing *something*, and not just willing, is the key; the objective of the will is never simply a formally defined goal, but a fulfilment of desires and anticipations that are imbued with emotional and moral values of which one is rarely aware. Indeed, awareness may result in willing *nothing*, as we know from *Hamlet*, because it makes us realize that there is no simple, unified goal of human action, no shared master motive that will eventually result in eternal bliss, if reason could only reign.

Anticipation: The Illusion of Wholeness

In a precursor to this chapter I have discussed 'illusion' as a key to understanding how society is realized in the actions of people, engaged in a gradual fulfilment of what they see as the current and relevant drama (Hastrup 2004b). Illusion is to be understood in the theatrical sense of 'suspense of form' rather than a suspense of plot; what makes the drama gripping (for both players and audience) is not uncertainty about outcome, but the process of getting there. Until the drama is over, the participants act in the interest of completing the story. This also applies to other social spaces, where agents gradually realize what they perceive as the 'play' *through their actions*. They play their part in a plot that transcends them because they are linked in space and time to other people, other moments and other stories. Conversely, the self emerges as a character within a plot structure that is always deeply social, as I suggested above. Social reality is not reducible to either the whole or the parts.

The notion of plot structure is originally owed to Aristotle, who in his work on drama simply defined it as the organization of events. The plot 'is the first principle and, so to speak, the soul of the drama' (Halliwell 1987: 37–8). For Aristotle, the plot structure is the organization of events into one whole drama and it is therefore only when the drama is over that the actions take on their true significance (Vernant 1992: 36). Characterization is secondary to plot because it is included only for the sake of the actions; in other words, the actions are not there to portray the characters. We cannot fail to notice the likeness to social life in general: we do not act in our daily lives in order to portray ourselves, but through our actions our 'character' stands out, more or less clearly. By stressing the pre-eminence of plot, Aristotle simply built upon the pre-eminence of action in real life (Freeland 1992: 112).

For the player, the connection is embodied; the wholeness of the plot is present in the individual action. There is only one action at a time, a hypothesis of character existing, as the actor Simon Callow explains, 'on the interface between you and what the author has written' (1995: 164). Through the embodiment of the play, players may even get to know the individual characters better than the writer; the writer wrote the characters with all due concession to the plot, but the players *are* them (ibid.). Their actions are *real* in this sense. If it is an imitation of action, it is still an imitation *in* action, as well. The emphasis is on the *making* of the representation, not on representation itself. It is an activity that deeply affects the player for whom 'imitation' becomes a lived experience. As Callow puts it, the player finds him- or herself in a state of 'ontological flux' (ibid.: 171).

The notion of ontological flux implies much more than simply switching between being oneself and impersonating another. For the actor, action is one whole thing, and there is little discussion of the primacy of either action or character; both are constituted within a plot that lends coherence and meaning to individual actions, while also achieving its reality from these very actions. The suspense of form premeditates a kind of cultural *engagement* – to use Michael Herzfeld's notion (1997: 3) – that breaks away from any notion of cultural determination while also giving room for an illusion of wholeness. In the drama, the representation of action (the act) and the organization of the events (the plot) fuse and make one whole play, a world. This actually qualifies the nature of 'imitation' at a vital point. The play achieves its realistic effect not by *copying*, but by making the audience vicariously experience real actions as intelligible only by way of emplotment – that is, by making a whole configuration out of successive events (Ricoeur 1991). In actual social life each moment and each action both expose and betray the absent 'social order'. The rhetoric of regularity is denied by the social experience that precedes it (Jenkins 1994: 452).

All social fields, ranging in scale from the global community to villages and families, depend on illusion (as suspense of form) to be real. To accept the 'rules of the game' an illusion of a whole, ordered by certain conventions and of a shared interest, is a precondition (Bourdieu 1990: 66ff.; 1996: 166ff.). The point is that by investing their own interests and actions in filling out the form, social agents make the community happen. Without a sustained (and shared) illusion about the social space in which one participates, no action makes sense. Society is a suspended form that precipitates particular actions, through which the illusion is gradually *realized*. Indeed, society does not exist except in its permanent seeking of form; in other words, a social space – be it a nation state, a university conference or a construction site – has no ontological status *as a whole* apart from what is collectively attributed to it and made manifest in action. Conversely, social spaces are naturalized and allowed to exert physical force over individual action.

Action is never simply a *re*action to what has already happened; it is also a mode of acting upon anticipation. Agency in this sense, I would argue, is closely tied to a vision of plot, to the anticipation of a story, a line of future development. It is a profound matter of *responding*; response being made within a moral horizon and within a social context that we interpret and project forward as we go along. 'Anticipation is also potentiation' (Strathern 1992: 178). Without a sense of plot, meaningful action would be precluded. The sense of plot is what integrates individual actions into a larger vision of the world, filled out imaginatively and acted upon. In that sense any social action is a creation, contributing to a history that outlasts (and outwits) our imagination.

We perform a world into being, acting as much upon anticipation as upon antecedent. We may even speak the world into occurring, because speech in itself is an act; *words are thoughts in action* (Berry 1992: 17). Words are not simply expressions of the world, they are means of dealing with it – after which it is no longer the same. Speaking – like seeing and thinking and other processes by which one appropriates the world – is bound up with time and history. To understand a mode of action or a form of life, we must bring figure and ground, or 'the passing occasion and the long story', into coincident view (Geertz 1995: 51). The unique event of the act and the 'long story' of the plot belong together. The 'frame' is always part of the event; the larger plot is incorporated into individual agents. It is not for them to fully comprehend their actions because the descriptions that are available to them from inside their experience cannot at the same time bring the complete story into view.

The illusion of a social whole is an efficient framework for social action; its efficiency is constantly reaffirmed in practice, where agents realize the whole as they engage in unique actions – with a view to a perceived plot and in anticipation of particular responses. In this sense, time is an integral part of what looks like pattern – but can only be so in retrospect or in anticipation. This, I would argue, is part of the reason why time and temporality tend to recede from view – for social agents and theorists alike – namely that the frame moves along with the act. The eventness of being concedes to the illusion of wholeness.

Creativity: The Accordion of Meaning

If anticipation is creative in the sense that responsible social action always contributes to the (re)shaping of the social, creativity as such must mean something different. Evidently, there are many possible ways of defining the notion of creativity; initially I shall take it to describe a way in which *perceived* newness enters the world (Hastrup 2001). Creativity is not cut loose from the world (in which case it would register as madness), nor is it simply a competent response to anticipated outcomes (putting it on a par with agency). For 'creativity' to retain a separate meaning, it must comprise both the unexpected and the recognizable, both newness and anticipation.

The creative agent is one of those 'gifted individuals who have bent the culture in the direction of their own capacities', as Ruth Benedict has phrased it (1932: 26), echoing Sapir, who suggested that 'creation is a bending of form to one's will, not the manufacture of form *ex nihilo*' (Sapir 1924: 418). In this respect it differs from magic, which Mauss identified as precisely that: a creation *ex nihilo* (1972: 141). Creative agency brings the unprecedented into effect by way of imaginative power and thus expands the community's awareness of itself. The expansion is possible due to the inherent flexibility of the social. Bateson has defined flexibility as 'uncommitted potential for change' (1972: 497); and I would argue that all social worlds have such uncommitted potential – outside of the commitment to uphold the illusion of wholeness and dramatic closure. The illusion is necessary for 'the social' to make sense, and for individuals to see themselves in the frame.

This illusion provides a safety net for creative agents to experiment with form. Bateson provides the parable of the acrobat on a high wire to illustrate his point about flexibility (ibid.: 498). To maintain his position on the wire, the acrobat must be free to move from one position of instability to another, and his arms must have maximum flexibility to secure the stability of more central parts. If the arms are locked, the acrobat will fall. During the period when the acrobat is learning to walk on the wire, and thus learning to move his arms in an appropriate way, a safety net is necessary; this gives him the freedom to fall off the wire. 'Freedom and flexibility in regard to the most basic variables may be necessary during the process of learning and creating a new system of social change' (ibid.). Both freedom and flexibility are provided by the social. Thus, even the lonesome and eccentric acrobat depends on a sense of the communal to engage the high wire.

In general, creativity deliberately parts company from anticipation; the former presents the truly discontinuous, while the latter is at most inadvertently transformative (Friedman 2001). An example of such transformation is found in Sahlins' work on the historical reworking of Hawaiian mythical themes (1981). The point is that social creativity cannot be a mere fact of novel combinations, making it a wholly intellectualistic enterprise (Friedman 2001: 60). It must also contain a sense of semantic and emotional newness, in which others are prepared to take interest – and invest themselves – in spite of its being unprecedented and discontinuous.

The reason for action, whether or not on the high wire, is not of course located in the mind alone. There are lots of hidden causes and preconditions, many of which are beyond cognitive understanding. Once again, fieldwork teaches a lesson. By engaging other worlds, ethnographers experience how they are caught in a web of apparently irrational behaviour. They act as if 'out of their mind', or as if they are not really themselves. They are not, of course, if by 'selves' we refer to fixed ontological beings. Through their own sensation of acting 'between' worlds, anthropologists experience a glimpse of a larger truth of people being concurrently engaged in 'incontinent actions', that is, actions that go against better knowledge, as it were (Davidson 1980: 21ff.). Most often, such actions are deemed out of the ordinary, out of the domain of reason. Yet – as irony does in the domain of language – such incontinent actions show the potential crack in individual agency and the creative surplus in any moment.

We may add to our understanding of this crack if we consider the proposition made by Donald Davidson (1980: 43ff.) that the identification of an action involves a 'third event' – which is where irony, individuality and unpredictability reside. Agency plays 'accordion' between intention and consequence. Davidson's example is the statement that 'Brutus killed Caesar by stabbing him'. It seems clear enough that the stabbing resulted in Caesar's death (thus linking agency to causality), but we still have that 'third event' whose relation to other elements of the sentence is unclear, namely the killing itself. Killing is not a description of the act, but a concept compounded of the intention and consequence of the act of stabbing. In fact, most actions are described in terms that include their consequences. This gives rise to a recurrent mistake:

> The idea that under the assumed circumstances killing a person differs from moving one's hand in a certain way springs from a confusion between a feature of the description of an event and a feature of the event itself. The mistake consists in thinking that when the description of an event is made to include reference to a consequence, then the consequence itself is included in the described event. The accordion, which remains the same through the squeezing and stretching, is the action; the changes are in the aspects described or descriptions of the event. (Davidson 1980: 58)

Once we describe particular events or speak of agency, we incorporate a good many things that have little to do with the simple bodily act, and much to do with ways of perceiving oneself in social space in a constant process of reorientation through actual social performance. I would suggest that creativity resides in the ability to play the accordion – to act – without incorporating an anticipated consequence into the perception of the action, or to make the event break free of the frame while still allowing it to be recognized. In that sense creativity belongs outside of historical time; it refuses simply to realize a preconceived illusion.

Imagination: The Link Between Action and History

In this final section I shall tie together the preceding paragraphs by suggesting how agency, anticipation and creativity are linked up with imagination, and how imagination itself plays with time. Gaston Bachelard suggested that 'A phenomenology of imagination must do away with all intermediaries ... it is not a question of observing but of experiencing being in its *immediacy*' (Bachelard 1994: xx). In this view, imagination is an inherent element in the eventness of being as defined above and is part and parcel of the immediacy of agency. Imagination and agency are two sides of the same coin.

Immediacy transcends the moment, however. As Richard Kearney has it: 'Imagination promises to present "absent" value in the immediate here and now. It encourages consciousness to defy historical postponement of meaning. Imagination resolves to create its own meaning, out of nothing, even if it has to invent an unreal world in which to do so' (Kearney 1998: 6). In any historical moment, imagination is a precondition for anticipation and for the illusion of wholeness – both of them preconditions for social action. The challenge for anthropology is to invent a language that will not betray this insight by subsuming the eventness of being under narrative closure.

Let me approach this by way of an example. All of us know Malinowski's now almost mythical arrival story: 'Imagine yourself suddenly set down surrounded by all your gear, alone on a tropical beach close to a native village, while the launch or the dinghy which has brought you sails away out of sight...' (Malinowski 1922: 4). We also know that being 'alone' was maybe not a social fact, but a mental one. What I want to stress in particular is his invocation of beginnings: 'Imagine further that you are a beginner, without previous experience, with nothing to guide you and no one to help you' (ibid.: 4). Beginners are normally qualified as unskilled (as yet); they do not have the corporeal knowledge necessary for acting appropriately in the situation. We know what Malinowski means because we recognize the feeling of 'beginning'. Closer inspection, however, reveals that Malinowski profoundly misleads his readers in the interest of presenting himself as a hero. No one is without previous experience, and there are lots of people in the field to help you. They may not help you directly or knowingly in your immediate interest, but in pursuing their own interests they are there for you to engage with.

What, then, is Malinowski's point in casting himself as an absolute beginner, apart from underscoring his act of heroism? Without being too speculative, I think it is safe to suggest that by emphasizing the beginning, he establishes a zero-point by which one can measure his later perfection. The beginning is constructed *retrospectively* at the precise moment it is described. We need pasts to tell our stories of fulfilment; this also applies when we are telling stories of

Agency, Anticipation and Creativity

our own discoveries or theoretical innovations. Thus, anthropological creativity itself works through a particular play on temporality. The problem lies in the introduction of a narrative deception that configures the 'beginning' as absolute, when actually its consequence becomes part of the description of the event.

At a general level, narration is always a construction with time – as is social life. In most cases, narratives depend on linear representations of time (Ricoeur 1984); this implies that they are generally related to the directional. It is part of the Enlightenment legacy that history was also seen as directional or progressive, as the story went (Hastrup 1992a). History and the writing of history became conflated, and the early anthropologies conceptually transformed difference in space to distance in time (Fabian 1983). This is a well-known story, which was targeted in the critique of modernism. The critique was not without merit, but perhaps it went too far in suggesting that no history has a direction – even if direction can be established only retrospectively.

The moments that make up history are 'total historical facts', in a similar manner as those undivided actions discussed above. They are simultaneously action and meaning, past and future, and are generally portrayed in categories that incorporate the consequences in the description of the events. For true creativity (historical discontinuity) to happen or to be perceived, the storyline must be broken. In this case, the microhistory of the act cannot simply amplify the macrohistory of social structure – to use Sahlins' (2005) notions – but must challenge it.

Language is inherently deceptive because it tends to portray the world in categories that make us believe that even actions are fixed and ordered, while in fact they are accordions in perpetual movement. Thus language itself privileges the safety net over the flexibility of the high wire. The latter, however, is found in the mode of irony. Irony embodies a certain detachment from the world as represented in ordinary language and speech, and facilitates the imagination of a possible otherness. 'Irony plays with the possibility of limitless alterity' (Rapport and Overing 2000: 212). Ironic imagination is a universal human capacity for expressing and exploring the possibilities for reforming practice and refining knowledge.

Irony treats the world as inherently contingent, and it therefore comes closer to experience than those categories that are normally used to describe it; yet irony only works within a language that provides the safety net for the explorer of new ways of understanding, new tightropes of achievement – just as creativity works within a social field where most of the time the appropriate actions can be anticipated. I would suggest that social creativity is irony in the mode of action as well as speech.

For both anticipation and creativity, imagination provides the link between action and history – because imagination is what makes present actions meaningful by making anticipation possible; and because imagination also makes the creative agent perceive that intention and consequence are not one and the same. As distinct imaginative modes, anticipation and creativity work upon different temporalities: the first relates to perceived continuities; the second hinges on discontinuity.

To explain how the world *works* is to make new connections between individual imagination and social 'facts', and between the unique event and history. One such connection that often passes unacknowledged concerns the excess of social experience at any point of time, that is, experience which is not captured by current categories, and which potentially points to alternative ways of seeing things and acting on them. This 'historical surplus' comprises possible sites of social resistance or creativity, as the case might be. In both cases, we can see how temporality and imagination are inseparable from human agency and the eventness of being. The future is crammed into present action, just as the past is.

References

Bachelard, G. (1994), *The Poetics of Space*, Boston, Mass: Beacon Press.
Bakhtin, M.M. (1993), *Towards a Philosophy of the Act*, Austin: University of Texas Press.
Bateson, G. (1972), *Steps to an Ecology of Mind*, New York: Balantine Books.
Benedict, R. (1932), 'Configurations of culture in North America', *American Anthropologist*, 34: 1–27.
Berry, C. (1992), *The Actor and the Text*, London: Virgin Books.
Bloch, M. (1956), *The Historian's Craft*, Manchester: Manchester University Press.
Bourdieu, P. (1990), *The Logic of Practice*, Cambridge: Polity Press.
—— (1996), *The Rules of Art*, Cambridge: Polity Press.
Callow, S. (1995), *Being an Actor*, Harmondsworth: Penguin.
Davidson, D. (1980), *Essays on Actions and Events*, Oxford: Clarendon Press.
Evans-Pritchard, E.E. (1961), 'Anthropology and history', in *Social Anthropology and Other Essays*, New York: Free Press.
Fabian, J. (1983), *Time and the Other: How Anthropology Makes its Object*, New York: Columbia University Press.
—— (1991), *Time and the Work of Anthropology*, London: Harwood Academic Publishers.
Freeland, C.A. (1992), 'Plot imitates action: Aesthetic evaluation and moral realism in Aristotle's Poetics', in A.O. Rorty (ed), *Essays on Aristotle's Poetics*, Princeton, NJ: Princeton University Press.
Friedman, J. (2001), 'The iron cage of creativity: An exploration', in J. Liep (ed), *Locating Cultural Creativity*, London: Pluto Press.

Geertz, C. (1995), *After the Fact*, Cambridge, Mass.: Harvard University Press.
—— (2000), 'Thinking as a moral act', in C. Geertz, *Available Light*, Princeton, NJ: Princeton University Press.
Halliwell, S. (1987), *The Poetics of Aristotle*, London: Duckworth.
Hastrup, K. (1992a), 'Introduction', in K. Hastrup (ed), *Other Histories*, London: Routledge.
—— (1992b), 'Out of anthropology. The anthropologist as an object of dramatic representation', *Cultural Anthropology*, 7: 327–45.
—— (2001), 'Othello's dance: Cultural creativity and human agency', in J. Liep (ed), *Locating Cultural Creativity*, London: Pluto Press.
—— (2004a), *Action, Anthropology in the Company of Shakespeare*, Copenhagen: Museum Tusculanum Press (Copenhagen University).
—— (2004b), 'All the world's a stage. The imaginative texture of social spaces', *Space and Culture*, 7(2): 223–36.
—— (2004c), 'Getting it right: knowledge and evidence in anthropology', *Anthropological Theory*, 4(4): 455–72.
—— (2005), 'Social anthropology: Towards a pragmatic enlightenment', *Social Anthropology*, 13(2): 133–49.
Herzfeld, M. (1997), *Cultural Intimacy*, London: Routledge.
James, W. (2003), *The Ceremonial Animal: A New Portrait of Anthropology*, Oxford: Oxford University Press.
Jenkins, T. (1994), 'Fieldwork and the perception of everyday life', *Man*, 29: 433–55.
Kearney, R. (1998), *Poetics of Imagining: Modern to Post-Modern*, Edinburgh: Edinburgh University Press.
Kermode, F. (2000), *Shakespeare's Language*, London: Allen Lane.
Malinowski, B. (1922), *Argonauts of the Western Pacific*, London: Routledge and Kegan Paul.
Mauss, M. (1972), *Towards a General Theory of Magic*, London: Routledge and Kegan Paul.
Nietzsche, F. (1991), *Ecce Homo: How One Becomes What One Is*, Harmondsworth: Penguin Classics.
Rapport, N. and Overing, J. (2000), *Social and Cultural Anthropology: The Key Concepts*, London: Routledge.
Ricoeur, P. (1984), *Time and Narrative*, Chicago: Chicago University Press.
—— (1991), 'Life in quest of narrative', in D. Wood (ed), *On Paul Ricoeur: Narrative and Interpretation*, London: Routledge.
—— (1992), *Oneself as Another*, Chicago: University of Chicago Press.
Sahlins, M. (1981), *Historical Metaphors and Mythical Realities: Structure in the Early History of the Sandwich Islands Kingdom*, Ann Arbor: University of Michigan Press.

—— (2005), 'Structural work. How microhistories become macrohistories and vice versa', *Anthropological Theory*, 5(1): 5–30.

Sapir, E. (1924), 'Culture, genuine and spurious', *American Journal of Sociology*, 29: 401–29.

Shakespeare, W. (1994), *Complete Works of Shakespeare: The Alexander Text*, London: Harper Collins.

Singer, A. (1993), *The Subject as Action: Transformation and Totality in Narrative Aesthetics*, Ann Arbor: University of Michigan Press.

Strathern, M. (1992), 'Reproducing anthropology', in S. Wallman (ed), *Contemporary Futures*, London: Routledge.

Taylor, C. (1985), *Sources of the Self: The Making of Modern Identity*, Cambridge: Cambridge University Press.

Vernant, J.-P. (1992), 'Myth and tragedy', in A.O. Rorty (ed), *Essays on Aristotle's Poetics*, Princeton, NJ: Princeton University Press.

–10–

'Tradition and the individual talent': T.S. Eliot for Anthropologists

Felicia Hughes-Freeland

This chapter is about artistic creativity, particularly embodied performance, in relation to time and established practice. I begin with the poet, playwright, essayist and critic T.S. Eliot's seminal essay 'Tradition and the individual talent' (1946 [1920]) to frame a discussion of creativity in relation to history, innovation and self-invention, and to answer the question '*who* is the creative agent?' I also make some comparisons with a phenomenological model of creative performance. The second part of the chapter explores my ethnography of Javanese performance in the light of Eliot's ideas about creativity. I close by suggesting that anthropological pluralism in theories of creativity and agency allows for the coexistence of different temporal styles, and raise some more general points about the relationship of temporality to structure and agency.

Creativity may be applied to two kinds of action: innovations that mark a change in direction from previous practice; and ongoing problem solving (Carrithers 1992; Davis 1994). The assumption that creativity is a constant has been used to support an improvisational model of action, according to which it yields 'a series of ramshackle contraptions which serve to get us through from one day to the next... The analogy is with Heath-Robinson rather than Palladio' (Davis 1994: 107–8). This idea of social action as a series of creative improvisations is reminiscent of Lévi-Strauss's (1966) notion of 'bricolage', which he contrasted to 'engineering' as a more systematic and methodical mode of thought. If all societies have both modes of thought (Lloyd 1990), then creativity might also have more than one style. My focus will be on innovations, but it will become clear that the contrast between innovation and ongoing improvisation is less clear-cut than it might first appear.

Tradition and the Individual Talent

In Western discourse, artistic creativity has been associated with the individual since the eighteenth century. The personalization of authorship was intensified

Romantic movement, in contrast to the idea of social creativity. ?hilosophy of John Dewey that sees self-criticism as the way to ..,ity, Joas has argued that 'now that there are no longer any metasocial ,.,arantees to underpin the creation of social orders, reflection causes us to turn to the creativity of human action itself' (1996 [1992]: 258). Even if 'metasocial guarantees' and indeed history have changed (or ended) since 1920, the poetic practices of Eliot are relevant to theorizing the (post)modern multiple person (Battaglia et al. 1995). In particular, Eliot's arguments about impersonality in the creative enterprise prefigure post-structuralism's 'death of the author', and remind us that postmodernist claims about the individual rest on a false contrast: abnegation and deconstruction are themselves at the heart of modernity (Hughes 1979; Strathern 1990; Appignanesi and Garratt 1995).

Eliot asserts the importance of tradition in creative writing over and above that of the personality of, in this case, the poet, taking up four themes that are relevant to my argument. First, a tradition 'cannot be inherited', it must be worked at; it involves 'the historical sense', based both on 'his own generation in his bones' and on 'the whole of the literature of Europe from Homer and within it the whole of the literature of his own country'. By compressing time in himself, the poet becomes more of his time: 'a sense of the timeless as well as of the temporal and of the timeless and the temporal together, is what makes a writer traditional. And it is at the same time what makes a writer most acutely conscious of his place in time, of his own contemporaneity' (Eliot 1946 [1920]: 14). Eliot repeats this theme in *Four Quartets* (first published in 1944), coming close to suggesting that change is defeated by time as a process of accretion which produces a tradition. But with his growing interest in Hinduism and Buddhism, most strongly evident in *The Waste Land* (1969; first published 1922) there is also the sense that this accretion is cyclical, as we rehearse, rewrite and re-enact the same core dilemmas (or myths or archetypes) over and over again. *Four Quartets* (Eliot 1969) is a Christian meditation on this inexorable cycle of life, death and rebirth, and opens with the oft-quoted lines: 'Time present and time past / Are both perhaps contained in time future, / And time future contained in time past' (*Burnt Norton*). The poem is also about 'the intolerable wrestle / With words and meanings' (*East Coker*), but the last quartet offers reconciliation as time and place become unified: 'History is now and England' (*Little Gidding*). You might be thinking that Eliot's concern is with how the creative interacts with the past, whereas anthropologists are concerned with how individuals interact within the group, socially and mutualistically (Carrithers 1992: 117), but our topic invites a consideration of personal creativity within the temporal context of action. Eliot's understanding of time presents concepts that will be familiar to anthropologists: linear and cyclical time (Howe 1981). His views about culture and cultural unity being founded on a 'common faith' (Eliot 1948: 82) are less helpful to anthropologists; thus my remarks here concern his ideas about tradition in the sense of conventions deriving from a shared literary past.

Eliot's second theme is the centrality of innovation to artistic production, and raises questions about texts and genres. A new work changes the whole of the existing order: 'the past should be altered by the present as much as the present is directed by the past' (Eliot 1946 [1920]: 15). Tradition is not a constraining factor but an enabling one, which is transformed even as it is built upon in time, as has been made clear in a useful discussion of metamorphosis and change in 'the permutations and creative acts' generated by the *Agganna-suttanta*, a 2,400-year-old Buddhist text (Carrithers 1992: 118–45). The literary critic Tsvetan Todorov appears to share this view; he has written that 'no text is the simple product of a pre-existing combination but is always the transformation of that combination ... double-movement, from work to literature (or genre) and from literature to work' (Todorov 1990, cited in Curti 1998: 34). In this he opposes Croce's view of genre as anti-creative, anti-original, and of necessity violated by artistry (Curti 1998: 184).[1] Eliot's poetic practice exemplifies this in *The Waste Land*, a polyphonic, multi-voiced work, which includes quotations, allusions and references from many genres and traditions, Hindu and Buddhist included, and, famously, was the first poem to come with its own footnotes. This poem was a palimpsest, and rewrote pre-texts. It was also a dialogic work; Eliot redrafted extensively after feedback from his friend, the poet Ezra Pound, another enthusiastic recycler of previous texts. Tradition – or in this case, genre – is dynamic rather than deterministic, inspirational rather than ideological. This has implications for the relationship of agency and structure, to which I return below.

At this point I draw attention to some points of comparison between Eliot's approach and that of the philosopher of science, Robert Crease (1997), in which creativity depends on the product's gaining value (or reception, or meaning) in relation to the larger whole. 'Let us call creativity the process by which new phenomena are sought and brought into the world. Performance is one means by which world enrichment can happen' (Crease 1997: 220). Innovation, in turn, is a process that Crease calls 'carrying-forward', in which 'I apply everything that has been culturally and historically transmitted to me, and inevitably wind up acting originally and with fresh involvements' (ibid.: 222). This 'carrying-forward' is similar to Eliot's vision of temporal depth, but comes closer to anthropological models of constant creativity as a prerequisite for sociality (Carrithers 1992: 67; Davis 1994: 98). Creative performance is part of a '*responsive order*' (Gendlin 1995, cited in Crease 1997: 222, my emphasis). Rather than thinking up an idea in advance, scientists and artists are 'involved in an interactive process in which putting together a performance involves accommodating oneself to diversions, obstacles, and responses that are not *exactly* what we expected... A new phenomenon shows itself as more than a program or theory, but not apart from it' (Crease 1997: 222). This is relevant to general thinking about creativity in the social as well as the temporal field, because it attempts to explain the relationship between the agent and the collectivity in the creative process: ideas come not from sitting alone, but from 'working on a subject, working on an experiment, that gives the idea' (Perl 1996, in Crease 1997: 222–3).

This leads to Eliot's third point: that a work of art must do more than conform to be new. A test of its value is 'its fitting in' (Eliot 1946 [1920]: 15). Although the boundaries of acceptability and the notion of a 'canon' have altered since Eliot was writing, reception and recognition are central to how anthropologists might model creativity as innovation and as social. They also serve to inscribe a creative work into time, so that it ceases to be a momentary one-off, an idiosyncratic solipsism or eccentricity, and becomes available as a reference in the fabric of the sociocultural world. The creative person draws on what is already there in the hope of adding to the whole, which will continue into the future. Newness is meaningless unless it can be received: recognition is one of the 'three essential characteristics of performance' (Crease 1997: 218).[2]

The fourth and final point is that the poet works not from Wordsworth's 'emotion recollected in tranquillity', but from 'a continual surrender of himself ... a continual self-sacrifice, a continual extinction of personality' (Eliot 1946 [1920]: 17). Poetry is 'an escape from emotion ... an escape from personality' (ibid.: 21). Here Eliot rejects a subjectivist (or individualist) ground of poetic creativity and gives it instead a relational and collectivist significance: the individual artist gathers to himself the sum of history. Given what an *innovator* Eliot was, it is revealing that he nonetheless prioritizes continuity over innovation in the act of creation, and detachment over the personal. This is more than a self-legitimizing tactic: his criticism consistently asserts the links between the individual work and its predecessors. For example, Shakespeare's *Hamlet* is

> a stratification, it represents the efforts of a series of men, each making what he could out of the work of his predecessor. The *Hamlet* of Shakespeare will appear to us very differently if, instead of treating the whole action of the play as due to Shakespeare's design, we perceive his *Hamlet* to be superimposed upon much cruder material which persists even in the final form. (ibid.: 142)

Eliot notes that it is in 'depersonalization that art may be said to approach the condition of science' (ibid.: 17). Interestingly, where Eliot depersonalizes art, Crease personalizes science, and develops a phenomenological, first-person, experienced-based account of embodied creativity as performance in relation to temporality: 'A performance in this sense is not merely a *praxis* – an application of a skill, technique or practice that simply produces what it does

– but a *poesis*; a bringing forth of a phenomenon, of something with presence in the world' (Crease 1997: 214). Creativity in the dramatic arts and science share a performative process which is not a metaphor but actually 'assists in the encounter with the new' (ibid.: 216), even if it does not completely determine the outcome.

It could be argued that the characterization of temporality in Eliot's and Crease's accounts, as in anthropological ones, fails to take into account time as a system of power (Mills 2005: 350). Eliot's time is metaphysical, and slips away from political constraints, just as Crease comes down towards the optimistic end of phenomenology's view of the world as a good place to be, rather than one where carrying-forward might be forbidden by officials or the force of circumstance. For instance, for Crease a new performance is 'mysterious'; it 'imposes itself', transforms us and is 'celebratory' (Crease 1997: 220–1); but is this newness at the level of form or experience? Just as disjunction is minimized in the view of time as flowing and fulfilling (albeit ultimately destructive of human life in Eliot's vision), the constraining factors on creativity, and the relations between creativity and constraint, are not explored. There is no possibility of a Khmer 'Year Zero' in their models.[3]

The crucial point in Eliot's essay is that at the height of modernism, a key modernist innovator is claiming continuity with an august classical line of forebears, and yet displays a recognition of a key issue in self-making, what Battaglia calls 'the tension between the rhetorics of an individuated, autonomous self and rhetorics of a collective or relational self' (Battaglia 1995: 7). Eliot's essay can be summed up in the following passage:

> The poet cannot reach this impersonality without surrendering himself wholly to the work to be done. And he is not likely to know what is to be done unless he lives in what is not merely the present, but the present moment of the past, unless he is conscious, not of what is dead, but of what is already living. (Eliot 1946 [1920]: 22)

In thinking of the dead not as gone, but as having contributed to the living, Eliot echoes Comte's view that 'the majority of actors are the dead'; and thus agents are not necessarily individuals (Archer 1995: 73). This gives tradition a different character: rather than being assumed to take a deterministically structuring form that impedes creativity, tradition (the products of the agentive dead) is itself a form of agency. So at the very least, Eliot's essay demonstrates that when we think about creativity in relation to agency, we need to be careful how we think about creativity in relation to what already exists, and also not to overstate the contrast between societies which could be characterized by Western individualism and those with what might initially appear to be a more collectivist social style.

Performing Continuity and Innovation

Drawing on the ideas outlined above, I now turn to agency and creativity in Javanese dance traditions of the court city of Yogyakarta, to consider where creativity might be said to reside in a tradition in which the degrees of freedom for innovation and individual expression might appear limited (Hughes-Freeland 2001a).

In high art traditions in Indonesia and elsewhere, the role of the dancer has been to conform to a pre-existing movement text by working to perfect the execution of dance figures: to repeat, not to innovate or improvise.[4] Such practices have been seen as expressions of regimes of discipline, not self-expression. Scholars of different dance and drama traditions in Indonesia have often compared the performer to a puppet, explaining that what is at issue is not the dancer but the danced, rather as poetic work for Eliot involves the 'extinction of personality'. In the case of Java, genres are at issue. Dance forms have names that refer as much to circumstance as to anything inherently generic. Human dance is referenced back to a prior puppet form, though not in the case of ceremonial female dance. A second problem of comparison here is that whereas Western criticism has a literary taxonomy (baroque, Gothic, etc.) and a critical apparatus, Javanese discriminations and evaluations have worked differently. For instance, particular sultans of the colonial principality of Yogyakarta are associated with particular 'cultural phases': thus Sultan Haměngkubuwana VIII's reign (1921–39) is variously associated with the heyday of dance theatre, its renaissance or its degeneration into kitsch. Authorship of specific dance works has been attributed to the sultan, and not to the choreographers and practitioners who created them. Considering the relationship of physical texts to performances, it is important not to obscure or compress the processes of production that link any performance to its other versions (see Hughes-Freeland 2005). Such processual data are central to elucidating more generally how performances are produced out of prior texts and in turn generate subsequent texts.

The classical dances of Java as performed in the royal courts require the dancer to efface visual expression and to fit his or her body movements to prefigured sequences, in a manner which suggests a Foucauldian sense of discipline (see Hughes-Freeland forthcoming for a critique of this approach). In court dance, performers had to satisfy the rigorous scrutiny of a sultan like Haměngkubuwana VIII, who is remembered as a disciplinarian and a stickler for detail. In most court dances, the dancer does not aim to stand out but to fit in to the group, which can be seen as an image of the body politic moving in harmonious accord under the scrutiny of the sultan's gaze. Women's ceremonial dance forms reproduce the restraining clothing and behavioural codes for speech and comportment that characterize formal social interaction, and they do so at a pace which is almost slow motion. The aesthetic goal of dance movement is to achieve a quality called *alus*, which is often glossed as 'refined', although words like 'gentleness' or 'restraint' better communicate this feeling, experienced in dancing as well as in social interaction.

Performance practitioners explained that *alus* is achieved through a correct relationship to measure (*wirama*). This can be illustrated by *ngĕndherek*, one of the simplest movement sequences from Saritunggal, the training dance for the feminine style. It is accompanied by the musical form *kĕtawang*, in which there are sixteen beats to each stroke of the big gong (*gong agĕng*). The intermediary eighth beat is marked by the *kĕnong* (vertically hung gongs), and every other beat by small horizontally hung gongs (*kĕthuk* and *kĕmpul*). The dancer fits her movements to the music by attending to these instruments, notated below as *gong*, (*kĕ*)*nong*, (*kĕ*)*thuk* and (*kĕm*)*pul*. The numbers are how the sequence is counted out (here in Javanese) in dance training: *si-ji, lo-ro, ti-ga, pa-pat, li-ma, ĕ-nĕm, pi-tu, wo-LU*, the *LU* indicating the accent of the gong on the sixteenth beat. For the dancer these sixteen beats are counted as eight, as shown in the following example; the dashes indicate the places filled by basic and elaborating instruments and the rhythm-directing drum (*kĕndang*).

1	2	3	4	5	6	7	8
-	[thuk]	-	pul	-	thuk	-	nong

1	2	3	4	5	6	7	8
-	thuk -		pul	-	thuk	-	nong/gong

1. Knee bend, look right, left hand *ngruji* (palm forwards, thumb diagonally across), flick back right sash (the dance sash is tied around the waist and hangs to the floor in two lengths).
2. 'Kick' (*gĕdrug*) left foot (the foot comes forward, draws the fold of the *bathik* skirt back and puts the toe down behind). The *thuk* is not sounded on this beat of the cycle.
3. Up on toes (*jinjit*), body weight slightly forward.
4. Knee bend, left foot back a little, right sash held, body leans left, look left.
5. Prepare to
6. Kick right foot, flex left wrist.
7. Lean right.
8. Flick back right sash and look right, left hand unchanged.

This sequence is performed three times, with the gong falling on the first and third repeats.

This dance sequence was described to me as a musical sentence: 'the *kĕnong*, *kĕmpul*, and *kĕthuk* are commas, the big gong a full stop; one musical sentence is then filled in with two or three motifs' (Gusti Suryobrongto in conversation, 1983). But this punctuate grammatical analogy is inconsistent with the desired aesthetic of dance movement, which is of 'flowing water' (*toya mili*), the result of sustaining dance movement across these counts (Bu Yudanĕgara in conversation, 1987). A less experienced dancer will interpret the counting in *ngĕndherek* literally, and make the mistake of rushing the shift of body weight at the fourth beat and then either executing the kick too soon or being left with a hesitation between the fifth and sixth ones. Flowing water means that the dancer's movement should never cease: she is always turning a hand or letting her chin lead her neck in a graceful turn after the transfer of body weight has been completed, sustaining movement which centres on an incessant shifting of weight from one leg to the other. When turning onto the dance floor in entrance marches, trainee dancers turn their chins too far ahead of moving their weight into the advancing leg, and run out of movement before the rest of the body has followed. The physical precision required of the dancer calls for an anticipation that comes only with experience, as does the ability to exploit the lack of coincidence between the layers of musical texture, between the percussive gongs noted above. The experienced dancer moves with a fluency that is at once continuous, sustained and measured, not rigidly set against the musical structure, but in a flexibly responsive way: the relationship between movement accents and musical accents should be what Gusti Suryobrongto called *nggampuh*, 'late but not late' (in conversation, 1983).

This detailed example conveys something of the relationship between the text and the enactment, or between the genre and the work, to reiterate Todorov. The form may be prescribed, but there is a highly dynamic and ongoing need for responsiveness by the performer, who loses herself in the dance, extinguishing her personality while performing creatively out of hard work and practice, not through abandonment to an externally conceived agent (as in the case of possession). During the performance, the highly controlled and formalized movement ideally frees the dancer, who transcends any mechanical determination of movement: 'the movements move by themselves, and the dancer faces God' (Rama Sena, in conversation, 1987). In contrast to Eliot's idea of extinction, this effacement occurs in the present moment of collective performance, with the prescribed movements becoming automatic, and the creative presence freed to transcend constraints (Hughes-Freeland 2001a). So although to an outsider court performance might exemplify social constraint and the repression of any creative personality, for individuals within the tradition, creativity, liberation and even immanent subversion were central to their understanding of the tradition in which they worked. Discipline and expression, far from being opposed, are here united in a creativity that dissimulates itself in the process of 'getting it right'. The signs of creativity are not always obvious, so here we find that Crease's specifications of multiple horizons, freshness, thrall and attention (Crease 1997: 219) need modification. Indonesian performances are rarely the sole focus of attention, and only sporadically involve an audience experiencing the 'edge-of-the-seat' quality of thrall and attention. When we turn to consider the work of the choreographer, we find again that innovation is not always visible.

Innovation in a Local Tradition

I now outline the relationships of three individual choreographers to the classical Javanese court tradition of Yogyakarta.

Bu Yudanĕgara (Yuda), the widow of the present sultan's uncle, is a leading choreographer of female court dance forms.[5] Her *bĕdhaya* dances appear identical to ones seen in 1924 colonial footage taken by the Dutch cinematographer, Tassilo Adams, among some samples of performance documentation brought back to Java in the 1980s by the American dance scholar and performer Deena Burton for purposes of elicitation, and she tends to work in the temporal scale which had become the norm by that time. However, although each tradition of Javanese ceremonial dance involves the principle of *mutrani*, 'being the child of (the previous work)', they are never just imitations. Bu Yuda also 'revives' older dances, but modifies them to include specific gestural and choreographic references to the event they represent. For example, the Accession Bĕdhaya dance of 1989 referenced the older Bĕdhaya Durma, but the lyrics were new, albeit written in a conventional style. The costumes diverged from the usual ones, and included large orange bows (which met with royal disapproval as not in keeping with traditional values of feminine modesty in dress). Yet orange bows apart, these innovations were barely perceived as new. Bu Yuda does experiment with new forms, however, usually by changing the numbers of dancers performing a set genre, which entails creating new floor patterns, as for example in her *Saritunggal* for six dancers (see Figure 10.1). Her *bĕdhaya* dances tend not to breach the scale and substance of 'traditional' form, nor are they attributed to their choreographer. She operates in a system of service where individual effort is neither recognized nor rewarded financially, but takes place in terms of generalized exchange. Like the choreographer in my next example, she has also taught in state dance academies.

Rama Sasmintamardawa (Sas) was, until his death, an expert in feminine dance, and a court choreographer of female dance. Since the 1960s he ran a dance association which puts on shows for tourists. His dances look like court dances and have an enduring appearance of continuity: they appear to have the same pace and tempo, the same costumes, musical and choral accompaniment, and so forth. But they differ in two ways. First, they are fundamentally different for the dancers to perform. Rama Sas's stance requires the dancer to pull her shoulder blades together and tighten her torso, as I discovered when I moved

Figure 10.1 The *Saritunggal* for six dancers. Photograph by Felicia Hughes-Freeland

from his dance school to take classes with Bu Yuda, who taught me to take a softer stance. Second, his choreography increases the number of transitions and weight shifts which occur in an eight-beat cycle, sometimes doubling them.[6] He also choreographed many solo female *golek* dances (which in the colonial period were performed by males). These dances are shorter, often lasting only fifteen minutes, and are easier to memorize than the court versions. They are immensely popular with dancers in Yogyakarta who often complained about the 'difficulty' of learning and performing the longer court forms. Rama Sas has been linked to performance though a process which is absorbing the royal family into the institutions of the post-colonial state, and before he died some of his innovations had fed back into the court, in terms of dance style and choreography.

Innovation varies in scale and in the extent to which it appears. These two examples of classically practising court choreographers would both be classed as working within an identical tradition. But their choreographies and comportments are by no means identical. Rama Sas's creativity is more marked than that of Bu Yuda, but, like her, he innovated within a generally recognized repertoire. It is important to note that within the court itself, these two choreographers collaborate in productions, although the dance will have been designed by one or the other. Variations on the tradition are passed down as former pupils of these teachers take on the mantle of court choreographer. So the effects of individual creativity are here blended into the collective enterprise, which continues to be branded with the stamp of the sultan, as it always has been in the Javanese court system since the eighteenth century (if not before).

Didik Hadiprayitno ('Didik Nini Thowok') plays with traditional forms to surprise his audiences with the ostensibly and demonstrably new. A classically trained innovator who is not part of the court centre, but marginal in respect of his ethnicity, religion and sexuality (Hughes-Freeland 2001b), he studies with the oldest practitioners of different regional traditions, to learn the technique appropriate to the genre he wishes to use (like Eliot's poet, working to get the historical sense in his bones). But rather than replicating the appearance of traditional forms, he uses aspects of their gestural and presentational resources in new forms. For example, in the *Walang Kekek* dance, he draws on Balinese masked dance, Sundanese music and dance movement and Western mime; in the 1987 *Dwimuka* 'Two faces' dance he plays with Sundanese mask dancing, and wears the mask on the back of his head (see Figure 10.2). A more extreme

Figure 10.2 Didik Nini Thowok plays with Sundanese mask dancing. Photograph reproduced by permission of Didik Nini Thowok

example of his innovative approach is the 'Sandal Dance', *Tari Teklek*, which he devised for the carnival to open the Yogya Arts Festival Week in July 1989. The dance was inspired by the noise made by the wooden sandals that were standard bathroom wear in Java before plastic flip-flops were introduced. As the band of children from his dance school, wearing comical heart-shaped sunglasses, processed down the main street past the seated dignitaries and standing crowds, they did not so much dance as clatter. Cleverly, Didik had taken an unassuming and everyday traditional rural object, recognizable to any Javanese, and made it the instrument of a completely new performance. And yet everyone (except possibly a handful of overseas tourists) understood the idea and appreciated the humour of its minimalism. This example epitomizes how he works: to produce a new performance in the future out of a dialogue with established practice. His dances look new and different, but are invariably based on extensive immersion in their traditions of embodiment. He himself also plays with the interface of genre- and gender-bending, simultaneously continuing the 'tradition' of male dancers representing females in Yogya court performance, and extending them into something new. A recent experiment was to present a male *bĕdhaya* (unseen for fifty years), made new by using Japanese influences in dress and fan-work.

Innovation is not always apparent, and technical expertise can dissimulate newness behind the appearance of similarity. Tradition thus appears to continue in a legitimized manner, but underneath the surface there has been a radical restructuring, in one example, of the number of movement transitions within a cycle of eight beats. Although there might appear to be a very big contrast between these forms of creativity, there is also considerable interaction between the three in their engagement with tradition. One difference is Didik's highly professional approach to his work, and his ability to generate a considerable income from his performances (Hughes-Freeland 2001b: 223).[7] Of the three, he is closest to Eliot, as his work is historically grounded, but the surface is new and surprising, and requires the audience to readjust their expectations. The only difference between these choreographers and Eliot's artist is that they do not have access to the texts of the past as the dance traditions are largely oral. What they were in the past can only be inferred from what has survived in the present, and the depth of that past is less than Eliot's (Hughes-Freeland 2006).

Conclusions: Creativity and Temporality

I have argued that creativity and constraint are complementary, not opposites; they are co-present and co-dependent in performance. T.S. Eliot's literary critical essay presents a modernist and humanist view of the person, not as a highly individuated subject, but as one susceptible to the pressures of the past. Both

he and Crease give grist to anthropology's attempt to balance a col.
with the creative individual as a framework for dealing with different
creativity in relation to the 'way of the ancestors'. Although it is not yet clear what a distinctively anthropological take on creativity would be like, it is heartening that when Keith Sawyer could not find enough psychologists to contribute to his book on performance and creativity, he was able to find anthropologists working in this field (Sawyer 1997: 1).

I have drawn from Eliot a model of creative yet historically defined personhood, and applied it both to Javanese court choreographers, making dances to fit the classical canon with different degrees of innovation, and to the ostensibly innovative choreographer whose aim is to entertain and surprise his audiences and also attract new pupils. These examples show how creative performance work builds on previous practices, and dissimulates individual innovations to varying degrees. In all cases, what is new and individual is the tip of the iceberg: the size of the tip may vary, but what remains common is the proportionately vast section hidden under water – the past. The ways in which each practitioner engages with the past are quite individual. In Eliot's argument, creativity is not a question of moving away from social structure; rather it is understood to be moving the past forward. Eliot's artistic model conjoins with the social model of creativity in emphasizing the effect of the action in the world – 'fitting in' or 'recognition'. If an idea or an artefact is too new, or too singular, it risks failing to enter into the field of social relations, failing to connect to an audience or to a market. Isolated and unrecognized, it becomes solipsism and will not survive the test of time. So creativity becomes a strategy for moving away from the past while retaining a link with it.

I close with a general theoretical point about temporality and creativity. Archer (1995) has made a case for placing temporality at the centre of social analysis. She criticizes Anthony Giddens' structuration theory for 'conflating' structure and agency into a timeless present, using words that could have come from Eliot's *Four Quartets*: 'it is the past *in* the present which matters for him ... a continuous flow which defies periodization'. What is lacking in Giddens, and arguably too in Eliot, is 'the length of time between the "moment" and the "critical phase" – in which the slow work of structural elaboration is accomplished and needs theorizing about' (Archer 1995: 89). Crease, conversely, would be found guilty of 'upwards conflationism' by privileging agency over structure (ibid.: 84). Social conditioning works on transformative moments of agency which are then reintegrated, morphogenetically, into a temporal developmental line. Structure and agency work together in this model to make creativity possible *across time*. Anthropologists might have reservations about the value of the model for explaining emergent phenomena as opposed to historical data and about its specifically linear understanding of temporality; they might also wish to consider creativity as a special kind of agency. Nonetheless, we would do well to attend to Archer's warnings about the delusions of structural determinism – because 'the world of people props the door permanently open' – or of becoming 'floored by flux' in the quagmires of process, because the properties of structures are different from those of people (ibid.: 70). Most importantly, the model endorses my argument that the relationship between tradition and individual talent is not a simple correspondence between structure and agency; instead, tradition can act as an agent, not just in a structural and constraining sense. There is value in considering how to bring in the context of time to separate out the aspects of the personal agency of the creative subject and the systemic, structural or cultural collectivity which emerges in a different timescale, even as we go about our more personal, particular, present view of the world, manifest in the I-witnessing of fieldwork in the Malinowskian tradition.

Acknowledgements

The author is grateful to Faber and Faber for permission to quote from the works of T.S. Eliot.

Notes

1. Despite Marxist assertions that genre has ideological power, Curti argues that while we may not be able to escape the power of the text, there is room for manoeuvre. By playing with genre in a Derridean style, we can find the counter-law behind the conventions: 'The very same essence of genre, repetition, engenders variation, deformation, proliferation and decomposition ... Genres become quotations, frames, thresholds and, at the same time, parody, contamination and play with form. In this function or absence of function, they remain essential elements of the game' (Curti 1998: 33, 40). This statement resonates with Eliot's own (pre-postmodern) play of genres and quotations, in both *The Waste Land* and *Four Quartets*. The dynamic 'self-referential' understanding of genre challenges a strong critique of genre as represented in Bakhtin's notion of 'chronotypes' (Hobart 1991: 208 and *passim*).
2. The other characteristics are 'presentation ... original rather than representative ... revelatory and disclosive rather than imitative [and] representation – through text, script, technique etc. – [which] has a "*fragility*" because in use these elements are often modified to fit what works in performance' (Crease

1997: 217-8). A discussion of fitting-in moves newness away from the producer (one might ask whether a performance is ever new *for the performer*, because performances are rarely one-offs) to the audience, who might be experiencing something for the first time, but alternatively may be experiencing a different version of what is already familiar, as my ethnography shows.
3. As Crease observes of performers, 'their purpose is internal to the process, and if some other motive is involved – money, prestige, problem solving, career advancement – it provides no indication as to how to perform well' (Crease 1997: 217). However, in another essay in the same volume, Hanna (1997) describes how externality can constrain exotic dancing: both the physical body and the legal code impinge on how to perform *acceptably*, i.e. to permit recognition.
4. As Joy Hendry observed at the ASA 2005 conference, creativity resides as much in getting it right as in making it new.
5. Since writing this paper I have learnt the sad news of Bu Yuda's death.
6. Experts recognize this immediately; some claimed that these were not Rama Sas's own innovations, but a return to choreographies and performing styles from a dance school set up outside the court in 1918 by two princes, on the sultan's instructions, so that outsiders could learn court forms.
7. Didik works in a professional capitalist style, but one that needs to be distinguished from the 'capitalist creativity' of exotic dancers in the USA (Hanna 1997).

References

Appignanesi, R. and Garratt, C. (1995), *Postmodernism for Beginners*, Cambridge: Icon Books.

Archer, M. (1995), *Realist Social Theory: The Morphogenetic Approach*. Cambridge: Cambridge University Press.

Battaglia, D. et al. (eds) (1995), *Rhetorics of Self-Making*, London, Berkeley and Los Angeles: University of California Press.

Carrithers, M. (1992), *Why Humans Have Cultures*, Oxford: Oxford University Press.

Crease, R.P. (1997), 'Responsive order: the phenomenology of dramatic and scientific performance', in R.K. Sawyer (ed), *Creativity in Performance*, Greenwich, Conn. and London: Ablex Publishing Corporation.

Curti, L. (1998), *Female Stories, Female Bodies: Narrative, Identity and Representation*, Basingstoke: Macmillan.

Davis, J. (1994), 'Social creativity', in C. Hann (ed), *When History Accelerates: Essays on Rapid Social Change, Complexity and Creativity*, London and Atlantic Highland, NJ: Athlone Press.

Eliot, T.S. (1946 [1920]), 'Tradition and the individual talent', in *Selected Essays*, London: Faber and Faber.

—— (1948), *Notes towards the Definition of Culture*, London: Faber and Faber.

—— (1969), *The Complete Poems and Plays of T.S. Eliot*, London: Faber and Faber.

Hanna, J.L. (1997), 'Creativity in Ubakala, Dallas Youth, and Exotic dance', in R.K. Sawyer (ed), *Creativity in Performance*, Greenwich, Conn. and London: Ablex Publishing Corporation.

Hobart, M. (1991), 'Criticizing genres: Bakhtin and Bali', *Bulletin of the John Rylands Library*, 73: 195–216.

Howe, L. (1981), 'The social determination of knowledge: Maurice Bloch and Balinese time', *Man (NS)*, 16: 220–34.

Hughes, S. (1979), *Consciousness and Society*, Sussex: Harvester Press.

Hughes-Freeland, F. (2001a), 'Dance, dissimulation, and identity in Indonesia', in J. Hendry and C.W. Watson (eds), *An Anthropology of Indirect Communication*, ASA Monographs 37, London: Routledge.

—— (2001b), 'Performers and professionalization in Java: between leisure and livelihood', *South-East Asia Research*, 9(2): 213–33.

—— (2005), 'Visual takes on dance in Java', *Oral Traditions*, 20(1): 58–79, with eCompanion at www.oraltradition.org

—— (2006), 'Constructing a classical tradition: women's dance in Java', in T.J. Buckland (ed), *Dancing Across History and Ethnography*, Studies in Dance History, Series of the Society for Dance History Scholars, Madison: University of Wisconsin Press.

—— (forthcoming), *Embodied Communities: Dance Traditions and Change in Java*, Oxford: Berghahn.

Joas, H. (1996 [1992]), *The Creativity of Action*, trans. J. Gaines and P. Keast, Oxford: Polity Press.

Lévi-Strauss, C. (1966) *The Savage Mind*, London: Weidenfeld and Nicolson.

Lloyd, G.E.R. (1990), *Demystifying Mentalities*, Cambridge: Cambridge University Press.

Mills, M. (2005), 'Living in time's shadow: Pollution, purification and fractured temporalities in Buddhist Ladakh', in W. James and D. Mills (eds), *The Qualities of Time: Anthropological Approaches*, ASA Monographs 41, Oxford and New York: Berg.

Sawyer, R.K. (ed) (1997), *Creativity in Performance*, Greenwich, Conn. and London: Ablex Publishing Corporation.

Strathern, M. (1990), 'Out of context: the persuasive fictions of anthropology', in M. Manganaro (ed), *Modernist Anthropology: From Fieldwork to Text*, Princeton, NJ: Princeton University Press.

–11–

Back to the Future: Temporality, Narrative and the Ageing Self

Cathrine Degnen

Introduction

Western stereotypes about old age include the notion that older people are 'lost' in the past.[1] Such representations effectively employ different temporal relations as a marker of oldness itself. In this chapter I explore intergenerational differences in people's relationships with time and how temporality becomes a marker of social difference and distinction. While I argue on the one hand that such notions contribute to the stigmatizing of older people as no longer fully adult, on the other hand, subjective temporal positioning does appear to shift as people age. The ageing self exists in a time universe which differs from that of younger and middle-aged adults, not just in its frames of reference, which determine how people position themselves, but also in the extent to which the past informs the present, as well as in a certain insouciance about the future. This difference offers insight into a temporal positioning of the self that may be unique to this part of the life-course. This chapter explores the dynamics of these differing temporal relationships and their implications for the construction and maintenance of the ageing self. In particular, I examine the characteristics of narrative style used by the older people I came to know during the course of my fieldwork; I consider the ways in which these characteristics challenge narrative conventions and temporal ordering; and I call into question my own initial supposition that these narrative styles were a creative form of resistance to social stereotypes.

Theorizing the Construction of Self

One thread of anthropological research on the self has emphasized both the contextual and shifting nature of selfhood and the central role of narrativity in constructing the self. This approach to understanding the creation of a sense of self is predicated on a processual and interpretive framework, led by influential authors such as Rosaldo (1980, 1984), Turner (1985) and White and

Kirkpatrick (1985). This paradigm perceives the self as created in its telling, in its performance and in its reception by others (Bruner 1984) through time in a particular sociocultural context. Self formation is not a uniform nor a necessarily chronological process (Boyarin and Boyarin 1995: 28), but is rather experienced as a cyclical, multi-stranded web of relations. Senses of self vary depending on whom they are being performed for, and the self is forged in a dialectical relationship with others.

Temporality (experience of and experience within the passage of time) figures powerfully in the creation of the self because narrations of the self occur not once, but repeatedly in many moments. The self is in perpetual motion and is constantly being reinterpreted and recreated across multiple moments in time. Indeed, it behoves us as ethnographers to remember that such moments include the research context, created during interviews and participant observation. By narrating experience, individuals create self-representations which are neither unitary nor fixed, but rather fragmented and partial, as well as perpetually under construction (Peacock and Holland 1993; Bruner 1984, 1986).[2] As a result, how the self is narrated depends on circumstance, level of discourse and context. While authors of anthropological literature concerned with the self, experience and subjectivity have paid careful attention to cross-cultural differences in these topics, they have given little consideration to the impact ageing may have on the construction and experience of self. Indeed, it strikes me that a middle-aged, universalized self is taken as the baseline for discussion about experience, but that the losses of 'unprecedented seriousness ... [such as] retirement ... death of lovers, friends and kin' (Thompson 1992: 27) faced by older people are largely absent from the literature. Perhaps under such conditions a certain rewriting of the self could be anticipated, but this possibility has gone largely unexamined.[3]

In a separate body of literature concerning the anthropology of old age, questions about personhood and the self have been framed in a very different way. Here, issues of dementia, role-loss or loss of status have been of central concern. While research on these topics has been valuable for expanding our understanding from a cultural perspective of pressing issues such as Alzheimer's disease (Herskovits 1995), it can also reproduce a problematic tendency to see the self and personhood in old age only in terms of fragility and decay. Such a powerful paradigm ultimately reproduces the notion of old age as a 'problem' and is at the expense of the majority of older people who are neither 'demented' nor needing care.

Drawing on the theoretical insights offered by these two areas of anthropological research, respectively on selfhood and old age, I aim to explore how aspects of the self particular to old age but not specifically linked to illness or disability, such as temporality, identity and narrativity, play out in everyday life. Such an approach is necessary in order to better understand what the future and the past actually signify in older people's notions of self. The ethnographic examples on which I draw come from fourteen months of fieldwork (2000–1) in a South Yorkshire village called Dodworth, near Barnsley. The village is situated in an area that used to be known for coal mining. Until the late 1980s, coal was still being mined on a large scale in and around Dodworth. The subsequent closure of the mines has caused deep socio-economic and cultural rupture. How people make sense of their lives under the erasing pressures of post-industrialism is a question that runs alongside and fundamentally intersects with my interest in the experience of ageing. The demise of the mining industry and subsequent social transformations that these erasures provoke also bring into focus the ways larger global changes play out on the local level. Issues orbiting around selfhood become particularly relevant within this context as the excruciating shift out of heavy industry into post-industrialism threatens the foundations on which the self was written and understood locally, quite apart from those reorientations due to the subjective experience of old age itself. Here I can only signal the importance of this contextual background, which I have examined more fully elsewhere (Degnen 2003). I turn now to an exploration of the distinctive forms of temporal experience and its implications for the ageing self, as they emerged from this fieldwork.

Narrative Style

Researchers have commented on the extent to which older people engage in what Myerhoff has termed 'narrative activity', something she describes as 'intense and relentless' (1979: 33). Hazan writes that

> The 'invisible social worlds' (Unruh 1983) of the elderly are ... often based on ritualized forms of talk (e.g. story-telling, discussion groups, proverbs, etc., ...) ... the question of why elderly people are so pre-occupied with the oral, and the various forms this preoccupation takes in the postmodern, could arguably define a new agenda for a sociology of ageing that is sensitive to its narrative moment... (Hazan 1996: 27)

My research experiences were similar in this respect to Myerhoff's and Hazan's. I spent a great deal of my time during fieldwork happily listening to such forms of talk and spontaneous narrative accounts, both inside and outside the interviewing context.[4] While the *content* of these narratives has been central to my work, I turn my attention here to three distinctive characteristics of narrative *style* among my research participants. These are shifting temporal frameworks, 'irrelevant' information and the decoupling of background information from narrative accounts.

Shifting Temporal Frameworks

The first distinctive characteristic of narrative styles employed by many of the older people who took part in this research has to do with the movement between past and present and their mutual integration. For example, one afternoon in July 2000, Anne and I were sitting together at her kitchen table having a cup of tea and catching up, having not seen one another for about a week. We had known each other by then for about six months and usually met at least twice a week, often for several hours at a time. I was telling her about things I had been up to or that I was worrying about: trying to find someone to remove the rotting timbers and the stone slabs that formed my kitchen floor and replace them with a new wooden floor before they collapsed; the wedding I had been to in Lyme Regis; and a part-time teaching job I had been commuting to in Hull.

In marked contrast to my talk about the present, Anne listened politely and then went on at length about how her husband had told her once they started dating and then once they were married that she could not go out with her girlfriends any more, especially not dancing. He felt strongly that once they were a couple, they would do couple things together. This was something she had trouble accepting at first, but eventually (and especially after having kids) she got used to. She told me how her granddaughter is enjoying her new job as an assistant at a nursing home and then started talking about the changes in her own life after marriage. This led to her telling me what it was like when her husband, at the age of fifty (over thirty years ago), had to quit his job on the railway and take another job due to his angina.

Her narrative about these past moments, events and worries in her life was not at all self-consciously different from when she was talking about the present or listening to me speak, but rather was seamlessly integrated into our chit-chat about contemporary everyday concerns. Although Anne may weave different historical periods in and out of her narratives, she is by no means 'lost' in the past and lives a very active, present-oriented life. She does incorporate a great many past events from long ago into her narratives about the present, however, as do the majority of her peers. The temporal frameworks bookmarking Anne's conversation with me shift much more than my own.

This aspect of narrative style of older people that I became accustomed to during my fieldwork is different from the one I use myself. It is also distinct from that used by middle-aged and younger adults in Dodworth (which largely parallels my own). It often seemed as though I and the older people I had come to know were speaking in different forms of the same language. By and large, I was employing a linear form whereby small talk is about present-day occurrences, experiences, hassles, problems, worries and pleasures. Conversation is carried out in a more or less reciprocal kind of exchange where both parties get a chance to contribute, which moves the conversation on to further topics. For the most part, however, my research participants used a much more circular form of small talk that brought in a great deal of information from the past, and was recited from a repertoire of narratives that were often strung together in long chains rather than interjected into a conversation where interlocutors alternated between the roles of speaker and listener.

Sally, another woman I came to know very well during my fieldwork, made an offhanded comment to me one day about how 'losing the art of conversation' was one of the consequences of old age. While she did not elaborate further, I believe that more than any other of the people who participated in my research, she is aware of some of the narrative shifts that occur in old age. These narrative shifts are linked to shifts in temporal perspective. However, while Sally talks about them as a loss (not surprisingly, given her overwhelming concern with the experience of disconcerting memory blanks which disrupt her conversation), she was alone among the older people I knew to do so. For this reason I have chosen to conceptualize these shifts as a reconfiguration of narrative style rather than as a loss per se.

'Irrelevant' Information

A second aspect of narrative style, the introduction of what I call 'irrelevant' information, covers a wide range of conversational topics that I encountered during my fieldwork. I have purposefully placed the word 'irrelevant' in inverted commas since my reflections on this narrative behaviour are premised on the disjuncture between the assumptions of younger and middle-aged individuals and those of older people about what belongs within the parameters of a particular conversation. I intend here not only to problematize the notion of 'irrelevant' information in narrative strands, but also to examine it as a feature of narrative discourse that emerged periodically among my research participants. What I am referring to are verbal *faux pas* that were experienced as moments of particular social stress. Although intermittent rather than continuous, these stressful moments formed a pattern that was repeated many times throughout my fieldwork. Indeed, the discomfort they occasioned was so marked that in my field notes I came to refer to it as 'the cringe factor'. In these moments I felt that my own everyday parameters of social discourse were being disrupted in a way that they usually were not when engaged in conversation with younger people. Such feelings indicated that these situations called for closer attention. What was it about the interaction that was provoking discomfort on my part? What could the dissonance reveal about the ways in which old age is constructed in interaction between generations and between individuals?

My chosen example of 'irrelevant' information comes from a woman I came to know named Olive. When chatting one day, Olive told me that she had no one to go with her to the hospital for a diagnostic test that was worrying her. The test was to assess her heart rate after she had experienced a series of troubling falls over the course of a few months. I said I would be happy to accompany her. Olive insisted that I come for lunch first, and then we would go to the hospital together. On the day, after eating together at her home, we went to catch the bus to the hospital. It never arrived, so we went back to her house to call a taxi.

This disruption to her plan made Olive anxious. When we got back to her house, it seemed as though she was transforming into a slightly different version of herself, one no longer certain and no longer in charge. Instead of going inside her own home to call a cab, she went directly to the next-door neighbour's house in distress to tell Linda (a middle-aged woman) all about what had happened. Linda came out (rolling her eyes and smiling at me) and went with us into Olive's house. By this point, Olive was so anxious that she could not think how to call the taxi firm or where to find the number. Linda used the telephone book to find the taxi number and then Olive asked Linda to call for her, which Linda did. The taxi seemed to take for ever to arrive and Olive was increasingly tense because it was clear that we would be late for her appointment.

Then, when Olive and I finally got to the hospital, I thought we were going to ask for directions for where to go, but she sped off, certain that there was a staircase nearby (and, I think, she thought that a help desk was near the staircase) even though we'd just gone past the help desk and there was no staircase where she insisted there would be. I made her stop when I realized how far we had gone in the wrong direction. By this time we were already ten minutes late for the appointment, adding to her stress. I asked her the name of the department we needed. She said she did not know and started searching through her pocketbook for her appointment slip. Once she found it, she gave it to me without looking at it and I read that it was with the cardiology department. Then, while this was happening, she stopped a man at random in the hallway we were standing in to ask for directions, but began by telling him about the bus and the taxi not coming and being late rather than asking him for directions to cardiology. She was about to tell him all about what a good neighbour Linda is when I put my arm around her shoulders. I think I meant to calm her and help her focus on asking the 'right' question, but what happened in effect is that I took over the conversation so that she would not embarrass herself with this stranger. I was afraid that he would judge her unkindly as old, senile and incoherent. By the gesture of my arm, however, I gave away much of my own assumptions about the boundaries of old age and about 'old' comportment.

Although we found our way to the correct department in the end, what struck me most was my own assessment of Olive's rapid decline into behaviour and a narrative style that is culturally codified as old. Her stream of narrative directed at the stranger seemed to me to be completely irrelevant to the situation and indeed, given the time pressures we were under, counteractive to our goal of finding the correct department. Olive, however, was understandably nervous about the state of her health and what the unknown test would be like or what the results might portend. Furthermore, the irritation of the bus not arriving meant the added expense and hassle of the taxi. Her reactions, however, extended beyond the bounds of nervousness into comportment that I read stereotypically as characteristic of old age, compounded by her narrative style with the stranger that was off-topic and unfocused.

Olive's loss of control over her comportment was mirrored in her increasingly fractured discourse and in my perception of her use of 'irrelevant' information, aspects of behaviour which lead to oldness being attributed to her by her interlocutors. This example also shows how anxiety-producing situations can sometimes threaten the normal ordering of one's relationships with the world. When under too much pressure, the carefully constructed balance of order can start to crumble. To regain some control, Olive appears to seek refuge in the reassuring narration of details of ordinary life. These details provide a sort of soothing framework, even if from the outside they appear jarring and 'irrelevant'. Such moments reveal a certain fragility of the self, but one that is probably much more evident to the outside observer than to the person herself.

The Decoupling of Background Information from Narrative Accounts

The third and final stylistic characteristic of the narratives of older people that I explore here is a tendency to refer to people and places that are not fully contextualized or explained in the course of conversation. These decouplings mean that it is not always easy to follow a narrative account without learning more about the other people, connections and experiences in the narrator's life. A brief initial example comes from a taped interview with Emma:

> *Cathrine*: And you used to help your mom out with her housework after you got married?
> *Emma*: Yeah, I used to come to hers every Thursday and I used to bring 'em, but when they started school, I used to be home for coming out.

When Emma said 'they started', I knew that by 'they' she meant her two children, even though she does not say so at this point in the narrative and had not spoken of them previously in the interview from which this passage is excerpted.

This tendency to decouple background information was common during my fieldwork. I became used to it, mentally filling in gaps in meaning such as this on a regular basis in a variety of contexts as I came to know more about each individual as a person. I was not aware of what I was doing, however, until I visited two of my older friends at home in Dodworth with a younger third friend, Diane, who was visiting me and staying over for the weekend. Both older women included a number of blanks in their conversation which assumed my friend's familiarity with topics such as their family members and local place names as well as local history, seemingly forgetting that Diane would not know any of this, let alone that she had only just met them herself. Diane's confusion and subsequent reaction to them as 'old dears' made this dynamic much more evident to me.

Reflecting on this event made me think that perhaps the context was decoupled from the narrative because the information backgrounding the narrative had become irrelevant to the subjective place occupied by the narrator in recounting her stories. Over the course of my fieldwork, narrative accounts would often open up for a short while without a beginning, ending or context. Stories were told like this as if the listener knew the tale already, leaving much background information unsaid and placing the listener in a potentially confusing position. Sally might call this narrative style part of 'losing the art of conversation', which implies that the usual rules of narration are transgressed. This transgression can cause discomfort and confusion for the younger listener. Critically, however, the narrative styles I am describing here gave no cause for stigmatization in interaction among older people themselves, but were normal aspects of their conversation. Moreover, although Emma could stereotypically be described as being 'scattered' on the basis of the blanks in her narratives, she may very well have assumed that I had all the same background information about her life and memories that she did, so that filling in the contextualizing information and constructing an explicitly (rather than broadly) linear narrative was not a priority for her.

Conclusions

Some of the episodes I recount here may seem banal when considered individually, with microscopic attention to descriptive details in the recounting of unremarkable events of daily life. I have demonstrated, however, that as these episodes accumulate, patterns emerge that are lodged in cultural praxis and come to define the limits within which daily life is lived and experienced by older people. Some of these patterns also intersect with the way experience is narrated and with the temporal rhythms that underpin this experience.

Ultimately, the decoupling of background information from the narrative being told, combined with 'irrelevant' information and shifting temporal frameworks, can destabilize younger interlocutors, leading at times to disruption in the transmission of meaning. This destabilization is due to a rupture between the temporal rhythms and the conventions of narrative accounts and positionality used by older speakers, and those used by younger co-conversationalists. In asserting that there is something distinctive about older people's narrative lives, mannerisms and experiences of time as compared to younger people, I may appear to be reverting to an essentialist argument after trying so hard to lay out an interpretative, processual framework for understanding ageing, lodged in subjectivity and experience. This, however, is not the case.

As outlined above, I take the self to be created through narration and dialectical relations. This self in narratives of older people tends to be an 'ageless self' (Kaufman 1986) and people rarely identify themselves as old, particularly because ageing and old age are heavily stigmatized in Western societies. Older people are perceived as if they are locked either into the past or into a motionless present. This evokes a particular stereotype about older people – one that turns around issues of temporality, and an interrupted temporality at that. Rather than experiencing the forward motion of time attributed to younger or middle-aged people, those who are categorized as old are, broadly speaking, taken to have stepped *out* of the flow of time and, in particular, to have their backs to the future and to be preoccupied instead with the past.

This does not simply marginalize older people as fringe members of society in a relatively powerless position, but creates a different, lesser category of being human, in comparison to a vision of the middle-aged adult whose temporal positioning becomes the standard against which older people are judged and ranked. The implications for maintaining personhood and full adult status under such cultural pressures are stark. Indeed, it is not a coincidence that ageing is perceived both as a movement out of personhood (Hockey and James 1993: 87) and as a stepping out of time, and that ruptures in selfhood and temporality go side by side in cultural constructions of old age. However, while older people are not lost in the past, the past does enter into their narrative accounts and style in a much more fluid way than it does for younger speakers. Past experiences can be used as a way of making conversation, as a way of staking a claim to knowledge based on experience, as a way of maintaining connections and as a way of performing identity.

Problematically though, these narrative styles are also taken, among members of the wider society with whom older people interact, as proof that they are old. This is because the particular non-linear features of the narratives, their shifting temporal frameworks and their decoupling from contextual information are read by younger adults as signs of senility and of a loss of self. This may be the case for a minority of older people suffering from pathologies. However, the people I knew in Dodworth, and whose narrative styles I evoke here, were emphatically not suffering from such conditions. Despite this, the patterns and rhythms of their narratives approximated the stereotyped assumptions about older people enshrined in mainstream notions of old age, in terms of the repetition and temporal flux which meant that a conversation about the present day could quickly shift into a different temporal framework located in the distant past, and back again. There are thus two issues at stake in discussing the construction of self through narrative in terms specific to old age. The first concerns the ways the self is created, worked and reworked through narration, with certain stories being used to say 'this is me'; the second concerns the ways in which certain stylistic attributes of telling these stories are interpreted by younger people as characteristic of old age itself, with the corollary that people using such stylistic patterns are themselves judged to be old.

Rapport and Overing argue that conventions of narration are based on a set of fundamental principles which, following J. Bruner (1990), they call 'time or sequentiality, narrative voice or "agentivity", narrative structure or canonicality, and point of view or perspectivity' (Rapport and Overing 2000: 287). Through these principles, individuals come to share a collective way of 'organizing, presenting and remembering information, and so knowing the world. The narrative stock of a culture is thus seen as embodying what are socially recognized to be typical behaviour patterns' (ibid.: 287–8). However, while such ways of knowing the world through shared conventions of narrative are assumed by these authors to be consistent for all members of a particular culture or society, my fieldwork data show that narrative conventions can and do change with age, particularly with a relaxation of the rules delimiting time and linearity. Ironically, this can become a double-edged sword, since the disjuncture between the conventions of middle-aged speakers (that narratives should concern the past, present and future; be orderly, linear and thus 'rational'; and non-repetitive) and those of older speakers (that narratives may well convey knowledge about the past; need not be linear; and may be repetitive) ends up *reinforcing* younger people's assumptions that older people are confused and unreliable sources of information about the present day.

Finally, and to loop this discussion back to the theme of creativity, I had hoped that an approach to ageing that privileged narrativity and temporality would also permit me to attend to the creative agency that I felt older people would exercise over the stereotypes governing old age. As these stereotypes are so negative, I wanted the older people I came to know to be freed from such stigmatizing labels. While older people are able to a certain extent to resist the deeply negative connotations of old age by refusing to accept the label of old in relation to themselves, over time I came to admit to myself that perhaps their scope for creativity in this respect is severely limited. This is partly because of the ways in which some aspects of the narrative style of older people are interpreted as confirmation of their being 'lost' in the past, but also because temporal dimensions do appear to shift for many people as they age. I nevertheless persisted, wanting to see the play with time and the multiplicity of selfhood in old age as creative responses to the pressures imposed on older people to maintain an ordered self despite the physiological and cultural pressures of ageing. In the years since finishing this fieldwork, I have come to wonder if my affirmative stance may have led me instead to participate in the occlusion of the darker sides of ageing and the fragility of experience on the margins of social life. The circularity of self, other and expectation may indeed mean that my hopes for creative channels out of social stigma were perhaps only an echo of what older people themselves are attempting to achieve (a clamping down on the infringing, threatening aspects of ageing), blinding me to the more tragic aspects of self-erasure experienced in old age. The minutiae of daily life for many of the older people I worked with were genuinely reconfigured by a sense of loss. To leave unspoken the pressures it engendered would be to misrepresent their everyday experiences. These pressures should not be muted for the sake of preserving a uniformly positive portrait of ageing.

Acknowledgements

I would like to express my thanks and appreciation to all the people in Dodworth who participated in the research project on which this chapter is based. My thanks to Ellen Corin for our many discussions about ageing, temporality and the self, and for her reminders to me that difference does not equal inequality; her insight and guidance have added immensely to this chapter. I would also like to thank Colin Scott and Colin Duncan for their careful reading of this material as it took shape, Elizabeth Hallam and Tim Ingold for their precise editing work, and Sharon Macdonald and Eric Hirsch for organizing the ASA 05 conference panel on 'Creativity and Temporality' at which I presented a version of this chapter. Funding from McGill Faculty of Graduate Studies, McGill Department of Anthropology, the Radcliffe-Brown Trust Fund and STANDD are all gratefully acknowledged.

Notes

1. Although I use the monolithic terms 'Western' and 'the West' throughout this chapter, I wish to signal here my discomfort with the largely unproblematic way these are usually employed and the homogeneity they imply. Although

there are strong cultural similarities and frameworks throughout the so-called Western world, blanket use of the term masks significant differences and nuances between the cultural groups that make up the West, as well as the even more local levels of experience and meaning within these groups themselves. Class, gender and age issues also go unsignalled. On the other hand, it does act as a sort of shorthand to express certain shared tendencies which lie behind the questions posed in this chapter. Additionally, I purposefully adopt the term 'older people' rather than 'elderly' or 'old' or 'the aged' in an attempt to move away from labels that demarcate old age in tidy compartments (and that connote chronological age).

2. Not only do individual selves shift, but cultural notions of what is accepted as 'the self' are perpetually shifting as well. Several authors (resisting earlier work in the school of culture and personality studies) make this explicit by problematizing the notion that there is a 'unitary discourse of selfhood pervasive in an entire society' (Kondo 1987: 241). Similarly, Nancy Abelmann argues that 'by assuming various and blurred epistemologies in the (traditional anthropological) field against a unified selfhood in advanced capitalist societies... we impoverish our understanding of selfhood everywhere' (Abelmann 1997: 789).

3. Consideration of some characteristics specific to the ageing self offers the chance to widen theoretical conceptualizations of the Western self. These include dynamics such as the uneven and multi-directional process of selfhood creation and an increasing rigidity in representations of self that I discuss elsewhere (Degnen 2003).

4. As an aside, while people tend not to talk explicitly about the self under normal conditions, the interview context opens up a particular sort of social space to reflect on one's self. This raises important contextualizing points about the presentation, construction and staging of self unique to interviewing. My research, however, relied as well on intensive periods of time spent with older people outside of the interview settings over many months, which balances the potential skewing effect of relying only on interviews.

References

Abelmann, N. (1997), 'Narrating selfhood and personality in South Korea: Women and social mobility', *American Ethnologist*, 24(4): 786–812.

Boyarin, J. and Boyarin, D. (1995), 'Self-exposure as theory: The double mark of the male Jew', in D. Battaglia (ed), *Rhetorics of Self-Making*, Berkeley: University of California Press.

Bruner, E. (1984), 'The opening up of anthropology', in E. Bruner (ed), *Text, Play, and Story: The Construction and Reconstruction of Self and Society*, 1983 Proceedings of the American Ethnological Society, Washington, DC: American Ethnological Society.

—— (1986), 'Experience and its expressions', in V. Turner and E. Bruner (eds), *The Anthropology of Experience*, Urbana and Chicago: University of Illinois Press.

Bruner, J. (1990), *Acts of Meaning*, Cambridge, Mass.: Harvard University Press.

Degnen, C. (2003), *Mining Experience: The Ageing Self, Narrative, and Social Memory in Dodworth, England*, unpublished PhD thesis, Department of Anthropology, Montreal, Quebec: McGill University.

Hazan, H. (1996), *From First Principles: An Experiment in Ageing*, Westport, Conn.: Bergin & Garvey.

Herskovits, E. (1995), 'Struggling over subjectivity: Debates about the "self" and Alzheimer's disease', *Medical Anthropology Quarterly*, 9(2): 146–64.

Hockey, J. and James, A. (1993), *Growing Up and Growing Old: Ageing and Dependency in the Life Course*, London: Sage.

Kaufman, S. (1986), *The Ageless Self: Sources of Meaning in Later Life*, Madison: University of Wisconsin Press.

Kondo, D. (1987), 'Creating an ideal self: Theories of selfhood and pedagogy at a Japanese ethics retreat', *Ethos*, 15(3): 241–72.

Myerhoff, B. (1979), *Number Our Days*, New York: E.P. Dutton.

Peacock, J. and Holland, D. (1993), 'The narrated self: Life stories in process', *Ethos*, 21(4): 367–83.

Rapport, N. and Overing, J. (2000), 'Narrative', in N. Rapport and J. Overing (eds), *Social and Cultural Anthropology, the Key Concepts*, London: Routledge.

Rosaldo, M. (1980), *Knowledge and Passion: Ilongot Notions of Self and Social Life*, Cambridge: Cambridge University Press.

—— (1984), 'Toward an anthropology of self and feeling', in R. Shweder and R. LeVine (eds), *Culture Theory: Essays on Mind, Self and Emotion*, Cambridge: Cambridge University Press.

Thompson, P. (1992), '"I don't feel old": Subjective ageing and the search for meaning in later life', *Ageing and Society*, 12: 23–47.

Turner, V. (ed E. Turner) (1985), *On the Edge of the Bush: Anthropology as Experience*, Tucson: University of Arizona Press.

White, G. and Kirkpatrick, J. (eds) (1985), *Person, Self, and Experience: Exploring Pacific Ethnopsychologies*, Berkeley: University of California Press.

Part IV
The Creativity of Anthropological Scholarship

Introduction
Mark Harris

During one of the sessions of the conference that gave rise to this volume, a panellist remarked with some exasperation that 'research is almost the opposite of creativity'. The remark was made publicly and, of all those present at the session, neither I nor anyone else challenged it. There appears to be a deeply and widely felt sense that real creativity lies beyond the realms of science, whether human, social or natural. If it exists in these realms, it is but a pale imitation or a sham. The correct place for creativity, it is often assumed, is in the world of high art and literature. The panellist seemed to be saying that the work of scholarship is about collecting data, applying methods, refining ideas and in general contributing to the accumulation of knowledge. And in the main, it is dreary labour. The production of high culture, by contrast, fizzes along with its own abundant inventiveness. Creativity is understood as typically the preserve of the individual author or artist. Scholarly work, even though often carried out by a single person, effaces individual identity since it is by definition a contribution to a larger body of learning. The research that we do as anthropologists cannot then be creative because it is characterized by various checks on creativity. We have to use theories developed by other people at other times and places; we are trained to avoid the idiosyncratic; we have to fit in with existing scholarship so that our argument is recognizable. To cap it all, 'audit culture' restricts any residual creative or experimental tendencies (Strathern 2000). Not only do we have to comply with the rigours of scholarship; we also have to do what our managers expect us to do.

This bleak picture is, I hope, a caricature. Many contrary examples could of course be adduced, from both anthropology and neighbouring disciplines, reminding us of Collingwood's (1993) insistence that history cannot be done without imaginative empathy. But the idea that research is 'dull', and that it requires nothing of the creative imagination, persists in various guises. We are thus in a rather odd situation, for while we can study the creativity of others, we are reluctant to recognize it in our own accounts. Whatever creativity the discipline may have remains implicit in the methods and procedures that have driven studies of other people's creativity, such as those described in previous parts of this book. In introducing the present part, I shall argue that the separation of research and creativity is unnecessary – a depressing reflection of certain aspects of academic labour that effectively mystify what anthropologists do and how they go about their work. Given the nature of its inquiry, as the study of humanity, critical reflexivity is not an end point of anthropology but integral to its overall project. Giambattista Vico was the first modern author to make this argument in his criticism of Cartesian rationalism, in his *New Science* of 1725 (Vico 1999). Vico insisted that the study of humanity requires its own methods and theories, different from those needed for studying the world of nature. Since nature has not been created by humans, he argued, it must always remain to some extent unfathomable. The history of human societies, however, fashioned through imagination and reason, can be understood through the exercise of these same faculties. Central to Vico's thought is the idea that societies and individuals follow a sequence of development that is not random, but logical and cumulative (Berlin 2000). The study of this historically situated progression is critical to the proper understanding of the creative impulse of humanity. In the following I take inspiration from this idea to argue for an expanded notion of 'the field' to include the creative spirit of research and teaching.

What are we discussing, then, under the rubric of the creativity of anthropological scholarship? It could be the range of creative ethnographic writing, taking in such works as Gregory Bateson's *Naven* (1958), Hugh Brody's *Maps and Dreams* (2002), Ruth Landes' *City of Women* (2005), Michael Taussig's *Shamanism, Colonialism and the Wild Man* (1987); a list less definitive than exemplary. Or it could be the creative and responsible uses to which anthropology can be put by anthropologists, such as in political campaigns, in teaching and in critical interventions in public debate. Alternatively, creativity could be sought in the development of specific concepts or methods in order to analyse more effectively old topics or new social formations, as exemplified in Richard Vokes' innovative use of the radio as a research tool in Uganda (Chapter 14), or in Amanda Ravetz's exploration of the uses of photography (Chapter 12).

If creativity is to mean anything it has to be framed by concrete situations rather than abstract propositions. Moreover, we have to decide whether the creative process in anthropology is different from any other kind – bearing in mind Edmund Leach's (1982: 53–4) comment that anthropologists are usually bad novelists. This is precisely the issue that Robey Callahan and Trevor Stack address in Chapter 13 comparing the work of fiction writers, anthropologists and advertising creatives. By way of introduction, I want to refocus on creativity by expanding on and reinvigorating the notion of the field. In particular, my concern is to integrate the activities of teaching and research. Conventionally, the field refers to the location in which an ethnographer conducts empirical research, typically a dense network of people defined geographically. This notion of the field is rooted in structural functionalism and its attendant literary form, the monograph, which focused on the bounded field as a set of relations (Hart 2004). What does a field site mean

Part IV, Introduction

in contemporary anthropology? Can a monograph capture that place? What form might be better suited? These questions should be practical and methodological, rather than abstract.

In the study of Latin American peasantries – my own regional interest – the conventional notion of the field came under attack over fifty years ago. The defining intellectual moment was when Julian Steward organized the People of Puerto Rico project in the early 1950s. New methodological and theoretical questions were catapulted to the forefront of the study of non-tribal peoples caught up in labour migrations, agricultural modernization and class inequality. In this and subsequent work concerning peasantries in Latin America, innovations were made in the form of writing and method; for example, the life history method, used by Sidney Mintz (1960) to look at both personal and global change, and Eric Wolf's (1959) synthetic use of anthropology, archaeology and history to study ethnicity in Guatemala and Mexico. This was not a case of losing sight of the village, but of understanding that it was, in important ways, shaped and constrained by processes and movements of people outside the immediate area. New forms of anthropological engagement were necessary to understand these processes. Fieldwork-based ethnography was too limited. Complementary techniques and sources were required, such as films, novels, archives and journalism, to express the intertwining of different ways of knowing the world.

More recently, another development has produced similar innovation in scope. Although not uniquely responsible, Michael Jackson's *Paths Toward a Clearing* (1989) pioneered an approach in which experience was foregrounded, both as a participatory method (active involvement in practical life) in the field and as an epistemological orientation (phenomenology). This argument helps to open up the stages in which anthropological knowledge is made, running from field site to academy, since it forces a reflection on the move from unarticulated experience to explicitly articulated, representational forms. Moreover, it drew attention away from the text – that is, from preoccupations with 'writing culture' – towards and into the world itself. In my terms, the emphasis on experience is a way of reclaiming Vico's project for the study of humanity, grounding it in what humans share as their common heritage and in what connects them to one another. The field, in effect, comprises the manifold pathways connecting varieties of subjective experience.

Another consequence of the experiential turn was to question the boundaries between common-sense knowledge, of the everyday kind that ethnographers collect, and the sort of expert knowledge (for example, of kinship systems) that was supposed to result from specialist analysis by trained anthropologists and that they alone could understand. The focus on experience threatened this division by refusing to allow that knowledge, since it is always connected to perception and sensation, could ever escape the world. Moreover this 'radical empiricism', as Jackson (1989) called his approach, forced a consideration of whether an ethnographer's apprenticeship in another way of life is really any different, in principle, from a child's learning the business of life amongst family and neighbours. Is the fieldworker's education so different from the interpersonal encounters in which all social and cultural life subsists? Although they are organized and valued differently, they intertwine in ways that reveal an innovative dynamic that has always been important to anthropology. I shall illustrate this point briefly by turning to the relation between creativity and teaching, again with reference to the notion of the field.

It is uncommon for anthropologists to reflect on their teaching experience, and even more uncommon for them to write about teaching as a creative exercise. I could not, for instance, find anyone willing to present a contribution on teaching to the conference session on 'the creativity of anthropological scholarship' on which this part of the book is based. There are, however, some exceptions in the history of anthropology. Edmund Leach, who had much to say about the clear communication of ideas – especially in teaching – and devoted significant time to students (Hugh-Jones 1989; Tambiah 2000), said in his fifth Reith lecture, delivered on BBC radio in 1967:

> Certainly the young need to be educated; they need to be taught to gain confidence in the astonishing power of their imaginations. But they don't need to be loaded down with the clutter of useless information which is all that traditional scholarship has to offer. Only those who hold the past in complete contempt are ever likely to see visions of the New Jerusalem. (Leach 1968: 76)

Although this passage was of its time and spoke to the generational tensions of British society in the 1960s, it should still provoke any teacher who wishes to release the power of students' imaginations. I assume that pushing the past to one side (which is to say that conservatism is a matter of choice and not of scholarly necessity) and working things out for oneself is creative. Indeed, I believe the spirit of Leach's argument is that nobody learns without trying something out for him- or herself. With this experimental approach to pedagogy, Leach saw anthropology as a personal skill requiring training, and not as a series of theories or facts to be learned (Leach 1984). Yet how can this approach possibly work as a teaching programme in universities, policed as they are by quality assurance and audits? There have been many examples in Britain over the last decade or so, but few of them have been reflected upon sufficiently to make their way into print (see, for example, the C-SAP website; Grimshaw et al. 2000; Ingold with Lucas forthcoming). Interestingly, these experimental programmes have taken place mostly in departments of anthropology linked to a specialist centre: visual anthropology (Manchester, see Ravetz, this volume, Chapter 12), ethnomusicology

(Belfast), computing (Kent). At the heart of these moves is an attempt to make the teaching process more like the research process. This is to encourage students to become researchers, discovering their subjects for themselves, with their teachers guiding them along the way.

There is nothing new about seeing teaching and research as complementary activities, but this has been more from the point of view of the academic than from that of the student. The recent switch towards a more student-centred view has been motivated by a theoretical emphasis, noted above, on the experiential aspects of social life. Learning, according to Tim Ingold (forthcoming), is an exploratory practice that generates its own knowledge and understanding. If this argument works for learning in social and cultural life, then why should it not be applied to more formal educational environments, such as the teaching of anthropology? In this light, learning becomes tantamount to acquiring the skills of perception, observation and imagination. Together with Ray Lucas, Ingold has taught a course at Aberdeen along these lines. It naturally raised a host of questions, not least of which was how to assess student work. But in its rejection of the division between learning and research, theory and practice, discovery and creativity, it forces an awareness of the process of making an anthropological argument. It throws into relief the changes a student undergoes in the course of learning, along with the methods and resources used and social relations engaged to make progress. Learning then becomes a journey in which knowledge is not so much passed down ready-made as continually produced under conditions that, far from being obscured and mystified, actually propel students forward. The same kind of journey is entailed in postgraduate and established academic work, even though we may wish to deny or distort it.

All these points come together in a superb article by Alberto Corsín Jiménez (2004), which considers the author's experience of researching mining communities in Chile, in the same place as the university where he was also working. As well as teaching his students the classical texts, he engaged them with some of his own research to the extent that some of them became his informants – hence the title of his essay, 'teaching the field'. However, they were also throwing back at him some of the concepts and theories first encountered in teaching. This, he argues, was a 'reduplication of knowledge' that reversed the normal flow of information from the field of observation to the analytical field of writing up. Students used ideas they encountered in teaching to make sense of their own lives and those of others. Corsín Jiménez argues that this aspect of teaching gives it a special 'ethnographicness', uniting the different fields of anthropological work such as the fieldwork site, the canteen, the seminar room, office, and so on. Ethnography does not produce knowledge as such; rather it mobilizes knowledge across places (Corsín Jiménez 2004: 154). Following Marilyn Strathern (1995), this can be seen as a 'rescaling of knowledge', that is, a movement between orders of signification. The notion of the field in this argument is reinvigorated through its emplacement with the ethnographer (who could be the student or the professional anthropologist) as he or she moves between different contexts and relations. The field is like a map on which paths of knowledge are inscribed, echoing Ingold's (2000) argument that knowledge-finding is a form of wayfaring or the tracing of a continuous line.

Newly established teachers, fresh from their recent doctoral fieldwork, make better teachers, according to Corsín Jiménez. They are keener to engage in the ethnographicness of teaching, to encourage students to think with and apply the categories and concepts of ethnography (Corsín Jiménez 2004: 155). Older teachers are likely to be less conversationally inclined, which is to say that they might be further from the dialogic and relational contexts of participation in their field site, though they may otherwise be better read and intellectually more rigorous. This contention is not as polemical as it seems: it was made by Edmund Leach in his 1967 Reith Lectures – no teacher of young people, Leach declared, should be over forty-five years of age. Teaching, Corsín Jiménez tells us, is the 'paradigmatic form ... of anthropological knowledge' (2004: 159). In the terms I have introduced here, fieldwork is not grounded in a specific location. We can open out the notion of the field to include the work of teaching, where a teacher and student also engage in the activity of ethnographic labour (deploying concepts in new contexts and making the effort to explain an unfamiliar argument). And if we see the university contexts in which we work as another kind of field, then we can open up the movement of knowledge to methodological scrutiny.

I have shown briefly how research and teaching have been subject to innovations and reflections that have moved beyond a restricted notion of the field and academic labour. These developments have been methodological in character and have been intended to demystify the conditions in which ethnographers come to understand their subjects. The movement, as Corsín Jiménez shows, is between different orders of understanding. Instead of squashing the creative process into an end point, such as the written ethnography or the classroom lecture, we can see it as a continuous path connecting places and persons. Those paths are anthropological ways of knowing. So long as we persist in seeing a specific kind of fieldwork as the initial experience of anthropology, I believe we reduce the creative potential of the discipline. This understanding of fieldwork is too often linked to the toolbox image of methodology, as though it consisted of an assortment of instruments to be picked up and put down, or left lying around in the field, rather than embodied skills requiring education, inseparable from their users. I do not mean to negate the significance of fieldwork or its data, or to imply any anti-science sentiment. On the contrary, I maintain that the creativity of anthropology lies in its fidelity to experience and the world, and its revelation of the connections of subject and object.

Part IV, Introduction

The three chapters here provoke a rethinking of methodology. They argue for more openness and more analytical attention to the process of making anthropology. While the discipline is no longer committed to the kind of fieldwork-based ethnography that aimed to uncover social structures and reveal their functions, it is not yet clear what has replaced it. This is partly due to the growth and subsequent partitioning of anthropology into subdisciplines. A common aim has become fragmented. The chapters in this part, in their different ways, reveal what an eclectic and methodologically sophisticated anthropology could look like (and there are other examples, to be sure). Each one engages in a conversation between anthropology and another subject: radio broadcasting, photography and creative writing. This framing is intended to be an advance on the 'anthropologies *of*...' that turn every other subject into an object of investigation. Instead we have 'anthropology *and*...'. Every such combination opens a debate, an interrogation perhaps, but always on a more equal footing. This explicitness concerning method and theory is a formalization of what has always been at the heart of anthropology. With its two-sided nature, one foot in the field and the other in the academy, anthropology's creative motor has been its unique and ambivalent identity. As Grimshaw and Hart argue (1996: 54): 'it might be said that, compared with the other sciences and humanities, anthropology has remained in important ways an anti-discipline – taking its ideas from anywhere, striving for the whole, constantly reinventing procedures on the move'. Nevertheless there is an opposite tendency with which anthropologists struggle: the move to formalize these informal procedures, and to institutionalize the anti-discipline – in short, to keep anthropology going as a university-based subject. The following chapters exemplify this struggle and the innovative and improvisational spirit of anthropology. They are not so much concerned with creativity per se in anthropological scholarship as with some aspects of the way in which anthropology can work creatively.

Acknowledgements.

I thank David Mills for his reading of a draft and his astute comments, and the Leverhulme Trust for the funds that made writing a pleasurable experience.

References

Bateson, G. (1958), *Naven*, Stanford, Calif.: University of Stanford Press.
Berlin, I. (2000), *Three Critics of the Enlightenment: Vico, Hamann, Herder* (ed H. Hardy), Princeton, NJ: Princeton University Press.

Brody, H. (2002), *Maps and Dreams*, London: Faber and Faber.
Collingwood, R.G. (1993), *The Idea of History*, revised edition, Oxford: Clarendon Press.
Corsín Jiménez, A. (2004), 'Teaching the field: the order, the ordering and the scale of knowledge', in D. Mills and M. Harris (eds), *Teaching Rites and Wrongs: Universities and the Making of Anthropologists*, Birmingham: CSAP.
C-SAP (Centre for Sociology, Anthropology and Politics), http://www.c-sap.bham.ac.uk.
Grimshaw, A. and Hart, J.K. (1996), *Anthropology and the Crisis of Intellectuals*, Cambridge: Prickly Pear Pamphlets.
——, Harris, M., Ravetz, A., Solomons, N., Liebnit, M., Grasseni, C., Walker, N., Ward, C. and Dibb, M. (2000), *The Child in the City: A Case Study in Experimental Anthropology*, Manchester: Prickly Pear Pamphlets 13.
Hart, J.K. (2004), 'What anthropologists really do', *Anthropology Today*, 20(1): 3–5.
Hugh-Jones, S. (1989), *Edmund Leach 1910–1989: A Memoir* (unpublished manuscript), King's College, Cambridge.
Ingold, T. (2000), *The Perception of the Environment*, London: Routledge.
—— with Lucas, R. (forthcoming), 'The 4As (anthropology, archaeology, art and architecture): reflections on a teaching and learning experience', in M. Harris (ed), *Ways of Knowing? Anthropological Approaches to Crafting Experience and Knowledge*, Oxford: Berghahn Books.
Jackson, M. (1989), *Paths Toward a Clearing*, Bloomington: Indiana University Press.
Landes, R. (2005), *City of Women*, Albuquerque: University of New Mexico Press.
Leach, E. (1968), *A Runaway World?*, London: British Broadcasting Corporation.
—— (1982), *Social Anthropology*, London: Fontana.
Mintz, S. (1960), *Worker in the Cane: A Puerto Rican Life History*, New Haven, Conn.: Yale University Press.
Strathern, M. (1995), *The Relation: Issues in Complexity and Scale*, Cambridge: Prickly Pear Pamphlets 6.
—— (ed) (2000), *Audit Cultures: Anthropological Studies in Accountability, Ethics and the Academy*, London: Routledge.
Tambiah, S. (2000), *Edmund Leach: An Intellectual Biography*, Cambridge: Cambridge University Press.
Taussig, M. (1987), *Shamanism, Colonialism and the Wild Man*, Chicago: University of Chicago Press.
Vico, G. (1999) *New Science* (trans. D. Marsh, introd. A. Grafton), Harmondsworth: Penguin.
Wolf, E. (1959), *Sons of the Shaking Earth*, Chicago: University of Chicago Press.

–12–

From Documenting Culture to Experimenting with Cultural Phenomena: Using Fine Art Pedagogies with Visual Anthropology Students

Amanda Ravetz

Introduction

In *Raw Histories*, a collection of essays about photography, anthropology and museums, Elizabeth Edwards (2001) shows how the points of fracture in the ethnographic images she presents admit contested histories and practices at odds with the forms of closure attempted by their makers. Understood as material objects with their own social biographies, photographs have an ambiguous character (as also discussed by Berger 1982: 85–92) that challenges the idea of the archive as an embodiment of homogenizing metadiscourses: 'Meanings are made through dynamic relations between photographs and culture that do not stop at the door of the archive' (Edwards 2001: 11). This ambiguity allows the photographic image to be used as a tool to interrogate contemporary Western museums' representations of post-colonial and minority cultures. Here, 'shifts in assumptions about the role of photography, especially in ethnographic museums, can function as an interpretative strategy or as a site of translation within the public space of the museum' (ibid.: 183).

At the intersection of museum, anthropology, photography and culture, it is increasingly the figure of the artist who stands as an intermediary, facilitating a critique of museum practice and revealing 'the epistemological base of collecting and the museum ... through counter-narrative' (ibid.: 199). Artists' work, specifically their use of photography, can become a means to question authoritative forms of cultural appropriation and representation. The ability of artists to take up this position reflects a dominant strand of contemporary art practice that has its roots in the twentieth-century avant-garde and which puts particular emphasis on 'art as a verb'. Art in this mode is thought to *do work*, and to do so through self-consciously contingent, affective and interrupted means (Ravetz, forthcoming).

Against the privileging of affect that characterizes much contemporary art practice, anthropologists might be said to strive for an indexical effect in the production of photographic images, desiring to close the gap between signifier and signified, and control the way images are subsequently read. In this chapter, I set out to establish some of the effects of this strategy on the relationship between anthropology and photography and then to suggest that the heterogeneity that surrounds the reception of photographs *could* become a more explicit part of the process of producing ethnographic images themselves.

The chapter grows out of a one-day workshop held for students at the University of Manchester's Granada Centre for Visual Anthropology where I used pedagogies familiar to art students as a way of introducing anthropology students to the use of the stills camera. I wanted to see whether, by presenting them with the ambiguity of the photographic document as an aspect that could be used and explored as well as contained and controlled, their confidence in using a camera for the first time in a 'fieldwork' situation would be enhanced, giving them additional insight into the character of the photographic image. How would this approach sit with the rest of their anthropological training? Instead of showing students images from an ethnographic and documentary corpus, I introduced them to the work of a number of conceptual artists whose use of photography in the 1970s went against the grain of a canonical fine art photography tradition. Using fine art pedagogies such as the 'silent crit' to review the work the visual anthropology students subsequently brought back, my aim was to allow them to engage with the affecting qualities of photography and to experience some of the tensions between the ways anthropologists try to qualify photographic images and the ways images work to escape closure.

The Photograph as Evidence

There are a number of ways of recounting the historical relationship between anthropology and photography. But running through narratives of photography's changed fortunes within the discipline are indications of a strong impulse on the part of anthropologists to emphasize photography's indexical capacities, its ability to *point* to the world, at the expense of images' silence – their powerlessness, impotence and abjection (Mitchell 2005: 10). At the end of the nineteenth century the camera's ability to make a record of the world was for a time used in an interrogatory way and as a means of constituting knowledge; but this dialogue between photography and anthropology was later restricted by the requirement that the image not be seen as 'wanting', giving rise to more static forms of visual mimesis. This attempt to control the photographic image, to deny its double nature, seems implicated in what MacDougall (2005) has called the 'dark age' in visual anthropology, beginning during the 1910s and lasting until the 1950s. During this period photography and film disappeared from mainstream anthropology, along with the excitement that had surrounded them; photography was effectively stripped of its earlier status as anthropology's progressive face.

Photography arrived on the scene in both American and British anthropology at a time when drawing, engraving, painting, watercolours and sketches were the established means of representing what was known and seen of 'other races' (Griffiths 2002). From the beginning, photography was embraced as a medium of ethnographic evidence and as an accurate and scientific way to 'picture empire' (Ryan 1997). In the context of visual methodologies requiring the intervention of hand and eye, photography took on a new burden of empirical proof; photographs were praised for being objective and immediate. By contrast, engravings and drawings were demoted to the level of subjective interpretation. They took time to produce and involved the subjective vision and error-prone skill of the artist. At best, these 'human' methods of visualization were difficult to generalize from; at worst they were misleading (Griffiths 2002).

Photography was thus readily absorbed into the collective quest for ethnographic data. Photographs and other materials of anthropological interest were circulated amongst and between committees, and images were collected and exchanged 'for the common scientific good', comparison and categorization being paramount (Edwards 1992: 4). The uses made of the stills camera in this period were intimately caught up with the power relations of colonialism, and photography functioned as both a symbol for and an instrument of technological control. A number of historians have noted that the photographing of human subjects involved practices analogous to those used to survey and classify territories and land, so that anthropometry, for example, treats the racialized body as a territory to be charted and controlled through mapping.

It was not unusual for nineteenth-century anthropologists to be trained in medicine and the natural sciences. The convergence of photography with laboratory-based science inaugurated a new phase in the relationship between photography and anthropology, culminating in the Cambridge Expedition to the Torres Strait in 1898. The expedition leader A.C. Haddon and his young assistant A.W. Wilkin took approximately three hundred photographs and several minutes of ethnographic film footage. Haddon was a convert to anthropology from zoology; in 1888 he had visited Torres Strait to study the marine zoology of the area. The 1898 expedition was motivated in part by his concern that the customs and rituals of the Islanders were threatened with imminent disappearance. With a scientific background that gave him a familiarity with work in both the laboratory and the field, he assembled a team of leading scientists and equipped the expedition with the latest recording instruments. One of the methodological aims of the expedition was to extend the conditions of the scientific laboratory into the field. Cutting-edge laboratory practices of the 1890s involved the isolation and subsequent imitation or recreation of natural phenomena under controlled conditions. The conversion of raw phenomena to data frequently involved processes of mimesis and visualization. Photography, with its indexical relationship to a referent, offered a means of replicating and verifying the results of scientific observation (Edwards 2001: 162).

The Torres Strait Expedition was poised between an earlier paradigm of photography, understood as a chemical process producing material images that were 'flattened', and that correlated to regimes of colonial control (MacDougall 2005), and a more radical conception of the photographic process as a site of experimentation and interrogation – the latter moving away from typologies created on the basis of visible surface appearances. The inclusion in the expedition team of W.H.R. Rivers, a doctor who played a key role in developing the field of experimental psychology, underlines the assessment of Torres Strait as a pivotal moment in anthropology, and in its relation to photography. Rivers was to carry out a number of psychological tests concerned with visual perception; if the procedures he used involved the elicitation of drawings from Islanders and requests that they discriminate between colour samples and the lengths of vertical lines, then the differences he detected between their skill in these areas and that of his English 'control' groups were explained not through notions of evolutionary difference, but through environment and habit (Schaffer 1994). Classification was moving away from visible surfaces towards social and psychological 'depths'.

From Surface to Depth

The years following the Torres Strait Expedition coincided with a declining anthropological interest in photography. The concern in Rivers' work with an 'invisible' dimension to experience is emblematic of a more general shift in anthropology towards social structure, depth and the singular fieldworker; there was a slow reduction in the numbers of photographic images used in monographs to the point of their virtual disappearance after the 1930s (MacDougall 1997: 281).

Photography became increasingly associated with an earlier era in the development of the discipline, particularly evolutionism, and with anthropology 'at a distance', as in the study of art and material culture (Banks and Morphy 1997: 9). Not everyone abandoned the camera, but its use began to be seen as additional to rather than constitutive of anthropological inquiry. In America, Mead and Bateson pioneered the use of photography in a way that was underpinned by observational science. But each had a different assessment of the camera's value. Mead believed that photography revealed more than it obscured and preserved an event for re-analysis (Banks and Morphy 1997: 10). MacDougall suggests that Bateson wanted to apply an exploratory approach to using film and photography, consistent with his experimental text *Naven* (1958), and that as a consequence Mead's and Bateson's work was compromised: it was a use of photography that extended neither the mind nor the eye (MacDougall 2005: 224). In the 1960s photographer John Collier perpetuated this stance, advocating the medium not only as a means of seeing, but also as a means of 'storing away complex descriptions for future analysis' (Collier 1967: 8).

A number of explanations have been offered for the turn away from visual matters in these years. Christopher Pinney's much-quoted suggestion has the work of photography magically transposed onto the body of the newly constituted fieldworker. Malinowski, the first 'lone anthropologist with a notebook' (Grimshaw and Hart 1993), advocated exposure to the field in a way that uncannily recalls the exposure of emulsion to the imprint of light (Pinney 1992). Anna Grimshaw (2001) has made a strong case for the effects of the Great War on an age that had faith in vision's ability to reveal the truth – a belief that was traumatically undermined by the chaos of the trenches. Other suggestions have included the costliness and difficulty involved in photography and its association with vulgar popular entertainments from which, in the establishment of its academic identity, the discipline of anthropology was anxious to keep its distance (Griffiths 2002; Pratt 1986). A rising interest in 'invisible' aspects of the social, for example in kinship, is the explanation favoured by MacDougall, and one he finds both intriguing and unsettling, since these 'deeper' conceptions of sociality coincide with an increased interest in environment, perception and observable social behaviour – all eminently suitable subjects for visualization. MacDougall suggests that the reasons for the disappearance of photography after the turn of the century probably included a shift to abstract thinking at a time when the technologies of film and photography were too undeveloped for anthropologists to know how to make use of them in this new context. In the 1950s a small number of anthropologists turned to film – Jean Rouch being the most celebrated example. But photography, while it kept some small presence within the discipline, did not have an equivalent champion, and the subdiscipline that emerged in the 1970s, and which became known as 'visual anthropology', was identified with ethnographic film rather than photography.

Photography, Anthropology and the Domestic Snap

Little systematic information is available about the extent or character of anthropological uses of photography since the 1970s, making it hard to assess the current relationship between the two fields. Some anthropologists undoubtedly have clear intentions of what they want to do photographically (see, for example, Banks 1997; Loescher 2004; Pink et al. 2004); the majority of us take a camera to the field to use as we would at home, though perhaps with one difference: in the field the camera may, in Collier's words, 'record material that the camera operator himself [*sic*] cannot recognize or yet understand' (1967: 8). Others indulge in a practice criticized by Collier, using the camera to provide illustrative evidence for existing ideas and conclusions. On the surface, little seems to have changed since George and Louise Spindler commented in an introduction to Collier's book that 'most anthropologists take a camera with them into the field ... but too often with no clear concept of what to do with the camera in the field or what to do with the pictures once they are taken' (Collier 1967: x).

What began as an active and optimistic relationship between anthropology and photography during its earlier years in the late nineteenth century, and became with Rivers a search for an exploratory and interrogatory photographic method that could be considered constitutive of knowledge, declined as knowledge was increasingly detached from appearance. But what remained constant throughout photography's presence in the discipline was an attachment on the part of anthropology to the camera's capacity to record, whether the strategies pursued by anthropologists in their uses of the medium were informed by a laboratory aesthetic, an ideal of 'unmediated spontaneity' as promoted by Mead (Edwards 2001: 171) or a more ambivalent use of the camera as domestic recording device.

Given the diminished use and presence of photography in anthropology, it is hardly surprising that many anthropologists are unsure of what to do with a camera, falling back on familiar kinds of usage. This in turn raises the question of what makes an image specifically ethnographic. Judgements of anthropological likelihood, as Elizabeth Edwards (2001) calls them, rely heavily on images being embedded in recognizably anthropological commentaries and texts. The fact that a photographer's intentions cannot realistically hope to withstand the photograph's subsequent readings may help to explain why photography has declined to the extent that it has in anthropology. If authorial intentions are likely to be effaced and the question of anthropological 'likelihood' is almost wholly dependent on the contexts in which images occur, why take photographs at all? This may be why so many of the images that relate to fieldwork are used like footnotes in the more 'serious' business of anthropological analysis. Yet if we look beyond anthropology to the field of contemporary art, we find that similar questions about the documentary uses of the photograph, and about its indexical and iconic properties, have been approached in intriguingly different ways. Artists in the 1970s believed that there *were* ways to work intelligently and imaginatively with the historical loss of intention, with the characteristics of the domestic snap and with the properties of photography itself.

Photography and Conceptual Art

In an important essay on the history of conceptual art, John Roberts shows how between 1966 and 1976 the photographic document opened art up to the 'unconscious place' of photography, making possible 'a representational art that avoided many of the problems of iconophilia' (Roberts 1997: 45). Roberts argues that photography underlines one of the paradoxes of this aspect of the avant-garde. Conceptualism was an attack on the primacy of the visual; and yet many of the forms that went under the heading involved photography, either as primary work or as means of reproduction. But as Roberts suggests, rather than this revealing the failure of conceptual art, photography was able to deliver a new reading of the pictorial.

Conceptual art in the late 1960s set out to reveal the prejudice involved in the ascription of quality to certain kinds of abstract painting and sculpture. It presented artists not as exemplars of taste and aesthetic judgement, but as thinkers – producers of 'ideas about ideas' (ibid.: 11). Roberts identifies two strands of conceptualism, analytical and stylistic. Analytical conceptualism drew heavily on Wittgenstein's anti-mentalist accounts of meaning to demonstrate the temporal nature of understanding. This furthered the disengagement of judgements about the visual from the requirements of aesthetic immediacy and put in place new requirements for the viewer of art. If modernism had sought to shore up the space-time differentiation involved in the production and consumption of art, then conceptual art tested this distinction, identifying the viewer not only with the spatial, the traditional site of aesthetic pleasure, but also with 'reading'. The viewer of conceptual art was someone on the move, exposed through their (in)ability to read what they knew or did not.

In the 1960s discourses on photography in art were limited to institutional attempts to have photography divested of its functionality so that it could be validated as a modernist form. It was in stark opposition to this that the commonplace qualities of photography attracted conceptual artists. For his book *Twentysix Gasoline Stations* (1963), Ed Ruscha took images of filling stations and used them in a format that demonstrated a kind of wilful ignorance of the aesthetics of presentation. The appearance of filling stations in a book by an artist was suggestive of the status of everyday forms as artworks; but the photographs themselves – similar to technical images found in manuals – were also being appropriated in the manner of the 'readymade' (Edwards 2004: 143). Ruscha claimed to be aiming for a book with a commercial or industrial feel. Steve Edwards suggests two things are at issue. One is an ambiguity over how the piece is to be viewed – as a collection of photographs or as a collection of objects. The other concerns the way the book looks like a technical manual; we are presented with everyday forms without knowing to what use we should be putting them. An 'interpretative industry' has developed around this and other books by Ruscha. *Twentysix Gasoline Stations* has been seen as a road movie; a journey across the USA from west to east and back, which involved the consumption of a full tank of gas for every photograph taken; and as a pun by Ruscha, a lapsed Catholic, on the stations of the cross, including the 'station' of his home town of Oklahoma. Ruscha himself claimed to be after 'no-style or a non-statement with no-style' and Steve Edwards (2004) reads this no-style as an attempt to break the link between the artist's intentions and the imputed meaning of a work. Exemplified in Ruscha's work is the tension between the photograph as raw information and as image. By fixing on utilitarian objects, by presenting them in a low-key way more akin to the manual than high modernism, Ruscha produced and exploited uncertainty about the artwork's proper context and about the status of the photographic image. His work exemplifies the way that artists then and since have attempted to escape convention by rejecting existing competencies and skills. The strategy of attempting to evacuate the image of artistic intention and then seeing what rushes in to fill the gap proved to be influential in the uses to which artists put photography in the years to come.

Twentysix Gasoline Stations works against the 'witnessing' ethos of documentary photography. Thus one of Ruscha's images came from a picture archive and he claimed that he would have been happy to use other such images if necessary. In the years that followed, other artists attempted to politicize the photographic document by critiquing its purported neutrality and objectivity. The German artist Hans Haacke, an advocate of General Systems Theory, caused a stir with his work *Shapolsky* et al. *Manhattan Real Estate Holdings, a Real Time System as of May 1, 1971*. The subject was the Shapolsky Group, a family-run empire that bought and sold rented property and raised mortgages between apparently independent businesses. The work was made up of 142 panels that mixed black-and-white images of the buildings with texts giving details of ownership, mortgage details and tax value, and a series of charts giving information about organizations used to cover up the identities of the building's owners. The work was originally scheduled to be shown as part of a solo show at the Guggenheim Museum, but six weeks beforehand the director of the Museum, Thomas Messer, called it off, claiming that Haacke's focus on 'ulterior ends' compromised the work's aesthetic integrity (Edwards 2004: 148). When Edward Fry, the curator, publicly defended the work, he was immediately dismissed. Messer's refusal to regard the photographic document as 'aesthetic form' ran counter to a strong strand of contemporary art at the time that privileged structures, systems and series above content. By deploying this procedure to address a politically contentious issue, Haacke questioned whether this work should be viewed as art or as political document. The ambiguity and uncertainty into which the viewer is thrown – something difficult to recapture in a contemporary context – reflected back on the art institution whose refusal to validate the work as art revealed it as unequal to its own aestheticizing logic.

Martha Rosler's piece of 1974, *Two Inadequate Descriptive Systems*, combines text panels with photographic images taken around the Bowery, an area of New York known for its use by alcoholics and the homeless. It was important to Rosler's project to work in an area of the city that was haunted not only by 'down-and-outs', but also by documentary photographers. Steve Edwards notes that the images, which are black and white, 'play with the rhetoric of Evan's depression pictures' (2004: 150). They feature store fronts, photographed front-on, and texts listing words used as metaphors for drunkenness, for example: boozehead, juicehound, boiled owl, whale. Rosler brings us close to the traditional sites of documentary photography, but makes us question this imagery by withholding the kinds of visual information we have come to expect, recording only the traces of people's habitation – empty bottles, cigarette packets. She troubles the codes through which viewers of documentary images lay claim to social knowledge: 'Stripped down to the document's most basic protocols, documentary emerges here as an empty marker rather than a site of plenitude' (Edwards 2004: 150).

A different response to the documentary tradition took the shape of a gradual move towards studio photography. Victor Burgin's photographic work embodies a commitment to go beyond the art world ghetto into a wider social sphere as a proper context in which to question the perceptual systems and modes of communication at work in media representations. He saw artists as one of a number of groups whose job it is to alter the apprehensions of another social group (Paoletti 1984). His work UK76 consists of eleven units, each combining a photographic image with text. In *St Laurent Demands a Whole New Life Style* an Asian woman worker on an electronics assembly line is pictured with an integrated text that uses the language of an advertising campaign: '…by night black velvet camisole bodices extend down over the hipline then the bright taffeta skirt springs out free…' Burgin's objective was, he said, to 'deconstruct these [media] codes, to unpick the apparently seamless ideological surface they present' (Edwards 2004: 154). However by the 1980s, Burgin was himself critical of this strategy, feeling that it did not provide a sufficient critique of the ideology of the documentary form itself – its claims to show things as they really are. He began to produce work with studio constructions that allowed him to address issues such as constructions of fantasy and sexual identity.

Cindy Sherman also worked with the idea of staged photography in her series produced between 1977 and 1980, *Untitled Film Stills*. Sherman acts as both model and photographer, taking on various identities and different locations to construct images that reference movies and celebrity publicity photos of the kind common in the 1950s and 1960s. Working at a time when art critics and artists were considering the ways in which reality is produced through the media, the work was taken up by feminist theorists as exemplary of an analysis of female subjectivity constructed in media representations. 'By staging a range of powerful and prevalent images of femininity, Sherman revealed something of its ideological effects' (Edwards 2004: 157). Both Burgin and Sherman took an existing imagery of cinema, painting and advertising as their starting point, and used this to question ideas of authorship, originality and ownership.

In the hands of these artists, then, and in the context of contemporary art practice, indexicality was not linked to the triumph of photograph as document – although artists did use photography in part to document ephemeral and performance work. Rather, the indexical properties of photography were linked to the banal, everyday and ordinary, making the photograph a possible vehicle for the re-engagement of art and life. The judgement of likelihood that Elizabeth Edwards talks about with regard to anthropology and photographic images relied on subtly different criteria in art of this kind. The snapshot was used by artists to test and expand conventional judgements of likelihood through being marked as an unskilled and aesthetically undemanding trace of the real; to anthropologists, by contrast, it was valued for its ability to index reality and verify presence, reflecting the anthropological requirement of 'being there'. Whereas for art the relationship between the genre and its banality was elaborated and used as an interrogatory tool – with reference to the authority of the image, its status as fiction or fact and the relationship between image and text – for anthropology, the ability of the photograph to index the everyday was a means of insulating reality from fiction. The inherent vulnerability of the photographic image to the imaginings of the viewer was kept in check primarily through the photograph's proximity to titles, captions and text. While some artists were enthusiastically embracing the image's propensity to suggest untruths and then celebrating its ability to lie, this same possibility had produced anxiety in anthropological circles, forcing photography in anthropological fieldwork into retreat.

The Workshop

I turn now to the workshop and to the way I used images and work by conceptual artists to prepare students to go out and take their own photographs. I began the day by introducing students to a number of images, beginning with photographs by Bronislaw Malinowski, scientist and anthropologist, and his friend Stanislaw Witkiewicz, the artist and surrealist who was almost to become Malinowski's fieldwork photographer. The different approaches of these two contemporaries are suggestive of the two broadly contrasting approaches of art and anthropology to the photographic document. As Young has pointed out, it was by working against everything that Witkiewicz stood for that Malinowski developed his own photographic approach (Young 1998: 12).

These images were followed by a selection of photographs by American and British conceptual artists of the 1970s. These artists' acceptance of the ambiguity of the photographic image, and the difficulties this presented, provided a foil to anthropological anxieties about reality and closure. Going through a selection of images by Ed Ruscha, Hans Haacke, Martha Rosler, Allan Sekula, Victor Burgin and Cindy Sherman, I talked through some of the questions raised by their work: for example, the tension between photographic image and the referent; the entanglement of art and the everyday; representation and visual culture; the polarities of aesthetics and political content; and the problems of re-enactment, visual pleasure and the clash of documentary aesthetics with the fictions of the studio. Rather than trying to circumvent the problem of how photographs are subsequently viewed, interpreted and understood, I argued that the work of these and other artists suggested ways in which the ambiguity of the photographic image could become part of the productive process.

Students were then asked to consider the 'strategies' exemplified by these artists, as they went out to take photographs in Manchester. I wanted them to be aware of how any use of a camera demands choices from the user, and how – although these may not be wholly conscious or easy to articulate – they are circumscribed by existing genres, forms and ideologies, all involving ambiguities and problems. The aim here was to give students alternative and conscious choices to the kinds of strategies that result from copying domestic or journalistic forms.

After questions and discussion, students had three hours to go out either together or individually and to take photographs. They were instructed to obtain fast-process prints and to choose how to display one or more of these, or, if using digital cameras, to print off images or use a data projector. It was emphasized that the choice of image and means of display was as critical as the production of the photographs and that there should be some connection between them. On their return students were given half an hour to arrange their photographs; and they were introduced to the rules of the 'silent crit'.

Fine Art Pedagogies

The 'Crit' is central to the pedagogic approach in art schools in the UK. It can take many different forms: it can be silent; it can involve advocacy by one student of another's work; be presented by students themselves or led by members of staff. What all these forms have in common is the centrality of the relationship between the audience – comprising students, staff and invited others – and the work. The artist may sometimes be invited to describe their intentions for the work, but in the silent crit this is left to the end, when others have given their responses uninfluenced by stated intentions. It is the *affect* of the work as relayed through the audience that takes priority and is valued.

In the silent crit the student observes while the others respond to whatever is presented for critique. Often responses begin with descriptions of what can be perceived – this can be as seemingly banal as 'it's a photograph', or 'it's a text, Blu-tacked to the wall'. This banality has the effect of making every detail and every element relevant and underwrites the expectation that all that is presented as 'the work' has been included purposefully. Beyond descriptive responses, students may talk about how the work feels, what meanings they take from it, its connections with other artwork, the references it makes to the social, to different genres, and so on. The silent crit, performed in the way described above, privileges affect and the idea that 'art is a verb'. Rather than searching for stable meaning embodied in an object, the idea of art as a verb places emphasis on the contingent and changing character of meaning and its situational nature in the relationship between viewer and work. Although from the perspective of the audience we might talk about artwork as if it is 'about' something, the emphasis on affect suggests that it is we who bring meaning to the work (Ravetz forthcoming).

Student Work

The majority of the students seemed to find that going out to take photographs with a chosen strategy in mind had enabled them to feel confident about using the camera in public, and in many cases with the public. A number brought back engaging bodies of work; I will briefly discuss two examples as a way of reflecting on the question I raised at the beginning of this chapter – how to embrace, rather than suppress, the ambiguity of photographic images in a field that carries a responsibility for cultural mediation and understanding.

A sense of responsibility was a key issue for Pete Conteh, who made a large number of photographs and had difficulty deciding which to present. Those he showed were located firmly within the documentary genre, while seeming to take on board the critique of the form apparent in the work of artists such as Rosler, Burgin and Sekula. He used a digital camera to make images on an estate where he had been living since coming to Manchester to study, and presented the images as a slide show on a data projector.

Conteh looks directly at a subject that is at least partially familiar to him and congruent with his own social experience. In many of the images, people return his (camera)gaze directly, as if he and they shared an agreement or piece of information to which we are not party. Although the images have been taken in a poor area of Manchester, the subjects are chosen so as to emphasize the positive

Documenting Culture Using Fine Art Pedagogies

Figures 12.1, 12.2 and 12.3 © Peter Conteh

self-presentation of the people who appear in the photographs. This is brought out through the clarity of visual information, the absence of distracting detail and the way in which the subjects occupy the centre of the image, with an eye-line level with or above that of the viewer.

At the end of the silent crit, students were allowed two minutes to make a statement. Conteh said that he wanted to give a positive image of the estate without glossing over reality. Having heard a number of different responses to the images he said he would like to caption them in order to anchor their interpretation in ways he felt were appropriate. There was a discussion about how much slippage in meaning could be tolerated in relation to the images and whether meaning could in fact be pinned down in the way the photographer would like. Conteh showed a strong desire to integrate the experience of taking and viewing images with other aspects of his anthropological training. He understood the challenge to documentary represented in the artists' work seen earlier in the day, but his images reveal his decision to discharge his responsibility to his subjects through a documentary ethos that holds on to the act of 'witnessing' and to a belief that representation can be 'got right'.

Nadia von Christierson and Lynn Morris used a basic point-and-shoot Olympus camera with a 35 mm colour film that they then had developed at a local one-hour service. After some discussion they decided to display the prints on the wall of the seminar room, using a simple grid format and placing paired images together. For each pair of images the women took it in turns to take the photograph of the other wearing the same wig while looking into a mirror.

Seeming to reference Cindy Sherman, the photographs are playful, but carefully structured. In each image we see the photographer in the background, to the left or right edge of the image, and in the middle ground the 'subject', both viewed through the reflection produced in the large mirror on the changing-room wall. The foregrounds of the photographs reveal close-up rear views of the wig wearer. Each pair of images contains a reversal, the women having taken it in turns to wear the wig and take the photograph. A number of reflections are involved here, not only those produced in the mirror in the changing room, but in terms of mathematical symmetry, so that each pair of images is built around a central axis. In the manner of Cindy Sherman, the students have become subjects of their own photographic construction. But they have also introduced the idea of the repeat, so that the question of identity becomes entwined with that of repetition, mass production and the ready-made. Taking the staged image back to the site of documentary street photography, the students have found a recognizably anthropological/ documentary site from which to explore the dynamic between the indexical and the symbolic – if photography has an indexical relationship to the world, then identities *in* that world are constantly being manipulated. In the context of an anthropological exercise the images instantiate a proliferation of identities that

Documenting Culture Using Fine Art Pedagogies

Figure 12.4 © Nadia von Christierson and Lynn Morris

threaten to collapse into one another: photographer, ethnographer, subject, object, producer, consumer, self and other. This proliferation is spatialized across the grid that the photographers used. Working with their own images allowed the photographers to avoid some of the responsibilities involved in representing others. They have been freed to explore a space which is in some ways analogous to the space of photography – a space of disguise, mirrors, gendered representations and auto-ethnography that, like photography itself, asks 'is it possible to get it right?'

The approaches of Conteh and von Christierson and Morris play out some of the problems underlying anthropological representation that, as Elizabeth Edwards shows, meet in the photograph – that is, between the desire to get representation right, fuelled by responsibility to subjects and viewers, and the counter-impulse to exploit meaning as something that is only ever partial and fleeting, existing in the dialogue between viewer and viewed. If neither example resolves the question of how the heterogeneity surrounding the reception of images can become part of the production of ethnographic photographs, then both indicate rich possibilities for the extended use of photographic practice in the investigation of social worlds that are 'in the making', relational and unfinished, in an analogous way to acts of making and viewing photographs.

Conclusion

Elizabeth Edwards shows how the dynamic relations between photographs and culture generate meanings beyond the disciplinary function of the archive. She argues that shifts in assumptions about photography's role open up a site of translation. The work of a number of conceptual artists in the 1970s suggests that this dynamic could be addressed and used by artists in conscious ways through making photographs that engage (and often manipulate) the assumptions of the viewer. If artists' uses of photography can be a way of questioning the authoritative forms of cultural representation and appropriation, the workshop described here set out in a modest way to ask if anthropological uses of photography might usefully aspire to something similar. The thesis of this chapter is that one of the things that stands between anthropology and a more extended use of photography is the consistent ambition for the camera to act as a recording device.

Artists in the 1970s took this same feature and did something different with it; they manipulated the dynamic between image and how it is read, trying to find a space for reflexivity within the viewing of the image. This required what Catherine Russell (1999), in relation to experimental ethnography, has called a move from the documentation of culture to experimenting with cultural phenomena. This might be said to involve an ability both to be within a situation and to track your movements through it, as well as to understand image as affect – that is, to learn to read an image through a different set of coordinates than those conventionally assumed in the production and consumption of ethnographic images.

MacDougall concurs with Grimshaw's analysis that anthropology's 'lost vision' seems to have occurred at the same time as the Great War, a moment of spiritual and intellectual drama that alienated the senses, particularly vision. MacDougall points out that this may also have led to a more sophisticated understanding of the intersection of vision with language, body and mind – while modernism questioned surface appearances, it also celebrated the expressiveness of the visual: 'When anthropologists more or less stopped using visual images, it was not necessarily for the reason that they had lost the power of visual imagination but that they had not yet found the means to make visual expression commensurate with their new-found experiences' (MacDougall 2005: 245). It is right to refuse the conflation of the visual image with imaginative capacity, but I wonder too if there has not been a certain collective failure of the imagination within anthropology when it comes to understanding how visual images themselves work, or in Mitchell's (2005) terms, 'what pictures want'. Asking students to engage through practice, art school pedagogies and artwork with what images 'want' provides a powerful antidote to the double bind in which anthropologists using photography often find themselves – of either disciplining images at the point of consumption by pinning them down with 'voice-over' style texts, or abdicating responsibility at the point of production, hoping the camera will do the looking and thinking for them. Instead it becomes possible to enter into an imaginative dialogue with photography that takes account not only of its indexical properties and of how images are variously disciplined, but of how images 'want' and of the potential dialogue this opens up between photographer, reality, representation and audience.

Acknowedgements

I would like to thank Rupert Cox at the Granada Centre for Visual Anthropology, University of Manchester, for inviting me to lead the Photography workshop, and equally the MA students for taking part. I am especially grateful to Peter Conteh, Nadia von Christierson and Lynn Morris for allowing me to reproduce their photographic work.

References

Banks, M. (1997), 'Representing the bodies of the Jains', in M. Banks and H. Morphy (eds), *Rethinking Visual Anthropology*, New Haven, Conn.: Yale University Press.
—— and Morphy, H. (1997), 'Introduction', in M. Banks and H. Morphy (eds), *Rethinking Visual Anthropology*, New Haven, Conn.: Yale University Press.
Berger, J. (1982), 'Appearances', in J. Berger and J. Mohr, *Another Way of Telling*, New York: Random House.
Collier, J. (1967), *Visual Anthropology: Photography as a Research Method*, New York: Holt, Rinehart and Winston.
Edwards, E. (ed) (1992), *Anthropology and Photography, 1860–1920*. New Haven, Conn.: Yale University Press in association with the Royal Anthropological Institute.
—— (2001), *Raw Histories, Photographs, Anthropology and Museums*, Oxford: Berg.

Edwards, S. (2004), 'Photography out of conceptual art', in G. Perry and P. Wood (eds), *Themes in Contemporary Art*, New Haven, Conn.: Yale University Press.

Griffiths, A. (2002), *Wondrous Difference: Cinema, Anthropology, and Turn-of-the-Century Visual Culture*, New York: Columbia University Press.

Grimshaw, A. (2001), *The Ethnographer's Eye*, Cambridge: Cambridge University Press.

—— and Hart, K.J. (1993), *Anthropology and the Crisis of the Intellectuals*, Cambridge: Prickly Pear Press.

Loescher, M. (2004), 'Cameras at the Addy: speaking in pictures with city kids', in A. Grimshaw and A. Ravetz (eds), *Visualizing Anthropology*, Bristol: Intellect Books.

MacDougall, D. (1997), 'The visual in anthropology', in M. Banks and H. Morphy (eds), *Rethinking Visual Anthropology*, New Haven, Conn.: Yale University Press.

—— (2005), *The Corporeal Image: Film, Ethnography, and the Senses*, Princeton, NJ: Princeton University Press.

Mitchell, W.J.T. (2005), *What Do Pictures Want? The Lives and Loves of Images*, Chicago: University of Chicago Press.

Paoletti, J. (1984), *The Critical Eye/I May 16 – July 15 1985*, New Haven, Conn.: Yale Centre for British Art.

Pink, S., Kürti, L., and Afonso, A.I. (2004), *Working Images*, London: Routledge.

Pinney, C. (1992), 'The parallel histories of anthropology and photography', in E. Edwards (ed), *Anthropology and Photography, 1860–1920*, New Haven, Conn.: Yale University Press in association with the Royal Anthropological Institute.

Pratt, M.L. (1986), 'Fieldwork in common places', in J. Clifford and G. E. Marcus (eds), *Writing Culture: The Poetics and Politics of Ethnography*, Berkeley: University of California Press.

Ravetz, A. (forthcoming), 'A weight of meaninglessness about which there is nothing insignificant: abjection and knowing in an art school and on a housing estate', in M. Harris (ed), *Ways of Knowing? New Anthropological Approaches to Method, Learning and Knowledge*, Oxford: Berghahn.

Roberts, J. (1997), *The Impossible Document: Photography and Conceptual Art in Britain 1966–1976*, London: Camerawork.

Ruscha, E. (1963), *Twentysix Gasoline Stations* (black offset printing on white paper), 17.9 × 14 × 0.5 cm (closed), 48 pages, 26 photographs) first edition: 400 numbered copies.

Russell, C. (1999), *Experimental Ethnography: The Work of Film in the Age of Video*, Durham, NC: Duke University Press.

Ryan, J.R. (1997), *Picturing Empire: Photography and the Visualization of the British Empire*, Chicago: University of Chicago Press.

Schaffer, S. (1994), *From Physics to Anthropology – and Back Again*, Cambridge: Prickly Pear Press.

Young, M. (1998), *Malinowski's Kiriwina Fieldwork Photography 1915–1918*, Chicago: University of Chicago Press.

–13–

Creativity in Advertising, Fiction and Ethnography
Robey Callahan and *Trevor Stack*

> You're asking about creativity here [in the creative department of this advertising agency], but you know it's really everywhere. People use it every day to do all sorts of things.
>
> Verity, an art director

More than seventy-five years ago, Edward Sapir (1993: 23–39) went to some trouble to define for his students the term 'culture', in part to distinguish between what we may call 'culture-as-elite-tradition' and 'culture-as-academic-abstraction'. Anthropologists in his day, he notes, often found themselves drawn to the ritual specialists among the peoples they studied – fascinated by the relative sophistication of their knowledge of local origin myths, curing lore, judicial precepts and supernatural esoterica. As much as we may wish to believe otherwise, things have not changed all that much in the intervening decades.

For many of us, information gleaned from such specialists forms a rather disproportionate share of our ethnographic data and enjoys a level of evidentiary privilege in our accounts that is frequently at least on a par with its local valuation. Yet precisely because elite forms are generally esteemed locally, this preferential treatment need not skew our interpretations unduly. In fact it can often provide us with sufficient material to do a rough sketch of a group's culture-as-academic-abstraction – to get an initial feel for its dominant cultural patterns, even if that depiction were to need later refinement in the light of analyses of the significance of more quotidian behaviours, including those implicated in the transmission of elite forms.

Like 'culture', 'creativity' is a troublesome but useful word.[1] In the epigraph above, Verity reminds us that human beings are by nature creative. We produce on a daily basis innumerable micro-innovations, reflexive adjustments to the ephemera of our physical and social environments. Any one of these micro-innovations would no doubt deserve to be seen as an example of creativity. However, while it may receive impetus and direction at least partly from prevailing cultural patterns, and while it may prove of definite benefit to its creator, it would not in itself necessarily be of lasting cultural value. To acquire such value, according to Sapir, it would have to gain currency beyond both the moment and the individual.

At the opposite extreme to the micro-innovations of everyday life, we encounter examples of creativity of another intensity entirely – examples we may sense as unequivocally cultural in character, as pertaining to culture-as-elite-tradition, 'high culture' or 'expressive culture'. We refer to institutionalized or conventionalized forms of novelty, which under other circumstances would likely be classed as dangerous eruptions of lunacy. Our purpose in this chapter is to examine the experiences of creativity for those who produce culture-as-elite-tradition (cf. Amabile 1996: 5–15; Freud 1970 [1908]; Gardner 1982: 352–68). We focus on three such forms: advertising, fiction and ethnography.

We are concerned, however, less with the 'obvious' creativity of the final products of these forms (ads, novels, ethnographies), than with the practical steps people take to come up with relevant ideas and how they commit those ideas to paper in the hope that they will eventually achieve wider circulation. These practical steps, many of which are more or less established 'tricks of the trade', themselves exemplify creativity at work. Many of them are clearly cultural in both source and ultimate significance; others are of a more ambiguous character, seeming, perhaps to some, too 'individual' or 'psychological' to warrant anthropological attention.

What, though, if we follow Sapir's thinking more closely? If we do, we find that even the most personal of such creativity-enhancing techniques is likely to bear the impress of prevailing cultural patterns. In other words, any given method may be useful only to a single person and only for a limited time, and yet within it would be manifested something of the logic underwriting more or less established tricks of the trade – a logic which would also reflect wider cultural patterns. Indeed, even if that method subsequently proves of no discernible consequence to culture, its presence nonetheless contributes, if only for one individual at one moment, to the often amorphous feeling that those tricks of the trade and those wider cultural patterns are inherently sensible.

Inspired by Urban's (2001) work on metaculture, we take the quest for newness to be a key motive-bearing schema (D'Andrade 1992) of the culture-as-academic-abstraction – in Sapir's sense – of modernity. We therefore expect to find it expressed not only at the level of metaculture (and the elements to which metaculture refers), but also within the more intimate, everyday experiences of individuals operating creatively, in whatever capacity. In other words, this core cultural pattern – the drive for novelty – motivates our elite forms, the techniques that give rise to those forms and, beyond them, our more general attitudes towards life.

Even core patterns within a culture, however, can manifest themselves in different forms. For instance, Strauss (1992) demonstrates that although both blue- and white-collar workers in America are motivated by what she calls a general 'success' schema, this central pattern of American culture is expressed quite differently, in both practical and ideational terms, on either side of that particular economic class divide. The same may be said about the 'quest for newness' that broadly characterizes modernity. While as an abstraction the idea has heuristic utility, its real-world instantiations vary in intensity and quality among particular domains – our focus here being on the three domains of advertising, fiction and ethnography.

Undoubtedly there are many ways one could proceed to compare and contrast the manifestations of the quest for newness within these three domains. One could, for instance, examine the finished products that emerge from them – the different forms of culture-as-elite-tradition we routinely consume by way of a wide range of media. Our concern here, however, is with the practical steps people take to stimulate their creativity in order to produce these forms of culture-as-elite-tradition. Among these practical steps we shall also encounter differences in people's attitudes towards their particular brands of creativity – their ideas about the creative processes behind their productions.

Understanding these steps and the reflexive commentaries that give them practical sense is, we have found, easier if they are conceptualized in terms of the spaces, literal and figurative, in which producers operate. We organize these various spaces according to two axes of variation. The first runs between two contrasting modes of creative thinking, which we call 'flux mode' and 'focus mode', with the former (more often) being punctuated by what are commonly known as 'eureka moments'. The second runs between contrasting manners of being in the world, which we call 'engagement' and 'disengagement'. Although there is always slippage in practice, flux mode, in which the conscious mind is usually (but not always) occupied in matters other than the creative problem at hand, most often occurs during engagement, a species of openness to the world and its distractions. Focus mode, in which the creator is actively putting pen to paper (or fingers to keys), is most often characterized by disengagement with the wider world, a kind of deliberate and controlled desensitization to ambient confusion.[2] At various points in between, we find what we may call 'focused-flux mode', in which (usually) two or more creators conjointly contrive to generate a hybrid space between engagement and disengagement, a sort of halfway house in which the eureka powers of an individual's flux mode can potentially be kick-started and partially directed towards the creative problems at hand.[3]

Through analyses of such spaces we may gain insights into the mysterious workings of the creative 'machine' – the myriad ways culture and psychology commingle and from which new things of wider cultural import may arise. We begin our survey with a focus on the spaces, physical and mental, in which advertising creativity occurs. As this particular creative domain is likely to be least familiar to our readers, we include in our discussion some relevant background information.[4]

Advertising

The core product of any advertising agency is creativity that helps sell things, and this commercial end strongly influences the spaces in which such creativity occurs. The people largely responsible for producing this form of creativity are collectively known in the industry as 'creatives'. Although much in this section pertains to all types of advertising creativity, here we are concerned particularly with the efforts of creatives working on direct-marketing ads – think here of anything with a 'call to action' (e.g. almost all 'junk mail' and any television ad with a telephone number that viewers are urged to 'call now!').

Creatives come in two main varieties: copywriters, whose focus is the text of ads; and art directors, whose remit is their design. Normally, each team in an agency's creative department comprises one copywriter and one art director, and any given advertising job begins life for such a team with a 'brief' devised by agency middlemen ('account handlers') in conjunction with representatives from the company commissioning the ad. A typical brief contains information about the product at hand, its benefits, its intended audience, the type of advertising desired, the available budget, production timings, past creative treatments (and results data, if available), branding issues, legal disclaimers, and so forth. Key amongst all this information is the 'proposition', or central selling message (e.g. 'consolidate all your debts into one easy monthly payment' or 'sponsor a child for £2 a month') of the ad-to-come. It is up to the creative team to transform a brief's proposition into an advertising 'concept' – a clever and concise idea that makes that proposition interesting and appealing to potential customers, and an exciting fusion of text and design that stands out in a world of commercial clutter long enough to have the chance of making a sale.

Of the three creative domains examined in this chapter, it is within advertising that we find creative modes (flux, focused flux and focus) and manners of being (engagement and disengagement) most powerfully demarcated in experience.

Flux, as we have noted, foregrounds the originality arising from eureka moments. When, for whatever reason, a new approach to a particular project is deemed necessary, the assigned team will make use of a wide range of creativity-enhancing and idea-generating techniques to form new concepts that meet the brief's proposition.[5] Most of these techniques require creatives to withdraw from the routine spaces of their work – to free themselves physically and mentally from the more mundane tasks (and reminders of such tasks) that clutter the bulk of the working day, in order to open themselves up to the stimulating distractions of engagement.

Focus, on the other hand, emphasizes technical expertise over originality. For copywriters this means grammatical proficiency and a facility with registers and literary genres; for art directors, this refers to visualization skills and a fluency with media and formats. Here, the role of creatives is either to follow through with ads based on new concepts, or to refine existing ads organized with reference to already proven concepts in ways that, it is hoped, will generate even stronger consumer response. On the whole, the tasks of focus mode occur within the everyday physical and mental spaces of agency life; for copywriters this normally means at a desk and in front of a computer screen.

Although some creatives work better in flux and others in focus, these two modes are not mutually exclusive. Rather, they are both key phases of the overall creative process. Those refining old ads have their eureka moments too, even if such moments tend to be less pronounced and celebrated; and those creating new ones rarely seriously consider concepts which fall beyond their technical skills (or the project's budget) to realize. On rare occasions, one or both members of a creative team, after receiving a brief, may be required to do some fieldwork – perhaps spending a weekend away at a 'luxury Highland retreat' to help sell a timeshare, or a longer period travelling to Africa to help sell a development charity. Such research excursions are periods of great flux and engagement for creatives, as the new spaces and stimuli provide fruitful ground for new ideas and connections. More usually, however, creatives must contrive their own spaces in which to work.

After a creative team has received a brief calling for a new approach, they play about with a few initial concepts, but these tend to be the most manifestly obvious possibilities and so are usually rejected, for there is always the fear that they may have been done before, perhaps many times. More often, the team will return to other tasks needing their attention, such as refining other projects in later stages of production. After a significant delay, they will regroup in focused-flux mode to direct their attention to the new project. For such a brainstorming session, a novel setting (e.g. cafe, pub or empty meeting room) is often preferred, both because the team is less likely to be disturbed by others and because a change of scene itself can help stimulate the flow of ideas. Some creatives also brainstorm on paper with spider diagrams, pursuing clever metaphors or tantalizing puns across the page. Most pore over old ads, industry magazines and photo sourcebooks, searching for something they will only know when they see it – an image or a turn of phrase that sparks a new thought.

Should useful concepts still not be forthcoming, a larger ad hoc brainstorming session may be formed. Here, the greater number of participants can enlarge, often geometrically, the number of possible creative 'answers' to the brief. Although the flow of ideas in such a group is often rather chaotic, with each person throwing out ideas as they come, sometimes a modicum of organization is imposed upon this anarchy via some form of turn-taking (e.g. moving clockwise or anticlockwise around the room or tossing a ball randomly from one participant to another).

Returning to the issue of the delay between receiving a brief and actually beginning to brainstorm it, we see that it is of no small significance to understanding flux mode, particularly its more enigmatic aspects. Verity tells us that during this delay the facts of the brief drift back to a 'mulling point' in her mind where they are actively, if unconsciously, sorted and creatively pondered.[6] Wherever she goes, she keeps herself 'open to the aesthetics of everyday life, very sensitive to images and colours and ideas', and she views this openness as enhancing her creative powers. Ideas, for her, often come surging forth from that mulling point when she is in motion – walking or cycling, for example – and she suggests that increased serotonin levels may be involved. Others present a similar view of their eureka moments, although Verity was one of the few to identify the source of her inspiration with such clarity. Jason holds that his moderate dyslexia helps him 'to see the world from a different angle' and so to generate better, more interesting ideas. He is, in his estimation, naturally more adept at entering what we are calling 'flux mode'.

Often, such eureka moments come unbidden. One can nevertheless increase their likelihood by reminding oneself of the task at hand and then doing something else entirely unrelated. Robert, for instance, tells himself he needs to solve a creative problem just as he is starting a session at the gym. He then 'forgets' about it, gets on with his exercises, and, as often as not, is rewarded at some point during or after his session with one or more solutions which seem to have come out of the blue. Movement, characterized invariably by engagement and often by flux, can in itself be stimulating: Nigel often experiences eureka moments on his motorcycle; Mark, while riding home on the train or walking his dogs. Many creatives find that ideas come to them in sleep, when only their minds are in motion.

Inspiration, in sum, appears at times to arise as a result of active, conscious (and often social) commotion; and at other times, of passive, unconscious, quasi-magical (and seemingly private) mental activity. In either case, the eureka moment usually occurs when flux is in the ascendant, at a physical or mental remove from the day-to-day routine of the office. Universally, it is experienced with delight (or at least relief) – as a puzzle solved, a new connection made, a brief 'cracked'.

Focus mode for creatives normally occurs in the office setting. Unless they wish to take their work home with them or remain after hours (as some do), they must find ways to respond to interruptions by others while simultaneously disengaging from the distractions which inhibit the realization of their work – the transformation of concepts into ads. While different creative modes of operating in advertising are explicitly distinguished, it is also recognized that one can become 'stuck' in focus mode. Working on another project, or re-entering flux (perhaps simply by going out for a coffee), can help.

The industry is keenly aware that creatives need 'space' in which to operate, so they are often given considerable freedom of movement relative to their co-workers. Many behavioural eccentricities are likewise tolerated so as not to stifle their creative capacities. However, the fact remains that an agency's creative department forms part of a larger, highly structured, commercial environment. Delivering the goods on time is ultimately what counts, so creatives must be able to switch between creative modes effectively on demand. Yet they are only human, and while most achieve a sense of fulfilment when they produce good ads, many do not feel their needs as creative people are fully met within such a 'mechanical' environment. Some seek recognition for their talents within other creative domains. Copywriters, for instance, may take to penning poems, plays and novels. Within such diversionary activities, they are free to move as they wish among creative modes, and worries over deadlines rarely disturb their efforts. Let us now consider the creative spaces which give rise to works of fiction.

Fiction

The process of taking a novel from an initial idea to the bookshop shelf is long and complex, and not unlike the conception, gestation and birth of an ad. Whereas in advertising, however, we saw a relatively strict division of creative modes organized within a highly institutional setting, here in fiction we find individuals who enjoy a great deal of freedom in how they arrange their creative endeavours. It is, as novelist Emma explains, 'a part of life under their control as opposed to work where you do what others say'. It would indeed be difficult to imagine writing fiction – at least of noteworthy quality – under the 'factory' conditions found in advertising agencies. For one thing the ideas underwriting novels are far more complex and harder to come by than the concepts which give sense to ads.

There are, of course, exceptions: successful writers are often more closely tied into relationships with publishers, and they may routinely experience the anxiety of deadlines. In general, though, any pressure most fiction writers feel is of their own making. Although hopes of financial reward and critical recognition form part of most writers' motivation to write, the act of writing fiction for many is mainly an act of personal exploration. This is certainly why some advertising creatives choose to write fiction in their spare time – it is difficult to imagine wanting to produce ads as a hobby.

The poet Annie Sexton says 'I do not write for ... [others]. Nor for you. Not even for the editors... Reaching people is ... important, I know, but reaching the best of me is most important right now' (Amabile 1996: 10). Kevin, a novelist and chief editor at a publishing company, likes 'the process [of writing itself], the feeling of subsuming [himself] in ideas – it becomes like waking dreaming, when the process is going really well, and the ideas and words are flowing... Writing for [him] is a form primarily of expression, but also of escape'.

The image of the fiction writer as someone disengaged from the wider world, working away in a room of his or her own, is a quite common and largely accurate sketch of focus mode. Certainly some such practitioners, like Juan Rulfo (1992: 383), may write solitarily in focused-flux mode until something appears – a word that provides the 'key' to what is to follow. (We are reminded here of advertising creatives and their spider diagrams.) Others may join groups or take classes in which something akin to focused-flux mode likewise predominates. Still others may conceive of their writing as social, at least in the sense that they engage with 'imaginary' characters and their worlds. Yet all write in some sense alone most of the time, and this is what we should expect given that their motives often arise from an interest in self-exploration. While Marjorie, a novelist and former copywriter, says, 'I guess any kind of writing is solitary except maybe advertising which is best when it is a collaborative process', Kevin tells us that 'only in the process afterwards, involving feedback and revision, can other people help you out'.

Creating a 'room of one's own' – a space of disengagement and focus – is something every writer must be able to do.[7] Mary, a fiction writer, finds herself all too often distracted by 'kids, drum and bass, life, telephone, lists of other things ... [she] should be doing, housework, earning a crust, doing questionnaires on writing'. Yet she still somehow manages, usually in the quiet of an odd late night, to carve out the space she needs. Marjorie's room has 'a sleeping cat or two, a few windows to look out every now and then, a green plant on ... [her] desk, an area to pace, [and] lots of books'. Novelist Francisco reminds us, however, that 'if you decide that it is a room of your own, of course it is'. In other words, a cafe, public park or library may 'work' for some writers. Thus, Kevin tells us: 'Normally I like it quiet – no music or television in the background, [t]hough I must admit there is a certain something about being in a public place.' Some writers are quite sensitive to colours and lighting and so arrange these environmental aspects to best effect. Others have music playing, often on repeat, quietly in the background to help stimulate a feeling of disengaged tranquillity and a sense of timelessness. For some, steadily sipping coffee or smoking is particularly conducive to focus. For others, a coffee or cigarette break can signal a small shift into flux, a temporary reprieve from the tyranny of the page or screen.

On the whole, however, most eureka moments, big or small, occur outside the 'room' – in flux and engagement. None of our interviewees mentioned the disorientating effects of alcohol or drugs, but clearly some authors (e.g. Aldous Huxley, Ernest Hemingway, Ken Kesey, Hunter S. Thompson and Paul Bowles) have found insight in intoxication (cf. Pritzker 1999: 731–3). More often, it seems, inspiration emerges at unexpected yet otherwise unremarkable moments, when anything – sight, smell, sound, taste, touch – can take on extraordinary significance and elicit a response, a connection sought or unsought. Kevin explains: 'Generally

I will be doing something banal and not very stimulating: showering or shaving or driving a well-known route. This opens my mind to other concerns. I've had some of my best ideas while brushing my teeth.' Ethnographer/fiction writer Jeremy tells us: 'Pretty much all of my ideas arise ... when I am detached from the writing process in some way, engaged in some non-intellectual activity such as gardening, walking, sometimes lying in bed at night or first thing in the morning.' Marjorie says: 'There is no pattern to ideas "coming into my head". It has happened when reading, walking, sitting outside.' For Mary, 'riding a bike is good for letting the mind flow freely'. Fiction writer and ethnographer Steve has, like advertising creative Nigel, had 'some of ... [his] best ideas ... while riding a motorcycle'. Emma finds train travel particularly stimulating and concludes that 'most people are moving at the time' when they have their flashes of inspiration.

Fiction writer/ethnographer Hannah discovers her inspiration in both flux and focused-flux modes. She tells us:

> Any circumstance might trigger an idea... It's not the specific circumstance but more so one of two things: a) down time completely independent of a specific writing project such as a long plane ride or free time at home or b) a situation where I am brainstorming with others in an artefact rich environment where we are building on each other and the material context.

Suspicious of mystical readings of eureka moments, novelist James holds that 'most writers probably tend to view life through the prism of its potential for their fiction, picking up on literary structures cropping up in real life'. Such a claim reinforces our view that focused-flux mode need not occur only in brainstorming groups. Consider, for instance, the expert photographer who sees, with requisite diminution of (among other things) peripheral vision, the world in terms of its potential to yield striking and saleable images. While for a novelist this ability may well represent a shift towards the esteemed 'mature art' phase characteristic of, say, a later Graham Greene, for an advertising creative it all too often signifies a transition to what is somewhat disparagingly known as the 'pipe and slippers' stage of a career – a period in which veteran reliability and technical skill supplant youthful exuberance and marketable spontaneity.[8]

Though we have seen that some advertising creatives on rare occasions undertake something akin to fieldwork, their research is normally much more 'bookish', drawing on old ads, their briefs and other supporting materials (most products for which they devise ads are not terribly complex, but they must still understand them in order to make ads for them). Most fiction writers emphasize the importance of reading 'good' works of fiction as the best general starting point, and most also draw inspiration from non-fiction sources. Many engage in their own forms of fieldwork. Blanca, a novelist (and ethnographer), spends considerable time in the settings she describes, eating the food, meeting the people, taking photos and even making audio recordings – all in order to help her future readers suspend disbelief.

Yet research is clearly not a prerequisite for such writers. Carolyn, another novelist/ethnographer, does some research for her fiction, but she tells us: '[I only really need] my brain, my imagination and my computer.' Kevin has found in the past that too much research into one subject can lead him astray, to abandon his original plans in favour of others. Mary has found that her readers prefer the works she 'just wrote off the top of ... [her] head' to those she has researched: she assumes the former come across as 'less contrived'. More common and seemingly much more productive for fiction writers is a less programmatic approach, one in which they simply 'dirty themselves', to use Francisco's words, in social interaction. Marjorie reports that 'a particular scene ... witnessed or a conversation ... overheard' can spark her creativity, and she is by no means alone. Emma is not unusual in collecting 'scraps from newspapers' and writing down her 'dreams on waking'. Whatever form of research a fiction writer pursues, odds are that he or she will keep a journal to record random thoughts and ideas which may at some point prove useful in resolving as-yet-not-encountered creative problems.

In advertising, the vast majority of eureka moments are rather 'small'. They involve transforming simple selling messages into entertaining concepts. Fiction writers, too, experience a great many such small flashes of inspiration, most often to help them over the sorts of minor hurdles which inevitably arise, for example, to resolve a contradiction in a character's motivation, to rationalize a temporal sequence, to introduce pivotal pieces of information with the most effective degree of emphasis. A 'big' eureka moment that provides a powerful grounding idea for an entire novel is another matter entirely. Such a moment, according to Kevin, is 'universally rare and envied, but hardly essential', for one can always find form in strict adherence to genre. It may be of central importance to the creativity behind an ethnography, however, so now we turn our attention to this rather peculiar literary form.

Ethnography

Long gone are the times when one could produce a simply descriptive (or at least largely descriptive) ethnography. Nowadays, a strong mixture of theory and data, united by a guiding and ideally novel theme, is required in order for the thing to count as a worthwhile contribution. When Callahan returned from his doctoral fieldwork in Yucatán, his advisor told him that he should not feel under too much pressure to begin writing his thesis straight away; rather, he should give himself 'six months to let things settle' in order 'to get a sense of perspective'. After trying to write in both the USA and the UK, he returned to Mexico in search of his muse. The first night there, while dazedly awaiting sleep in a cheap hotel in Cancún, he had a big eureka moment – the outline of his thesis appeared to him in a flash, with startling clarity. At that instant, a great weight lifted, and everything began to come (relatively) easily.

We anthropologists, however, if we are to believe books on how to write ethnography, conceive of our creativity largely in terms of focus and disengagement. Not only do such books rarely touch on the subject of eureka moments, we also seem hesitant to acknowledge the true extent of the creativity behind our works. Perhaps talk of flux and engagement seems too unempirical, too much of a threat to our authority as social scientists. Yet we regularly read with a critical (and creative) eye the published works of our predecessors and contemporaries, and in classroom discussions, conferences, symposia, cafes and pubs we routinely enter into focused flux, much as advertising creatives do in brainstorming sessions. Ethnographer Mark, for whom newspapers and documentaries also contribute importantly to the mix, concludes: 'We have to deal with the world around us, and the world around us is very good at giving us ideas.' In common with advertising creative Verity and novelist James, he sees the eureka moment as a rather complex entity: it 'is not actually a spontaneous thing that just pops up ("look at me, I am your idea!!!"), but rather takes hard work and a sponge-like soaking up of ideas around you, both academic and popular'.

Most important of all, though, for our own special brand of creativity is the pure flux at the core of the fieldwork experience. In it we 'dirty' ourselves, to borrow again from Francisco, in social interaction. But unlike most fiction writers, we do much more than simply dip our collective feet into the water. Our immersion in – or better, our exposure to – alien socioscapes is often so intense that it cannot help but inspire us. Like special versions of Victor Turner's 'edgemen', we find ourselves freed from the world of 'status incumbency and role-playing' in which we have previously lived our lives, and 'enter into vital relations with [a much wider range of] other men [and women] in fact ... [and] imagination' (Turner 1969: 128).[9] Like fish who have just come to suspect the substance of the water in which they swim, we are confronted with profound glimpses into the surprising contingency of existence.

In fieldwork we quickly lose control of events. We are rendered, whether by choice or default, vulnerable to all manner of disorientating happenings: suspicion of our motives; simmering hostility, stigmatization and perhaps even overt physical violence; unwelcome interest from authorities and gossips; political and perhaps even sexual intrigue; illness and personal traumas there and back home; and unexpected displays of kindness from odd quarters. It can be a heady mix. Some of us take a long time to recover, or at least to gain any kind of useful purchase on the experience.

Our time in the field is often one of near-continuous flux and engagement. Carolyn, in common with many of us, found that, with all the 'things [that] happen ... in fieldwork', she hardly ever had time to withdraw and reflect – to disengage and focus on writing field notes. Like a fiction writer's journal, an anthropologist's field notes represent a sort of halfway house on the road to a publishable piece, and yet they are so much more. Within the relative safety and distance they provide, the many failures and triumphs of daily life in the field are brought into some semblance of temporary order, for ends not simply academic. The task of writing field notes is more than one of recording, and perhaps codifying, data on a piecemeal basis. It requires a sort of 'room of one's own' for many, although the 'walls' of that 'room' usually need not (and cannot) be as solid and impenetrable as those of our room 'back home'. Yet the field-note space can also be a vital form of personal therapy – a way of communicating, even if only in fantasy, with those who share our own values and norms and who may sympathize with our plights in ways our subjects perhaps cannot.

The 'writing stage' in anthropology is normally considered quite separate from the 'fieldwork stage'. Before writing of the ethnography proper can begin, however, the ethnographer must have some grounding idea to guide his or her efforts. For Trudy, as for most ethnographers, this idea begins life within her original proposal, and then 'develops and changes as ethnographic material is collected'. If a big, transformative eureka moment did not emerge in the flux of the field, then ideally it should come, unbidden yet desired, afterwards. Assuming that it has come, there remains the task of finding the right conditions in which to write. Andrew, an ethnographer/novelist, speaks of the need to strike a balance between 'emotional proximity' (as a stimulus to writing) and 'critical distance' (as a stimulus to writing *ethnography*).

The writing stage often takes place at great physical remove from the field. For some ethnographers this distance is essential for focus, and their flux periods occur while wading through field notes or simply going about their lives, as they do for advertising creatives and fiction writers. Their 'rooms' resemble in most respects those of the fiction writers we have already met: some prefer the solitude of office or home, while others find comfort and focus in the white noise of public spaces. For Mark, it is a combined space of focus and flux – a quiet place that is also 'somewhere ... you can just let your notebooks, binders, documents, records, what-have-you explode'.

Some ethnographers, however, feel drawn to write some or all of their ethnographies in the field and find it possible to achieve a sense of distance by other means. While for Jeremy 'there is a certain clarity in thinking about something from afar..., there are benefits ... in being present [in the field] and ... detached [in some other way]'. Stack wrote his doctoral dissertation in the field, but enjoyed a good deal of privacy in that west Mexican town, full of large and often empty houses – many residents having left to work in California while other houses were owned by weekenders from the city. Callahan, by contrast, had much less privacy in his Yucatecan village, but still felt somewhat detached by the simple fact of writing in English. Again, there are many ways of building a 'room of one's own'.

At the end of the day, every ethnographer, in common with every advertising creative and every fiction writer, has his or her own ways of creatively accomplishing the tasks before him or her. Some of these methods are uniquely personal and perhaps not even open to conscious reflection; others are more or less culturally established. All arise from and give new life to our abiding sense as moderns that newness is inherently valuable.

Conclusion

All cultures emphasize tradition and novelty to some degree. One cannot, in any meaningful sense, have one without the other. The innovation can only be recognized and acknowledged as such by contrast to the standard from which it deviates. However, some cultures are far more resistant to novelty, while others feel its seductive pull in nearly every domain of life. Sapir (1993: 28) notes that, among the Navajo, a chant perfectly rendered in line with traditional expectations may accord prestige to the performer. We know that, among ourselves, a clever ad, a thought-provoking novel or a ground-breaking ethnography may bring recognition and respect to its creator.

Modern culture's 'quest for newness' not only finds expression in the elite forms consumed by various specialist and non-specialist audiences; as we have seen, it also gives the creativities implicated in the production of those forms their peculiar characters. While we could have focused solely on the products of creative activity for evidence of this ubiquitous pattern, we have chosen to investigate the differences in the creative processes behind the products.

Time and again we have seen the importance of mimesis, of the replication of tradition, of the mastery of generic forms, in the creation of novelty: advertising creatives draw on past ads, particularly those which have proved commercially successful, to give direction to their own works; fiction writers stress the importance of reading 'good' books as a guide to producing 'good' fiction themselves; and ethnographers emphasize a familiarity with relevant academic works and evince a desire to situate their own efforts 'within the literature'. Yet caught as we are within the warp and woof of modernity and its quest for newness, we are just as much impelled to reproduce novelty as the Navajo specialist, whose culture underscores the potency of tradition, is impelled to seek distinction through the careful replication of past forms.

Reproducing novelty means embodying the practical steps, shared or otherwise, that liberate the individual to whatever degree from the burdens of tradition, and that leave him or her more open to unexpected turns of thought. It also means reflecting to some extent upon such steps, dispensing with some of them and modifying others in order to become better and more reliable creative producers. In each of the three domains explored in this chapter, we have witnessed what are clearly shared, properly 'cultural' techniques – tricks of the trade. Yet we have also witnessed at first hand the soft borders between shared culture and individual psychology.

Across the domains of advertising, fiction and ethnography, we have encountered both similarities and differences in people's experiences of creativity. In all cases we have seen that the creative process entails movement between spaces, literal and figurative, which are broadly characterized either by flux and engagement (and, sometimes, eureka moments) or by focus and disengagement, along with occasional forays into the middle ground of focused flux. There are differences too. In advertising, for instance, we find a great deal of attention paid to creative techniques involving collaboration. (Advertising is also probably the most creative when it comes to creating new ways to be creative.) The solutions of fiction writers tend, like their writings, to be more private and idiosyncratic. Yet both advertising creatives and fiction writers share a high regard for creativity, and they view themselves and their best works as sometimes clever, sometimes profound and sometimes simply entertaining – but *always* innovative.

Our own brief explorations have led us to suggest that we as ethnographers too often downplay the importance of creative processes that draw their special qualities from the unique intensity and flux of our 'dirtying' exposure in fields foreign to those of our 'normal' lives. Although Jeremy, along with many of us, is 'strongly motivated by a sense of scientific creativity', it seems that we are at the same time somewhat suspicious of thinking about our work as being fundamentally creative. Perhaps, though, we can serve ourselves, our discipline and our audiences better not only by acknowledging our creativity, but also by actively seeking to enhance it, both through paying greater attention to our own traditional creative 'spaces' and through opening ourselves up more to the tricks of other creative trades. We anthropologists are, after all, what Barth (1967) calls 'entrepreneurs'. We are unifiers of disparate domains of value, translators, linkers and innovators. In short, we create.

Acknowledgements

We are grateful to the participants in our study, some of whom kindly offered feedback on earlier drafts of this chapter. Callahan would like to thank, in addition to his co-author, Jim Gilbert (a good friend, excellent writer and unusually creative force) for his help.

Notes

1. Useful collections and syntheses of literature on creativity include Vernon (1970), Glover, Ronning and Reynolds (1989), and Runco and Pritzker (1999). One of the few anthropological collections is Lavie, Narayan and Rosaldo (1993).
2. Csikszentmihalyi (1990) uses the term 'flow' for the state in which individuals – on their own or in groups – manage to remain focused on something and to pursue that thing in a particular direction. In other words, he uses 'flow' for what we call a state of 'focus'. He gives little importance to what we call 'flux', which is a very different kind of mental movement, not in one direction but in several shifting directions.
3. Our discussion of modes of being in the world has obvious resonance with the literature on phenomenology (e.g. Heidegger 1977), while the notion of the mind working below the level of consciousness is resonant with psychoanalysis (e.g. Brophy 1998). We intend to address these literatures in future publications, together with the political economy of creativity (e.g. Negus and Pickering 2004), the history of the concept of the 'creative imagination' (e.g. Engell 1981) and the critique of authorial intention in literary studies (e.g. Barthes 1977).
4. This information is derived from Callahan's observations from his time as a copywriter working in agencies in Edinburgh and London. The material on which our study is based is drawn from taped interviews with, and completed questionnaires from, more than two dozen respondents.
5. Some of these techniques are discussed in O'Looney et al. (1989: 314–17).
6. Verity's comments here are a beautiful rendition of the mathematician Poincaré's (1970 [1924]: 81–8) experience of his own creative processes, later developed by Wallas (1970 [1926]) into his theory of the 'stages' of creativity: preparation, incubation, illumination and verification. Particularly relevant is their concept of 'incubation': after an initial conscious attempt at creativity, usually fruitless, ideas continue to gestate unconsciously or semi-consciously (cf. O'Looney et al. 1989: 314).
7. Some writers, like Julio Cortázar, enter into extreme states of disengagement, separating themselves from others and the world for lengthy periods of time

(Cortázar 1998 [1977]). This is less common, but not unknown, among academics, who are afforded such spaces in sabbaticals.
8. This, of course, raises the issue of creative 'peaks'. More specifically, the sorts of creativity valued in fiction, as indeed in ethnography, mean its practitioners tend to peak creatively rather later in life than those working in advertising.
9. Our use of Turner here is inspired, though to a somewhat different purpose, by Shostak (1992: 54), who provides one of the few anthropological accounts of creativity.

References

Amabile, T.M. (1996), *Creativity in Context: Update to The Social Psychology of Creativity*, Boulder, Colo. and Oxford: Westview Press.
Barth, F. (1967), *The Role of the Entrepreneur in Social Change in Northern Norway*, Oslo: Universitetsforlaget.
Barthes, R. (1977), *Image, Music, Text* (trans. S. Heath), New York: Hill and Wang.
Brophy, K. (1998), *Creativity: Psychoanalysis, Surrealism and Creative Writing*, Melbourne: University of Melbourne Press.
Cortázar, J. (1998 [1977]), *Julio Cortázar (entrevista con Joaquín Soler Serrano)*, Madrid: Editrama.
Csikszentmihalyi, M. (1990), *Flow: The Psychology of Optimal Experience*, New York: Harper Perennial.
D'Andrade, R.G. (1992), 'Schemas and motivation', in R.G. D'Andrade and C. Strauss (eds), *Human Motives and Cultural Models*, Cambridge: Cambridge University Press.
Engell, J. (1981), *The Creative Imagination: Enlightenment to Romanticism*, Cambridge, Mass. and London: Harvard University Press.
Freud, S. (1970 [1908]), 'Creative writers and day-dreaming', in P.E. Vernon (ed), *Creativity: Selected Readings*, London: Penguin Books.
Gardner, H. (1982), *Art, Mind, and Brain*, New York: Basic Books.
Glover, J.A., Ronning, R.R. and Reynolds, C.R. (eds) (1989), *Handbook of Creativity*, New York and London: Plenum Press.
Heidegger, M. (1977), *Basic Writings: From Being and Time (1927) to The Task of Thinking (1964)* (trans. D.F. Krell), New York: Harper & Row.
Lavie, S., Narayan, K. and Rosaldo, R. (eds) (1993), *Creativity/Anthropology*, Ithaca, NY and London: Cornell University Press.
Negus, K. and Pickering, M. (2004), *Creativity, Communication and Cultural Value*, London: Sage.

O'Looney, J.A., Glynn, S.M., Britton, B.K. and Mattocks, L.F. (1989), 'Cognition and writing: the idea generation process', in J.A. Glover, R.R. Ronning and C.R. Reynolds (eds), *Handbook of Creativity*, New York and London: Plenum Press.

Poincaré, H. (1970 [1924]), 'Mathematical creation', in P.E. Vernon (ed), *Creativity: Selected Readings*, London: Penguin Books.

Pritzker, S.R. (1999), 'Writing and creativity', in M.A. Runco and S.R. Pritzker (eds), *Encyclopedia of Creativity*, San Diego, Calif.: Academic Press.

Rulfo, J. (1992), *Toda la obra* (comp. C. Fell), Mexico City: Archivos.

Runco, M.A. and Pritzker, S.R. (eds) (1999), *Encyclopedia of Creativity*, San Diego, Calif.: Academic Press.

Sapir, E. (1993), *The Psychology of Culture: A Course of Lectures*, Berlin: Mouton de Gruyter.

Shostak, M. (1992), 'The creative individual in the world of !Kung San', in S. Lavie, K. Narayan and R. Rosaldo (eds), *Creativity/Anthropology*, Ithaca, NY and London: Cornell University Press.

Strauss, C. (1992), 'What makes Tony run? Schemas as motives reconsidered', in R.G. D'Andrade and C. Strauss (eds), *Human Motives and Cultural Models*, Cambridge: Cambridge University Press.

Turner, V. (1969), *The Ritual Process: Structure and Anti-Structure*, New York: Aldine Publishing Company.

Urban, G. (2001), *Metaculture: How Culture Moves Through the World*, Minneapolis: University of Minnesota Press.

Vernon, P.E. (ed) (1970), *Creativity: Selected Readings*, Harmondsworth: Penguin Books.

Wallas, G. (1970 [1926]), 'The art of thought', in P.E. Vernon (ed), *Creativity: Selected Readings*, London: Penguin Books.

–14–

(Re)constructing the Field through Sound: Actor-networks, Ethnographic Representation and 'Radio Elicitation' in South-western Uganda

Richard Vokes

Anthropology and 'Science Studies'

Over the last decade or so, a number of anthropologists have begun to engage critically with the 'science studies' of Bruno Latour. Particularly for those anthropologists working in the field of science and technology studies, and especially in the sub-field of medical anthropology, Latour's (and Callon's) concept of the 'actor-network' has proved particularly useful for analysis, and has opened up new ways of thinking about interconnections between people and the material objects of science (not only DNA, viruses, plants, animals and the like, but also the apparatus, machines and other objects which furnish the scientific 'laboratory'). At the heart of the actor-network model lies an attempt to dissolve any categorical distinction between people and non-human social actors, both of which are included within a single category of 'actants'. As Latour argues at length in *We Have Never Been Modern* (1993), such a distinction is little more than artifice, one that has been particularly influential in Western scientific thought from the Enlightenment onwards, but which is nevertheless problematic. Instead, he draws attention to the complex ways in which people and other orders of actants continually constitute and reconstitute each other, in an endless production of different sorts of 'hybridities'. The argument is that while human action endlessly shapes and reshapes the material world, so too the objects of that world impact upon both the individual human body and the social domain. So fundamental are these interactions, Latour argues, that it makes little sense to privilege either people or non-human 'actors' over the other. Instead, the two must be conceptualized as equally important elements within identifiable assemblages – or actor-networks – of relations. These ubiquitous assemblages, and not people or non-human actors alone, produce social effects (see also Latour 1996).

Science studies emerged as a distinct area of anthropological concern in the mid-1990s. Following the various critiques of the politics and poetics of ethnography that had occurred in the preceding two decades, many anthropologists were at that time attempting to redefine their objects of analysis, away from studies of (apparently) politically powerless, territorially and temporally bounded, non-Western 'others', towards a focus on 'multiperspectival points of view, local and transnational sites ... the changing velocities of space and time, the historical conditions in which capitalism [has been] reshaping global power on an unprecedented scale, and the historical conditions of Western theory and practice' (Weiner 1993). It was in pursuit of the latter part of this agenda, in particular, that a number of anthropologists began to study the sites of scientific production themselves, and this led them to engage with actor-network theory. For one thing, Latour himself had first developed several of his key ideas through an ethnographic study of a neuroendocrinology research laboratory at the Salk Institute in California. His seminal work (with Steven Woolgar) *Laboratory Life* (1979) was one of the first detailed ethnographic accounts of scientific practice to appear in print. But more importantly from the anthropological point of view, the concept of the actor-network provided a model for theorists to think about scientific innovation not only as an outcome of technical processes, but also as a combination of the technical and the social. It drew attention to the fact that the instruments used in any given experiment are not neutral 'windows on the world', but are instead – as are all objects of material culture – socially located. Furthermore, they are used in clearly demarcated and socially meaningful spaces: 'laboratories' (including not just designated rooms and buildings, but any space in which deliberate experimentation takes place). In addition, within the experimental context they are used – through the execution of certain well-defined practices – to produce yet more types of objects known as data. Thus the experiment itself is an assemblage that yields additional hybrids as its outputs. A wide range of social constructs, from the scientist's own academic training to departmental funding agendas, subsequently combine with these new outputs to produce yet more effects: research outputs, patents and the like. The argument can be extended here to ever widening scales or 'levels' of complexity. Thus, depending on the length to which one wants to take the analysis, one could widen the scope to include such additional factors as state research strategies, disciplinary objectives, and so on. Indeed, so extensive can these networks become that the challenge for analysts is to decide at what point they should be 'cut' (Strathern 1996), while still doing justice to the object of study. From the mid-1990s onwards, anthropologists working in the field of medical anthropology, in particular, found this way of thinking particularly useful for unpacking a specifically social dimension of scientific practice.

The present chapter, however, is *not* a contribution to the anthropology of science. Instead, it is an attempt to explore some of the broader implications of actor-network theory for the discipline of anthropology as a whole. I show that the types of practices identified by earlier theorists as central to the scientific method can also be seen as fundamental to anthropological work. Specifically, I will demonstrate that all ethnographic fieldwork involves the mobilization of both people and things into networks of relations that actor-network theorists would term hybrids. In effect, all anthropological representations emerge out of precisely these sorts of assemblage. I will explore this argument through a detailed discussion of the history of 'elicitation' research techniques in ethnographic fieldwork: those interviewing methods in which objects are used as a means of focusing responses around a given topic or issue. In particular, I will discuss the new technique of 'radio elicitation', a method of interviewing I developed during twenty-seven months of fieldwork in rural south-western Uganda between 2000 and 2005.[1] However, I will go on to argue that these insights concerning elicitation have further implications for all types of anthropological fieldwork.

Representations, People and Things

In the two decades or so since the emergence of the 'textual critique' in anthropology, issues of representation have become key epistemological concerns for all anthropological fieldworkers. Once the preserve of specialist sub-disciplines such as visual anthropology and museum ethnography, debates surrounding the politics and poetics of portraying cultural 'others' – in textual, visual or other forms – have preoccupied ethnographers from across the anthropological spectrum and beyond (Clifford 1988; Clifford and Marcus 1986; Marcus 1998; Marcus and Cushman 1982). Nevertheless, over the last twenty years, the locus of these debates has shifted significantly. Responding to the critique of 'naive realism', which was one of the early strands in the 'crisis of representation', many ethnographers initially explored various concepts of reflexivity as possible means of forging more representative accounts of the field (cf. Austrin and Farnsworth 2005: 149). In an effort to disrupt both the conventional objectivism and the political naivety of previous styles, this new generation of ethnographers frequently included elements of multi-vocalism or dialogism in their written accounts (for critical discussions of these attempts, see Crapanzano 1990; Tedlock 1987). In most instances this dialogism took the form of local 'voices' appearing alongside that of the anthropologist (for an overview of this literature, see Clifford 1988: 41–54). In others it involved the anthropologist developing multiple authorial positions of her own (Wolf 1992). Such approaches, however, soon came under attack for being themselves politically naive, guilty of overestimating the ability of any local voice to compete with that of the anthropologist (see, for example, Fabian 1990: 763–7; Marcus 1998: 112–14). After all, practically all ethnographies continued to be edited only by anthropologists themselves, and all continued to be subject to the textual and stylistic constraints of Western publishing conventions. Such dialogical approaches therefore proved to be somewhat short-lived. They were soon replaced by alternative experimental styles, each of which tried to further the twofold agenda of producing both more critical and more politically engaged ethnographies. One key development here involved a problematization of the entire genre of ethnography, a move which led to a number of anthropologists experimenting with alternative generic styles, including poetry and fiction (Fabian 1990; Geertz 1988; Taussig 1997, 2004). Another took the form of a general reassessment of the political position of ethnographic readers, with a view to engaging them in different sorts of ways. Thus, rather than simply 'imparting knowledge' about other cultural groups – a knowledge now known to have been implicated in the processes of colonial domination – ethnographers tried to elicit other sorts of responses from their readers: sympathy, empathy, and so on (Jackson 2004; Prattis 1985).

These various experimental approaches have made important contributions to the overall anthropological project. Nevertheless, all have also made one key omission. Specifically, by only emphasizing the social and political dimensions of ethnographic representation, the 'new' ethnography has failed to attend to the role of material objects in shaping the construction of those representations. Yet if the new 'science studies' have taught us one thing, it is that the agency of objects is crucial to the production of all empirically based academic knowledge. This much is demonstrated by Latour, in one of his key explorations of the processes through which scientific knowledge is constructed, an essay that describes a fieldwork trip in which he participated to the Boa Vista forest, on the edge of Brazilian Amazonia, in 1991 (originally published in 1995, the essay is reproduced in Latour 1999: 24–79). The purpose of the expedition – which included a pedologist, a botanist, a geomorphologist and Latour himself (as observer) – was to determine whether the Boa Vista forest was advancing into, or retreating from, adjacent savannah regions. At the outset, the presence of isolated trees, located several metres beyond the treeline of the forest proper into the savannah zone, appeared to pose an intractable problem. From the pedologist's point of view – and following a general theory of soil fertility according to which earth necessarily degrades from rich to poor, from clay to sand – the presence of such outliers surely indicated a retreating forest. For the botanist, on the other hand, the fact that some of the outlying trees were savannah species, and that examples of these species could also be found several metres into the forest proper (within which, by rights, they should not have been able to survive for long), suggested that the forest might instead be advancing.

Latour's purpose in his essay on the expedition is to examine the ways in which each of the three scientists – with his or her own theoretical frameworks and methodological procedures – goes about collecting the evidence deemed necessary for answering this particular research question, of whether the forest is retreating or advancing. The resulting account is a fascinating description of the variety of ways in which different disciplinary practitioners approach a single problem. Yet it also highlights how these approaches nevertheless share certain key features. Specifically, each involves the scientist literally placing – or inscribing – some preformed symbolic template onto the physical world of the forest/savannah. Thus the pedologist places a series of strings and posts across the forest floor in order to recreate a grid of transects he has already drawn on a piece of graph paper. The botanist pins numbers on trees to map out samples that correspond to her predefined classifications of species, and so on. The purpose of these various techniques of inscription is for the scientists to fix, and to give meaning to, various physical objects that are then removed from the forest/savannah by the researchers. Thus the inscription of transects recasts the individual lumps of soil that the pedologist goes on to remove as 'samples' (of given locations). Similarly, the tagging of trees recasts the individual leaves that the botanist collects as examples of species distribution. All this is significant, as these same objects subsequently go on to form the very basis of the scientists' research accounts, providing the necessary evidential foundation for the various tables, graphs and conclusions they construct. (The forest, it turns out, is probably advancing after all. The scientists conclude that this is possibly the result of the activity of earthworms, although further research would be required to confirm this.)

For Latour, this example of a small research trip to the Boa Vista forest demonstrates, contrary to common sense Western understandings of cognition, language, and so on, that symbolic representations are not necessarily ontologically distinct from the physical world to which they refer. Rather – within the limited domain of academic scientific knowledge, at least – the two exist in a necessary state of complex and dynamic interaction. Just as symbolic constructs are invariably inscribed within the physical world, so too the incorporation of specific objects of that world is central to the construction of further symbolic schemata. In this sense, all scientific representations (at least) are necessarily hybrid; all require some process of incorporation of material objects in order to be convincing. To put it another way, all accounts are translations of the networks of relations – of both human and non-human actants – that have brought them into existence. Hence they are all 'actor-networks'. This conclusion has important implications for theorizing the process of anthropological fieldwork as well, whether or not one thinks of anthropology as a science. Certainly most anthropologists would not, as the pedologist and the botanist in the above example, inscribe preformed symbolic schemata onto their objects of study. Although more or less all ethnographers, especially those newly arrived in the field, do create maps, genealogies and the like, often according to preconceived categorical criteria, rarely do they attempt, as the botanist with her markers, literally to inscribe these on the reality to which they refer (you can peg labels to trees, but not, under normal circumstances, to people).[2] Nevertheless, many anthropologists frequently mobilize material objects as part of the normal process of ethnographic fieldwork. Furthermore, the presence of these same objects is also key to the later construction and stabilization of ethnographic representations. Thus, ethnographies are no less hybrid than the accounts produced by pedologists and botanists. Ethnographies, too, are actor-networks.

Fieldwork, Elicitation and Objects

All ethnographic fieldwork – all, at least, that is practised within a Malinowskian or Boasian tradition – involves a necessary mobilization of material objects. To begin, I want to draw attention to those interviewing strategies commonly bracketed under the term 'elicitation'. Interviewing techniques that involve some element of elicitation – that do not ask questions directly of the respondent, but instead seek his or her thoughts on a given practice, event or issue through the use of an object connected with it – have a long history in anthropological field research. As early as 1915, Malinowski remarked: 'my experience is that direct questioning of the native [*sic*] about a custom or belief never discloses their attitude of mind as thoroughly as the discussion of facts connected with the direct observation of a custom or with a concrete occurrence' (1915: 652). This effect was most easily achieved, Malinowski argued, through the use of some object associated with that custom or occurrence. A quarter of a century later, Siegfried Nadel's guide to fieldwork interviewing made a similar point. Basing his discussion on the Royal Anthropological Institute's *Notes and Queries* of 1929, Nadel argued that asking abstract questions of a respondent did have some utility, in that answers often revealed normative principles. However, if one wanted to understand how respondents actually thought and behaved in practice, then it was necessary to have them talk about real-life events. This reflected the fact that 'the trend of native [*sic*] languages, and indeed of the native mind in general, is towards the concrete, and consequently ... a discussion centring on concrete instances and events is usually more likely to yield reliable information' (Nadel 1961 [1939]: 320). Again, such instances and events were best approached, Nadel thought, through the various objects and paraphernalia associated with them. These acted, in the interview context, as essential aides-memoire.

It was not until the early 1950s, however, that elicitation interviewing techniques began to gain widespread appeal. At that time a number of more psychologically minded – especially American – anthropologists became interested in various techniques of 'projective' interviewing, which were at that time in vogue in clinical psychology. Projective interviewing was, in essence, a form of elicitation (cf. Whyte et al. 1982: 118). In clinical psychology interviewing, the types of objects used tended to be of the researcher's own making, designed to offer some insight or other into the 'inner personalities' of individual respondents (the most famous of these was the Rorschach ink-blot test). However, among anthropologists, given their more empirical predilections, it was held much more useful to use artefacts derived from the social environment under investigation. They were also much less concerned with their respondents' 'inner selves' than with group sentiments and socially constructed world views. Thus they were more likely to turn to artefacts such as productive tools, ritual implements and the like (Kemp, in Ellen 1984: 234). However, the key development in the history of anthropological elicitation occurred from the mid-1950s onwards, as a growing number of anthropologists began to advocate the use of photographs as an especially good artefact around which to structure sociological interviews. Of particular importance here is the work of John Collier (especially 1967; see also Ravetz, this volume, Chapter 12).

Notwithstanding their Eurocentric and at times overtly racist language, Malinowski and Nadel were right, as others since have been also, to draw attention to the advantages of elicitation techniques for the anthropological researcher. On the one hand, getting a respondent to discuss a specific practice, event or issue through a physical object invites a degree of self-expression over and above that which could normally be achieved in an interview context. In other words, this technique certainly does help the anthropologist to 'elicit' fuller and more detailed responses than might otherwise be possible. This is especially true if the respondent has particularly strong views about the practice, event or issue in question. But it is also a function of the fact that people simply feel more relaxed if they do not perceive themselves to be the object of the interview. After all, with the introduction of an extraneous object, one is questioning the respondent *about something*, rather than questioning him or her directly. And this also makes note-taking easier, because the anthropologist is ostensibly taking notes about the object, rather than about the respondent him- or herself. Also from the interviewer's point of view, the use of an object helps to structure the interview, by providing a concrete and explicit point of reference to which one can constantly return, should the interview drift too far from the main topic of interest. In addition, the introduction of the artefact tends to heighten the respondent's self-expression (hence the term 'elicitation'). This is because the object tends to dominate the interview space, and thereby invites the respondent to take the lead in interview discussions. It is also important that the object can be looked at, touched, smelled, tasted, or – as in the case of radio, described below – listened to.

In his seminal work on 'photo elicitation' John Collier argued that the use of photographs as objects for elicitation confers further advantages still (over the use of other types of artefacts for the same purpose). Collier talks of the 'hypnotic pull' of the photograph, as something that triggers particularly heightened self-expression, to the point where a respondent might betray 'very great confidences' (Collier 1986: 107). For example, he talks poetically of the photograph's ability to momentarily place the informant 'back on his [*sic*] fishing boat, working out in the woods, or carrying out a skilled craft' (ibid.: 106), such that he momentarily forgets himself. Further, he argues that the peculiar qualities of photographs mean that this heightened self-expression can be maintained over a number of interviews (whereas other artefacts tend to provide diminishing returns in this regard). However, the key difference between photographs and other types of artefacts stems from the particular social effects they create. According to Collier, photographs create a peculiarly intense interaction among informants as they are passed round, and as discussions take place over their content and meaning (ibid.: 105–7). This inherent contestability of the photographic image is of more than just observational interest for the anthropologist. It also creates a possibility for more dialogical approaches to interviewing, in which the anthropologist's own interpretations may be explored in relation to those of his or her respondents.

Thus from the time of Malinowski onwards, anthropologists have made regular use of interviewing techniques in which questions focus on the discussion of material objects. In other words, ethnographers have often found it useful to approach other social and cultural worlds indirectly, through various kinds of objects produced by the people being studied. In this, the objects in question are cast as key mediators, a crucial bridge between the anthropologist's own perspective and that of the people among whom he or she works. They are, as an actor-network theorist would put it, agents of translation between the two perspectival domains. Yet as such, they also exert an influence on the descriptions that result, shaping representations in important ways. In the remainder of this chapter I wish to explore this notion further, through a discussion of the use, in my own work, of the method of 'radio elicitation'.

Radio Research in South-western Uganda

Over the course of twenty-seven months of fieldwork in the village of Bugamba, south-western Uganda, I conducted a wide-ranging project of radio and media research. Reviewing the data from this project some months later, I realized that it was possible to identify three distinct methods that I had used, throughout the project, to examine local uses of radio. The first involved what might be termed 'radio walks'. As the phrase suggests, these walks involved me moving around the village along a predetermined route about three miles long. The route was designed to take me past a range of households of different socio-economic status, as well as through various public spaces, through the swamp and hilltop rangelands (this part of Central Africa being characterized by steep hills and valleys), across the road (at various points), past the church, past the school, and around several bars and shops. Walking with a notebook and pen, the idea was to build up a record of the village 'soundscape', by noting down all the sounds that could be heard along the way. Particular attention was paid to radio noise, and whenever I came across a radio playing, I did my best to ascertain from where it was coming, what station was playing and – where possible – what programme was being listened to. I also tried to ascertain who was 'in control' of the set, how many people were listening to it and what other things they might have been doing at the same time (i.e. whether or not they were listening exclusively, or were doing so while cooking, digging, etc.). I repeated these walks along more or less the same route – although at different times of day and night, and (eventually) at different times of year – on dozens of occasions. I should note here that I did not begin these 'walks' until some months into my fieldwork, when people were already used to my presence, and when the sight of me moving around no longer caused people to break their usual routine. In this way, I was able to build up a detailed, and objective, picture of the village soundscape, how this changed over time, and how radio noise was 'located' within this.

The second method I used involved what might be termed 'unstructured radio elicitation'. To begin with, this involved little more than sitting with people as they listened to the radio as part of their normal daily routines. On these occasions I would try to keep very quiet and still, often sitting in a corner – even in the shadows – so as not to break the flow of people's interactions with the radio, or with each other in the listening group. At this stage my actions were effectively the same as those of any researcher trying to do a typical 'reception' study. As time went on, however, I began to pose one or two questions to the listeners, related either to the physical radio set or to the content of the programme then playing. Gradually, over very many of these sessions, I began to 'take control' of the listening situation, by asking more and more questions of the other listeners. Although I never had control over the radio set, or the content of the radio broadcasts, I could use certain types of shows – health programmes, political broadcasts, for example – as anchors for questioning on those same topics. Little by little, I began to introduce a notebook to the sessions as well. Of course, the whole interviewing effect was easier to achieve in some listening environments than in others. In this regard, it was especially important how other listeners placed me. For example, the process worked more naturally when I was in a listening group in which I seemed to 'belong' (for example, in a group of young Catholic men) than when I was in a group to which I clearly did not (such as a group of elderly Protestant women). The intended effect was also achieved more easily with certain types of programmes than with others. For example, phone-in shows proved much better than music programmes. The time of day also made a difference.

The third of my methods involved a more formal mode of 'radio elicitation' based on the classic focus-group model. To begin, I would invite to my house a number of people whom I had pre-selected to comprise a representative sample based on age, gender, religion, or whatever. Gathering them in my living room, I would place a radio on a central table and play them a series of clips from various radio shows, which I had edited down in advance. At the end of each clip I would ask the group a series of prepared questions on the material they had just heard. In this way, I was able to generate discussion on often quite focused subjects, with my role being recast as that of facilitator. Most of these sessions involved selections from various sorts of 'cultural-historical' shows.[3] However, I would also use other clips, which were often selected to be as provocative as possible (for purposes of generating debate). For example, for one session I did on local politics, I selected part of an interview which had just been recorded for Monitor FM in Kampala with Milton Obote. This was purposely designed to cause as much debate as possible.[4] Obviously, a high degree of judgement is required in these matters, and for this reason I conducted most of these sessions towards the end of my fieldwork, when I knew all my respondents very well. This was also important given my desire to tape the discussions in all these sessions, rather than to use a notebook and pen.

Judging from my experience of using these methods, I would conclude that the claims Collier makes for photo elicitation are equally applicable to 'radio elicitation'. Like photographs, radios certainly do have something of a 'hypnotic pull'. Indeed this may be even more pronounced with radio, given the content of much radio programming (and especially that of international broadcasters). Even the simplest radio set has the ability to bring in exotic stories from imagined, faraway places. I am reminded of Graham Furniss's anecdote at the beginning of *African Broadcast Cultures*, in which he recalls once meeting an old Hausa man, in the remote mountainous part of the Nigeria–Cameroon border, who, as a result of having listened to the BBC World Service, had developed a particular fascination with the politics of Pakistan (in Fardon and Furniss 2000: 2). Like Collier's photographs, radio sets also generate an intense sociality, in that they too are handled and passed around, and broadcasts also generate keen discussion and debate among groups of listeners. Furthermore, unlike photographs, which are usually seen in very specific, often quite formalized contexts, radios are everywhere in Africa, a common part of the normal, everyday flow of social relations. Thus an anthropologist trying to construct dialogue around a radio programme is employing a medium of sociality with which people are already familiar and comfortable. From the anthropologist's point of view, the nature of radio programming means that radio is often the primary medium through which people gain knowledge of, and in a sense interact with, the 'outside' world (and by extension with 'outsiders'). In addition it is noteworthy – and of greatest relevance to an anthropologist in the early stages of his or her fieldwork – that radio programmes are the medium through which most people have their most regular exposure to multilingual environments (ibid.: 3–7).

More importantly for my discussion here, the three methods outlined above demonstrate different ways in which the radio, as both material object and broadcast signal, might be mobilized in the course of ethnographic fieldwork. In the first instance, that of the 'radio walks', no direct contact was made with any radio set or with any listening group. Instead, the sound from the sets was used indirectly to map out such things as villagers' uses of space (in particular their public and private domains), as well as the types of interactions and activities associated with those spaces. In the case of 'unstructured elicitation', again no contact was made with the radio itself. This time, however, the radio sounds were used more actively to manipulate relations within the listening environment. This was done somewhat speculatively at first, but more and more boldly as I began slowly to take control of the various listening groups (in the sense of my 'controlling' the flow of conversation). Finally, with the third method, that of 'radio elicitation' proper, I made direct contact with the radio set, as I actively manipulated – or 're-versioned' – its signal, with a view to steering the focus group conversation in a particular direction of my own choosing. Each of these shifts was facilitated by a conscious reflexive shift in the positioning of myself as ethnographer, by a change in the constitution of the 'ethnographic I'. In the case of the radio walk, the 'I' was that of the (metaphorical) spy, one who seeks to gather information primarily through overhearing rather than intervention. In the method of unstructured elicitation, I became instead the professional stranger, one who intervenes – from a position of ignorance – in pursuit of elucidation. Finally, with the method of structured radio elicitation, the 'I' had become that of the scientist, one who is able to recreate reality – under controlled conditions – in order to isolate specific and predefined objects of research. (In this sense, the setting of the structured elicitation sessions had indeed become my own 'laboratory'.)[5]

Over the course of these researches, there were also key shifts in my interaction with the radio set itself. I had ever greater contact with it, and made increasing interventions in the flow of radio – and radio-related – sounds. Or to put it another way, I mobilized the radio to assemble different sorts of hybridities in each of the different methods. The prediction here, from the point of view of the actor-network theorist unwilling to cast the social world as an outcome solely of *human* agency, would be that over the course of these shifts the radio would gain more and more social agency in its own right. In other words, it would become an increasingly important agent of translation between the social world and my descriptions/representations of it. As a result, these descriptions/representations would become, to an ever greater degree, accounts of hybrids. And this was indeed what transpired. Looking back over my notes from the radio project with the benefit of hindsight, I realize that the radio *did* indeed become more and more important over time. Thus in my notes from the radio walks, the radio – and its signal – is scarcely mentioned. Apart from a few words of general description, on issues such as where the set was physically located, who owned it and what station was playing, these notes are taken up with descriptions of social activities and social relations. Consider, for example, the following excerpt from 'Radio Walk' (17 September 2000, 5.50 p.m.):

> Crossed the swamp by the bridge behind Bwente's house, [took the] path through [the] *orutookye* [plantation] behind her compound. Radio playing – I think it's Bwente's own – very loud, tuned to Radio West, *ebirango* [announcements].[6] All present listening, in between discussions. As I come into view, I'm greeted by Bwente, sweeping the compound. Tells me that Bakyenga is not around [Bakyenga is Bwente's son, and my current research assistant]. Also present = Florence [Bwente's daughter], six small kids, Modesta [a neighbour], Tweheyo [a friend], several other old men I don't know. Modesta and men sitting in a line along the small wall. Stop to say hello, Florence translates [this being just a few months into my fieldwork, my own Runyankore was not very good]. She tells me that Modesta and the other men are here to talk about a cousin who has just died (not Tweheyo, he was just passing). Seems to be some dispute about land; part of it is adjacent to Bwente's plot, and they are thinking of putting in a new boundary marker, but there have been some   problems ... [and so it continues].

As I move into the unstructured elicitation, however, these general descriptions are replaced with more and more detailed accounts of both the movements of the radio set and the content of its broadcasts. Furthermore, throughout the notes from these sessions, descriptions of the radio are more or less interspersed with descriptions of discourse and social activity:

> Returned home from interview with Busenene, wrote up notes etc. Grace [the head of our household] out, probably drinking up in the trading centre. Not much going on, so decided to have another go at radio interviewing. Kekyerunga [our 'house girl'] is cooking with my radio on, listening to a health phone in show for young people on Capital Radio (talk interspersed with songs – Britney Spears again!!).[7] Also Bob and Aruwo [Grace's sons], Rukanga [a young man who lives at our house], Ziwade [a young man who lives nearby]. As I'm sitting, a couple of others drift in (attracted by the radio?) – Sebugirigiri's new herd boy (name?) and Tweheyo's eldest son (name?). They're all sitting around the hill bit at the back of our house, a couple of them on the

veranda. Kekyerunga is preparing the food, others just talking etc. Ziwede holds the radio. Aruwo etc. dancing. I sit on a stool on the edge of the group, don't really say anything. A caller to the health show asks a question about condoms 'is it true that you can still get HIV while using one'? Rukanga says that he's heard that as well. Ziwede says that Kihura Nkuba says that as well [Kihura Nkuba is a prominent commentator on another local radio station]. He thinks that condoms are useless. I come in and ask if they're told anything about condoms at school? Rukanga says that they talk about it all the time. There is a teacher there who gives classes in health issues. Rukanga goes over and takes the radio off Ziwede and continues, saying that there is also a government health advisor who visits the school from time to time. And since the current chairman has taken over, there is also talk about HIV/AIDS at some public meetings etc. (some connection here between holding the radio and speaking? I notice throughout the session that the person currently holding the radio seems to talk the most about the issue at hand?) The next caller to the phone-in asks if someone suffering from malaria is more likely to contract HIV/AIDS? ... [and so it goes on]. (Excerpt from field notes, 1 May 2001)

Finally, by the time I get to the structured elicitation, the transcripts refer *primarily* to the radio output.[8] Furthermore, where other people 'speak' in the transcripts, their words are completely dependent on the radio content, in that what they say simply cannot be understood independently of it. The following excerpt (from transcript of 'structured radio elicitation' session, 31 January 2001) is taken from a session which aimed to open up discussion of the Virgin Mary, and local practices of Marian devotion. The group – all older women – are being played, and are responding to, a section from a lecture broadcast some months earlier by Kihura Nkuba.[9]

Presenter: To repaint the Sistene Chapel in Vatican, in St. Peter [*sic*] Square. St Peter's Basilica – there is a special chapel that had ancient images of a black Jesus and a black Mary and Pope Julius II...
Participant 1: Black! Huh!
Participant 2: No! Huh! This guy [Kihura Nkuba] tells lies! [Group laughter]
Presenter: ...commissioned Michelangelo to repaint the Sistene Chapel and change the images from black to white. Michelangelo uses the image [*sic*] of his auntie as Mary, his uncle as Jes..., as Joseph, and an anon child as Jesus. That is why some pictures of Jesus show him with blue eyes, others show him with brown eyes, others show him with black hair, others show him with brown hair, others show him short... And Jesus was not white.
Participant 3: Eee! Is it so?
Participant 1: No!

Presenter: So in that year, up to today [*sic*], if you go in that museum in Berne in Switzerland, there is an image of a black Madonna and child, a black Mary and a black Jesus. If you go in Nuestra, in Spain [*sic*], Our Lady ... or in the Pyrenees, a black Madonna and a black child. If you go in Kazan, in Russia [*sic*], Our Lady of Kazan, a black Madonna, a black Mary and a black Jesus, and in fact in Poland, they have what they call [*sic*], Our Lady of Shostakova.

Participant 2: Also here, also here. Up there, there in the hills. There, there, up in Ntungamo [District]. It's the truth. That one [indicating informant 1], she'll tell you...

Presenter: Every year the Pope celebrates mass in Poland, before the feet of Our Lady of Shostakova ... [and so it continues].

Comparing the three examples presented above, it can be seen that the radio – as both physical object and broadcast signal – has indeed become more and more active, playing an ever greater role as an agent of translation. Further, the notes themselves – as descriptions, representations of fieldwork – have also changed. Whereas in the first example they refer primarily to a social world, by the third example they reference a hybrid network of people and machine. In other words, they have become an account of hybridities.

Conclusion

Of course it does not end there. In the above example radio acts as an agent of translation between the world of the village and my representations of it by inscribing other sorts of objects, initially a notebook, but later an audio cassette tape as well. And these objects will in due course go on to be agents of translation themselves, in the subsequent construction of further sorts of representations, namely academic ethnographic accounts. After all, only with reference to the inscriptions in these notebooks, audio recordings, and so on, can such accounts be drawn up. More radically, one might note that when ethnographers refer to 'the field', they are referring not so much to some specific place and time (the location of their fieldwork during the time they were there) as to a series of objects – notebooks, cassette tapes, and so on – which, although inscribed in that place and time, are now most likely locked away somewhere in their university office. This is not to say that their accounts convey nothing of the empirical reality of the field site during the time of their visit. Rather, it is to suggest that how much they convey, and how convincingly, depends on the qualities of those objects, not least on how well and in what ways they had been inscribed – possibly by other sorts of objects – in the first place.

Yet neither, of course, does it begin there. After all, these chains of translations between the material world and representations of it do not begin with the anthropologist. On the contrary, they are the very stuff of all human social life. I am here reminded of my radio walks, and the people I observed on them, often gathered in groups around some radio noise. Such groups tend to form around radio signals wherever they are playing, given the association between broadcasting noise and public space. In this sense radio noise is used to mark out – physically to 'inscribe' – domains of public and (by association) private space in the village of Bugamba, which then become meaningful for social praxis. In other words, even before the radio was mediating the relationship between the world and my descriptions of it, it was already doing exactly that for local people. To go still further, the radio's capacity to mark out domains in this way is itself the outcome of an earlier set of translations, in which 'broadcasting posts' had been used, by the British authorities from the early 1940s onwards, as a tool of 'education' for rural Ugandans.[10] Located outside administration buildings, these posts established an initial connection between public space and broadcasting noise. And no doubt earlier sorts of translations had had similar effects beforehand. Indeed it might even be argued, as some actor-network theorists have done, that such chains of translations continue in all directions, possibly ad infinitum. The assumption is that these chains are always present, even though the terms of each individual translation might themselves become erased. A key problem for the analyst is then to decide at what point to stop. Where can we 'cut the chain' without doing violence to the object of study?

This broader question is beyond the scope of the present chapter. Instead, my intention has been to highlight a few of the ways in which physical objects have exerted – and continue to exert – an influence on anthropological representations of the world, by acting as key agents of mediation between the two. Over the last couple of decades, many anthropologists have posed the question of whether or not, or in what ways, anthropological methods resemble those of the 'hard sciences'. I have shown that in one key way, at least, anthropological representations do resemble those of the pedologist or the botanist, in that they too involve a mobilization of both symbolic schemata – our own, and those of our informants – and various sorts of physical objects as well. Whether or not we always acknowledge the fact, anthropological accounts are just as entangled in the material world.

Acknowledgements

The research on which this chapter is based was funded substantially by the Economic and Social Research Council, UK (grant nos: R00429934453 and

PTA-026–27–0254). Specific elements of the project were additionally funded by the Tropical Agriculture Association, the Godfrey Lienhardt Fund (Wolfson College, Oxford), the Radcliffe-Brown Fund (of the Royal Anthropological Institute), the Vice-Chancellors' Fund (University of Oxford) and the Ioma Evans-Pritchard Junior Research Fellowship (St Anne's College, Oxford). I would like to thank all these funders for their generous support.

An earlier version of the chapter was presented to the North-East Africa Seminar at the Institute of Social and Cultural Anthropology, University of Oxford, in March 2004. I would like to thank Professor Wendy James for the invitation to speak at the seminar, and all those who took part for their useful questions and comments.

Notes

1. The fieldwork for this project was conducted in Bugamba Village, Rwampara County, Mbarara District, in five separate periods between March 2000 and May 2005.
2. One exception might be ethnographers' field photos. Much contemporary photographic theory has argued that all photographic practices can be understood as acts of inscription (see, for example, Bean 2006; Ravetz, this volume, Chapter 12).
3. The 'cultural-historical' format has become particularly popular in south-western Uganda following the establishment of the Greater Africa Radio (GAR) station in Mbarara Town in March 1999. The highlight of GAR's programming was a nightly show, hosted by the station's charismatic owner, Kihura Nkuba (lit. 'the unveiler of thunder'), which took the form of a lecture on some point of local historical or cultural interest.
4. The interview was very controversial in Uganda at the time because it was the first time that the former President's voice had officially been allowed to be broadcast in the country since his deposition in the mid-1980s (although there is some evidence that his supporters had broadcast speeches before that, using a range of illegal shortwave frequencies).
5. I thank Terry Austrin for clarification of these points.
6. *Ebirango* are broadcast several times a day on all Ugandan radio stations, to announce births, deaths and marriages. Throughout all parts of the country, they are an essential means of information and communication, especially among dispersed families.

7. A note here on languages: Capital Radio broadcasts throughout Uganda, mostly in English. For example, the health phone-in show being discussed here is in English. The group I am with includes a number of senior school students who speak English, and they translate the show's content for the others present. Discussion between the group then proceeds mostly in the local language, Runyankore. My own interventions involve a combination of both English and Runyankore.
8. As noted above, I did not write notes during these sessions, but instead recorded them on a digital sound recorder.
9. Another note on languages: for various reasons the lecture itself was given in English but simultaneously translated into Runyankore. Thus the original broadcast – and therefore the tape being played back here as well – included both the English and the Runyankore versions. For ease of transcription, I transcribed the original English lecture. However, the women – none of whom spoke English – were instead listening to the Runyankore, and responding in that language also. Their words here are my own translations of their responses.
10. In Uganda, as elsewhere in British colonial Africa, public radio was introduced following the publication of the Plymouth Report in 1937. At that time, the cost of radio sets was prohibitively high (the most common form of radio, at that time, was the crystal set). Thus the authorities decided to disseminate broadcasts via 'listening posts' – loudspeakers attached to flagpoles – a majority of which were sited in the grounds of local administration buildings (*gombolola*). These remained the primary mode of radio delivery until the advent of mass-produced (and cheap) transistor radios in the mid-1960s.

References

Austrin, T. and Farnsworth, J. (2005), 'Hybrid genres: Fieldwork, detection and the method of Bruno Latour', *Qualitative Research*, 5(2): 147–65.

Bean, R. (ed) (2006), *Image and Inscription: Essays on Contemporary Photography*, Toronto: Yyz Books.

Clifford, J. (1988), *The Predicament of Culture: Twentieth-Century Ethnography, Literature and Art*, Cambridge, Mass.: Harvard University Press.

—— and Marcus, G. (1986), *Writing Culture: The Poetics and Politics of Ethnography*, Berkeley: University of California Press.

Collier, J. (1967), *Visual Anthropology: Photography as a Research Method*, New York: Holt, Rinehart and Winston.

—— (1986), *Visual Anthropology: Photography as a Research Method*, revised edition, Albuquerque: University of New Mexico Press.

Crapanzano, V. (1990), 'On dialogue', in T. Maranhao (ed), *The Interpretation of Dialogue*, Chicago: University of Chicago Press.
Ellen, R. (1984), *Ethnographic Research: A Guide to General Conduct*, London: Academic Press.
Fabian, J. (1990), 'Presence and representation: The Other and anthropological writing', *Critical Inquiry*, 16: 753–72.
Fardon, R. and Furniss, G. (2000), 'African broadcast cultures', in R. Fardon and G. Furniss (eds), *African Broadcast Cultures*, Oxford: James Currey.
Geertz, C. (1988), *Works and Lives: The Anthropologist as Author*, Stanford, Calif.: Stanford University Press.
Jackson, M. (2004), *In Sierra Leone*, Durham, NC: Duke University Press.
Latour, B. (1993), *We Have Never Been Modern* (trans. C. Porter), Cambridge, Mass.: Harvard University Press.
—— (1996), *Aramis, or the Love of Technology*, Cambridge, Mass.: Harvard University Press.
—— (1999), 'Circulating reference: Sampling the soil in the Amazon Forest', in B. Latour, *Pandora's Hope: Essays on the Reality of Science Studies*, Cambridge, Mass.: Harvard University Press.
—— and Woolgar, S. (1979), *Laboratory Life: The Construction of Scientific Facts*, Princeton, NJ: Princeton University Press.
Malinowski, B. (1915), *The Natives of Mailu: Preliminary Results of the Robert Mond Research Work in British New Guinea*, Adelaide: Royal Society of South Australia.
Marcus, G. (1998), *Ethnography Through Thick and Thin*, Princeton, NJ: Princeton University Press.
—— and Cushman, D. (1982), 'Ethnographies as texts', *Annual Review of Anthropology*, 11: 25–69.
Nadel, S. (1961 [1939]), 'The interview technique in social anthropology', in F. Bartlett, M. Ginsberg, E. Lindgren and R. Thouless (eds), *The Study of Society: Methods and Problems*, London: Kegan Paul.
Prattis, J. (ed) (1985), *Reflections: The Anthropological Muse*, Washington, DC: American Anthropological Association.
Strathern, M. (1996), 'Cutting the network', *Journal of the Royal Anthropological Institute*, 2(3): 517–35.
Taussig, M. (1997), *The Magic of the State*, New York: Routledge.
—— (2004), *My Cocaine Museum*, Chicago: University of Chicago Press.
Tedlock, D. (1987), 'Questions concerning dialogical anthropology', *Journal of Anthropological Research*, 43(3): 325–44.
Weiner, J. (1993), 'Anthropology *contra* Heidegger; Part II: The limit of relationship', *Critique of Anthropology*, 13: 285–301.

Whyte, C., Constantopoulos, C. and Bevans, H. (1982), 'Types of countertransference identified by Q-analysis', *British Journal of Medical Psychology*, 55: 187–201.

Wolf, M. (1992), *A Thrice Told Tale: Feminism, Postmodernism and Ethnographic Responsibility*, Stanford, Calif.: Stanford University Press.

Epilogue

–15–

A World Without Anthropology
Clara Mafra

What would it be like to live in a world without anthropology? It is worth remembering that anthropology has not always been around. It is a relatively modern phenomenon, a by-product of Western history. Ancient Greece had its poets, philosophers, artisans, priests and physicians, but not anthropologists. Among the Greeks anthropology did not exist as a subject, on account of a general incapacity to recognize the Other. Only with the advent of the Enlightenment, and the transposition of 'primitive man' from the plane of ideas to the plane of experience, did the modern anthropological project achieve its own shape and expression (Duchet 1971). If this was how anthropology began, however, then the same formula should allow us to predict its end. Granted that anthropology is driven by a desire to know and understand alterity, we can postulate that at some time in the future, in a world that has already come to terms with difference, the discipline will disappear. The success of anthropology presupposes its own dissolution. Yet nowadays this is not what we find. The evidence is very much to the contrary. We hear of wars, misery and destruction among people, along with an increase in the number of anthropologists and a proliferation of anthropological institutions around the world. Paradoxically, this expansion of the discipline seems to be accompanied by a decline in its vigour.

Though the reasoning that predicts the end of anthropology may seem precise and crystal-clear, it sets out from a conception of the discipline that some critics might see as rather innocent and old-fashioned. After all, the idea that anthropology has a mission to rescue the world surely harks back to a romantic notion of the anthropologist as hero that we have long since left behind. No academic discipline can be so piously committed to such a utopian project as the formation of a new society. That, of course, was the commitment of thinkers of the Enlightenment, yet the closest they came to fashioning a portrait of the Other was in the highly idealized figure of the 'noble savage'. This idealism was counterbalanced by the cruelty shown by colonial explorers and administrators, who perpetrated the most widespread genocide of foreign peoples ever known: in the Americas, Africa and Asia.

The sceptical reader may be more inclined to find fault with the reasoning set out above on account of the utilitarian connection it presupposes between the disciplinary project of expanding our knowledge of the human condition and the political project of changing the world. The human sciences, the sceptic will remind us, only gained consistency and vigour once they had dissociated themselves from any contingent political project. To be more emphatic, in this view *anthropology does nothing in the world*: it is a discipline of thinking, a set of methods and a certain approach to the production of knowledge. To subordinate anthropological knowledge as a means to the end of political intervention in the world would be retrogressive in terms of the discipline's development, tying it to a ball and chain that would thwart freedom of thought and creativity.

In the following paragraphs I shall present an argument in the form of a dialogue in which I shall first take up my own subject position as author, and then respond with the imagined words of a sceptical reader. I shall also include interventions from an anthropological novice and a critical listener who, we may suppose, have also been following the conversation. Through this dialogue, I aim to elaborate on the idea that although the project of anthropology is not to *intervene* in the world, the discipline is nevertheless one that *undergoes development* in the world.

In the Words of the Author

I would like to ask sceptical readers to suspend their disbelief for a while. Had I regarded anthropology as a discipline that is more political than academic, ever ready to intervene in the world, I would of course have been the first to welcome the expansion of anthropology, both in the numbers of its practitioners and in the spread of its institutions in the most diverse regions of the world, along with the growth in the volume of research that should be expected to follow from this. I began, however, from the observation that precisely the opposite has occurred, namely that despite the global increase in the number of anthropologists the vigour of anthropological scholarship appears to have declined. This negative evaluation of disciplinary expansion, however, does not mean that I would align myself more closely with the sceptic who would favour an anthropology indifferent both to the little events that underlie the progress of fieldwork and to the public policies that guide the institutions in which we teach, compensating for this lack of attention to detail with a commitment to universal, advanced and abstract theoretical knowledge. Skilful anthropologists, I believe, not only allow themselves to be educated by the world, especially through their engagement in fieldwork, but are also attentive to the conceptual debate that drives the discipline's theoretical agenda. Nor is this latter debate disconnected from its worldly setting: just like fieldwork, it entails elements of improvisation and of resonance with the rhythms of life, lying as it does in the productive tension between occidental speculation about what human life should be, what our life actually is and how it is for particular groups of people in certain places and periods of history (Ingold 1994: xvii). And this brings me back to my initial thesis, namely that anthropology is a discipline that undergoes development in the world. It was not born as a pre-specified set of representative investigations, but rather gains strength and vigour from remaining flexible while articulating emerging questions within the various traditions of scholarship represented in different centres of education and research around the globe.

The Sceptical Reader Responds

Your formulation is interesting and apparently goes to the point; however, it forgets that the discipline today is highly polymorphous. Few colleagues would allow themselves to be taken in by your proposition: it supposes a critical flexibility and organic coherence that are hard to combine within a single discipline. Being a sceptic, I propose to the contrary that we define anthropology as whatever kinds of activity people may engage in as members of anthropological institutions. Though this definition may look tautological, it is not trivial, since it has the merit of emphasizing the framework or context in which anthropological work is produced. This allows us comfortably to accommodate the polymorphism I mentioned previously, granting any institution or author in the field the freedom to declare that 'we do anthropological work here' in any way deemed appropriate. It also allows us to accommodate the competition between authors and institutions – which is embarrassing to those with a more traditional and self-centred conception of disciplinary production – as a way of maintaining a more or less flexible field that is nevertheless reasonably capable of resisting the wilder flights of fancy of its exponents. Thus if an author like Clifford Geertz, an association such as the Northeastern Anthropological Association and a postgraduate programme such as the one at the State University of Rio de Janeiro all refer to something as anthropology, then that something may be acknowledged as such.

The Author...

But things do not happen like that! Established writers can be discredited, institutions can change their name, appearance and position, and good work can be done even in peripheral contexts. Although the framework in which we operate is important to our disciplinary practice, and has guaranteed the almost spontaneous reproduction of anthropology in many places and in multiple forms over the last few decades, knowledge of this framework is not sufficient to allow the neophyte to navigate through it. To say that anthropology is what anthropologists do is too vague and protean for those who want to learn how to guide themselves through the disciplinary terrain, and to find their way along its alternative pathways.

The Sceptical Reader...

I am certainly not thinking of the beginner as an interlocutor. A novice who lacks experience, who carries no theoretical baggage and who is unfamiliar with the history of anthropological thought would be unable to comprehend the enormous polymorphism of contemporary anthropology without either retreating into a particular corner whence he or she would produce a general map based on local colours, or becoming swept up in the whirlpool of options, revealing nothing but arbitrariness and chaos. Were we to invite him into our conversation, we would have to abandon key questions, for example, about the status of anthropological knowledge, about the hazy margins between reality and fiction, discovery and creativity, truth and fantasy. To make sense for the beginner we would have to return to the familiar but exhausting quagmires of the border between objective and subjective worlds.

The Novice Intervenes

I am surprised that you think my participation in the debate is going to diminish its quality. Since you profess to be a sceptic, I would have thought that your view would diverge from those of more conventional interlocutors, and that you would express some reservation in relation to established authors and institutions. Allow me to introduce myself: I am from the rock generation, and I cannot imagine any of my idols affirming that there is but one reality or that he [the idolized figure] was privileged, or that, by virtue of possessing some unusual equipment, he had 'access to reality'. Like many of my generation, I have a relativist perception of the world. Still, the lyrics of rock music are strangely different from anthropological articles. Throughout my undergraduate years, I have read innumerable articles and some ethnographies; for the most part, however, I am much better able to jot down rock lyrics than outline an anthropological article. Why is the latter so difficult?

The Author...

I am delighted to include you in our debate, especially because you can help us curb our tendency towards excessive intellectualism, something all too typical in a discipline that values the skills of reading and writing above all others. Moreover as a beginner you present us with a great challenge: maybe we should try to define anthropology by the knowledge it produces. It would indeed be strange if an author of rock lyrics were to explore such conceptual tensions as between society and culture, art and ethics, the individual and the person. Would we rock out to such themes on a Saturday night? As with other poets and writers, the language of lyricists draws from the realms of everyday life, of the bakery and the drugstore.

But in their practices of writing, anthropologists do not inhabit this realm. Where, then, do they belong? We turn again to the masters: what makes Malinowski – and not Rousseau – a model author for modern anthropological work? Rousseau sought to know men and their different habits only very cursorily, in order to lend support to a project for the construction of a utopian, future society. The image of the distant man was crucial to the Enlightenment project, since it bore the mark of the primitive – that is, of the simplest, most basic, primordial and original state of humanity. The savage, for Rousseau, was not a man of flesh and blood, but rather the vehicle through which he formulated a set of insights into humanity in general (Rousseau 1992 [1754]). Malinowski, by contrast, tied his writing to a narrative thread that follows his own experience of a singular encounter. In this sense, the element of fantasy entered into his work more discreetly than it did into work of Rousseau. Nevertheless, it was not so discreet as to lead to the abdication of his position as the subject and hero of a modern enterprise. Indeed it is possible to construct an inventory of the several strategies that Malinowskian ethnographic writing employs to strengthen its authority, including its insistent pretension of omniscient presence, its appeal to actual encounters as a basis for its legitimacy and its focus on alterity (Rabinow 1985; Clifford and Marcus 1986). Beyond his peccadilloes of Victorian vanity and blindness, Malinowski preserves the idea of *description*: what he registers is an encounter that actually took place in the world.

Consider, for example, *Argonauts of the Western Pacific* (Malinowski 1922), in which Malinowski uses several strategies to affirm the value of 'having been there'; a detailed description of the place where the encounter occurred, the use of the ethnographic present, the accurate placement of the anthropologist in the field and in specific situations, the use of native words in analysis, the gathering of evidence on particular topics and the dovetailing of descriptive accounts so as to make them fit with one another. It is all as if to declare: 'other white men have seen the Trobriand Islanders before me, but nobody has seen them the way I do!' When Malinowski sets out the rules for anthropological knowledge in the introduction to the work, he places himself as someone whose comprehension of the Other is based on systematic and rigorous inquiry. Such inquiry, he suggests, both distances him from his contemporaries and brings him closer to the Islanders themselves and to his disciplinary heirs, for – as he goes on – no matter how the Trobriand world might change through the years, the next generation of Islanders, along with anthropologists of the future, will be able to count on his description to study other aspects of that society. Much of his effort to provide an exhaustive, multilayered description is based on the idea that the work indexes a real and persistent structure of events (including the landscape as an event), which can be seen and recognized from several perspectives on a path of reciprocal familiarization that later generations of natives and researchers will be able to follow. At the same time, the ideal of descriptive accuracy invites modern readers to share in the experience of 'having been there'. Indeed Malinowski's quest for descriptive accuracy, in *Argonauts*, had a major influence on the anthropological work of subsequent generations. Much of the transformation that ethnographic writing has undergone over the years has been part of a process of improvement in what the Brazilian writer, João Moreira Salles (2005), calls the 'non-fictional interpretation' of a situation.

William Whyte's *Street Corner Society* (1993 [1943]), written some two decades after the publication of *Argonauts*, places even further restrictions on the kinds of imaginative flights in which Malinowski engaged. The writing follows a less journalistic pattern, purporting to listen to all sides of the story and engaging at greater length and more attentively with its time and place. Whyte seems to opt for less in order to give more: he restricts himself to a neighbourhood in the city; to the description of just a few characters (who are given names and personalities) with whom he actually had contact; he reduces the number of topics developed (the gang, politicians and the racketeers); and reduces generalization to a minimum. From the evidence of everyday actions and fleeting social interactions, the 'non-fictional interpretation' of the social structure emerges in a powerful and consistent way. Thus non-fictional writing has changed over the years, in response not only to debates among its authors, but also to the transformations that both 'natives'[1] and target readers have undergone.

The Critical Listener Intervenes

The transformation you have described was surely not driven by the aim to improve non-fictional writing. It was rather the result of a shift in dominant explanatory paradigms – in the example you have given us, from British functionalism to North American interactionism.

The Author...

Well, had the debate been on a purely epistemological level, as you suggest, the publication of Malinowski's fieldwork diaries (1967) would never have had the powerful impact that it did. When we are made aware of Malinowski's personal intolerance, his white man's pretension, we can no longer take his account 'on trust'. The implicit, background agreement that gives us confidence in the non-fictional character of the work is undermined. A great deal of the critical anthropology that developed after the diaries were published hinged on concerns about the interrelation between author, context and episteme. Moreover there were experiments in ethnographic writing that sought to deconstruct the contractual underpinnings of non-fiction, whether by operating *inside* the work (making it a meeting place with an anthropologist as author and the natives as co-authors), by manipulating its *content* (making an anthropological work a narrative of the Other's dreams or a fiction based on the experience of the encounter) or by means of its *form* (making the work a collage of different moments and situations with multiple narrative threads).

These daring experiments, and even the impact of Malinowski's field diary, do not seem to have reduced the influence of the *Argonauts* model. What makes it so vigorous? My argument is that we can find the answer in two principles of non-fictional writing that Malinowski himself enunciates. The first exploits the homology between the respective narrative structures of the encounter in the field and the written text. This enables the latter to acquire the characteristics of a novel, by means of a temporal linearity that allows the reader to immerse him- or herself in the author's experience with the natives. The second principle lies in the possibilities for reflection opened up by our manipulations of the materials we collect. Such a reflective attitude was uncommon in the 1920s, when *Argonauts* first appeared. Together these two principles made it possible to resolve some of the dilemmas that recurrently arise in ethnography, for example: How will I know if the impression that my informants made on me is intended? When and how does a shared situation occur? Is the author's assessment of meaning in line with the natives' own perception of the events experienced? How will I know that my creative flow is not idiosyncratic? In solving dilemmas such as these, Malinowski paved the way for writing to become a means to recreate the singularity of the ethnographic encounter.

Of the above two principles, much has been said about the first and I shall not pursue it further here. Instead, I shall concentrate on the second. I realize that issues concerning the manipulation of field materials in the process of non-fictional interpretation have long been mired in epistemological debates about truth and falsity, or originality and artificiality. Even without taking sides in these arguments, however, we can safely say that we anthropologists manipulate certain materials in collecting them, by making observations, conducting interviews, transcribing and translating these, developing photos, engaging in a dialogue with other writers and in writing ourselves. In doing all this, we 'handle the material' in a way that is clearly distinct from the manipulation of fictional matter, even when the latter draws on personal experience. In this connection, it is worth recalling the testimony of a visual anthropologist like David MacDougall, who recognizes the transformation undergone by the material that he himself manipulates:

> A person I have filmed is a set of broken images: first, someone actually seen, within touch, sound, and smell; a face glimpsed in the darkness of a viewfinder; a memory, sometimes elusive, sometimes of haunting clarity; a strip of images in an editing machine; a handful of photographs; and finally the figure moving across the cinema screen. (MacDougall 1988: 25)

MacDougall reminds us of a fundamental difference: whereas the reader tends to perceive the text as a whole – a finished work, the author knows all about the processes of improvisation, arrangement and rearrangement that have gone into its production.

Knowing this, the author might doubt his ability to keep faith with the reader: can he be sure that he is talking about something that really happened? If this issue is not faced adequately, self-criticism could lead to self-deprecation and eventual loss of confidence. One way to address the problem would be to transfer the dilemmas surrounding the handling of material from an epistemic or political to a pragmatic level. Indeed it is clear that novelists on the one hand, and both sociologists and anthropologists on the other, can and do incorporate non-fictional materials in the development of their work. However, while novelists can manipulate their subject matter by inserting fantasies, stylistic elaborations and fictionalized dialogues, quantitative sociologists will take the material as a basis for calculation, in terms of more or less artificial schemes of measurement. Interviews, observational diaries and photos may all be grist to the mill of either novelistic writing or sociological analysis, but by the end of the process they have been transformed into something else (either fiction or tabulation), never appearing as such in the final work. In both cases the approach is one of 'non-literal intervention'.

I would argue that anthropologists aim at a 'milder', more literal treatment of their material. If the term 'realism' were not so overused, we could resort to it to designate this 'mild manipulation of the material'. When seeking to describe Van Gogh's almost vital attachment to objects, Shapiro did resort to this notion, stressing, however, that his was a kind of 'personal realism':

> I do not mean realism in the limited and disgusting sense that it has nowadays, which is – with extreme kindness – referred to as photographic but rather as the feeling that external reality is the object of strong desire or necessity, as a possession and potential means to the self-realization of human beings and, thus becomes the necessary space for art. (Shapiro 1996: 140)

This is the kind of realism entailed in the 'mild manipulation' characteristic of ethnographic writing. Indeed it is common in ethnographies to find chunks of collected material – such as fragments of interviews, diary excerpts, photos or schematic drawings – that have been left almost unaltered, despite having been handled over and over again before they were incorporated into the final work.

The Sceptical Reader Interrupts Again...

This long digression presents anthropology as a discipline in search of realist writing. But this is, at most, only partially true. In recent years, as you have already pointed out, we have seen enormous advances in the development of a constructivist anthropology, one that does not take the surface of things at face value, or apprehend them photographically.

The Author Continues...

In fact this definition of anthropology is partial, and restricted to a line I share with some colleagues. We defend the idea of a non-restrictive realism that rests on a background agreement between us (the 'tribe' of professional anthropologists), the Other (about whose lives we write) and a readership, and that allows us to share in the confidence that what we write is non-fictional. The most vulnerable and yet crucial component of this agreement is in the relationship between 'us' (anthropologists) and 'them' (the Other). If this relationship is denied or broken off, on account of the manner in which the encounter is recorded or due to people's disappointment – on reading ethnographic work – with what is written about them, then the agreement can be jeopardized. In others words, a disastrous ethnography is not corrupted by technical inaccuracy, poor writing, incongruous formulation or intimations of anthropological heroism. We tend to forgive these peccadilloes, but we cannot accept work that fails in ethical terms, revealing a lack of humane commitment in the 'us/them' relationship.

Indeed, everything indicates that what we might have thought to be relatively autonomous aspects of anthropological practice appear to be correlated: namely, establishing an ethical understanding between observer and observed; seeking a 'mild' manipulation of the material; and maintaining a background agreement that allows all parties to have confidence in the veracity of the resulting work. An integration of these three aspects is commonly achieved as follows: deepening the ethical understanding between anthropologist and natives reinforces the demand for a mild manipulation of the material, which in turn tends to strengthen confidence in the reception of the work. It seems to me that the search for this integration means much more than just gathering knowledge about the Other, in the literal sense, but that it is nevertheless essential to fulfil the promise of anthropology.

For the neophyte who wants to know how to guide himself on the unknown path that opens up before him through the tunnel of anthropological practice, the good news is that by seeking this integration he can from the outset – and even with precarious skills – make his own way. Thus, even though the manipulation of non-fictional material is intrinsic to anthropological practice, such manipulation – as the adjective 'mild' indicates – has certain limits: it is only acceptable if it does not break the very fabric of the relationship between observer and observed. This is a guiding principle because, after all, an anthropological non-fictional work tends to be focused on the Other's world: therefore, ethical understanding must lie in agreed procedures governing the encounter, the collection of material, the recordings, the systematization, the collage, the juxtaposition and recomposition. How can the neophyte tell, however, if he risks going too far, threatening to 'break the fabric of the relationship'?

Though this critical point is ill-defined, it is there nonetheless. It involves a variety of creative answers and attention to the literality of the situation. It is worth mentioning here an anecdote from my own field research in Coimbra where I simulated a situation in an interaction with my informants. Did I go too far and 'break the fabric of the relationship' by manipulating it?

My doctoral dissertation dealt with the Universal Church of the Kingdom of God, a Brazilian neo-Pentecostal church established in Portugal. The church is plagued by questions about the place of money in its ritual system. As a researcher, I was pressured for answers from an eager public, but I preferred to keep the issue in context. The church promoted itself by means of sermons about prosperity. Among other public invocations, ministers enjoyed repeating the motto, 'Just like the blood of Jesus makes the world go round, money moves our church'. In my fieldwork I had already gathered much evidence to show that money was an important element, but I was wavering between a view of the church as a 'school' of capitalism for a population with scarce resources and traditionally outside the market, and as an institutional machine or 'marketer' of faith. To better understand this issue, I needed to know the ministers' position with regard to financial operations: were they immersed in a larger system, reproducing it in a limited and automatic manner, or were they actively and creatively co-responsible for its reproduction?

Uncertain about the interpretation and having to accept the church leaders' veto on carrying out the research, I chose to simulate a situation: I decided to have a 'consultation' with the minister at the church in Coimbra and to present myself as a church member. At the end of a summer service, I presented my dilemma to a pastor who attended to members in a queue. I was, I said, a Brazilian student in

Portugal and had scarce financial resources. I had brought along with me some savings that were given to me by my mother. Months had passed, everything was going smoothly and I had not needed to use the savings. In the meantime, my youngest brother, who was trying to earn a living in a Brazilian town, wrote me a letter telling me about the enormous difficulties he was having. Upon reading his letter, I felt compelled to give my savings to him, but I knew that my mother would be against it: according to her principles, being a man he should manage on his own. If I did not use the money, it should be given back to my mother. What should I do?

The minister did not hesitate: he said I should give the money neither to my brother nor to my mother. I should instead use it for my own prosperity and join a Prayer Chain for my brother.

Some will say that I went too far as a researcher, acting like an informant, even if only occasionally. From the outset however, the context of my field research had been especially ambiguous and tense – I could hardly ever present myself as a researcher. Furthermore, the answer that the minister gave me, which was elicited by a simulated situation, shed more light than expected on an appropriate and true-to-life interpretation of the material I had collected. Without the simulation, the interpretation would probably have been too vague or schematic (Mafra 2002).

Conclusion

I began this chapter by noting that anthropology is a relatively new academic discipline, and that the promise of its fulfilment lies in its self-dissolution. A discipline dedicated to producing knowledge of the Other would be redundant in a world where alterity had ceased to be problematic. Such a formulation and its underlying promise, however, only make sense if we look at anthropology in its relation with the world. The emphasis on the autonomy and compartmentalization of knowledge in universities in the last few decades has distracted us from this necessary relation. With the imaginary help of a sceptical reader, a critical listener and a passionate beginner, I have laid out in this chapter some of the answers to being-in-the-world of anthropology.

Along this path we have considered some leading exponents of modern ethnography, leading us to the reasonable consensus that anthropology involves the production of non-fictional interpretations of events that have occurred in the world. This may seem an obvious conclusion to reach, until we stop to consider on what basis – if not on some notion of truth – we can have confidence in the status of our accounts as non-fictional. How can we speak of an encounter between a European citizen and a Trobriand expert seaman without coming up with an account that is either overly fantasized and vague or too systematic and literal?

My argument suggests that the answer to this kind of question does not necessarily lead us to a debate about epistemes or styles of discourse. It leads to an analysis of the agreement between author, native and reader, all of whom rely on the anthropological work as the non-fictional record of an actual encounter between author and native. We can even monitor changes in the ethnographic process by recovering the different terms of the agreement. In the attempt to validate non-fictional writing, one key element that has been maintained over the years is the exhaustive attention to detail, with an almost literal description of situations and events. Such attention serves as a constraint on the inflationary power of words so as to secure a more balanced position whenever interpretations are contested, curbing the flights of meta-reading that author and native are inclined to perform of themselves and of each other in recounting the course of events. Literality is particularly advantageous in unfamiliar and problematic situations, as it helps us to understand what is involved in a given situation without immediately affixing an asymmetrical interpretation on a scene.

This characteristic of literality, however, is not enough to secure agreement. As Jorge Luis Borges observed, a completely literal map is no longer a map, but the very thing it indicates and signifies. In a trend opposite to that of precision, modern anthropologists have become increasingly aware of how the manipulation of their material is intrinsic to their practice, and the work involved in it. Some anthropologists, with whom I have more affinity, aim instead to perform a mild manipulation of the material collected. In other words, they seek to maintain an explicit relationship with the 'sources' of non-fictional interpretation. This mild manipulation serves to protect and corroborate the agreement between author, natives and readers of non-fictional writing. We cannot ignore the fact, however, that there remains an asymmetry between author, natives and readers. The ethical commitments binding author and natives on the one hand, and author and readers on the other, are crucial to identifying the hurdles that, if left undiscovered, would allow this asymmetry to creep back into the contents of the work.

In this description of anthropological practice, the prerequisite for its exercise lies in a combination of three aspects of the relationship between author, natives and readers. The first involves the non-fictional quality of the work; the second has to do with the mild manipulation of the material collected; and the third grounds the coherence of the whole in a set of ethical commitments. These aspects together entail a certain disciplinary restraint, or even a deliberate abdication of the power of logical reasoning, pertaining either to efficient knowledge or to pragmatic action. For this very reason, anthropology is a discipline capable of grasping and teaching something about a world in process (Ingold 1993), to which we belong as much as every Other. My hope is that such an approach will eventually become so commonplace that people will cease to need anthropology as an institutionalized discipline.

Note

1. In this chapter I have used the term 'native' very liberally, closely following Viveiros de Castro's definition, in the sense of affirming the '"anthropologist" as someone who discourses on a "native's" discourse. The native doesn't need to be especially savage, or traditionalist, nor need he be a native of the place where the anthropologist encounters him; the anthropologist need not lack for excess civility, or modernism, nor for being a foreigner to the people about whom he discourses. The discourses, be they the anthropologist's and above all, the native's, are not forcibly texts: they are all practices of meaning. What is essential is that the discourse of the anthropologist (the "observer") establishes a certain relationship with that of the native (the "observed"). This relationship is a relation of meaning, or, as one would say when the former's discourse has scientific pretensions, a relation of knowledge. Yet from the very start, anthropological knowledge is a social relationship, since its effect is reciprocally to constitute a subject who knows and the subject that the subject himself knows, and the cause of a transformation (all relationships are transformations) in the relational constitution of both. This (meta) relation is not a relationship of identity: the anthropologist always says, and thus does, something other than the native, even when he has no other pretensions than restating "textually" this native's discourse, or tries to engage in dialogue – a questionable notion – with him. Such a difference is the effect of having knowledge of the anthropologist's discourse, the relationship between meaning in his discourse and the native's' (Viveiros de Castro, 2002: 113–14, my translation).

References

Clifford, J. and Marcus, G. (eds) (1986), *Writing Culture: The Poetics and Politics of Ethnography*, Berkeley: University of California Press.

Duchet, M. (1971), *Anthropologie et Historie au Siècle des Lumières: Buffon, Voltaire, Rousseau, Helvétius, Diderot*, Paris: François Maspero.

Ingold, T. (1993), 'The art of translation in a continuous world', in G. Palsson (ed), *Beyond Boundaries: Understanding, Translation and Anthropological Discourse*, Oxford: Berg.

—— (1994), 'General introduction', in T. Ingold (ed), *Companion Encyclopedia of Anthropology: Humanity, Culture and Social Life*, London: Routledge.

MacDougall, D. (1988), *Transcultural Cinema*, Princeton, NJ: Princeton University Press.

Mafra, C. (2002), *Na Posse da Palavra: Religião, Conversão e Liberdade Pessoal em Dois Contextos Nacionais*, Lisboa: ICS.

Malinowski, B. (1922), *Argonauts of the Western Pacific*, London: Routledge and Kegan Paul.

—— (1967), *A Diary in the Strict Sense of the Term* (introd. R. Firth, trans. N. Guterman), London: Routledge and Kegan Paul.

Rabinow, P. (1985), 'Discourse and power: on the limits of ethnographic texts', *Dialectical Anthropology*, 10: 1–14.

Rousseau, J.-J. (1992 [1754]), *Discours sur l'origine et les fondements d'inégalité parmi les hommes*, Paris: Hatier.

Salles, J.M. (2005), 'A dificuldade do documentário', in J. Martins, C. Eckert and S. Caiuby (eds), *O Poético e o Imaginário nas Ciências Sociais*, Bauru: EDUSC-Editora Sagrado Coração.

Shapiro, M. (1996), 'Sobre um quadro de Van Gogh (1946)', in *A Arte Moderna: Séculos XIX e XX*, São Paulo: Edusp.

Viveiros de Castro, E. (2002), 'O Nativo Relativo', *Mana – Estudos de Antropologia Social*, 8(1): 113–48.

Whyte, W.F. (1993 [1943]), *Street Corner Society: The Social Structure of an Italian Slum*, Chicago: University of Chicago Press.

Index

actor-network theory, 285–7, 289–90, 292, 295, 299
adultery, 167, 177
advertising, 12, 268–70, 272–3, 275–6, 279–80
ageing, 223–4, 231
agency, 36, 57, 75, 185, 187–9
  abduction of, 145
  creative, 7–8, 220
  displacement of, 52, 74, 112
  extended, 128
  and imagination, 202, 204
  individual 18, 51, 108, 151–4, 158, 161–2, 201
    versus social, 193, 296
  and intentionality, 187, 196–7
  of persons and things, 52, 94–6, 288
  self-conscious, 120
  sources of, 20
  and structure, 219
  and time 195, 199, 204
  and tradition, 211, 220
anthropology, 52, 139, 193, 245, 307–11, 315, 317–18
  creativity of, 244
  emergence of, 134, 137–8
  at home, 128–9, 144
  medical, 286
  as modern social science, 140, 145, 147
  and photography, 248–52, 256–7, 315
  and reflexivity, 240
  visual, 242, 248–9, 251, 287
  see also knowledge, anthropological
anticipation, 187; 193–4, 197, 199–200, 202–4
appropriation, 119
Archer, Mary, 219–20
architecture, 3–5, 8–9
archives, 128–9, 138, 144, 247, 262
Aristotle, 196–8
art, 46–8, 82–3, 210, 239, 248
  and anthropology, 21, 252, 256–7
  and calligraphy, 51, 96
  concept of, 80
  contemporary, 96, 254–5
  and literature, 186, 239
  as a verb, 247, 258
audit culture, 190, 239, 241
authenticity, 121
authorship, 20, 144–6, 207, 212

Bachelard, Gaston, 202
Bakhtin, Mikhail, 18, 194
Baptist ministry, 167–72, 176, 179
Barber, Karin, 13, 20–1
Bateson, Gregory, 46–8, 187–8, 190, 200, 240, 250–1
Battaglia, Debbora, 28, 211
Bauman, Richard, 29
being
  and becoming, 194
  eventness of, 193–5, 199, 204
Benedict, Ruth, 200
Benjamin, Walter, 82
Bergson, Henri, 11, 47–9, 52, 186
Best, Elsdon, 139, 144–5
Bible, 168–70, 173–5
Bloch, Maurice, 39
Boden, Margaret, 8–9, 14
Borges, Jorge Luis, 318
Bourdieu, Pierre, 15
Brand, Stewart, 4
bricolage, 46, 49, 207
Bruner, Edward, 2, 7
Bruner, Jerome, 51, 232
brush (in calligraphy), 89–90, 93–4
building, 3–5, 8, 10, 28
Burgin, Victor, 255–8

cabinets of curiosities, 17–18, 135
Callahan, Robey, 12, 21, 240, 276
calligraphy, 13, 19, 80
  Chinese, 81, 86
  Japanese, 5, 49–52, 82–3, 86–9, 92–5
  and music, 88
  see also handwriting; writing
Callow, Simon, 198
Certeau, Michel de, 7

Index

Chamberlain, Basil Hall, 81
change
  awareness of, 151–2
  versus continuity, 7, 25–6
  creative, 185
  and growth, 16, 27–8
  notion of, 152, 161–2
  social, 16, 120, 154
  technological, 16, 109
  versus tradition, 6
character, 195–6
Chennai (Madras), 55, 58, 60–1
Chomsky, Noam, 30, 46
choreography, 89, 189, 193, 212, 215–16, 218–19
  see also dance
Christierson, Nadia von, 260–1
civilization, 106–7, 110, 138
Clark, Andy, 9
Collier, John, 251–2, 291–2, 294
Conquergood, Dwight, 29
Conteh, Peter, 258–61
continuity, 119, 121, 146, 152, 204
  versus change, 7, 25–6
  versus discontinuity, 120
Cook, Nicholas, 13, 31, 39
copying
  creativity of, 5, 81
  in dramatic performance, 198
  of original, 50, 85–6
  patterns 48, 61
  as plagiarism, 144–5
  as replication, 6, 51
  see also imitation; reproduction
Cory-Pearce, Elizabeth, 13, 20, 121–3
Crease, Robert, 209–11, 214, 219–21
creation, versus revelation, 45–8
creationism, 4
creatives, 270–3, 275
creativity
  in advertising, 270, 280
  and agency, 8, 18, 151–2, 162, 189
  and anticipation, 193–4, 204
  and change, 185
  concept of, 1, 100, 108, 110, 119–21, 187, 191, 200, 240
  and culture, 113, 267–9
  in design, 55
  human capacity for, 16
  and imitation, 5, 80
  and improvisation, 3, 19–20, 25, 207
  location of, 136
  and modernity, 3, 16, 50, 107

  of organic life, 4
  versus revelation, 45–8
  rhetoric of, 99
  versus society, 7, 123
  sources of, 37, 109
  and teaching, 242
  and time, 201
  and tradition, 5, 7, 189–90, 207–8, 214
culture, 36, 106–9, 121, 239, 267

dance, 13, 50
  Javanese, 5, 14, 19, 189–90, 212–19
  see also choreography
Daston, Lorraine, 16–17
Davidson, Donald, 201
Davis, John, 20
Degnen, Cathrine, 10, 188
Delaney, Carol, 108
description, 311–12, 318
design
  architectural, 3–4, 8, 10
  innovation in, 5
  kōlam, 48, 55–9, 62–6, 70, 74–5
  see also pattern
Dewey, John, 208
dialogism, 287–8, 292
Dobzhansky, Theodosius, 45–6

Edwards, Elizabeth, 247, 252, 261–2
Edwards, Jeanette, 4, 19, 121–3
Edwards, Steve, 253–5
elicitation, 287, 290–7
Eliot, T. S., 189, 207–11, 214, 218–20
Enlightenment, 51, 104, 106, 203, 307, 311
entextualization, 29–31, 33, 36–7
Eriksen, Thomas Hylland, 190
ethnography
  authorship in, 129
  auto-, 143
  creativity of, 268–9, 280
  fieldwork-based, 241, 245
  genre of, 288
  heroism in, 191, 202, 311, 315
  monograph form of, 137
  museum, 287
  as non-fiction, 313, 315
  in teaching, 243
  as writing, 12, 128, 138, 144, 244, 276–9
  see also fieldwork
Evans-Pritchard, E. E., 194
evolution, 4, 45–6, 106, 137, 250

Index

fatherhood, 174
  see also paternity
fiction, 12, 268–9, 273–80, 288, 310, 314
  versus non-fiction, 312–13, 315–18
field-notes, 278, 298
  see also notes
field, ethnographic, 21, 28, 240–5, 298, 313, 317
fieldwork
  and actor-networks, 287, 289–90
  by advertising creatives, 271, 275
  as basis for ethnography, 241, 245
  experience of, 201, 244, 277–8
  by fiction writers, 275
  images relating to, 252
  Malinowskian tradition of, 127, 137, 290, 312
  methods of, 128, 147, 294–5, 298, 308, 316
  among older people, 225
  settings of, 20
  see also ethnography
Firth, Raymond, 139
flexibility, 109, 187, 190, 200, 203, 309
flux, 269–72, 274, 277–8, 280
focus, 269–70, 272, 274, 277–8, 280
Fraser, Sir James, 139
Friedman, Jonathan, 6
future, 188, 190, 196, 199, 225
  versus past, 11, 195, 204, 208, 224, 231

Gatewood, John, 14
Geertz, Clifford, 194, 309
Gell, Alfred, 49, 52, 56, 75, 80, 82, 94, 145
genetic modification (GM), 100, 190
genre, 31–2, 36–7, 209, 212, 256, 288
Giddens, Anthony, 219
Grasseni, Cristina, 190
Great Exhibition (of 1851), 133–5
Grimshaw, Anna, 243, 251, 262
grotesque, 18
growth, 5, 16, 18, 26–8

Haacke, Hans, 254, 257
Hacking, Ian, 186
Haddon, Alfred Court, 249
handwriting, 13–14, 83–4, 128
  see also calligraphy; writing
Hardin, Garret, 105–6, 109
Harris, Mark, 21
Harvey, Penelope, 185, 188
Hastrup, Kirsten, 7, 33, 187–8, 191

Hendry, Joy, 190
heroism, 152, 154, 156, 158, 160–1
  in ethnography, 191, 202, 311, 315
Herzfeld, Michael, 198
Hidai Nankoku, 87–8
Hirsch, Eric, 15
Hirschmann, Albert, 101–2
history
  causal explanations in, 196
  creativity in, 8
  empathy in, 239
  progressive, 203
  and time, 9–10, 15, 194, 199, 208
Howe, Leo, 33
Hughes-Freeland, Felicia, 5, 19, 189
human nature, 102–6
hybridity, 17–18, 109, 285–7, 289, 295–6, 298

illusion, 198
  theatrical, 197
  of wholeness, 193, 199–200, 202
imagination, 186, 194, 202–4
imitation, 5, 50, 80–2, 198
  see also copying; reproduction
improvisation, 1, 27, 308, 314
  in copying, 5
  and creativity, 3, 25, 37
  dramatic, 35
  versus fixity, 29, 31, 33, 37
  in handwriting, 13–14
  by individuals, 19
  versus innovation, 2, 10, 33, 35, 207
  mental, 9
  musical, 32
  versus prediction, 15
  unscripted, 1, 12
individual
  as bounded entity, 18
  versus collectivity, 3
  concept of, 100, 135–6
  creativity of, 20, 152, 207, 239
  as hero, 158, 160–1
  primordial, 104
  self-interested, 106
  versus society, 6–7, 105, 119, 152, 186–7
  see also possessive individualism
information
  decoupling of, from narrative 229–31
  irrelevant, 227–9
Ingold, Tim, 8, 16, 243–4
ink, 52, 89, 91–3

Index

innovation
and agency, 57
as appropriation, 119
artistic, 209
creative, 3, 9, 37, 108–9, 267
in dance, 190, 215–16, 219
in design, 5, 66, 74–6
versus improvisation, 2, 10, 33, 35, 207
and intellectual property, 100
kinds of, 33, 49
and modernity, 16
and progress, 106
technological, 176
and tradition, 9, 19, 25, 95, 216, 218, 279–80
see also novelty
inscription, 33, 38, 289, 298, 300
intellect, 107–8
versus intuition, 49
intellectual property (IP), 100–1, 109, 144, 146
intentionality, 187, 196–7
interviewing, 290–1, 314
invention, 10, 17, 20, 47–8, 106, 109
versus convention, 19
irony, 190, 203

Jackson, Michael, 241–2
James, Wendy, 15, 28, 193
Jiménez, Alberto Corsìn, 190, 243–4
Joas, Hans, 208

Kabylia, north-eastern Algeria, 152–3, 155–6, 162–3
Kagame, Alexis, 37
Kimura Tsubasa, 84–5
kinship, 167–8, 172–4
Klee, Paul, 49
knowledge, 100, 109–12, 145–7, 243
anthropological, 20–1, 241, 244, 308, 311, 319
Kobayashi Hideo, 50, 80
Kōlam, 48–52, 55–8, 60–2, 64–75
Kpelle, of Liberia, 34
Kubler, George, 9

labour, 52, 103–4, 109
land, 52, 104, 110–11
language learning, 30
Latour, Bruno, 285–6, 288–9
Layard, John, 58–9
Leach, Edmund, 240, 242, 244
Leach, James, 15, 20, 51–2, 123

learning, 46, 50–1, 61, 81–3, 243
Lefebvre, Henri, 10
Leroi-Gourhan, André, 50
Lévi-Strauss, Claude, 46, 121, 207
Lewis, Gilbert, 29
Liep, John, 1, 16, 107, 162
life, creativity of, 4
linearity, 11, 13, 203, 219, 226, 231–2
of time, 10, 208, 313
see also lines
lines
calligraphic, 50, 84–5, 89
as gestural traces, 13, 50, 75, 244
growing, versus connecting, 10–11, 75–6
kōlam design, 48–9, 55, 57, 62–3, 75–6
of walking, 49, 244
literature, 186, 208, 239
Locke, John, 51–2, 99–100, 103–4, 106–7, 109–10, 112, 186

Macdonald, Sharon, 15
MacDougall, David, 248, 262, 314
MacPherson, C. B., 103–4
Mafra, Clara, 20–21
Makereti (Margaret Staples-Brown *neé* Thom), 121, 123, 129–34, 136–47
Malinowski, Bronislaw
fieldwork method of, 127, 251, 290–2, 313
as hero, 191, 202, 311
photography by, 256–7
on the Trobriand Islanders, 26–7, 312
Mall, Amar, 19, 48, 51
Maori (of Aotearoa, New Zealand), 130–4, 140, 143–5, 147
Marx, Karl, 155
materials, 11–12
see also objects
Mauss, Marcel, 200
Mead, George Herbert, 25, 32
Mead, Margaret, 250–2
medical anthropology, 286
memes, 6, 36
memory, 11, 26, 28, 31–2, 61, 82, 187
metaculture, 30, 268
Mills, David, 15
mind, 3, 9
versus material world, 12
Mintz, Sidney, 241
modernity
and creativity, 3, 16, 50, 107
and progress, 106

Index

and the quest for newness, 269, 279
   versus tradition, 120, 211
Monod, Jacques, 45–7
monsters, 17, 123
monuments, 28, 158–9
Morris, Lynn, 260–1
museum ethnography, 287
museums, 128–9, 136, 144, 247
   see also Pitt-Rivers Museum
music, 13, 31–4, 39, 50–1, 87–9, 96
myth, 30–1, 111, 155

Nadel, Siegfried, 290–1
Nakamura, Fuyubi, 5, 19, 49–50, 52
narrative
   in epic poetry, 34, 37
   and life-history, 187, 232
   mythic, 111
   styles of, 223, 225–7, 229–31
   and time, 194, 203
natives, 138, 319
natural selection, 4–6, 46–7
new reproductive technologies (NRT), 121, 167–8, 171, 173, 175–6, 179–80
Nietzsche, Friedrich, 194
notational systems, 12
notes, 293, 296, 298, 301
   see also field-notes
novelty, 2, 10, 16–17, 187, 268, 279–80
   see also innovation

object, 291–2, 298
   versus subject, 50, 244, 310
objects, 51, 110, 289–90, 299
   material, 247, 288
older people, 10, 188, 223–5, 231–2
Ostrom, Elinor, 105
ownership, 20

paper, 52, 89, 92, 94
Park, Katharine, 16–17
passions, 101, 105
past
   versus future, 11, 195, 204, 208, 224, 231
   versus present, 2, 10–11
paternity, 108, 174
pattern, 48–9, 57, 65, 75, 199, 232
   see also design
pedestrians, 7–8
   see also walking
Penniman, T. K., 140–4

performance, 28–9, 209–11
   calligraphic, 51, 87–9
   dance, 214, 216
   and genre, 32
   of self, 224
   social, 187, 193
   versus text, 26, 31, 33–4
personhood, 100, 113
   conceptions of, 20, 185, 188–9
   extended, 83, 128
   and self, 224, 231
   see also selfhood
photography, 245, 247–58, 262–3
   and anthropology, 248–52, 256–7, 315
   and conceptual art, 253–6
   indexicality of, 250, 260–1
   as means of elicitation, 291–2, 294
   theory of, 300
Pinney, Christopher, 251
Pitt-Rivers Museum, 129, 131, 135–6
   see also museums
plot, 197–9
Pocock, J. G. A., 104–6, 110, 113
poetry, 37, 210, 288
possessive individualism, 51, 103–5, 110, 112, 120
   see also individual
Pound, Ezra, 209
predictability, 14–15
printing, 13–14, 58–61
property, 15, 51, 99–101, 103–7
   intellectual (IP), 100–1, 109, 144, 146
Pye, David, 12–13

radio, 245, 292–9, 301
Rai Coast, Papua New Guinea, 52, 99, 111–12
Ravetz, Amanda, 21
realism, 314–15
recombination, 6, 16–18, 46, 51
Renaissance, 18, 80, 101
repetition, 10
replication, 6
   versus reproduction, 51
reproduction, 51, 81, 85–6, 144
   see also copying; imitation
research, 239, 243, 275–6
revelation, versus creation, 45–8
revolution, 121–2, 152–4, 155–8, 161
rhythm, 10, 50, 75, 232
Rivers, W. H. R., 250, 252
Roberts, John, 253
Rosler, Martha, 255, 257–8

–325–

Index

Rouch, John, 251
Rousseau, Jean Jacques, 102, 311
Ruscha, Ed, 253–4, 257

Sahlins, Marshall, 200, 203
Sapir, Edward, 200, 267, 279
Sassoon, Rosemary, 13
savage, 104, 311
  noble, 307
Sawyer, Keith, 219
Schechner, Richard, 39
Scheele, Judith, 6, 20, 121–3
Schieffelin, Edward, 29
science studies, 285–6, 288
script, 1, 12–13, 26, 29, 31
selection, *see* natural selection
selfhood, 108, 195, 223–5, 231–2
  see also personhood
self-interest, 101–2, 105–6
Sen, Amartya, 101
Shakespeare, William, 33, 195, 210
Shank, Theodore, 33
Sherman, Cindy, 255–7, 260
Sigaut, François, 14
Silverstein, Michael, 30
Siza, Alvaro, 4
Smith, Adam, 102
society, 123, 198
  versus individual, 6–7, 105, 119, 152, 186–7
soundscape, 293
Sperber, Dan, 36
Spinoza, Baruch, 102
subject, 50–1, 244, 310
  human, 107, 110
Stack, Trevor, 12, 21, 240, 278
Steward, Julian, 241
Strathern, Marilyn, 185, 188, 243

Tamil, of South India, 48, 55, 58, 60–1
Te Awekotuku, Ngahuia, 143
teaching, 20–1, 242–4
technique
  versus art, 80
  of calligraphy 82, 85–6
  of pattern construction, 48, 55, 57, 62, 74–5
temporality
  conceptions of, 188
  and creativity, 185–6, 191
  and the eventness of being, 199, 204
  of improvisation, 9–10
  linear, 219
  and selfhood, 224, 231
  of social life, 193
text, 26, 29–34, 36–7, 241, 256, 313–14
  movement, 212
  versus performance, 26, 31, 33–4
theatre, 35, 197
time
  and agency, 195, 199, 204
  and change, 185
  and history, 9–10, 15, 194, 199, 208
  inauspicious, 56
  and intergenerational differences, 223, 231
  linear, 203,
    versus cyclical, 189, 208
  objectification of, 186
  organic, 191
  passage of, 188, 224
  and power, 211
  and sequentiality, 232
  of social worlds, 193
  transcendence of, 36
  wasting, 190
Todorov, Tsvetan, 209, 214
Torres Strait Expedition, 249–50
tradition
  as agency, 211, 220
  continuity of, 6, 25
  creativity in, 5, 7, 189–90, 207–8, 214
  dance, 214–18
  discourses of, 20, 162
  inertia of, 6–7, 120, 152
  versus innovation, 9, 19, 25, 95, 216, 218, 279–80
  versus modernity, 120, 211
  versus novelty, 2, 10, 28, 279
  revolutionary, 157–8
tragedy of the commons, 105
transmission, 6, 36–7
trust, 190
Turner, Victor, 277

Ucko, Peter, 145
Urban, Greg, 29–30, 268

value, 187
Vanuatu, 110–11
Vernant, Jean-Pierre, 196
Vico, Giambattista, 102, 240–1
visual anthropology, 242, 248–9, 251, 287

Index

Viveiros de Castro, Eduardo, 319
Vokes, Richard, 20, 240

Wagner, Roy, 106, 124, 191
walking, 14, 293, 295, 299
 see also pedestrians
Weiner, James, 190
Whitehead, Alfred North, 47, 52
Whyte, William, 312
Wieman, H. N., 8
will, concept of, 197
Witkiewicz, Stanislaw, 256–7
Wolf, Eric, 241
wonder, 15–18
Wordsworth, William, 210

workmanship, of risk versus certainty, 12–14
writing, 13
 calligraphic, 80–1
 creative, 208, 274–5
 ethnographic, 12, 138, 144, 244, 276–9, 311–12
 fictional, 273–6
  versus non-fictional, 315–18
 and teaching, 21
 see also calligraphy; ethnography; handwriting

Yoruba, 31, 34, 37–8
Yugami Hisao, 79, 92–3